# PROCEEDINGS
## of the
## ELEVENTH
## INTERNATIONAL CONFERENCE
## on the
## STUDY OF SHAMANISM
## and
## ALTERNATE MODES OF HEALING

held at the
Santa Sabina Center, San Rafael, California
September 3 to 5, 1994

Conference Coordinator and Editor
Ruth-Inge Heinze
University of California, Berkeley

Typesetting by
Steven Zegas, Pages Publishing, Oakland, CA
Artwork by
Bob Bourdeaux, Design Etcetera, Gaithersberg, MD


**Library of Congress Cataloging-in-Publication Data**

International Conference on the Study of Shamanism and Alternate
Modes of Healing (11th, 1994: San Rafael, Calif.)
    Proceedings of the Eleventh International Conference on the Study of
Shamanism and Alternate Modes of Healing: held at the Santa Sabina Center, San Rafael, California, September 3-5, 1994, conference coordinator
and editor, Ruth-Inge Heinze
    p. cm
    Includes bibliographical references
    ISBN 0-945875-12-6    $25.00
    1. Shamanism - Congresses. 2. Spiritual Healing - Congresses.
3. Medicine, Magic, and Spagiric - Congresses
I. Heinze, Ruth-Inge, II. Title
BL 2370-55155    1994            S4-43549
291. 1'4—dc20                   CIP

# TABLE OF CONTENTS

# COMMITMENT

We have gathered to celebrate our meeting with the Sacred.

We are offering our Selves to the conference with the intention
to listen with the ears of our soul.

We are offering our Selves to the conference with the intention
to keep each other honest, aiming not only at perfection but wholeness.

We are offering our Selves to the conference with the intention
to support each other's path.

We want to be healed of the myth of separateness and become
filled with fierce compassion.

We consciously intend re-membering and re-storying.

We consciously accept responsibility for the continuance of life.

# PHOENIX RISING II

Ruth-Inge Heinze

Americans celebrate the New Year by tearing up their calendars, getting drunk, and making resolutions. Rosh Hashana is understood to be the day God created the world and the day God judges the world to decide who will be in the book of life next year. The holy season *(tashuva)* lasts ten days until Yom Kippur, the Day of Atonement. At the end of this self-reflective process, Jews traditionally fast for 25 hours and then celebrate with a Sukkot feast.

What relevance has this for our conference? Meeting for the eleventh time we have to reflect on our conference, too.

The first series of nine International Conferences on the Study of Shamanism and Alternate Modes of Healing was conducted under a flag Rowena Pattee Kryder created. She reminded us of the different forms of shamanism. Then Julien and I composed a commitment which was read at the beginning of each conference. (You will find the words on the last page of the List of Abstracts and at the beginning of this book.) This still did not seem to mean much for some participants.

I have called the second series of our conference, "Phoenix Rising," because we resurrected from the ashes of a fire which flared up at the end of the ninth conference and rose again briefly during the tenth conference.

Phoenix IS rising. I got more proposals than ever already by mid-October last year and we are overbooked. But there are still some ashes on the feet of the Phoenix which I will try to shake off right now.

At the bottom of human problems is ignorance. I won't go into all aspects of ignorance but use a simple example to explain what happens when, in critical moments, we allow ourselves to be deceived by ignorance in its most dangerous form. The regression begins with incomplete listening (hearing only what one wants to hear and editing out important information). This leads to distorted perceptions which lead to confused feelings which then cloud and overpower rational thinking. This process cannot but end in further confusion and chaos which then is exploited by individuals who themselves are blinded by their own drive for power.

It is important to recognize such situation as early as possible. The story I am going to tell will serve three purposes: (1) it will explain why I continue to make myself vulnerable, i.e., why I continue to call this conference. (It started with the vision that there is so much fear, anxiety, and confusion, especially about shamanism and alternative modes of healing, and ethics in general, that we have to increase our efforts to keep our world in balance.

My story will also (2) shed light on Jewish/German relationships and (3) offer a solution.

Now, the story: At the 1993 conference, a woman thanked Jurgen for expressing his deep concern about the holocaust. She said, she never expected a German male making such a statement. This surprised me. Why did she think that Germans would ignore the holocaust? I also felt this did not cover the issue adequately because Jurgen as well as the woman are one generation removed from the time when the atrocities were committed in Germany. To really address the issue, we should talk to somebody who lived at that time in Germany—and that is me.

Living for twelve years in a country ruled by a dictator with a sick mind is hard to imagine. Have you ever feared that the people who ring your doorbell may come not only to arrest you but to execute you quickly. Protest in the USA appears to be too easy, compared to young people under Hitler's regime who were executed for just distributing some flyers.

I was 13 years old when Hitler came to power. I never will forget the night of January 30, 1933, when Hindenburg, the president of the Weimarer Republic, appointed Hitler chancellor of Germany. Hindenburg was a military man of a stature like Eisenhower, popular, trusted, a rock of dignity and security. In 1933, thousands of storm troopers marched through Berlin and their burning torches evoked an image of doom. Shortly afterwards the German Parliament was scorched by fire and traitors were blamed for the crime. Purges occurred inside the government, however, Hitler gave work to millions of unemployed. Troops marched into areas which had been unjustly separated from Germany as the result of the Treaty of Versailles. So, for many Germans, Hitler restored the honor of the German people and provided prosperity for the working classes. The real dangers became visible much later. (I refer to an essay by Leland M. Wooton, "Albert Speer: How to Manage an Atrocity" (Fall 1981:21-38). Albert Speer's ideas are still considered exemplary at American universities, leaving students to wonder why a person of such genius served a corrupt government.

In 1936, the Olympic Games were held in Berlin and brought the world to my home city, at the same time some of my Jewish friends left for England. The Jewish teachers in my Junior College were replaced and then came the so-called "crystal night." Jewish shops were plundered and synagogues burned. I was horrified. There was no rational explanation for this criminal behavior. At the same time, at school, in the office, on the radio, and in public, representatives of the Third Reich began to talk about Germany's enemies. The inflammatory voices spoke of Jews being subversive, the main goal, however, was obviously to corrupt our minds.

I will mention here three criteria which allow us to recognize when somebody attempts to pervert our mind: (1) watch out for sweeping, general statements which cannot easily be checked up, (2) notice that no attempt is made to respect and understand the other; and (3) recognize that no hand is stretched out in love. There are three additional questions we should always ask of each other: (1) What is your essence? (2) What is your problem? and (3) What is your solution? We should not act before we get satisfactory answers. Remember, our motto is Respect, Relationships, and Reciprocity.

Let me continue to report on events in Germany. Jews were put into labor camps. We were told that these measures were necessary for reasons of national security, it was never openly known what happened in the camps. You had to listen to the BBC and this was punished by death.

Only somebody who has lived under a dictatorship knows what it means that everything you say can be held against you and any resistance or word of disagreement is punished by executing the perpetrator within days. You had to be careful whom you trusted. Most Germans adopted an attitude where they kept their thoughts to themselves.

In 1939, World War II broke out. Friends and relatives were drafted and quite a few died on foreign battlefields. November 1942, the air raids started and Berlin, for example, was attacked five times during the day and five times each night. The city was turned into a pile of rubble where the smell of burning flesh never left us. People died in the provisional air raid shelters, built under their houses. Buildings collapsed during the bombing and then were set on fire by incendiary bombs following the larger bombs. Bombs kept falling in a series of three. When the first bomb exploded close to us, we could be pretty sure that the other two would not hit our house. But when the first bomb exploded far away, the second or third could hit our house. We heard explosions around us every day and every night, not only for days, for weeks, for months, exactly for two and a half years.

With the rationing of food, under 1,000 calories a day, people became emaciated and even more lethargic. While the physical and moral destruction of my country was escalating, death became a welcome friend and suicide appeared to be attractive. In the desperation of watching my country being destroyed, physically, culturally and spiritually, I was looking for a sign why I should survive. How could the Christian God I had been introduced to allow such atrocities? He did not seem to have the power to intervene. I would like to refer here to the book, *The Concept of God after Auschwitz, A Jewish Voice* by Hans Jonas (1987). In essence, Jonas suggests that God withdrew at the day of creation and is now waiting for us to join him again.

Looking for something tangible I could hold on, I found this petrified sea urchin I had picked up on a beach of the Baltic Sea when I was a child. It had survived thousands, if not millions of years. It was, in its essence, perfectly preserved. It provided for me the metaphor that something survives.

The body can be destroyed and, at that time, death was considered a relief, but the essence cannot be touched. So I put everything of my culture—Bach, Beethoven, great painters, poets, philosophers, humanitarians—into this stone. I was holding this stone during the years when I waited for death in the air raid shelter under our house. I was holding the stone when I learned about atrocities by word of mouth. It could not touch the essence of what is German. The horror had to end some day or I would die with this stone in my hand. I think when Jews and Germans together can wash with their tears the atrocities from this stone, a real healing can take place.

At this time, I made a vow that, if I should survive, I would never again tolerate perversion of the human mind under whatever circumstances. When the Third Reich finally collapsed in 1945, I was twenty-five. Fifty years later, I am now seventy-five years old, but these twelve years are indelibly engraved in my mind.

I took this stone to America and to Asia wherever I lived and worked and put the essence of each culture into this stone. It contains also the essence of this conference—to share our knowledge, to balance what has got out of balance, to encourage creative work and to celebrate the joy of life. I devoted my life to infinite love and the mission to keep the essence pure and protected from contamination.

We all have to check ourselves for the Auschwitz inside of us. Auschwitz is not a single event in history. Invaders have destroyed whole populations in the past. Innumerable witches were burned in medieval times. We had thirty-year and hundred-year wars. Stalin killed over 25 million Russians, Pol Pot 2 millions, half of the population of Cambodia. What were our reactions at the time when atom bombs were dropped on Hiroshima and Nagasaki? What were our reactions at the time when the gulf war and the massive bombing of Iraq started? What are our reactions to the events in Bosnia and Rwanda? We live in a free country with all possibilities for individual and mass protest. None of these protests costs us our life as it was the case in Hitler's Germany. We should no longer apply double standards, also we don't need more conflict, we need peaceful solutions.

We have experienced ten beautiful and meaningful conferences on a wide range of topics and with a great diversity of people. We come to talk and to listen. When some of us come only to listen, this is alright too, because something may begin to germinate. But we have to look out for people who accuse us of something we have not done. We have to look out for people who only know one way to talk and that is theirs. Our conference is open to anyone who has something to contribute. Our conference is open to anyone who wants to restore balance and joy in the world. We can find solutions only when we all are ready to listen, to love and to be loved.

## References

Jonas, Hans. *The Concept of God after Auschwitz, A Jewish Voice* ["Der Gottesbegriff nach Auschwitz, Eine jüdische Stimme"]. Baden-Baden, Germany: Suhrkamp, 1987.

Wooton, Leland M. "Albert Speer: How to Manage an Atrocity," *Journal of Humanistic Psychology,* 21:4 (Fall 1981):21-

# SPACIOUSNESS: THE COMMON GROUND BETWEEN SCIENCE AND SPIRITUALITY

Jean E. Burns

One of the most important aspects of human experience is spaciousness, the ability to see the same particulars from different perspectives, and it is spaciousness that makes wisdom different from truth, justice different from the letter of the law, and tolerance different from the urge to conformity. Yet spaciousness is more than neutral possibility, for it is here, rather than in the particulars of experience, that awe, beauty, and the sense of the sacred reside.

The most important aspect of following a spiritual path is the ability to expand, to change past understanding and deepen your sense of who you are. Similarly, it is essential in doing scientific research to be able to change past ideas and develop new concepts. It is spaciousness that is central to both endeavors and their common ground.

Nowadays there are many attempts to justify spiritual teachings by relating them to scientific principles. However, it is more likely that spiritual teachings will deepen our understanding of science than the other way around.

Spirituality encompasses our experience of the sacred, our experience of connection with others, our freedom to be more than we are and to make choices. In these respects, spirituality is a matter of how an individual relates to the highest and best he knows and to his experience of the sacred. For some, spirituality emphasizes a personal relationship with God, or with a saint, savior or Buddha. For others, spirituality emphasizes a quest, inward to be a better person or outward to make the world better in some way. And any quest surely is spiritual whether a person refers to it that way or not, provided only that she always reaches for the highest and best in carrying it out.

Our experience of spirituality and sacredness dates back to prehistory, and organized religion arose out of this individual experience. Knowledge in the form of rational thought came later—for instance, in Greece of the sixth century B.C. The search for understanding of the relationship between spirituality, on the one hand, and science and rational thought, on the other hand, has occupied mankind since then (Tarnas, 1991). Nowadays it is often asserted that all aspects of experience, including spiritual experience, can be explained in terms of science. But placed in historical perspective, the view that science is primary and spirituality a derivative phenomenon is unusual.

Why should such a claim be made? The main reason is that there is a great deal of evidence showing that the content of our sensory experience and our ability to process information depend on the brain. For instance, vision is dependent on certain areas of the brain, and if one of these areas is damaged, through stroke or injury, there could be a blind spot in the visual field, loss of perception of color, or an inability to recognize faces, depending on which areas was damaged (Crick, 1994). Cerebral damage can also produce memory defects, the inability to read or to speak, or reduced ability to plan the future (Churchland, 1986).

The brain is a physical object and, therefore, must follow physical laws. If all aspects of conscious experience depend on the brain, then spiritual experience must be entirely reducible to brain processes and thereby to physical laws. But physical laws do not incorporate values and goals, so as personal search for the highest and best becomes embedded in a context in which there is no highest and best.

However, science is designed to study objective phenomena of the physical world, whereas conscious experience is subjective and is different in other ways from objective phenomena. If we are to study conscious experience, then we must ask what its characteristics are, and how these characteristics are similar to or different from those of physical objects.

One of the most important qualities in conscious experience is spaciousness, the ability to see the same particulars from different perspectives. It is this quality that distinguishes wisdom from truth, justice from the letter of the law, and tolerance from the urge to conformity. Our experience of it occurs throughout daily life, yet it is central to any description of spirituality. Because we are interested in the relationship of spirituality to physical laws, it will not be presupposed here that spaciousness reduces to physical laws. Rather, it will be described in spiritual terms, and we will inquire to what extent this description is compatible with presently known physical laws.

We will see that spaciousness, taken as a spiritual quality, is related to the concepts of infinity, infinitesimals, free will and possibility. To say that infinity is an aspect of spaciousness is to say that you can always find a fresh perspective on any situation. It implies that the search for truth never ends, because you can always find a new question.

Physics incorporates the idea of infinity in that space and/or time may be unbounded. However, aside from this consideration, physics has never had much to do with infinities. In fact, when infinities appeared in the formation of quantum field theory, great efforts were made to remove them, and their removal (via renormalization) was considered a great theoretical success (Pagels, 1985). Rather, it is mathematics that over the last century or so has explored the nature of infinity.

Infinity is that which is greater than any specific thing. For instance, there are an infinite number of positive integers, 1, 2, 3, ..., and no matter how large an number you specify, infinity is larger than that. One might think there is only one kind of infinity. However, it is now known that there is a series of infinities, each one greater than the last, with the infinity of integers being the smallest one in the series (Rucker, 1982).

Has infinity been tamed, now that its study has been brought into mathematics? Is it all neatly divided into compartments? Mathematicians do not agree on whether infinity exists as anything other than a mathematical concept, let alone whether it can be completely described in a finite way (Rucker, 1982). However, George Cantor, the person who brought the subject into mathematics, believed that infinity is not only a mathematical concept, but also part of our lived experience (Rucker, 1982:10). He made a distinction between infinities which can be labeled and Absolute Infinity, toward which all labeled infinities point, and some mathematicians hold a similar point of view.

An infinitesimal is that which is smaller than any non-zero number. Given any specific number, as small as you please, e.g., 1/4, 1/8, 1/16,...an infinitesimal is always smaller. Unlike infinities, infinitesimals are regularly used in physics. That is because the concept of continuity can be expressed in terms of infinitesimals, and most of the basic laws of physics describe continuous functions of time and space. However, physics takes for granted such concepts as continuity and infinitesimals, and it is mathematics that explores their nature (Davis and Hersh, 1981).

The concept of infinitesimals is closely related to our experience of idealization such as peace and happiness. Peace, for instance, manifests in degrees, but never as pure peace. If two countries are at war and declare a truce, there is peace. But if the people in the two countries do not trust each other, that peace can be improved on. If they trust each other enough to interact, there is a reasonable degree of peace. But if they don't feel bonds of friendship and connection, the peace can still be improved on. In lived experience, qualities such as peace and happiness are like *yin* and *yang*—they always have a bit of their opposite in them. We can conceptualize pure peace or pure happiness, but lived experience, no matter how close it comes, never completely attains the idealization.

But it is exactly in this *yin-yang* situation that spaciousness is important. If a situation isn't satisfactory, there is always room to improve it in some way. Furthermore, a situation can always come arbitrarily close to the ideal. Even though the pure ideal can never be attained, there isn't any finite separation, such that we can come so close but not closer. We are only separated by an infinitesimal. Thus infinitesimals are attributes of spaciousness.

Possibility and free will are connected to spaciousness because in any situation, changes can always be made to our internal point of view and nearly always to our external circumstances. Therefore, alternative possibilities always exist and we can select between them.

The basic laws of physics, as presently understood, have no place for the concept of free will. In fact, as several researchers have pointed out, the action of free will contradicts the second law of thermodynamics (Burns, 1993). For these reasons, many scientists assert that our actions arise entirely out of chemical processes in the brain, that mind cannot influence these processes, and that our experience of free will is an illusion (Dennett, 1984).

However, empirical considerations suggest that mind can act independently of matter. It is well known that conscious experience is associated with some brain processes, but not all of them. If consciousness is passive to the brain and has no independent function, we could be conscious solely of the details of our digestive processes and not of vision—we would be able to get around the room just as well. The fact that consciousness is associated with brain processes having to do with sensory input and the way we interact with our environment suggests that consciousness has become associated with these processes over the course of evolution and that it can produce more adaptive behavior than the brain acting alone (Burns, 1991). This conclusion is supported by the fact that when a person is not conscious, although s/he can carry out actions in an automatic way, as in sleepwalking or a petit mal seizure, s/he cannot respond in a meaningful way to new situations (Burns, 1991).

If consciousness can select some of the brain programs that determine our actions, then it must make its selections from alternative possibilities. There is no analog to the idea of alternative possibilities in classical physics. However, in quantum mechanics the wave function describing physical objects is expressed in terms of mutually exclusive possibilities. Obviously, mutually exclusive possibilities cannot co-exist in the physical world, and only one possibility at a time ever occurs; the latter fact is explained by a phenomenon called *collapse of the wave function* in which one of the possibilities described by the wave function is selected. In experimental measurements, the possibility that occurs is determined in a random way. However, the concept that a selection is made from different possibilities is at least present in quantum mechanics, and for that reason various physicists (Goswami, 1993; Herbert, 1993; Stapp, 1993) have proposed that consciousness can choose a desired action by selecting the wave function of an appropriate brain program.

In quantum mechanics objects can have correlations over very large distances, and for that reason some physicists (Goswami, 1993; Herbert, 1993) have proposed that our sense of connection with the rest of the universe derives from these quantum mechanical correlations. No information can be transmitted via these correlations, however, so they cannot account for psi phenomena such as telepathy (Herbert, 1993).

Thus possibility and our sense of connection may be related to quantum mechanics. The phenomenon of collapse of the wave function is not presently considered understood within physics; there are a number of differing proposals about its nature (Herbert, 1985), of which the proposal that an observer can cause collapse, and thereby exert free will, is only one. So free will cannot be said to be related to quantum physics at present, although such a relationship might be found in the future.

We asked earlier, does mind reduce to brain in all respects? Certainly, much evidence from the neurosciences shows that the specific content of conscious experience—what is seen, what is planned for—does depend on the brain and thereby on physical laws. But spaciousness is not a particular thing; it is a way of viewing and dealing with particulars. The statement that spaciousness exists is a statement that life is open-ended, that we are creators who can visualize a better existence and take action to make things better.

Because spaciousness incorporates qualities such as free will and infinity, it is not closely related to the laws of physics, as they are presently understood. Perhaps, some day our understanding of physics will increase, such that these qualities are incorporated into an expanded version of the basic laws. If that happens, it is likely that the change in our understanding of physics will be as great as the change that occurred when quantum physics was discovered.

On the other hand, it may be that the principles which describe consciousness are different from those which describe material objects. In that case, two sets of principles would exist, one describing the physical world and one describing consciousness, with some common ground between them. A model of this type has been developed by physicist Saul-Paul Sirag as part of a unified field theory (Sirag, 1993). This model uses a set of mathematical principles which describes fundamental particles in space and time. However, Sirag shows by means of a mathematical theorem that this set of principles must be associated with a second set of principles which describes something else, presumably conscious experience, that exists in time but not physical space.

However, the materialist would say that there is no need either to change the laws of physics or to develop a new set of principles for consciousness because spaciousness, as it has been described herein, does not exist. He would say that the brain has so many interconnections that it can describe a very large number of concepts, but certainly not an unlimited number. He would add that infinity is simply a concept, appropriate for mathematics, but otherwise just a confused way of talking about a large number of things we haven't counted. He would point out that within some 40 or 50 years computers will surpass the human brain in their number of interconnections, and assert that not only will computers be able to talk and act in a way that is indistinguishable from human behavior, they will surpass us in creative vision of the good, precisely articulating the nature of peace, happiness and truth and the way to achieve them.

One can imagine a test to show whether humans really partake of infinity, by comparing human ability to find new perspectives about an issue, such as the nature of peace, with the ability of a computer which has the same number of interconnections as the human brain. If the computer has more insight, producing relevant concepts which have more clarity, simplicity and usefulness than the human, then it would appear that the materialist is right. But if the human wins, the materialist is not proved wrong. He can say, "Well, I need better software. And the brain is more efficient than I thought. I need a bigger computer." One can imagine that somehow means are discovered whereby the entire universe can be converted into a supercomputer and the energy to power it, leaving only one small room where a few humans are gathered to test computer insight against human insight. Suppose the human wins again. The materialist can still say, "I know I'm right. And I could prove it if I had a bigger computer."

Thus the existence of spaciousness can never be proved, and if it is to be incorporated in an expanded set of physical laws or an independent set of laws which describe consciousness, it would have to be added as a postulate. Nevertheless, even though spaciousness is not part of present physical law, it is an important aspect of science in a different way. Science can be described either as an objective body of knowledge or the live experience of those who pursue the study of this knowledge. It is essential in doing scientific research to be able to change past ideas and develop new concepts, and it is spaciousness that is central to this endeavor.

The objective body of knowledge of physics consists of a set of basic principles which describe all physical phenomena which can be written in their totality on half a page of paper. These principles have a symmetry and simplicity which give them great beauty, and the fact that so few of them govern the workings of the entire physical universe gives them an awesome quality. It is not surprising that physicists, in working out new relationships which follow from these laws, often report that beauty and discovery go together.

Findings in other scientific fields are, as in physics, based on empirical investigation. The phenomena described by other fields, such as biology or psychology, often cannot be traced back to the basic laws of physics, but there is no reason to suppose they could not be, if we knew enough about them. As lived experience, these fields can have the same power and beauty as physics, through seeing the diversity of plant and animal life on this planet or the richness and complexity of the human psyche, for instance.

Mathematicians also find beauty in the truths they discover, and such is the power of these findings that over the centuries many mathematicians have asserted that God must be a mathematician (Davis and Hersh, 1981). In the present era, the great logician Kurt Godel has said that Mind is not localized or restricted to individual brains and that the ultimate goal of mathematics is to directly perceive infinity and the Absolute (Rucker, 1982:182-183).

In this way science and mathematics, as lived experience, are searches for truth and understanding, and spaciousness is central to these endeavors. If spirituality encompasses all quests which reach toward the highest and best, then science and mathematics must be viewed as a part of mankind's spiritual journey. This journey is multi-faceted and includes quests, such as that for greater peace and harmony between all peoples, which involve different concepts than those of science and for which we have so far not made as much progress. However, spaciousness enables the hope and optimism by which we continue all these endeavors.

It would not be surprising if, in the coming century, principles involving spiritual concepts were added to the laws of physics, or incorporated within a set of principles describing consciousness, as a way of exploring our spiritual nature. Even in the present search to relate consciousness to scientific principles, many scientists believe that spiritual ideas should be taken into account, and the present ripple of interest in this could well become a wave. Of course, if this happens, it will be spiritual teachings that deepen our understanding of science, rather than the other way around.

As mankind progresses on its quests, will we someday reach their end? Will we know all truth and plumb the depths of peace and harmony, such that there is nothing left to learn? If spaciousness is part of our existence, we will always have more questions and always find Infinite Mystery.

# References

Burns, Jean E. "Time, consciousness, and psi," *Silver Threads: 25 Years of Parapsychology Research,* eds. Beverly Kane, Jean Millay, and Dan Brown. New York: Praeger, 1993, pp.124-136.

_____ ." Does consciousness perform a function independently of the brain?" *Frontier Perspectives, 2:1* (1991):19-20, 29-30, 34 (published by the Center for Frontier Sciences, Temple University).

Churchland, Patricia S. *Neurophilosophy: Toward a Unified Science of the Mind Brain.* Cambridge, MA: MIT Press, 1986.

Crick, Francis. *The Astonishing Hypothesis: The Scientific Search for the Soul.* New York: C. Scribner's Sons, 1994.

Davis, Philip J. and Reuben Hersh. *The Mathematical Experience.* Boston, MA: Houghton Mifflin, 1981.

Dennett, D.C. *Elbow Room: The Varieties of Free Will Worth Having.* Cambridge, MA: MIT Press, 1984.

Goswami, Amit. *The Self-Aware Universe: How Consciousness Creates the Material World.* New York: Tarcher/Putnam, 1993.

Herbert, Nick. *Elemental Mind.* New York: Dutton, 1993.

_____ . *Quantum Reality.* New York: Doubleday, 1985.

Pagels, Heinz R. *Perfect Symmetry.* New York: Simon and Schuster, 1985.

Rucker, Rudy. *Infinity and the Mind.* New York: Bantam, 1982.

Sirag, Saul-Paul. "Consciousness: A Hyperspace View." Appendix to *Roots of Consciousness,* by Jeff Mishlove. Tulsa, OK: Council Oak Books, 2nd ed., 1993, pp.327-365.

Stapp, Henry P. *Mind, Matter and Quantum Mechanics.* New York: Springer-Verlag, 1993.

Tarnas, Richard. *The Passion of the Western Mind.* New York: Ballantine, 1991.

# THE SCIENCE OF GOOD AND EVIL

William C. Gough and Robert L. Shacklett

## Introduction

Can there ever be a science of good and evil? Certainly not under the current paradigm of modern physical science. There exists a wide gap between such human qualities as good and evil and what has been considered to date in the physical sciences. But before we begin to address what would be required to bring the qualities of good and evil under the umbrella of modern science, we will briefly describe how one of us (Bill Gough) learned the concepts of good and evil—since initially they are learned concepts taught to us by the society in which we are immersed.

I was raised during the Great Depression. There was no television and we had no telephone or automobile. I lived in the center of Jersey City, New Jersey and acted out the concepts of good and evil on the city streets. We played war games, cops and robbers, and cowboys and Indians. We used kitchen pots for helmets, garbage can covers for shields; broom handles were horses, swords were made from orange crates, and bamboo poles became lances. And, of course, we had cap guns. We learned our general ideas about good and evil from the family, the church, and the radio. However, to play our games we needed to be taught at our level and this was done through comic books and, even more effectively for me, through bubble gum cards since they told me about the "real" world.

The bubble gum cards told me that the Government is good—they fight the public enemies, the gangsters and robbers. Overseas, the Foreign Legion puts down the rebellions of the evil Arabs. Thus, I learned that the government in power and stability was good. But the good didn't always win! The Spanish Civil War ends with the Fascist rebels defeating the Loyalists government. And in Africa, the Italians invade Ethiopia and the government of Haile Selassie leaves as the Fascists win. Japan attacks China and many innocent people die. Why do the good suffer? Killing the evil invaders is good. It makes no difference what race does the killing, as my cards show the Moro tribesmen slaughtering the "Jap" invaders. Then came World War II. The Germans and the Russians invade Poland. This is clearly evil. But the evil doesn't always remain evil. The Nazis remain evil but the Russians become good when they fight the Germans. (Later they become evil again; now they are good.)

We also had bubble gum cards about the American Indians. They are evil when they are attacking the wagon train with its women and children. Yet they are also good—Pocahontas saves John Smith and, on the radio, Tonto helps the Lone Ranger fight evil. In fact, Tonto always seemed to be a little wiser than his masked companion. There appears to be good within evil. Forty years later, my son has Star War cards in which Ben (Obi-Wah) Kenobi represents good and Darth Vader represents evil. But Darth Vader seems to also have some good within himself. To understand the mystery of good and evil, Ben Kenobi takes Luke aside and says, "Learn about the Force!" This paper is about "the Force."

## An Expanded Paradigm

Science is not cast in concrete. It is and always has been an evolving search for truth. This search has resulted in a scientific process of ever expanding paradigms with their resulting world views. Figure 1 represents these expanding paradigms as a set of Russian dolls—each one encompassing the preceding one. Science has gone from a worldview in which the earth constitutes the center of the universe to our modern science worldview—one in which the entire universe consists of a "soup bowl" full of space and time in which there are chunks of matter.

Fig.1: The series of "Russian dolls" shows how paradigms arising from scientific thinking have evolved to encompass larger and larger perspectives. The nesting of the Russian dolls illustrates that the paradigms that have previously demonstrated a high degree of success will be included within a new, more encompassing paradigm. The last "doll" in the series represents an undefined new paradigm, one which the authors believe will include the current science of separateness and encompass it into a science of connectiveness.

To have a science of good and evil we will need a more encompassing scientific paradigm—one that extends beyond the limitations of space-time. In many fields of research there are "arrows" that point to the need for such an expanded science, as illustrated in Figure 2. The data from these diverse fields of human endeavor will help to find such a new paradigm. As many have noted, the seeds for such an expansion have already been planted by

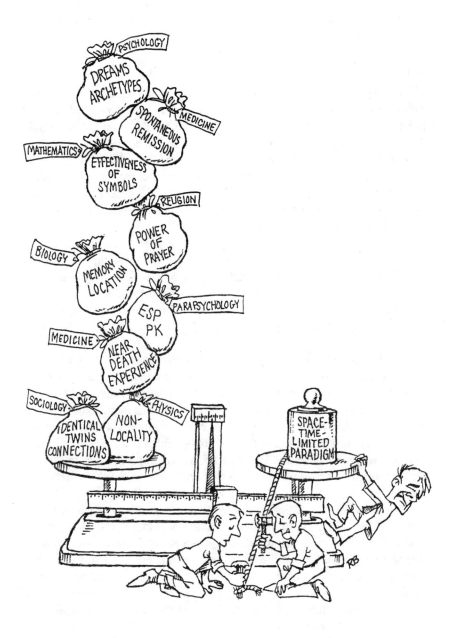

Fig.2: This cartoon illustrates the accumulating evidence that points to the need for an expanded scientific paradigm and the inherent resistance that will be encountered in the process of change.

modern physics itself—most notably in the research on non-locality. We will first discuss a model for such an expanded paradigm and then illustrate how the concepts of good and evil arise naturally.

## The Model

The model is designed to provide a basis for understanding the human experience in terms of connectiveness instead of separation, which is the prevailing Western paradigm. Furthermore, it is our intention to demonstrate that this connectiveness can be described in terms of conventional concepts used in physics and mathematics. Using the model, we have presented the basis for an expanded scientific paradigm that encompasses the existing space-time limited paradigm of modern science. The details of this model have been covered in a series of papers (Shacklett & Gough, 1991; Gough & Shacklett, 1993a, b, c, d, e).

We start by addressing the key simplifying assumption underlying modern science. That key assumption is that physical space and time represent a closed system and, hence, only patterns originating in the physical world need to be considered. Our essays have attempted to make a case for an expanded science that considers not only space-time patterns, but recognizes effects in the physical world, originating from "archetypal" patterns beyond space-time.

In addition to assuming that the creation process begins beyond space-time, our model assumes that mind is also located beyond space-time. We believe that there has been sufficient scientific research to support the concept that mind cannot be confined to the physical. This implies the possibility that our mind can interact with the creation process. In fact, humans appear to have an innate talent for interacting with and even adversely distorting this creation process. This may be the reason for the admonitions of the Buddhist and Taoist philosophies that one's actions should be in accord with the "flow."

Traditionally, physical science has studied the patterns of nature by assuming matter to be the starting point. Our model makes it possible to examine the nature and origin of the physical world from the opposite perspective. Matter results from a creation process originating beyond space-time, in realms where connectiveness rather than separateness dominates. Ordering principles beyond space-time that embody this connectiveness produce the archetypes from which arise the patterns of the physical world. These patterns can be classified into three types: fields that represent unmanifest form; matter that represents manifest physical form, and symbols that represent manifest mental form to which humans have assigned meaning. We believe that the mystery of why mathematics, and hence modern science, can so successfully model nature arises because the human mind can function beyond space-time and manifest meaningful symbols.

More specifically, our model assumes that the physical world is unfolding at the speed of light out of realms beyond space-time. Thus, the "weaving" of the fabric of physical reality (the patterns of matter, energy, and information) involves a continuous back and forth exchange between space-time and the higher realms. David Bohm called this process of undivided wholeness the holo-movement (Bohm, 1980:150-157). To elucidate how our model addresses this process, the relationship between light, space, and time will be discussed.

## Outer Light

Let us expand upon our assumption that the physical world is unfolding at the speed of light out of realms beyond space-time. We will now consider the entire physical world to be various manifestations of light. Modern physics has already found that under the right circumstances, light and matter can switch identities (Flam, 1994:2013-2014). In such a physical world, as David Bohm has stated, matter could be considered as "condensed or frozen light." (Weber, 1986:45, quoting Bohm). Hence, light becomes the manifestation of archetypes that take on physical form. This is not a new concept, having been proposed as long ago as the thirteenth century by Robert Grosseteste, the Archdeacon of Leicester, a churchman and scholar. Grosseteste wrote the book *De Luce* ("On Light") in which he considered light the first form from which all else followed. To Grosseteste, light was the medium chosen by God for his creation, thus, all of material creation was condensed light (Zajonc, 1933:52-56). In the present context, by light we mean the entire electromagnetic spectrum, not just the one octave that we experience as visible light.

To understand our basis for taking this position, we need to review what science knows about space, time, and light. the need to periodically review such basic concepts that serve as a foundation for the current paradigm of science is something that Einstein elegantly addressed:

> The eyes of the scientist are directed upon those phenomena which are accessible to observation, upon their apperception and conceptual formulation of the confusingly immense body of observational data, the scientist makes use of a whole arsenal of concepts which he imbibed practically with his mother's milk; and seldom if ever is he aware of the eternally problematic character of his concepts. He uses this conceptual material, or, speaking more exactly, these conceptual tools of thought, as something obviously, immutably given; something having an objective value of truth which is hardly ever, and in any case not seriously, to be doubted. How could he do otherwise? How would the ascent of a mountain be possible, if the use of hands, legs, and tools had to be sanctioned step by step on the basis of the science of mechanics? And yet, in the

interests of science, it is necessary over and over again to engage in the critique
of these fundamental concepts, in order that we may not unconsciously be ruled
by them (forward to the 1st edition, 1953, in Jammer, 1969:214).

Space-time is the foundation upon which modern science has built its
impressive structures. However, this foundation is not rock but sand. In fact,
space and time lose their meaning when one imagines traveling at the speed
of light, which is what Einstein did when he started thinking about relativity
theory. The deeper meaning of both space and time have remained unsolved
mysteries for modern science (Jammer, 1969; Morris, 1984; Shallis, 1982).
Our model challenges this foundation of space-time and suggests that we go
deeper to bed rock so that we can build an expanded paradigm for science
(Gough & Shacklett, 1993e).

Intimately associated with the scientific concept of space-time is our
understanding of light. Yet, to the scientific mysteries of space and time, we
must add this even greater mystery—what is light? The nature of light cannot be reduced to matter or its motions; it is its own thing. In fact, light is the
tool by which we have gained almost all the knowledge we have about our
universe (Ball, 1994:20). Neither of the great pillars of modern science, the
theory of relativity or quantum theory, reveal anything about the fundamental nature of light. Yet, all of modern scientific theory rests upon a foundation based upon an observed property of light—the fact that light always
travels the path that minimizes the time it takes to go from one place to
another. This observation has been generalized into the famous "principle
of least action" (Feyman, 1963).

If we cannot assign specific attributes to an object then the object loses
its identity—its individuality. A photon of light was the first object subjected
to this test. Since the photon has no mass or charge, light could be quantified
by four other attributes: polarization, wavelength, direction, and intensity.
However, science is now facing a dilemma. For each of the four attributes,
careful experiments in quantum optics have shown that "there is no truly
unambiguous attribute of light" (Zajonc, 1993:314)!

The photon interference experiments that gave these startling results
have now been performed with what we traditionally call matter, i.e., electrons, other atomic particles, and even atoms. These "matter" experiments
are showing that the quantum effects do not always diminish with increased
numbers of particles. Thus, at a deep level, "individuality" disappears and
connectiveness or oneness appears. Hence, the whole basis of scientific
thought that assumes that our physical reality is built upon well defined individual attributes of matter now seems questionable. We are suggesting that
the science of individuality be replaced by a "science of connectiveness"—a
connectiveness that emanates from beyond space-time.

We have chosen the twistor geometry as the mathematical basis for our model (Peat, 1988; Ward & Wells, 1990). An important aspect from twistor geometry is the term "null line." In space-time, it refers to a ray of light, with the "null" coming from the fact that, at the speed of light, time and distance intervals go to zero. This implies that along a null line, time and space have no meaning—the essence of non-locality. The twistor concept, therefore, is a symbolic way of representing the creation of the physical world of space-time via light rays.

## The Link to the Physical

Our model provides a mechanism for the introduction of structure into the quantum vacuum of space-time. This process originates from beyond space-time in the realm of archetypes (which contain the incipient patterns and forms of the physical world that lies next to the Planck length. The driving force behind this process has been called consciousness. It represents the universal intelligence that uses these archetypal patterns to modulate the light as it emerges into space-time and condenses or "freezes" into matter.

The electromagnetic spectrum (what we have called light) is normally represented as open-ended range of frequencies covering what scientific instruments have measured. To justify our extension of this frequency range, note that physics has identified four basic interactions—electromagnetism, strong, weak, and gravity—and has been moving toward a unification of these forces. The first three of these are now understood as aspects of a single force. Broadly speaking, this force can be considered to be an expanded version of electromagnetism. Even gravity, the maverick force, may eventually be brought into this fold (Puthoff, 1989; Sakaroff, 1968).

It is because of these unifying principles that we believe the physical realm is a manifestation of vibrations that span wave-lengths from the Planck length to "infinity." Of course, an infinite wavelength implies zero vibration or absolute stillness, which is impossible because of the Planck-length vibrations inherent in the wholeness. Figure 3 is a representation of an expanded EM spectrum that provide the basis for the manifestation of the physical realm interfacing with the knowledge realm beyond space-time.

## Choice and Magnetism

In order to understand life processes we will be concerned here with more than chemical reactions, which have been understood in detail through the powerful tool of quantum mechanics. We need to understand how the mind, which we locate in the knowledge realm beyond space-time, can affect the physics and chemistry of our bodies and how a concept like choice can be integrated into physical science.

A number of essays (Levin, 1993:77-85; Becker, 1992:53-72; Green,

# The Vibrational Spectrum
## (EXPANDED ELECTROMAGNETIC SPECTRUM)

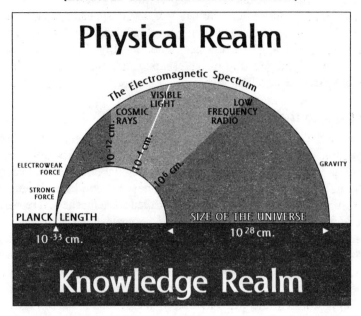

Fig.3: A representation of the physical realm as a spectrum of vibrations ranging in wave length from the Planck length to the size of the universe. This vibrational spectrum can be considered as an expanded EM spectrum. It is the vibrations emerging from the knowledge realm that create space, time, and matter.

*et.al,* 1992:65-103; Maxey, 1991:55-72) have dealt with experimental evidence pointing to the intimate connection of the magnetic part of the electromagnetic field to life processes. The obvious question at this point is, what characteristic of a living system appears most closely related to magnetism? The answer is its informational aspect, i.e., a living system's ability to make choices. This answer forces the next obvious question: what does choice have to do with magnetism? The question of choice (or free will) is one of the fundamental issues in the nature of consciousness that many scientists and philosophers have struggled with. Our model may be able to shed some light on this age-old problem. Consider the following sequence of arguments.

1. Choice can be reduced to a binary, left-right or yes-no type of process. A binary process is familiar to us; it is the basis for the information in our computers and music on our CDs. In the physical world, the smallest possible increment of binary change is Planck's quantum of action, and this amount of change (or larger) can be brought about through an alteration of

the constraints that determine the energy flow for a particular process. That is, a choice modifies a least action path in an organism.

2. Therefore, a physical or chemical process is altered when a choice is made. The more immediate consequences of choice are changes in the quantum states of atoms and molecules which then influence their chemistry. Tiny currents, arising from the dynamics of electron spin and orbital motion, exert magnetic forces on each other and are also influenced by external magnetic fields. Because of their quantum structure, some molecular systems can be flipped into different spin states by extremely small magnetic disturbances (Fano & Fano, 1959). A change in the spin "direction" represents a means for encoding information into the physical system.

3. So now the question becomes, how do such magnetic changes couple in from the mental realm? Dirac's quantum theory of the electron shows that magnetism (specifically, the "vector potential") affects the phase of the electron's quantum wave function. Under certain conditions, this phase alteration can affect the electron's location and thus the atomic and molecular structures of which it is a part. The twistor formulation provides for a "fiber connection" between the particle and higher dimensional abstract space (Gough & Shacklett, 1993d). Our model views these mathematical abstract spaces as symbolic representations of the knowledge realm beyond space-time. Since the knowledge realm includes the mind or mental realm, we can connect these abstract spaces ultimately to conscious thought processes.

To summarize: human choice (a conscious act in the mental realm) alters the constraints on chemical processes in the physical realm. The informational content of the system is changed. The diagram below, based upon our model, shows the intermediate steps.

| | |
|---|---|
| Mental Realm | (choice) |
| Groups | |
| Fiber bundles | |
| Twister space | |
| Penrose transform | |
| EM field | |
| Particles | |
| Chemistry | |
| Physical Realm | (behavior change) |

We propose that intention is focussed choice, i.e., intention uses the same mechanisms involved in choice except that they are amplified quantitatively. Figure 4 illustrates how the process of altering constraints works.

Quantum theory imposes a lower limit on "choice" by "quantizing" action (Young, 1976:20). Therefore, if choice cannot be broken down into

Fig.4: An illustration of how the life process relates to intention and constraints as implied by the model. The act of mental intention produces changes in one's brain/body which can often be experienced as "feelings." The target of intention can be one's self, another person, or any thing/object in the universe. The figure suggests how this non-local process can be understood in terms of standard physics concepts—the end effect is a change in physical constraints which alter the body's chemistry.

smaller units, the quantum of action may represent some kind of fundamental act of consciousness comparable to a basic "left-right" or "yes-no" decision. Support for such a position comes from the work and experiments of Dr. L. Mandel at the University of Rochester. Mandel describes experiments in which the result (a light beam interference effect) is influenced by the possibility that the experimentalist could take actions, even if he doesn't take these actions (Mandel, 1991:1882-1883). Thus, these data indicate that mental acts can influence future events. The research challenges the prevalent view of physics in which events are based on what *is* rather that what *could be*.

## Perception of Reality

Perception is about sensory *qualities*, not the *quantities* expressed by physicists. This can be illustrated by the research of Edwin Land (inventor of the Polaroid camera) who, in 1957, challenged the very foundations of contemporary color theory. Land did experiments in which the colors seen by a person could not be there, according to traditional physics. The importance of input from the mental level could no longer be denied. "Our every perception is literally colored by contexts, prior experience, indeed, by every aspect of our inner world. These are all active in producing color" (Zajonc, 1993:191, 198-199).

The model being proposed assumes that everyday reality is not simply out there nor is it within. Rather, we suggest, it is a perception we construct from aspects of the unity within which we are immersed. Science has demonstrated that, in the world described by quantum theory, human perception, when limited to the five senses, is not an adequate tool for explaining this universe. What our experience gives us is the "illusion" of direct, unmediated access to the external world. Cognitive science has demonstrated conclusively that there is no way for a human to "sense" or experience the physical world directly. What seems to be our experience of an objective exterior world is in fact a *subjective picture* that we construct (Rivlin & Gravelle, 1984; Bolles, 1991).

Human experience can be compared to a motion picture. We are continually interacting via both our physical behavior *and thought patterns* with the whole, thereby altering, however slightly, the next "frame." Our mind is subtly and usually unconsciously active in each of our five senses, constantly forming and re-forming the world we perceive. Everything we have previously seen or experienced affects what we presently see or experience (Shephard, 1990). We must accept the fact, that not only every individual, but every age and culture has crafted its own sensory reality. However, unlike ancient societies, most of the time we don't recognize that patterns/symbols can originate from the archetypal realm.

The model implies that our experience of everyday reality depends upon both the current physical world inputs and quantum linkages to the archetypal patterns of the mental and higher realms—linkages that have been constructed over time. Whatever our current reality is, and whatever meaning we attribute to it, can be altered by changing the focus of our intention and attention—therefore change our life.

## Love—A Least Action Process

The importance of focusing our intention on heart-felt love, and the impact it has upon the functioning of our bodies, was discussed last year in our paper on "Science and Symbols" (Gough & Shacklett, 1993b:25). We will repeat and expand upon this concept since love is an essential aspect for understanding a science of good and evil. In the ancient wisdom, there were three key centers in the physical body: the brain, the heart, and the generative system. Unlike Western society, to the ancients the patterns of the heart were considered the most important. "The secret doctrine declares that every part and member of the body is epitomized in the heart" (Hall, 1988:lxxv). The heart was considered the spiritual center, having a direct effect on the rest of the body. Such a position is reflected in the scriptures of many religions: "The heart of the wise teaches his mouth, and adds learning to his lips" (Holy Bible, Proverbs 16:23). "Out of compassion for them, I, dwelling in their hearts, destroy with the shining lamp of knowledge the darkness born of ignorance" (Bhagavadgita, 10:11).

Although there has been relatively little scientific research to uphold this position, some recent experiments that include an electrocardiogram (ECG) of the heart have been suggestive (McCraty, et.al., 1993; Tiller, et.al., 1994). The normally scattered and incoherent power spectrum of the ECG was observed to be dramatically ordered and coherent when a person experiences deep feelings of love, care, or appreciation. Hence, the deep feelings of love may create patterns in our bodies that connect us to an archetypal ordering principle beyond the mental realm. When this connection is invoked, an organizing essence or intelligence capable of restructuring the least action paths may be activated and thereby change the energy patterns of the system. Through the removal of constraints, this process could restore balance or bring greater harmony within a more encompassing whole.

The process by which this is accomplished in our physical body would have to be observable in space-time. Since the heart produces by far the strongest electromagnetic field in the body, all cells in the body exist in, and therefore could be affected by, this coherent electromagnetic field pattern and experience a physical force. This would lend support to the statement by the well-known mystic Alice Bailey that "The soul, seated in the heart, is— the central nucleus of positive energy by means of which all the atoms of the body are held in their right place and subordinated to the 'will-to-be' of the soul" (Bailey, 1979:469). Hence, the close linkage between love-symbolism and heart-symbolism may exist because the love experience represents a force which urges the lover towards a given center of a more encompassing unity (Cirlot, 1971:141-142).

## Good and Evil

In terms of system dynamics, we may thus consider love as a state of being that creates a balance or coherence with the dynamic force of consciousness, i.e., the dynamic of change emanating from the more encompassing realms beyond space-time. This force embodies the intelligence of the knowledge realm and has been called the life force or the God force. Hence, when one generates thoughts and emotions of sincere love, these inner symbols appear to create a resonant pattern that places one in contact with the knowledge of a universal wholeness.

Good could be defined as love in action—creating balance with the "force." In our model, the human mind resides beyond space-time and is linked to and directly affects the patterns of the body. A marvel of the human brain is its ability to rapidly change its inner patterns as it interacts with the force of consciousness. This flexibility enables us to either remain in balance with the creative "force" or not, through our choice and free will. It is the feedback from this process—the positive synchronicities or the stress, illness, etc.—that helps us learn, and steer our ship of life.

Our model implies that imbalance can exist in realms other than the physical. For example, such imbalance for an individual's spirit is known as 'karma'—a restoring drive requiring acts to reestablish balance. Karma represents a natural law of cause and effect that operates from beyond space-time. Its power does not disappear until it is resolved. Karma has been considered the driving force behind rebirth in the physical and the cause of events that are often assumed to be "by chance" (Rinpoche, 1993). Since karma is a cause and effect mechanism, not bound by the constraints of physical time, what appears to be good or in balance within the physical realm could be out of balance when considered from the perspective of the more encompassing realms.

Thus, good, at a deep level, can be learned only to a limited extent from others. Rather, to truly understand such a concept one must establish a personal coupling to the knowledge realm and obtain a knowing of the intelligence emanating from the creative force. With this inner knowing one's personal constraints, represented by one's belief systems, can be modified in ways that bring one into balance with a more encompassing wholeness. The result of shifting from the separateness of the physical realm to the connectiveness of the knowledge realm can be dramatic as the cartoon in Figure 5 illustrates. One's greatest friend in this process is fear since fear represents a physical feedback signal upon reaching one's constraint barriers. We recall how the shaman often uses fear to alter the belief system of an apprentice.

Evil can be considered a force resulting from an imbalance. Evil is thus the result of ignorance, i.e., ignorance of what is required to remain in balance with the creative force. In some cultures, they say there is no evil, everything is as it should be, In one sense, this is also correct, since evil can be considered as the restoring force necessary to reestablish balance.

Good and evil have implications regarding one's thoughts and feelings since these affect the creative process. Since imbalance can exist in realms

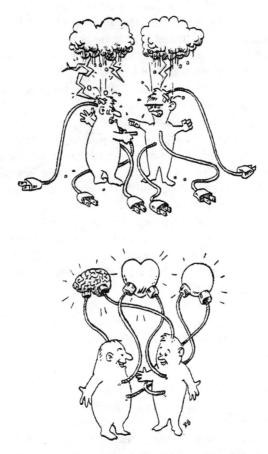

Fig.5: The first part of this cartoon illustrates how a failure to maintain a conscious connection of the body/brain system to more encompassng realms beyond space-time results in an illusion of separateness with its accompanying lack of balance. The second part shows that when this connection is established, the resulting balance leads to a more harmonious experience of oneness.

above the physical, focusing one's thoughts and feelings upon the spectrum of hate, hostility and strong aversion can manifest imbalance into one's physical body and life. The opposite effect is produced by focusing one's intentions upon love, compassion and appreciation, as the research data clearly show (McCraty, *et.al.*, 1993, Tiller *et.al.*, 1994).

## Summary

In summary, our model addresses the formation and creation of the physical world and how dynamic change is introduced from realms beyond space-time. Light and the electromagnetic spectrum are shown to be the underlying base for the structural patterns of the physical world. Choice and intention are related to the physical parameters of the magnetic field and spin. This ability to alter patterns, and hence information, in a two-way "feedback" manner is seen as a critical factor in the intervention of consciousness into the physical realm. It relates directly to our ability to alter both, ourselves and the world around us.

This expanded science recognizes (1) the unifying power of the pattern/symbol, and (2) mind and spirit as different, but not separate, from the physical. Mathematical concepts already exist for the physics of this expanded science. We therefore, outlined a conceptual model which illustrates that the realms beyond space-time and matter can be united, using connecting elements taken from conventional mathematical physics. An important factor in the model is the argument that space-time is not an impermeable barrier which confines human experience to the world of matter and that mind is located beyond space-time.

All models are simplifying suggestions or proposals on how to think about something that is more complicated. We have used the model to think about phenomena at the human level—to understand how we perceive "reality" and the role that the body/brain plays in connecting us to the appropriate patterns beyond space-time. The mental or archetypal patterns that form the basis of our belief systems and habitual thinking are thereby causative factors for the set of real physical constraints that govern the electrochemistry of the body. We now have a scientific model which illustrates how the physics of our outer world becomes the feelings of our inner world and visa versa. Thus, we have the basis for including good and evil under this expanded scientific paradigm—a paradigm that can encompass inner experience.

For further discussion of the "problem of evil," see Peterson's anthology (1992) in which he presents authors coming from different disciplines so that readers can compare aspects of evil, e.g., from logical, evidential, existential, point of views, including concepts of Augustinian, Irenaean, Process, Theoretical, and Practical Theodicy.

## Conclusion

We started this paper by discussing how a child *learns* about the concepts of good and evil and the many confusing signals that are received in our society. As one matures, the learning about good and evil must be supplanted by a *knowing* about good and evil. This knowing arises from an individual's coupling to a universal wholeness. Such coupling permits one to remain in balance with the changes emanating from that wholeness.

The strengthening of that coupling is achieved by a free will choice to focus one's intentions upon heart-felt appreciation, compassion and love. The result is a change not only in one's life but in the lives of others. Fortunately, there exists a universal feedback process to teach us when to shift from intellectual learning to inner knowing.

The feedback signals can be observed as symptoms of stress in an individual, society, and nature. Such stress manifests as disease in individuals and as "evil" for the overall society. The principle cause behind such stress resides in our belief systems—the constraints that operate upon our thoughts and hence upon our free will choices which are contributing to the creation of physical reality. The cure is to restore balance with the larger whole—a whole that encompasses more than the physical realm. The medicine required, as many of the ancient sages have taught, is sincere love and compassion.

## Acknowledgements

The authors wish to thank Robert Bourdeaux (8510 Brink Rd., Gaithersburg, MD 20882) for his artistic contribution to the creation of the artwork used in this paper. Some portions of this essay parallel material published in the copyrighted journal *Subtle Energies* and have appeared in the essay, "The Science of Connectiveness, PART III: The Human Experience (Gough & Shacklett, 1993e). They are being republished with the kind permission of the *International Society for the Study of Subtle Energies and Energy Medicine* (Golden, CO 80401).

## *References*

Bailey, A.A. *A Treatise on White Magic: The Way of the Disciple.* New York: Lucis Publishing, 1979.

*Bhagavad-gita.* New York: Bhaktivedanta Book Trust, 1972.

Ball, D.W. "Interactions of Light with Matter, *Spectroscopy 9:6* (July-August, 1994):20.

Becker, R.O. "Modern Bioelectromagnetics and Functions of the Central Nervous System," *Subtle Energies, 3* (1992):53-72.

Bohm, D. *Wholeness and the Implicate Order.* London: Routledge & Kegan Paul, 1980.

Bolles, E.B. *A Second Way of Knowing: The Riddle of Human Perception.* New York: Prentice Hall, 1991.

Cirlot, J.E. *A Dictionary of Symbols.* New York: Philosophical Library, transl., 1971. (Spanish edition, 1962)

Fano, U. and L. Fano. *Basic Physics of Atoms and Molecules.* New York: Wiley, 1959.

Flam, Faye. Lighting a Route to the New Physics—With Photons," *Science, 265* (September 30, 1994):2013-2014.

Feynman, R., R. Leighton & M. Sands. *The Feynman Lectures on Physics*. Reading, MA: Addison-Wesley, 1963. I-26 & II-10.

Gough, W.C. & R.L. Shacklett. "Physics, Parapsychology and Religion—Part I: The Reality Beyond Space-Time; Part II: The Quantum Linkage; Part III: The Human Implications," *Journal of Religion and Psychical Research, 16* (1993a):65-67; 126-134; 196-209.

____ . "Science and Symbols," *Proceedings of the Tenth International Conference on the Study of Shamanism and Alternate Modes of Healing*, ed. Ruth-Inge Heinze. Berkeley, CA: Independent Scholars of Asia, Inc., 1993b, pp.14-33.

____ . "The Science of Connectiveness, Part I: Modeling a Greater Unity," *Subtle Energies, 4:1* (1993c):57-76.

____ . "The Science of Connectiveness, Part II: Mapping Beyond Space-Time," *Subtle Energies, 4:2* (1993d):99-123.

____ . "The Science of Connectiveness, Part III: The Human Experience," *Subtle Energies, 4:3* (1993e; draft essay under review).

Green, E., P. Parks, A. Green, P. Guyer, & S. Fahrion. "Gender Differences in a Magnetic Field, *Subtle Energies, 3* (1992):65-103.

Hall, M.P. *The Secret Teachings of All Ages: An Encyclopedic Outline of Masonic, Hermetic, Qabbalistic and Rosicrucian Symbolical Philosophy*. Los Angeles, CA. Philosophical Research Society, 1988.

*Holy Bible*, authorized King James' Version. Philadelphia, PA: A.J. Holman Co., undated, Proverbs 16-23.

Jammer, M. *Concepts of Space: The History of Theories of Space in Physics*, 2nd ed. Cambridge, MA: Harvard University Press, 1969.

Levin, M. "Current and Potential Applications of Bioelectromagnetics in Medicine," *Subtle Energies, 4* (1993):77-85.

Mandel, L. "Coherence and Indistinguishability," *Optical Letters, 16:23* (1991): 1882-1883.

Maxey, E.S. "A Lethal Subtle Energy, *Subtle Energies* (1991):55-72.

McCraty, R., M. Atkinson, & G.Rein. "ECG Spectra: The Measurement of Coherent and Incoherent Frequencies and Their Relationship to Mental and Emotional States," *Proceedings of the 3rd ISSSEEM Conference*, Monterey, CA (June 1993):44-48.

Peat, F.D. *Superstrings and the Search for the Theory of Everything*. Chicago, IL: Contemporary Books, 1988.

Richard, M. *Time's Arrows: Scientific Attitudes Toward Time*. New York: Simon and Schuster, 1984.

Peterson, M.L., ed. *The Problem of Evil, Selected Readings*. Notre Dame, IN: University of Notre Dame Press, Library of Religious Philosophy, 8, 1992.

Puthoff, H.E. "Gravity as a Zero-Point Fluctuation Force," *Phys.Rev. A, 39* (1988): 92-93.

Sogyal Rinpoche. *The Tibetan Book of Living and Dying.* San Francisco, CA: Harper, 1993.

Rivlin, R. and K. Gravelle. *Deciphering the Senses: The Expanding World of Human Perception.* New York: Simon & Schuster, 1984.

Sakharov, A.D. *Dokl.Akad Nauk SSSR* [Sov.Phys. Dokl.], *12* (1968):1040 (referenced in Putoff, 1988)

Shacklett, R.L. & W.C. Gough. *The Unification of Mind and Matter: A Proposed Scientific Model.* Los Altos, CA: Report of the Foundation for Mind-Being Research, 1991.

Shallis, M. *On Time: An Investigation into Scientific Knowledge and Human Experience.* New York: Schocken Books, 1982.

Shepard. R.N. *Mind Sights.* New York: W.H. Freeman, 1990.

Tiller, W.A., R. McCraty, & M. Atkinson. "Cardiac Coherence: A New Noninvasive Measure of Autonomic System Order (in preparation, 1994).

Young, A.M. *The Reflexive Universe.* New York: Delacorte Press, 1976.

Ward, R.S. & R.O. Wells, Jr. *Twistor Geometry and Field Theory.* New York: Cambridge University Press, 1990.

Weber, R. *Dialogs with Scientists and Sages: The Search for Unity.* London: Routledge & Kegan Paul, 1986.

Zajonc, A. *Catching the Light: The Entwined History of Light and Mind.* New York: Bantam Books, 1993.

# THE ROLE OF FRONTIER SCIENTISTS' PERSONAE IN THEIR RESEARCH

Beverly Rubik

> I swear the earth shall surely be complete to him
> or her who shall be complete.
> The earth remains jagged and broken to him
> or her who remains jagged and broken.
> *Walt Whitman*

## Introduction

Over the past six years I have been in a privileged position of meeting and getting to know a substantial number of scientists worldwide, especially frontier scientists who are working at the cutting edge of science in areas of science that are not yet mainstream. These are a special type of scientists, high-risk takers whose scientific quest takes them in the furthest frontiers to blaze a trail where no one has gone before, committed to a path that is usually fraught with extraordinary difficulties. What appears as an outer quest for knowledge about the physical world is about an inner journey as well. I have come to see a strong relation between the work of frontier scientists and their personal evolution.

Perhaps this does not surprise any who are psychologists, as such a relation might be expected. But it is very surprising and unexpected for scientists who believe in the myth of objectivity, which is that any scientist could have asked the research questions, made the observations, and obtained the same results. Nothing to my knowledge has been published that contradicts this conventional view. However, it appears that the specific topics of inquiry that scientists choose are neither purely accidental nor purely intellectual. Scientists each have somewhat different questions they pose of nature, questions which in fact motivate them to engage in science in the first place.

Frontier scientists have a burning curiosity to pursue something novel and challenge mainstream dogma in the process. They do this despite extraordinary obstacles, such a difficulty in obtaining funding, lack of camaraderie, inability to publish their results in mainstream journals, loss of respect of their peers, difficulty in obtaining promotion, and loss of job security. On the other hand, work at the frontiers of science holds the greatest promise of future scientific breakthroughs. The risk is high, but the return can be a historical landmark in science. I propose that the nature of their pioneering question reflects deep psychological processes within themselves, a striving toward inner healing, integration and/or personal transformation. The nature of their maverick scientific questions, turned inward, relate to their quest for personal growth.

Scientists work by dialoguing with nature. We scientists pose questions of nature, and nature answers us as seen in the results of our experiments. Science is driven by new questions, and the nature of our questions—their quality, essence, and orientation—fully determine the science that we generate. Therefore, the scientific process, which reflects our unique perspective, must to some extent reflect our personal journeys. Therefore, we can examine scientific questions, concepts, models, and terminology in the light of the person or society that generates them. In the past I have reflected on the role of scientific community (Rubik, 1992:11-28); in this paper, I address the role of the scientist's persona.

## Some Examples

Theoretical physicist Emilio Del Giudice of the National Institute of Nuclear Physics, Milano, Italy, is a self-proclaimed communist who used to be quite active in the Italian communist party. His scientific work provides a radically new theory of condensed matter, developed for liquids and solids (Del Giudice, 1993:16-29 and 1988:1085). Compared to the mainstream view in which the particles of matter are considered completely independent of one another, it is a novel view in which the molecules are not individual entities but behave cooperatively like people in a communist society. The particles are, therefore, seen by him as dependent collectives that effectively lower their energy levels and gain more stability by behaving coherently. This type of "matter field" is analogous to a stage full of ballet dancers performing pirouettes all in phase, so that they are always performing the same motion in the same direction. Upon further interviewing him, I found that he has also had difficulty in personal relationships. He married relatively late in life and, after only two years of marriage, his wife developed cancer. She died of cancer after five years of marriage. He soon remarried, but his second relationship grew cold. Del Giudice expressed a need to be loved— not by one special person but by many, even by all. His physical theory reflects this—the projection of his innermost desires for a collective type of love onto particles of matter that exhibit a cooperative dance with one another and release energy in the process. Futhermore, when I pointed out this possible relation between his personal quest and his physical theory, he admitted that this seemed plausible.

The late David Bohm is another example that I would like to discuss. Since I cannot interview him, I am drawing on my relation with him as colleague for thirteen years, and also via F. David Peat, a physicist and author who worked with him and who is currently writing a biography of Bohm (personal communication, 1994). Bohm is noted for his unique interpretation of quantum theory and, to many, for his work on the mind/matter interface. The latter is a quest for wholeness: how the material world is interconnected with itself and beyond, in which an implicate order of reality is enfolded within the explicate order of ordinary space-time (1980). David Bohm struggled to bring wholeness to our fragmented scientific world view, but I would like to suggest that he was also struggling with self-integration. Peat, who is writing a biography of Bohm, told me that Bohm's mother was psychotic. Moreover, Bohm also revealed to Peat that he had felt betrayed by various important male colleagues or father figures. For example, Bohm had worked with the mystic Krishnamurti who claimed that he was celibate; however, after Krishnamurti had died, Bohm learned that the latter had had mistresses. Anyone who ever heard Bohm lecture found what appeared to be a dispassionate man addressing remarkable ideas. In my view, his intellect and his heart center appeared as separate compartments; the lack of passion in his self-expression was pronounced. One wonders further about the lack of emotional expression, since Bohm died of a heart attack and had long-term heart trouble. Furthermore, in his last few years of life, Bohm had been hospitalized for serious depression, and his brain was treated by electro-shock therapy. Toward the end of his life, he also revealed to Peat that he felt that his work was inadequate. The questions Bohm raised about how to bring wholeness into science, of how the universe can be regarded as one great seamless whole, perhaps grew out of his own brokenness as well as his concern over the fragmentation of the scientific world view.

In my own case, I also see trends in my scientific quest that reflect my personal journey. Some years ago, as a science student, I felt from the very beginning that there was something missing in the models of science, and I wandered from physics to chemistry to biology looking for the "juiciness" of life, but I never found it in conventional science, however, I persevered long enough to earn my Ph.D. in biophysics. I was then drawn to the subtle realms of nature that have not yet been much addressed in science: the interaction of subtle fields and living systems, the interrelationship between mind and matter, and alternative medicine. I was intent on pursuing these, despite numerous career difficulties. What these topics that appealed to me have in common is that they are softer, gentler, "low-impact" interactions that may be considered expressions of the feminine archetype in nature. In the past I have also made a presentation at this conference about a feminine view of nature, the missing feminine archetype in science (Rubik, 1992:11-28). Despite the successes of the women's liberation movement, it seems to me that what society has gained is not real gender balance, but that it is now okay for a woman to behave as a man. The masculine archetype dominates our science as it does our world. We have not gained much in the way of respect for nurturing, caring, or an understanding of the subtler, gentler ways of the feminine archetype. Moreover, as a career woman, I have had every reinforcement to behave as a man. I am under constant pressure to publish or perish, build an academic science empire by obtaining substantial grants, fulfill numerous speaking engagements, act rationally as a scientist, and be logical and cool, despite colleagues' other-than-logical reactions to my work. Also, because of my recent success and resulting numerous commitments as a professional, my personal life has withered for lack of time. I feel unbalanced. Something in me seeks to be expressed, and it is so strong that it has steered my scientific interests in a particular direction. It has been expressed in my dreams (see Appendix). It is also expressed in my quest to recover the missing feminine archetype in how we view nature. Thus, my work toward a gender-balanced science reflects my personal striving toward a balance between the gender archetypes inside myself.

A professor of physics, whose name I will not mention, is searching with great fervor to find the ultimate elementary particle, and he is also a con-

firmed atheist. Despite his denial of the spiritual realm, a search for the ultimate particle may be regarded as a search for the absolute, for "God" in the
material realm. His scientific work may reflect his anxiety, conscious or
unconscious, due to his inability to accept anything beyond that which can
be measured.

## Some General Observations

On occasion I have observed that personality obstacles in certain scientists may relate to their scientific quest in such a way that they also become
obstacles in their work, but they also offer them an opportunity for transformation. For example, someone working on cellular communication may
have a conspicuously difficult time in personal relations and communications, which hampers his scientific communications as well, although he
may remain blind to this. His research, if he reflected on its source, would
take him into the dark shadow side of himself, offering him an opportunity
for "alchemical transmutation" of darkness into greater self-awareness and
transformation.

Many enter science because they are good at it, but also because they are
not so adept at interpersonal relations, and science provides a convenient
escape. Scientists seek refuge from difficult human relations in the beauty
and comfort of nature, which becomes a mother archetype to them. Nevertheless, they project their own experiences with human relations into their
descriptions of nature. Consider that Newtonian science views objects in the
universe as discrete, separate, rigid bodies such as billiard balls, each with
their own trajectories, which interact only by means of collision and are
isolated by the vacuum of empty space all around them. If we project that
picture on the realm of human relations, we see how it reflects a certain
character structure, a *yang,* contracted state of independent beings fighting
to exert themselves amidst confrontations with others or seeking isolation to
find their own peace, aware of only the surface features, the hard exteriors,
the superficial aspects of things.

## Conclusions

To a large extent, research in the frontier sciences is "me-search," a way
in which various facets of ourselves seek to become expressed, integrated,
or transformed in our actions or ideas. Indeed, Paul Ricoeur wrote that our
psyche and our view of the cosmos are the convex and concave of the same
surface. The relation that I propose between frontier scientists' personae and
the nature of their scientific work, however, is very preliminary and also
speculative.

Moreover, I would not expect this relation to hold as strongly for conventional scientists because their motivations in performing scientific research may be quite different. Although most scientists are initially inspired to study nature because they are driven to ask new questions and discover something new about how nature works, this initial motivation is soon replaced by more pragmatic considerations as one matures in one's career. The scientific community is a conservative body that selects for members that maintain the status quo. Therefore, the research question posed by most scientists are those most readily accessible to inquiry, amenable to obtaining grants, that are obvious next steps to take, etc. Conventional scientists are shaped and groomed by perks from the scientific community that include financial rewards and professional status, and their research does not challenge the status quo. They are usually not the true pilgrims or mavericks as are the frontier scientists. Thus, their scientific quest may not represent a direct projection of their personal issues, as it is shaped by peer pressure and other factors.

I have not studied large numbers of frontier scientists to test for the relationship to their personal life struggles, nor am I able to perform statistical tests for reliability. But even if I had, what would come of it? Would scientists ever accept that their deeper personal quest may be reflected in their science? I doubt it, because scientists, like other human beings, reject that which deeply challenges their ego. It is one thing to read about consciousness and its role in science; it is quite another to apply it personally in our own discovery process. Humans, even scientists, at their core, are irrational beings. If I learned anything the past six year in my work to bring frontier science topics into the mainstream, it is that experimental data challenging the conventional world view do not convince anyone in and of themselves. Therefore, I am not particularly motivated to develop this idea further by studying large number of scientists, because the subjective realm that is involved here is not yet considered legitimate for scientific inquiry. Science has become what Karl Marx termed an "alienated concept," in that it does not take seriously any studies on its nature from outside its own scope or methodology of inquiry.[1]

Thomas Kuhn wrote that the transition between competing paradigms is not made step by step, forced by logic and neutral experience (1970). A paradigm shift is a conversion experienced within. Such a conversion experience starts with the decision to change on the inside, usually due to the "college of hard knocks"—real life experiences that challenge us or inner transformations. For example, many parapsychologists had personal experiences of what is conventionally considered to be paranormal earlier in life, and they became parapsychologists in order to understand and integrate these experiences into their body of knowledge about the world. However, those outside of parapsychology who have never had a personal experience, remain unconvinced, no matter how much good research data have been accumulated.

Returning to my basic thesis, the questions that we pose as frontier scientists are keys to our own personal transformation, which usually reflect our inner quagmire of unresolved issues. In our work to change the world, we must face our dark shadow—our unresolved issues, our hidden agendas—and by descending into the darkness, we bring back our own gems of wisdom into the light of the world for all to see. Work at the brink of the mind-matter interface within ourselves has the capacity to transform.

It would seem that various human emanations, whether they are skin rashes, fevers, tumors, emotional tantrums, or seemingly intellectual maverick questions posed about the external world have one commonality. They all help us recover balance, integrity, and health at the various levels of our being.

Finally, what does such an inquiry as the relation between scientists' questions and their personal development say about me? I wanted my work in science to be a very personal expression of myself, and I expected that to be the case for other scientists as well. Science may be objective knowledge for all to see just as art is, once it is revealed. However, the art of revelation is a deeply personal, mystical experience, part of one's self-actualization or self-realization. It might be fruitful for all of us to re-examine our questions or motivations underlying our work in the world and see how they reflect our innermost desires for personal integration and spiritual growth.

## Acknowledgement

I wish to acknowledge Marco Bischof of Biberist, Switzerland, with whom I had an extensive discussion on this topic in 1992. Working together, we developed a preliminary sketch for a jointly authored paper on this topic. The results I have, in part, incorporated here.

## *Note*

1.   All academic fields suffer from the lack of "I" in the work. Academics are not allowed to speak of themselves and their process in relation to their work and instead deny their humanity and the role it plays therein. Thus, to a large extent, the myth of objectivity goes even beyond science. In my opinion, a renaissance will begin when we admit to our humanness and observe its role in our work.

## *Appendix*

Dream written down upon awakening the morning of August 28, 1994:

I dreamed I was searching and finding coins lying under old slot machines, poking around in the dust between the cracks where no one else ever looks.

Suddenly, I heard a continuous trickle of coins from a machine on the other side of my row of slot machines that attracted my attention. No one was there that I could see, so I went over to take a look. I had to tilt the machine to gather all the coins. As the machine remained off kilter, even after I tried to push it back, I feared it would topple on me, but instead I became aware of a dead human hand, sticking out from the bottom. At first, I felt a slight aversion, but then I grasped the hand and got the "psychic" message that it felt good to this being, I lovingly encouraged its life. I stroked the hand gently and willed the spirit to be grounded once more in the body. In doing so, it gradually came to life.

I moved the slot machine away from it, maneuvering my hands gently over the whole body and then it revived completely. It was a young woman of about 30 years old who was from MA (Massachusetts? Mother?), a "pilgrim" of a sort who was from another era and could teach me about the past in a wonderful way. She was very tall, about six feet, with reddish-blondish-brown air, somewhat like mine, but shorter. I gave her the old coins I had been collecting from around the slot machines (they seemed to be from the 1800s), so that she would have some money to spend. Was she a feminine counterpart to Uncle Sam, the masculine soul of the U.S.?

Although she was grateful to be revived at first, she became difficult later and even cantankerous and disruptive. After a while, she was apparently together with some man, but spoke of wanting to "revive" her old boyfriend whom she said was very tall, over six feet 2 inches, in the same manner as she had been revived by me.

It had been a miracle that I could revive her, and I reflected on the biology of it. I had planned a meeting to present her to the scientific experts with all the evidence—but I soon gave up this idea. I no longer cared about teaching them something or showing them this remarkable feat. Instead I reflected on the power of gentle action of my hands, a sequence of light touch all over her body, with love and movement of my breath that together were able to rekindle life in a dead woman's body.

Is this woman symbolic of the feminine archetype that I am questing to revive in me and in science? I think so. However, it seems that I am no longer interested in convincing the experts. I am more interested in developing my capabilities in the subtle realms and in achieving greater understanding of them.

## References

Bohm, D. *Wholeness and the Implicate Order.* Boston, MA: Routledge and Kegan Paul, 1980.

Del Giudice, E. "Coherence in condensed and living matter," *Frontier Perspectives, 3:2* (1993):16-20.

_____, G. Preparata, and G. Vitiello. *Phys.Rev.Letters, 61* (1988):1085.

Kuhn, T. *The Structure of Scientific Revolution.* Chicago, IL: University of Chicago Press, 1970.

Peat, F.D. Personal communication, 1994.

Rubik, B. "Toward a New Science: A Feminine Perspective," *Proceedings of the 8th International Conference on the Study of Shamanism and Alternate Modes of Healing*, ed. R.-I. Heinze. Berkeley, CA: Independent Scholars of Asia, Inc., 1991, pp.11-28.

# DISCUSSION

With Burns, Gough, Heinze, and Rubik

*Goodman:* I am a multi-lingual researcher. When I listen to such discussions, my big problem is the fact that I don't ever hear any clear definition for either "mind" or "consciousness." I find this to be the basis for much confusion and I wonder whether the speakers could give us an idea of how they define "mind" and "consciousness"?

*Burns:* One of the reasons that we do not define these terms too well is that we really don't know what they are. You cannot explore something and, at the same time, try to pin it down. That's the problem. Publishing in various journals, people will talk about "what is mind?" and as soon as they pin it down, somebody else will say, "I don't think you got it pinned down right." Maybe some of us could answer your question in a more definite way, but it is kind of a problem.

*Gough:* I view "mind" as being beyond the physical. So whatever we describe, it will have limitations. "Mind" and "consciousness" are beyond the physical. All we can do is say what it is. We cannot give a definition other than what we are able to do for other physical objects. You have nothing to compare it to.

*Burns:* There are real problems with the question what is nameable and what is not. The mathematician Rudy Rucker has a book out which is called *Infinity of the Mind* (New York: Bantam, 1982). It just came out as a reprint in one of the older Walden editions. He does a beautiful job of pointing out the problem and what it has to do with objects of the mind. I talked about infinity, but infinity is just part of the problem. Some things are almost unnameable in our experience. You can point to them and you get better and better and do a wonderful job, but then spaciousness is coming up and you say, "I still have not named it." "Mind" probably has that quality. We do the best we can and get pretty far.

*Etchevery:* I am a science historians. Pockinghorn, a professor of physics and an Anglican priest, talked about the Einstein-Rosen paradox, the wave and the particle, Schroeder's cat in the box, etc. If you would say that consciousness controls the collapse of the wave, he would say, "I walk over to my book shelf and look up who won a cricket match at a certain year. The person who knows about that will have conscious control over it." And you have also to accept solipsism and the good Reverend Berkeley. The question is whether you have conscious control.

*Gough:* I don't think you have complete conscious control over anything. There is a coupling, in physics, too. Without a deep coupling, you will have little control. And in addition, you are interacting with a wholeness that may have and, I believe, does have an intelligence encompassing your own. When you talk about your control, you have to talk in broader terms.

*Etchevery:* It is not a paradox at all.

*Rudiak-Gillard:* Because of the nature of the work I do, I work with trauma, abuse and shock, I am really struck by the whole panel. It wove together some ideas which I wanted to voice, too, out of my own experience. I have not really a question but something to be put into the soup, using my words. In terms of defining wisdom, wisdom as coming from the realm of knowledge, evil is considered lack of wisdom. It has been a really interesting journey for me in terms of coming from a compassionate base. Most distortion, disturbance, and distress patterns come from ignorance. Lack of knowing, looking a lot at the natural tendency toward entropy will take people out of balance and what it means to stay awake, present, and alive. On the edge of that self-awareness, that self-sensing moment allows us to balance ourselves in the face of the ongoing process of entropy. That is not only a mental but also a physiological process. For me, the concept of destroying ego is about unraveling ignorance. The word "evil" is part of a dualistic paradigm, in which I am not really living, although I had some strong experiences and was affected by a lot of people who would classify as being evil. I guess it was my husband listening to something on Channel 9, "Alternative Medicine and Nature." To use a different word which I like because it is complimentary, for me, it feels like being inclusive and connected as opposed to something outside the realm. This is the way I would like to see things.

*Potts, Dominik:* I am a trial attorney. Beverly, I can relate to what you are saying. You talk about the myth in the scientific world. There is a myth of judiciality and fairness in the court system. Each judge brings to his bench his own prejudices, experiences, and sometimes clandestine considerations.

You see that a lot in the O.J. Simpson trial, for example. Any given judge can make a very dramatic difference on account of his experiences. Whoever presides shapes the trial process and the final outcome—the fair, objective process.

*Potts, Mena:* I enjoyed all your presentations which stimulated a question. You speak of "mind" and you speak of "consciousness" and I am wondering whether they are not perhaps the same? Do you see a distinction between them or are they the same?

*Rubik:* They have been used to describe different facets. Consciousness is awareness, and there is, of course, subconsciousness, unconsciousness, etc. Mind encompasses a bigger realm for all these more subtle features.

*Gough:* "Mind" is used as a limited area of those realms beyond space and time. "Consciousness" incorporates the wholeness coming from that realm which we experience.

*Groesbeck:* On this myth of objectivity, isn't it true that with the theories we have now, we have some basis for objectivity? Do we have evidence that the myth of absolute objectivity is true or not?

*Gough:* In the traditional science, objectivity is based on the physical world in space and time. I think we could get some objectivity in the sense of some individuals who could also encompass a larger wholeness. Then you could repeat the experiment from that larger level, but it would require the human being himself being part of that experiment. I don't see complete objectivity, it has a relative aspect.

*Burns:* I think that question is going to be more and more important and we will be hearing a lot more about it. For right now, Richard Tarnas has a wonderful book about the history of scientific thought, it is called, *Passion of the Western Mind* (New York: Ballantine, 1991). Toward the end, when he comes to the subject of post-modernness—hermeneutics—he brings this up. In science, yes, there is something objective we all can agree on. This is a podium, it is here and we all agree on it. But it is also kind of a paradox and somebody brought this up already. In science we are always involved in paradoxes. As Beverly said beautifully, this kind of lived experience of the scientist and the lived experience of the judicial system, how do you square things together? There is a very important movement here in postmodernism and hermeneutics that says, "look, what we do is really a set of agreements." It implicitly says that we live in a kind of infinity of mystery and we make agreements. Some agreements are very easy and very universal, like the existence of the podium and some are not that easy. We have to understand what does science relate to? How does the lived experience relate to certain statements?

*Leikam:* Of late, I have been trying to take in the bigger, and bigger, and bigger picture. Bill, you put the scientific world out there as a link between the physical world and the timeless-spaceless region. Has anybody done any work or thinking along the lines—beyond space, time, light, beyond consciousness, moving so far out, even to a bigger doll (like these Russian dolls) than the one you had? What might exist in such realms?

*Gough:* I will go back to the mathematics of infinity and to Cantor's final infinity, absolute infinity. You reach a point where there is nothing you can further describe.

*Olsen:* I love the setting in which you placed us all here—the context. The comment I have is that I love the book David Peat co-wrote with David Bohm, *Science, Order and Creativity* (New York: Bantam Books, 1987). This book outlines the whole topic for me. One of the issues I hear us talking about is the search for the absolute, the absolute infinity, which comes out of our insecurity. Even saying that God is absolute, is our way of pinning things down, rather than opening them up.

*Marks:* I want to thank Ruth for her incredible deep presentation, I feel we need to hear a great deal more about that. Ruth and Beverly's presentations come, in a sense, together. They bring us to the question how our own experience is valuable in relationship to our work. How to stay out of ego, too. I appreciate both presentations, especially Ruth's, because I feel this story should be told more and more by Germans. We all can learn deeply from this. It takes a lot of courage to tell these stories, especially when they surface at this time.

# INDIGENOUS SCIENCE FOR EURO-AMERICANS

Jürgen W. Kremer

This paper explores the possibility of an indigenous science approach or indigenous way of knowing for Euro-Americans. In order to understand what the term "indigenous science" means, we have to understand what indigenous consciousness or indigenous mind is. Consequently, I will proceed as follows:

First, I will discuss the need for Euro-Americans to recover their indigenous consciousness or mind.

Second, I will discuss the concept of indigenous mind.

Third, I will describe what indigenous science is.

Fourth, I will discuss the potential for retribalization or recovery of indigenous consciousness.

Fifth, I will discuss the recovery of an indigenous science approach for Euro-Americans.

Sixth, I will discuss the politics of retribalization and the recovery of indigenous science.

## I. The Need for the Recovery of Indigenous Consciousness or Mind

"I do not want people to adopt Indian rituals because I want people to own their own rituals. I want them to come to ownership out of experiences that are real to them. Then I'll come and celebrate it with them." This statement by Cattaugus Seneca John Mohawk (as recorded by Charlene Spretnak, 1991) is an adapt introduction to my topic. It shows that what I am talking about is really no news on this continent. Native American Elders have said it before many times in different ways: Euro-Americans (and by this I mean all people who have been socialized within that framework, irrespective of place of birth or race) need to remember their own traditions. Only then will there be the possibility of balance and harmony among all the people living on these lands. Only after such remembrance will there be the possibility of healthy communities and a balanced living with all our relations—humans, animals, plants and rocks. The recovery of indigenous consciousness means the recovery of indigenous ways of knowing or indigenous sciences. Rituals or ceremonies hold significant aspects of indigenous science and are part of its knowing and research process.

The issues at stake in the recovery of indigenous consciousness are the end of genocide, the end of ecocide, the honoring of spirit, the healing of communities, the honoring of woman, the balancing of the female and male and the healing of the children—all children. No small matter. It amounts to a shift in consciousness that is larger than any call for a new paradigm has encompassed. Maybe that is why it is so difficult (or threatening) to grasp the true meaning of what Elders say who are genuinely in their traditional minds. "Euro-Americans, remember your own roots!" These simple words spoken by traditionalists express a way of being, a way of seeing, and an epistemology and ontology which is unbelievable for the ways of the Euro-American mind. The traditional knowledge belongs to a paradigm which is different from that of humanistic psychology, transpersonal psychology, new age teachings and neo-shamanic approaches, postmodern anthropology or psychology, and liberal understanding of multiculturalism. This is the point most often missed by those who are seeking ecological knowledge from tribal people or who seek to emulate their healing approaches or who attempt personal growth through the use of what are commonly called "shamanic techniques."

Retribalization is the term which for me names the process in which the scientist or scholar gets to know who he is in ways which incorporate the split off parts (the choice of the masculine pronoun is conscious, since I am writing as a man and since the scientific paradigm is the masculinization of the phenomena): the result of such knowing would be called indigenous science. The retribalization of all those people who have bought into the Euro-American paradigm (whether this is here, in Africa, Europe or elsewhere) is a necessity for planetary survival. A person who remembers his or her tribal mind has stepped out of the addictive patterns of the "Western" mind. The simplest name for this addictive pattern is *progress.* It is no coincidence that the notion of progress has is roots in large scale agriculture—which early on served to grow sufficient amounts of hops for addictive purposes. The addiction of alcoholism and the progress addiction seem to spring from the same roots. The pervasiveness of the Euro-American paradigm is reflected in the pervasiveness of alcoholism. The split from the tribal mind is supported by the anaesthesia of liquor. Drunkenness helps to forget who we are. Intoxication is one of the simplest and most readily available means to maintain the split, the dissociation from those parts of ourselves which don't fit into the Euro-American paradigm with ease. The more we progress the less we know who we are. The more we dissociate the greater the need for drugs (in the form of alcohol, television, socially acceptable drugs, mind games, etc.) The remembrance of our tribal minds means the end of addiction.

## II. Indigenous Mind - What is it?

The first, and most important, thing which needs to be said about indigenous consciousness is that no list of its identifiable components can adequately capture what it is. We can define its significant aspects and coordinates, but its holistic functioning and nature escapes such attempts. What we can do, however, its circumscribe its nature and point to its depth and detail.

While it is true that individuals are (or are not) in their indigenous minds, it is also true that the indigenous mind is not individual. Individuals are in their indigenous minds if they understand how they stand in the weave of their ancestry, community, nature, spirit(s) and cycles. The individual gift from spirit(s) (medicine, endowment) of a person comes to life if, and only if s/he recognizes where s/he stands in this weave. Individuals embody the indigenous mind, which encompasses more than their individual self. Indigenous consciousness is participatory in reality. Reality is not out there and opposed to the individual, they are part of each other and each individual is challenged to maintain balance and harmony in this weave. It is important to emphasize that the indigenous mind is thus grounded both in spirit and matter. While it is a potential for every human being, this potential can only be realized if it is specifically grounded in the necessary conditions just listed (which means that it, ultimately, cannot be realized in an individualistic paradigm).

Looking out we track the seasons changing and know what can be gathered and hunted, and as we do so we acknowledge the spirit and the relation which gives away. This allows me to be in a relationship with nature, the plants I grow and the animals I breed which is sustainable, which provides for me while I provide for the weave.

I have given a description which identifies the necessary coordinates for the presence of indigenous mind. From these necessary conditions arise the specific indigenous mind.

Two presuppositions central to this exposition need to be mentioned:

1. The indigenous mind is a human potential which can be actualized by anybody and everybody.

2. the indigenous mind is not something of the past, but a consciousness present among various contemporary indigenous people.

Indigenous mind is thus understood as a human potential for all and everybody, and it is also understood as a worldview, or rather a particular way to participate in the world and to experience reality. The indigenous mind as a worldview does not so much signify a particular set of beliefs as it refers to a pragmatically, experientially grounded and validated way of being in the world. While this mind appears to rest in individuals (and needs their intentionality to be present), it only emerges when the individual rests in the weave of the ancestral heritage, the community, nature and spirit(s).

If people are in the mind set just outlined, then they could call it "the good mind" or what the Iroquois people call "the great peace," *skanagoah:*

> Skanagoah, literally interpreted as "great peace," is the term used to describe the still, electrifying awareness one experiences in the deep woods. This feeling or state of balance is at the heart of the universe and is the spirit of Native science (Colorado, 1988:52).

The loss of indigenous consciousness occurs through a process which I have called dissociative schismogenesis (Kremer, 1994), an increasing split from one's origin or roots. This addictive process lets us forget who we are and no longer places us in an understanding of the seasonal and astronomical cycles, the spiritual world, the power and meaning of sacred place, the local ecology and all our human capabilities. While the rational mind processes are valued, we are dissociated from emotional, somatic and spiritual knowing. What once was a part of us now is OTHER and strange—no longer a teacher.

This leads me to an important point: The world of the tribal person is not the world of the Euro-American person. A person who is in his or her tribal mind is not of this reality! This is neither a frivolous nor an outrageous claim. The fact is that the epistemology of the Western mind denies the reality of the indigenous mind and its world—it simply cannot see it. Individual pieces taken from the indigenous mind do not create tribal consciousness. The tribal mind does not rest in a feather, a sweat lodge, a sacred plant or a single prayer, acknowledging all our relations. While each of these things are part of the indigenous mind, they do not make it. The tribal mind is a way of being, not a technique or a particular set of techniques. The indigenous paradigm is so contrary to the western way of being that Euro-Americans have great difficulty grasping that something which is so obviously beneficial for the individual (the purification in a sweat lodge, for example) and which so obviously expands the Western paradigm, does not shift its fundamental consciousness. This shift can only occur once we cease to drink, once we surrender our addiction to progress. Then a new world will be there for the tribal Euro-Americans—a world which indigenous people have never left.

The differences between tribal mind and modern mind are significant indeed—but the differences lie in a particular pathology which denies the potentiality of tribal mind in all human beings. This splitting or dissociation from who we truly are is the runaway process of progress—dissociative schismogenesis—the split from our origin for the benefit of presumed rational control. These days it is more than apparent that this endeavor, also called evolution of consciousness, has failed in large measure. While the tribal mind and the modern mind live in different worlds or literally inhabit different realities, they can meet. The meeting place is the participatory process which all humans are capable of. Regaining participation with all our relations and with spirit means the remembrance of our origin for the future—retribalization.

These days a tribal person often times seems to get out of his or her native mind in order to share with a non-tribal mind. However, if we Euro-Americans are genuinely in our tribal minds than mutual sharing may happen in traditional ways. Being in our tribal minds is more than respecting tribal knowledge; it is more than seeing the traditional ecological knowledge which different tribal societies hold; it is more than appreciating their ways of healing: it is more than acknowledging the history of colonialism and genocide; it is more than loving tribal people; it is more than giving to needy native friends on the reservation. All this can be done as an amendment to the Euro-American addiction to progress. I am not talking about a change in attitude, like multi-culturalism or regrets about the histories of genocide. I am not talking about raising consciousness within a Maslowian framework. I am talking about stepping into a different mind so we not only see the world differently but so that we ARE in a different world.

## III. What is Indigenous Science?

The term "indigenous science" has been coined by Coloiado (1988, 1989) to validate the detailed and intricate knowledge which the indigenous people of this planet have accumulated over the millennia. We find extraordinary examples in Pacific navigation (Hostetter, 1991; Kyselka, 1987), archaeastronomy (Williamson & Farrer, 1991), agriculture and herbal knowledge and traditional ecological knowledge (Inglis, 1993). The construction of Stonehenge and Newgrange (Burenhult 1993:96-97; Wernick 1973:114-115) or the markings on Fajada Butte or the alignments of the kiva Casa Rinconada in Chaco Canyon are exquisite examples of ancient knowledge (Sofaer & Sinclair, 1983; Carlson, 1983; Williamson, 1983), Hopi dry-farming or the survival of Australian Aborigines in areas generally considered uninhabitable by others. Canoe journeying between Tahiti and Hawaii requiring detailed navigational knowledge is another astonishing example (Kyselka, 1987) which indicates why ancient indigenous knowledge should be considered on par with the scientific knowledge of the modern era; additionally, this approach avoids the continuing Euro-American denigration and takes it seriously. However, the paradigmatic differences between these two forms of science are not only significant, but they are highly relevant for our topic. Let me explain the differences between indigenous science and western science, primarily with reference to the healing arts (Colorado, 1988; Deloria, 1993).

The *skeptical* Euro-American researcher would be primarily interested in the efficacy of Native American healing and would try to isolate the element considered efficacious or a necessary condition in healing ceremonies. The *sympathetic* researcher would also, in addition to this analytical approach, pay attention to the "set" and "setting" as it were and would attempt to validate native approaches or find similarities, for example via psychotherapeutic approaches such as NLP (neurolinguistic programming) or Rogerian counseling, or via biochemical research of curative agents in herbs. The western scientific approach commonly entails a stripping away of what is considered extraneous and the isolation of what is considered effective. It is through this process that western science makes other what is essential for native understanding.

Indigenous science, on the other hand, would begin with the culturally specific, ecologically and historically grounded indigenous understanding of a balanced way of living in community on a particular land. Healing is needed when the "good mind" is out of balance for reasons which the cultural stories and myths can provide. Indigenous healing practices then are a synthetic, integral approach to what is out of balance. Native science guides the healer to the point in the fabric where it is rent and where wholeness needs to be reestablished. Trance narratives report the knowledge which indigenous people need and use as their personal gifts or medicine which helps them to be in balance. Indigenous ceremonies are the precise knowledge and practice designed to create balance on all levels and from all levels (within the person on the mental, physical, emotional and spiritual levels, and by doing so on the level of spirits, community and nature which hold the individual); they are indigenous science. Their efficacy comes through the integrity and the wholeness of the healing ceremony.

Colorado gives some coordinates for indigenous science:

> Just like western science, indigenous science relies upon direct observation; these are tests to insure validity and data are used for forecasting and generating predictions. Individuals are trained in various specializations, for example, herbalism, weather observation, mental health and time keeping. Unlike western science, the data from indigenous science are not used to control the forces of nature, instead, the data tell us ways and means of accommodating nature. Other critical distinctions include the following:

> 1. The indigenous scientist is an integral part of the research process and there is a defined process for insuring this integrity.

> 2. All of nature is considered to be intelligent and alive, thus an active research partner.

> 3. The purpose of indigenous science is to maintain balance.

4. Compared to western time/space notions, indigenous science collapses time and space with the result that our fields of inquiry and participation extend into and overlap with past and present.

5. Indigenous science is concerned with relationships; we try to understand and complete our relationships with all living things.

6. Indigenous science is holistic, drawing on all the senses, including the spiritual and psychic.

7. The end point of an indigenous scientific process is a known and recognized place. This point of balance, referred to by my own tribe as the Great Peace, is both peaceful and electrifyingly alive. In the joy of exact balance, creativity occurs, which is why we can think of our way of knowing as a life science.

8. When we reach the moment/place of balance, we do not believe that we have transcended—we say that we are normal! Always we remain embodied in the natural world.

9. Humor is a critical ingredient of all truth seeking, even in the most powerful rituals. This is true because humor balances gravity (1994:1-22).

The different motivations for inquiry in the case of western and indigenous sciences are of note. The researches of the native healer are done to increase the integrity and wholeness of the communal fabric and to benefit the individuals that are part of it. Western researches of native healing practices rarely seem to benefit the people researched directly, but they are a way to address the limitations of the western healing paradigm and to come to terms with events which western scientists commonly considered anomalous, inexplicable or nonexistent.

What is the precise knowing of the tribal mind that I am talking about? It is the way of being which our ancestors have created as the best possible way to live in balance with the environment using the guidance of spirit. This includes traditional ecological knowledge. It includes the ways of community. It is lived knowledge which is constantly maintained, strengthened and purified through the ceremonies which are the spirit life breath (*nilchi, pneuma*) of this way of being. Indigenous knowledge is not generic—it is a precise solution to the question of balance and beauty in the context of a particular ecology and its spirit. While there isn't just one "correct" solution which the tribal way of being of particular people represents is one "correct answer" to the existential question how to be who we are in beauty, balance and integrity. The tribal mind asks and answers all existential questions within the community context (rather than the separate individual). The answer is the world which a tribe creates with the spirit of where it lives.

As the voice of the indigenous other emerges within industrialized nations—however limited and distorted—through neo-shamanic techniques and the alternative interpretations which transpersonal psychologies and holistic medical approaches have to offer, a profound question arises: *Are (post)modern people trying to heal their western, Euro-American selves or are they trying to heal their indigenous selves?* This question is of utmost importance to indigenous people. If what they are doing is healing their Euro-American selves within the existing paradigm, then iatrogenic diseases which are an expression of the continuing dissociation from holism, and indigenous roots are the result (this is one of the reasons why natives are disturbed about the decontextualized use of their healing approaches; see Churchill, 1992:215-228; Durning, 1991:36). The correct technique used in a dissociated way is dangerous because it does not allow the appearance of a deeper healing (individual benefits notwithstanding). From an indigenous perspective, if western people are healing their indigenous selves through the remembrance of native healing ways, then individual healing is also the healing of community and paradigm.

## IV. If the Indigenous Mind is Lost—Can it be Recovered?

From an indigenous perspective the answer to this question is an emphatic "Yes!" The reasons for the possibility of the recovery of the indigenous mind are as follows and can be grouped in the five major dimensions of

1. the continued presence of cycles,
2. the continued presence of ancestral spirit(s),
3. the presence of artifacts and spiritually significant places,
4. the continued presence of nature, and
5. the psychological capabilities of the individual human mind.

Recovering the access to these areas can be called "retribalization." The term "retribalization" is not without problematic associations. However, it seems to he the best and most appropriate word available to point to the process of recovering the indigenous mind. Alternative terminologies could be the "archaeology of the (European, Asian, African, Australian) tribal mind(s)" or "becoming people again" (taken from the fact that most indigenous tribes seem to call themselves "the people"). However, retribalization has the advantage of startling most people in the modern minds (evoking many conflicted feelings). plus it communicates easily to people who are still in their indigenous minds (to them, naturally, the term makes eminent sense).

Retribalization then is the process of recovering one's indigenous roots using the avenues which were pointed out in the previous section. The indigenous mind is a human potential for everybody, however, not in the sense of the "human potential movement" of the 60s and 70s. Rather, the indigenous mind can only be present through spiritual and material grounding. One significant way of grounding is the acknowledgement of the grief and loss during the assimilation and accommodation to a dissociated Euro-American worldview. While the process of retribalization will look different for Asian-Americans, Afro-Americans, Australian Aborigines or Native Americans who are out of their indigenous mind, it will nevertheless have to deal with all the different dimensions used in my description above. It is important to remember that the indigenous mind is always specifically culturally and ecologically grounded; the generic descriptions thus capture only certain common aspects of the process of grieving remembrance. Each person and each lost tribe will have specific responses and needs during this process which are conditioned by their particular (personal) history.

Last year at this conference I described the remembrance process involved in retribalization and I mentioned the importance of confronting the grief and anger and the history of colonialism, genocide and imperialism. Retribalization is a process with uncertain results for all those who have lost connection to their indigenous roots entirely. If a contemporary indigenous culture is extant to which a person is related then the outcome is not as uncertain. However, when we have to look far back in order to discover our indigenous roots, then it is more difficult to anticipate the results. It is important to understand that the step of looking backward cannot be skipped; we need to look back in order to look forward. (Just dealing with the ecology or our abstract common humanity is insufficient and ultimately an avoidance maneuver.) If we don't grasp what our specific good mind might have been, then we don't know what it will be. The remembered indigenous mind (for the future) cannot and does not need to deny the history which has intervened. It surveys, critiques and integrates from the mutual perspective of the past and future indigenous mind.

People who are out of their indigenous mind, but whose indigenous roots are alive and present can reconnect with their contemporary heritage. For them grounding in a specific community, indigenous science, ecology and ceremonial practice is in proximate accessability. People who have been out of their indigenous minds, maybe even for centuries or millennia (like most Euro-Americans), have to begin as individual, based on the assumption that the lost tribe will gather in some form and the ancestral spirits will help out. It is not predictable, nor does it need to be predictable, what the community will be in which their indigenous minds will be grounded. Once the process of retribalization has begun, their world and the world will become different.

# V. The Recovery of Indigenous Science

Indigenous science and the recovery of indigenous consciousness imply a process of transformative learning. Such transformation would be the integration of that which postmodernists call OTHER (the culturally other, the body, the feminine, emotions, nature, etc.).

Let me use Newgrange as an example of indigenous science, which is the result of transforming and the facilitator of transforming. Newgrange, together with Dowth and Knowth is located in the ceremonial complex of the Boyne Valley, north of Dublin in Ireland (Brennan, 1980, 1983). The megalithic mound dates back to 3,200 B.C. and photos of the beautiful spiral patterns on its entrance stone have been reproduced many times. This neolithic ceremonial structure allows for precise seasonal tracking through the alignment of the altar with the winter solstice.

> Just once every year, at 9:45 a.m. on 21 December, a growing light spreads gradually in the pitch-dark burial chamber. Six minutes later, the sunbeam is at its broadest and bathes the chamber, situated 22 meters (72 feet) from the entrance, in a dazzling light. Then the light starts to fade, and by 10:15 am it has disappeared altogether. Behind this monument—one of prehistory's most advanced constructions—lie centuries, even millennia, of astronomical observations and cult ceremonies, the forms of which would have been transmitted orally from generation to generation (Burenhult, 1993:96-97).

The idea of a megalithic mound was obviously transformational and its idea must have been *preceded* by very careful tracking of the seasonal cycles. Such tracking would have led to an understanding where a new form would allow new tracking. The way of tracking changed and allowed a new level of ceremony. The megalithic mound was the result of a shift in meaning perspective, a shift in our habitual expectations governing perception, comprehension and memory (Mezirow, 1991:4); subsequently, the use of the mound became the catalyst not just for a different quality of tracking, but transforming learning, transforming as people moved through the seasons of their lives and as they observed the natural cycles. Newgrange never was a burial site [this is not completely true because ancient containers with bones and ashes have been found in the end chamber, the editor], but it may have been a ceremonial center for communication with the ancestors facilitated by the sun beam touching the hollow stone at the very end of the long passage at the time of deep recess and renewal. At the precise time of the resting point between cycles, the mound is entered by the sun, impregnated and renewed for the next cycle.

My remembrance of these events cannot only ground my own indigenous mind, but it can help me with the challenges posed by the dominant discourse. Seeing the precise understanding of the cycles then, seeing the precise understanding of the cycles now, understanding the record of knowledge in the megalithic mound I know how OTHER is me and how OTHER lives in the weave. I know—despite all contrary assertions—that OTHER has not left and I can develop a precise response to the discourse which denies OTHER. Going through my own process of retribalization, of transforming—learning—transforming. I have used the word "indigenous" for myself with great fear and trepidation. the reaction and reactivity of those who are part of the dominant Euro-American discourse in one form or another taught me how OTHER I truly am. Telling the story of my process and claiming my own indigenous mind has led to a paradoxical experience. My Euro-American listeners have frequently denied my right to apply the word "indigenous" to myself; they vociferously object as they fail to look at their own ancestry and indigenous mind (the myth of the new beginning and clean slate has created a big shadow). Often they react violently as if I have transgressed into an area which is taboo—thus paradoxically affirming how OTHER lives in me, affirming the possibility of my own indigenous mind, reacting to my transforming-learning—transforming. (Indigenous people generally have a different response.)

Transforming—learning—transforming is spirit shining forth in the mound, having shone forth in what is now called Newgrange, shape changing today in me through my tracking shapes changing as I pay attention to spirit making tracks now then and in the future. It becomes recovered knowledge in self. The transforming—learning—transforming of my new/old old/new indigenous minding now has the opportunity to understand the consequences of my acts within the weave. I track the cycles of the seasons and stars. I track what the Elders have said are saying and I track the stories. In transforming learning transforming I am looking back generations looking forward generations shape changing shapechanged within the weave. Throughout this tracking the mind of the *volva* on the megalithic mound looking into past—present—future tracking the cycles emerges in my mind as indigenous consciousness.

## VI. The Politics of Retribalization

For many people the term "retribalization" will evoke notions of chauvinism and nationalism. This represents a misreading of "tribe" as defined above by way of the coordinates of the indigenous mind. To explain further: Nationalism and chauvinism (as well as fascism, abusing indigenous terminology) are part of the dynamics of state capitalism and the economic dynamics of international corporations. For example, the virulent nationalism in some of the former East Block countries has to be understood as their claim to join the progress race for economic affluence. It is easy to evaluate each of these political movements on the above coordinates. It will quickly become apparent that the new nationalism is quite different from the good mind.

Politically, models for the indigenous mind in balance can be found among the foraging egalitarian hunter-gatherers in particular, who tend to be matrifocal and matrilineal (Lerner, 1986). There is no need to create a romantic image of an ideal history—even tribes we would consider very much in balance have committed atrocities. But this does not mean that we have to reject the indigenous mind and knowing wholesale. However, it raises the question of how to assess the state of an indigenous mind or the state of retribalization. My suggestion is that this can be done in the following dimensions:

Are the different aspects *within the human* in balance? What is the relationship or dialectic between cognition, emotion, the body, sexuality and spirit? How are these aspects bounded, how are they valued, and how are they made to speak to each other?

Is the relationship *between human beings* in balance? How is the relationship between genders defined? Are constraint-free and sincere interactions supported? Is there room for all aspects of the human being? Is open, respectful communication supported?

Is the relationship between *human beings* and *wilderness* in balance? What is the human impact on the environment? Are the spirits of the plants, rocks and animals heard?

What is the importance of the seasonal cycles? Are there any imbalances in the non-human wilderness which are caused by human impact?

The indigenous mind can assess *itself(!)* by way of "participatory concourse"—a coming together of indigenous minds using all the different ways of knowing represented in the coordinates above. Such an exploration includes all dimensions of human experience: somatic, sexual, emotional, spiritual, and cognitive. While words are important in participatory concourse, the knowing of the body, the knowing of the heart, the knowing of the rock, plant and animal spirits, and the knowing of the ancestors are valued equally. An agreement about the state of balance needs to be anchored in all these dimensions.

Human beings have always moved about this planet, at times over dramatic distances in short time periods. Tribes have met, mixed, blended, and conquered. Ancient and recent migrations are a reflection of the fundamental human interconnectedness (Colorado, 1991). Tracing these migrations and understanding the interconnections is appreciating human interconnectedness. Recovering the indigenous mind where it needs to be recovered means establishing bio-sustainable subsistence communities. These communities will be different and specific because of the ecology they are based on and the ancestral history they are connected with. Yet, these differences can be cherished if we understand our fundamental connections—not as an idealized image, not as nostalgia for a romanticized past that never was, but by way of the history of physical migrations throughout time.

Picking and choosing "useful" tribal symbols is an activity which shows the dissociated mind at work. While particular neo-shamanic practices or techniques may not even be wrong in their detail, they are misguided as endeavor as long the practitioners are not in their own indigenous minds. Then the guiding interest is the search for betterment *without* leaving the modern paradigm. It feeds the progress addiction. It is entirely a one-way street: Indigenous knowledge for the benefit of the Euro-American ways of being. Concerns for the tribal people and their survival, well-being and cultural integrity generally takes the back seat in this process. What tribal people share within their traditional ethics and obligations gets fed into a system which fails to comprehend the basis for the exchange. The sharing between the Euro-American and the traditional world is based on a fundamental inequity: The imperialistic deep structure of the western way of knowing conflicts with the obligatory openness of traditional people. This imperialism is at work not only consciously, but unconsciously, because it is part and parcel of the Euro-American way of knowing. No change of techniques changes a way of knowing and being but a change of mind changes the meaning of a technique. The progress addiction of the Euro-American mind feeds on the isolating, analytical, decontextualizing approach to the world; context is a confusing additive which disturbs the purity of knowledge. Recontextualizing means retribalizing; then the Euro-American shaman becomes a *volva, vikti, noadie,* etc. Now sharing can happen in an arena where traditional ways are honored: Tribal minds meet and exchange knowledge among realities which are fundamentally of the same mind. The Euro-American mind is thirsty for tribal knowledge, and, indeed, it is urgent for survival that this thirst be quenched—but the thirst will only be quenched once we are in our tribal minds. Otherwise no amount of traditional knowledge poured down thirsty souls will suffice—it won't stay. The science of modernity and postmodernity needs to become indigenous science if we are to recover global balance on the Mother Earth.

## References

Brennan, M. *The Stars and the Stones.* New York: Thames and Hudson, 1983.

_____ . *The Boyne Valley Vision.* Dublin, Ireland: The Dolmen Press, 1980.

Burenhult, G. "Newgrange: Temple of the Sun," *People of the Stone Age,* by G. Burenhult. San Francisco: Harper, 1993, pp.96-97.

Carlson, J.B. "Astronomical markings of three sites on Fajada Butte," *Astronomy and Ceremony in the Prehistoric Southwest,* by John Carlson and James Judge. Albuquerque, NM: Maxwell Museum of Anthropology, 1983, pp.71-88.

Churchill, W. *Fantasies of the Master Race.* Monroe, ME: Common Courage, 1992.

Colorado, P. "Indigenous science and western science—a healing convergence." Presentation at the World Sciences Dialogue I, New York City, April 25-27, 1994.

_____ . "A meeting between brothers," *Beshara, 13* (Summer 1991):20-27.

_____ . "'Indian science': from fire and ice," *New Voices from the Longhouse,* ed. J. Bruchac. New York: Greenfield Review Press, 1989.

_____ . "Bridging native and western science, *Convergence, XXI:2/3* (1988):49-67.

Deloria, V. "If you think about it you will see that it is true, *Noetic Sciences Review, 27* (1993):62-71.

Durning, A.Th. *Guardians of the Land: Indigenous Peoples and the Health of the Earth.* Washington, DC: Worldwatch Institute, 1992.

Hostetter, C. *Star Trek to Hawai'i.* San Luis Obispo, CA: Diamond Press, 1991.

Inglis, J.T., ed. *Concerns and Cases.* Ottawa, Ontario: International Program on Traditional Ecological Knowledge, Canadian Museum of Nature, 1993.

Kremer, J.W. *Looking for Dame Yggdrasil.* Red Bluff, CA: Falkenflug, 1994.

Kyselka, W. *An Ocean of Mind.* Honolulu, HI: University of Hawaii, 1987.

Lerner, G. *The Creation of Patriarchy.* New York: Oxford University Press, 1986.

Mezirow, J. *Transformative Dimensions of Adult Learning.* San Francisco, CA: Jossey-Bass, 1991.

Sofaer, A. and Rolf Sinclair. "Astronomical markings at three sites on Fajada Butte," *Astronomy and Ceremony in the Prehistoric Southwest,* by John Carlson and James Judge. Albuquerque, NM: Maxwell Museum of Anthropology, 1987, pp.43-70.

Spretnak, C. *States of Grace.* San Francisco, CA: Harper, 1991.

Wernick, R. *The Monument Builders.* New York: Time-Life, 1973.

Williamson, R.A. "Astronomical markings at three sites on Fajada Butte," *Astronomy and Ceremony in the Prehistoric Southwest,* by John Carlson and James Judge. Albuquerque, NM: Maxwell Museum of Anthropology, 1983, pp.99-119.

_____ , and C.R. Farrer, eds. *Earth and Sky.* Albuquerque, NM: University of New Mexico, 1992.

# THE MYTH
# OF THE VIRGIN MOTHER
# AND THE DYING GOD

Josephine A. Coffey

I will be talking today about ritual and myth, about something many people in this audience know first-hand. Through your teaching and the cere-monies you lead, you have been helping to revive experiences of the sacred in our too exclusively technological time. This is extremely important work. I think it is fair to say we cannot survive without it.

The importance of philosophical rumination about it, which is what I have to offer here, is less obvious. But perhaps it too has its place, I recently came across a definition, a kind of verbal self-portrait by Swiss artist Paul Klee (Stevens, 1987). He said the artist is one "[chosen] to come near to the secret places where original law fosters all evolution." This quotation pro-vides a motto for my talk today.

There is no mention of ritual in it, but we know now that all of what we call art—be it painting, poetry, drama, music, dance—had its origin in ritual, in people's experience of the sacred. Though insulated by thick layers of civilization, an artist may recover this original experience. There are a cou-ple of things I like about Klee's definition. First, there is the recognition that in the creative act—in the original ritual act—the person feels him- or herself chosen. It is not self-initiated.[1] Different names have been given to who is doing the choosing—god, the higher self—but I am not going to speculate about that. What is given in the experience is simply the fact of being chosen. We are accustomed to thinking of the artist as one who intuits the deep pulse of things. Klee describes this deep pulse as "the original law that fosters all evolution." Not "the unity of all things," not "the ineffable that transcends all things," not even "beauty itself," but "the law that fosters evolution." *Law* and *evolution* are scientific terms. But the artist's approach is different from the scientist's. Klee describes this approach as "coming near to secret places." Only coming near; the veil remains. This is different from the "clear and distinct" knowledge demanded by the scientist. To the scientist, the secrecy of nature is no more than the intractability of a hard problem. It is in principle able to be overcome. The scientist does not see as far as the mystery that the artist experiences. The scientist maps the territory; the artist hikes into it, dreams on its ground. So the artist and the scientist must speak differently about evolution. But at the same time, Klee is not speaking metaphorically; his word points to the same phenomenon, the same event, that the scientist studies.

Among beings that we customarily recognize as living, DNA has a dual aspect. As a holder of pattern, it preserves a configuration of atoms and allows a certain way of life to maintain itself across generations. But DNA is not identical with any particular pattern; it changes, and the change marks the coming into being of new forms of life. Among humans, there is very little difference in the DNA of different races,[2] but there is significant difference in the behavior of, say, a Yanomami Indian from the Brazilian rain forest, and an English country gentleman. We use the words "culture" and "cultural evolution" to describe such differences. The analogue of DNA in cultural identity and cultural evolution is ritual. Again, I am not speaking metaphorically. Ritual carries the force of evolution as truly as does DNA.[3] Like DNA, it has a dual aspect. Through periodic repetition, ritual preserves culture, but it can change, and such change marks new stages in the evolution of a population. We are experiencing such a change now.

I will be speaking interchangeably of ritual and myth. They are from the same dimension of being—the sacred. Myth is the verbal aspect of ritual. It may be the story line of a ritual or it may be a story that is told during a ritual, a story about the sacred events that brought things to the way they currently are. One of Joseph Campbell's books is called, *The Power of Myth,* and the title is apt. What we are learning now is not so much the sacred stories themselves, but their power. We are experiencing their power; their power is happening to us. I use that phraseology deliberately. We don't create myths. Ceremonies we put together may provide training or practice—they may prepare us, and that is helpful—but true myths or rituals happen to us; we find ourselves in them. An example of the difference between true and imitation ritual is Woodstock 1969, and Woodstock this summer. The ritual of 1969 wasn't created by the promoters or the artists or the audience. If they had created it, they could have done it again. Remember Joni Mitchell's song, "Woodstock"? She said, "I feel myself a cog in something turning." The experience brought her deep down into our mythic roots: "we are star dust, we are golden, and we've got to get ourselves back to the garden." The garden, before the fall, before the beginning of our history. That's what's turning. What's being transformed now are decisions we made, the path we took at the very beginning of our culture.

By "our culture," I mean western civilization, the culture that most of us here have been raised in. It may be, it is likely, that other cultures are going through a change of similar importance right now, but I am not speaking of them here. I don't know their story. I mention this because there continues to be a tendency to see the story of western civilization as the story of the species as a whole, or even the story of the universe.[4] We need to put such ethnocentricity behind us.

I will be talking today not about the myth of the garden, but about another fundamental myth of our culture, one that may be older and more widespread.

I am sure some of you have read Robert Graves', *The White Goddess* (1948). Perhaps, like me, you read it as part of a search for feminine roots. That book is about a myth which Graves summarizes as the story...

> of the birth, life, death and resurrection of the God of the Waxing Year; the central chapters concern the God's losing battle with the God of the Waning Year for love of the capricious and all-powerful Threefold Goddess, their mother, bride and layer-out (1948:11).

He says that "all true poetry... celebrates some incident or scene in this very ancient story" and continues with an observation Jung would appreciate,

> the three main characters are so much a part of our racial inheritance that they not only assert themselves in poetry but recur on occasions of emotional stress in the form of dreams, paranoiac visions and delusions" (1948:11).

Elsewhere in the book, he points out that in typical versions of the myth, the Goddess mother is a virgin. When I first read *The White Goddess* years ago, I thought his claim that all true poetry celebrates this myth was excessive and peculiar; obviously poets write about other things. But I have since come to think he is right, at least for Europe. I don't see that it holds for all cultures. It has been a theme for two major 20th century European poets—T.S. Eliot and James Joyce—Eliot in *The Wasteland,* and Joyce in *Ulysses.* In the notes published with his poem, Eliot refers to Jesse Westons' *From Ritual to Romance* (1957) and Frazer's *Golden Bough* (1890), both of which are about Grave's myth. Eliot, in *The Wasteland* as in other poems, seems to offer resignation as the appropriate response to myth's current state; Joyce, an Irishman after all, fights it, in the central moment of the novel, choosing the extinction of everything—light, space, time—over submission to the ghoul-white, dead-white goddess mother,[4] and, at its end, giving us Molly Bloom as her antidote.[5]

Graves finds the myth all over Europe, Northern Africa and the Middle East, in Mediterranean, Celtic and Scandinavian cultures. One telling of the myth is the Egyptian tale of Isis, Osiris and Horus.

Another telling of the myth is the following:

> I believe in one God, the Father almighty,....
> And in the one Lord Jesus Christ, the only begotten Son of God....born of the Father, before all ages....
> Who, for us men, and for our salvation, came down from heaven.
> And became Incarnate by the Holy Ghost of the Virgin Mary:

And was made man.
He was crucified also for us, suffered under Pontius Pilate, and was buried.
And the third day He rose again according to the Scriptures...
(Juergens, 1957:627).

This quote is from the summary of Christian beliefs drawn up by the Councils of Nicea and Constantinople in the 4th century. To this day, it is recited at every Catholic mass, the central Catholic ritual, and is professed by the great majority of European Christian denominations.[6] The Isis/Osiris myth and the Christian creed are generally recognized to be from two very different stages of European culture, the matriarchal or matrifocal stage from roughly 9,000 years to 4,500 years ago, and the patriarchal stage, from roughly 6,500 years ago to today.[7]

Some scholars hold that these two stages are fundamentally different. Marija Gimbutas said,

[t]he Old European [matrifocal] and Indo-European [patriarchal] belief systems are diametrically opposed (1991:396).

...[t]he functions and images of Old European and Indo-European deities,...and the entirely different sets of symbols prove the existence of two contrasting religions and mythologies (1991:401).

But if they are diametrically opposed, why is this central myth so similar? The continuity of the myth suggests that rather than two diametrically opposed stages, there has been instead a single project with two phases. Gimbutas sees radical discontinuity between the matriarchal and patriarchal phases because

The Indo-European warlike...patriarchal...pattern of social organization could not have developed out of the Old European matrilineal, matricentric... society.... The appearance of the Indo-Europeans in Europe represents a collision of two ideologies, not an evolution (1991:396).

Under our ordinary conceptions of evolution and history, she's right. But our ordinary conceptions are too superficial. History isn't simply the record of human activities, of the collision between people and their ideologies. People are called to their history; history is destiny. This is the same "calling" that Klee talked about. Whether they are aware of it or not, people's history is rooted in and pervaded by the sacred. Most people are aware of it, as the Bible and other people's legends attest. It is we children of rationalism that find it hard to see. Rationalism also prevents us from seeing the role of the land in history. To us, the land is mere backdrop, contributing only "resources" or "obstacles" to what is first and foremost a story of human activity. But I think that is backwards. History is first and foremost the destiny of the land, not just land-in-general, but the particular land on which it occurs. Myth is the telling of that destiny. The story of the virgin mother and the dying god has been the myth of Europe for the last 9,000 years, not just Old Europeans, not just Indo-Europeans, but Europe. I say Europe as shorthand; I mean the land associated with western civilization, the land around the Mediterranean which was perceived as the middle of the earth—the Middle East, North Africa as well as Europe.

Our story appeared at least once before in the history of the planet, this time not in myth but in the DNA. The insect order hymenoptera contains bees, ants and wasps. It includes almost all of the species that biologists have termed truly social or eusocial. Social species are those whose members communicate cooperatively for purposes beyond mere sexual activity. We are social; lions are social; tigers are not. Truly social or eusocial species go beyond this. With them, there is a reproductive division of labor, where more or less sterile individuals cooperate in caring for the young of others. Frequently reproduction is concentrated in one female—the queen bee, queen ant, or queen wasp. She lays eggs and the other females care of for the young, repair the nest, provide food for the community and defend it. Typically, males live off the fat of the land until it comes time for the queen to mate. In some species, all males join the queen in a nuptial flight during which they compete to mate with her. Then, their sole usefulness to the community having been served, they are abandoned. Sometimes, the community lives only one season; the inseminated queen alone survives the winter to start a new community the following spring.

Almost all eusocial insects are haplodiploid. Females are diploid, that is, they have a double set of chromosomes—DNA—one from their mother, one from their father; but males are haploid, they have a single set of chromosomes from their mother. The queen determines the sex of her offspring. After mating, she retains the sperm in her body, and when it comes time to lay her eggs, releases sperm for some eggs, thus producing females and keeps it from others, thus producing males. So far as males in typical eusocial species are concerned, their mother is a virgin, she is their lover, and mating with her—their sole ambition—is the immediate prelude to death (biological information, E.O. Wilson, 1980).

Thus we find something very like our virgin goddess—dying god myth in the DNA of the most social animals on the planet. The coincidence between this story and socialization in these species is striking. And when we look at the mythical form of the story, that is, when we look at western civilization, we find a similar striking connection with socialization. Human beings are social; they start out social. (I am using "social" here as sociobiologists understand that term, meaning that individuals communicate cooperatively for purposes beyond mere sexual activity.) Humans have always lived in groups, and these groups have probably always communicated with other groups, through trade if nothing else. But for the greater part of our

100,000 year existence, contact between people living at a distance of more than, say, fifty miles was rare, and contact across an ocean a singularity. Today though, we speak of the global village, united by the information highway. AT&T reminds us that we can communicate virtually anywhere on earth with "our true voice"; and though not all our communication is cooperative, we do seem to be moving in that direction. The technical side, at least the technical side of this extreme socialization, is due in large measure to western civilization.

Zulu Sanusi[8] Credo Mutwa has said that there is a "longing in this Earth, long isolated in a self-imposed exile, to rejoin the larger universe—to participate once again in the Song of the Stars" (Larsen, 1994:23). I think that the socialization of our species and the development of technology in general have been in pursuit of this, the Virgin mother—dying god myth has played a causal role in this socialization, the same role the DNA version plays in the socialization of bees and wasps. Since human socialization is largely complete, it is entirely appropriate that the myth is on its way out. And it is just as well it is on its way out because it has been extremely dangerous. It is a mutation that has almost wiped its bearers out.

It still might if it remains in power, and myths on their way out are like neuroses, on their way out, they tend to hold on. The virgin mother—dying god myth has to do with female and male, birth and death; sex, creation and extinction. Languages record the fact that people around the world experience things in the world around them—including what our culture calls inanimate things—as either male or female. (English is an exception, but modern English took form relatively late.) This includes beings felt to have great spiritual presence, like the sun, the moon and the earth. Interestingly, not everyone experiences these beings as the same sex. Most people experience the sun as masculine, but some, including the Celts, the Cherokee, the Germans and the Japanese, experience it as feminine.[9] But always there is the experience of both sexes, and there is a balance. For instance, to the best of my knowledge, the sun and the moon are experienced as opposite sexes. Sexuality implies sex, and sex is the way new beings occur. It has been the insight of thinkers in more than one culture that this is the way creation characteristically happens—through the coming together of male and female.[10] I suspect this is right. The universe just is. The only creation that exists is the rearrangement of elements into new forms.

Science has explored some of the forces responsible for this—gravity, electro-magnetism, etc.—but its spiritual blindness prevents it from seeing the forces involved in spiritual change. As its eyes open, I suspect it will see, as did the old philosophers and the even more ancient people who first spoke language, that spiritual change is more fundamental than material change, and that the driving force in spiritual evolution has been the spark between male and female.

It is against this background that we have to see the motifs in the virgin mother—dying god myth. The reason for its power and the reason for its danger is that it manipulates forces at the very center of life. The first thing to notice is that creation is gathered into one place. This happens in the DNA version, where maternity is limited to one female, and in the mythic version, where one being, first the mother goddess, then the father god, is seen as the source of everything. In this process, sex, the creative dance between male and female, is thrown out of balance, and is eventually shut down entirely. In the mother goddess version of the story, the male is robbed of a full role in creation, but something of his power remains in the love he arouses in his mother. It is a love that brings death, an unnaturally early death, so it is not surprising that in the transition to the masculine form of them this love is shut down. But like many reactions, this is an overreaction; the response is itself unbalanced, even more unbalanced. What is promised under this new form of the myth is eternal life, no more death. To do this, intercourse between male and female is shut down; celibacy becomes the mythic ideal.[11] But since the coming together of male and female is the source of any life, this path has exactly the opposite effect from what was intended. What the path leads to is not life but death. This is the state that Eliot describes in *The Wasteland:*

April is the cruelest month, breeding
Lilacs out of the dead land... (1948/1922).

The land is dead—spiritually dead—because of the impotence of its king, its male principal. This is not poetic dyspepsia we are talking here; we are talking about the grim effects of runaway technology, massive extinction, death, not of the earth—I am sure the earth can survive this—but of a broad swath of life,[12] and of western civilization. And, for the earth, that means that this attempt to "participate once again in the Song of the Stars," as Credo Mutwa put it, will fail. And that would be a tragedy. The earth will undoubtedly get there by a different path, but it would be a tragedy for us not to be there.

We are at a crucial point. The old myth is on its way out. Patriarchal excesses—hatred of the earth and other things feminine—are slowly being curbed. But there is a danger that we won't go far enough, particularly with respect to the central issues of male and female. Some of the danger signs are:

1. The continuing appeal of the myth: Recently, there have been two movies, two "liberal" movies, glorifying Christ as dying god—*Jesus of*

*Montreal* and *The Last Temptation of Christ.* As you may recall, the last temptation was sex. The movie reaffirmed the celibacy at the heart of Christ's mission. But it is not just the patriarchal version of the myth that expresses its power. In the last few years, the earlier, long hidden matriarchal version has been emerging. It is important for us to experience the goddess, but I think it is also important to move beyond her. A monotheistic goddess is as unbalanced as a monotheistic god.

2. The continuing rift between matter and spirit in sexuality: Ours has been a period of sloughing off old sexual values, and that has to happen, but for the most part, our new values haven't yet gone beyond rationalism and hedonism. For instance, it disturbs me to hear political allies describe abortion as simply a matter of choice. Sex has to do with creation and life, and they are sacred. This is by no means an endorsement of the right to life movement which only wants to stay with old, by now deadly values, but it is to say that our political deliberations will not be adequate until we honor the sacredness of sex.

3. The tendency to devalue erotic love and identify true love with compassion: I am not knocking compassion; certainly we need more of it. Knocking compassion would be like knocking motherhood. And that is just what compassion is. It is the nurturing acceptance of another being that is characteristic of motherhood. It keeps a being in existence, and, as such, is an authentic moment in love. But such love can't bring being into existence. The love that can is often a rogue—coyote in some Indian myths. It doesn't always domesticate well. Joyful, agonizing, ecstatic, abandoned, it is the wildness at life's deep core.

I have been talking about a European myth. While it is one most of us have been raised in, the land we live in is not Europe, and this land has its own destiny. When Europeans arrived here, wildness was what they saw, in the land and its creatures, including its two-legged creatures. It was a wildness that aroused passionate, destructive opposition. A 500-year holocaust was unleashed on native ways of life. It is a sign of their strength and of their importance to the land's destiny that those ways have nonetheless survived, and have begun again to flourish. It is entirely appropriate that we whites be ashamed of what our people have done here. Such shame should teach us humility and respect, but it should not make us look elsewhere for our spiritual roots. If the European migration to America had not been wanted, it would have failed. This is the place of our destiny as well. The Dineh or Navajo people migrated from Canada to the southwest fairly recently, sometime between the 12th and 16th century. Their myths record that migration not only as an emergence into a new world, but as the time they were first made human, by the gods of their new land (Locke, 1976, part 2). A comparable myth has not yet arisen among us, but it is coming; it has been coming.

## Notes

1.  Among the examples are the encounters between the god of the Israelites and Abraham and Moses, the encounter between White Buffalo Woman and the two Lakota warriors.

2.  According to Nei and Roychoudhury (1972), there is almost as much DNA variation within races as between them.

3.  How beautifully John Seed says it: "We call upon the spirit of evolution, the miraculous force that inspires rocks and dust to weave themselves into biology. You have stood by us for millions and millions of years—do not forsake us now. Empower us and awaken in us pure and dazzling creativity. You that can turn scales into feathers, seawater to blood, caterpillars to butterflies, metamorphose our species, awaken in us the powers that we need to survive the present crisis and evolve into more aeons of our solar journey (1988:3).

4.  This is true of some of the sources for this paper, i.e., Frazer, *The Golden Bough* (1890) and Graves, *The White Goddess* (1948). Such ethnocentricity is part of what western civilization has been all about, and is to be expected from someone writing in 1890 or 1948. But we are still not entirely free of it. There is so much to admire in Brian Swimme and Thomas Berry's *The Universe Story* (1992), and perhaps I am being persnickety, but it bothered me that they named every significant event in the story after a western god(dess) or personality (Tiamat, Aries, etc.). Of course, I would have been bothered even more if they had been politically correct and taken names, in the correct proportion, from all cultures. I guess what would have made me happy was an acknowledgement by the authors that they used names of deities meaningful to them, realizing that people from other cultures would name differently these experiences that are part of our common heritage.

5.  Joyce has been a particular hero of mine, and I try to keep his feast days: the day he was born: February 2; the day he died: January 13; and Bloomsday: June 16. Occasionally, lovely things happen, and I could convince myself that Joyce had a hand in them. Sometimes, I celebrate by copying the bible-reader. I open one of his books to a random page and look for a message in what I read. This February, what I read was the passage referred to here. I had not realized its significance before.

6.  I say "old world" because I don't think it is professed by the Christian schools that began on the American continent. It is not professed by the Church of the Latter Day Saints (Mormons) for instance. This leads me to believe that there is a distinction between the entities associated with the Christian religions—and I believe there are such entities—and the forms those religions take. The forms, including the myths, are specific to a time and place, but these are used by the Christian entities for their own purposes. What does unite the Christians religions is aggressive missionizing which, among the Mormons, extends to people no longer living on earth.

7.  These dates are from Marija Gimbutas (1991). There is an overlap in dates of the two stages because the rise of patriarchy happened at different times in different places.

8.  According to Larsen (1994), a *sanusi* is a holy man and lore-master. It is one category of holy persons among the Zulu. Others are *inyanga* (shaman, witch doctor or moon person), and *sangoma* (clairvoyant).

9.  The two major axis powers in the Second World War fought under sun symbols

and they both experienced the sun as feminine. I think this provides a clue as to what was happening in that war that we have yet to understand.

10. The western Pythagoreans say this (Kirk and Raven, 1957), as does the Chinese Lao Tzu (1979/500 B.c.). The *I Ching* (Book of Changes; Wilhelm, 1967) defines differences in states of being as differences in the way male and female come together.

11. It seems unnecessary to point out the Catholic Church's commitment to celibacy. Catholicism is the oldest European Christian school, founded closest in time to the original occurrence of these mystical events. By tradition, Christ was celibate, as was Mary his mother. All the apostles were celibate or became so after they joined Jesus. Like other sons in the myth, Christ dies, but his is the last death. His death conquers death itself and wins eternal life for his followers. Since the son always dies, it cannot be Christ's death that is important. Eternity, the absence of change, is achieved by turning off the source of change and new life—love, sex.

The Christ story is not the earliest masculine transformation of the virgin mother—dying god myth. Graves (1948:352) cites Agamemnon as an instance of the dying god. Agamemnon, brother-in-law to Helen, and one of the Greek leaders of the Trojan War, is killed upon his return by his wife Clytemnestra. Aeschylus' continuation of this story vividly captures the transition to patriarchy. Orestes, Agamemnon and Clytemnestra's son, kills his mother for murdering his father. He is pursued for this matricide by the snake-haired, female furies. He appeals to Athena who convenes a jury of Athenians to decide the question of his guilt. The jury is evenly divided and he is freed by Athena's vote. The winning argument is made by Apollo, one of the new generation of gods, representing the light of intellect against the dark passion of the ancient, earth-bound furies: "The mother is no parent of that which is called her child, but only nurse of the new-planted seed that grows. The parent is he who mounts" (1967:172; 6th century B.C.). This theft from mothers of their maternity prevailed in Western thinking until biologists with microscopes discovered the roles of egg and sperm. It is a point of view that does not simply devalue the feminine, it denies creativity to the coming together of male and female.

We shouldn't leave this point without talking about another famous Athenian, Plato, perhaps the most influential spokesman of the patriarchal themes of celibacy and eternity—transcendence from the world we live in. His *Phaedrus* (1963; 5th-4th century B.C.) is one of two dialogues he wrote about love. "Platonic love" has come to mean a somewhat anemic relationship, but that isn't at all what Plato had in mind. As Socrates experienced it, love was the hot blooded desire of a mature man for a younger one, a divine madness, kin to prophecy and poetry. In such love, and only there, a person comes to his true self. His true self belongs not here on earth, but in a place "beyond the heavens." Life in a body is a fall from that place, and the soul's task on earth is to return. Love gives it the wings it needs to fly there, but bodily satisfaction of that love will keep it chained to earth and is forbidden. This is the original meaning of "Platonic love." It is not a relationship between two people who are, at most, fond of one another. It is rather a deliberately celibate relationship between two men on fire for one another, a relationship prized as the surest path to salvation.

Plato says our true home is "beyond the heavens." As we know, the heavens are unimaginably vast, but there isn't anything beyond them. What is beyond them is nothing. What Plato is recording here is a transference of spirit from real space to non-space, from real time to non-time, from being to non-being, and all this in the context of eros aroused and denied.

Interestingly, there may have been a sense that this was coming. Parmenides (Kirk & Raven, 1957:266-276), who lived two generations before Socrates in Italy, then part of the greater Greek world is remembered for a vision, a meeting with the Goddess Truth, in which she warned him at length against following the path of non-being. I think this may have been a mythic warning about what was beginning to happen. We were beginning to look to a transcendent source of reality, changeless and eternal, of which the world we inhabit is a pale and more or less miserable reflection. Long centuries of this habit of mind, encouraged by fire and sword when necessary, ensured that when thinkers again turned their attention to the world around them, they saw matter purged of spirit. This has left us burdened with a materialistic and inadequate science.

Interestingly, there was a premonitory objection then as well and, again, it arose in Italy. Giordano Bruno (Yates, 1967:405-406), who came from the same area in southern Italy as Parmenides, was an early champion of the Copernican view that the sun was the center of the earth's world. But he had a Pythagorean sense of the spirituality of matter (and yes, the Pythagoreans also came from southern Italy). He objected vehemently to the purely mechanistic interpretation later adopted by Galileo, Kepler and other founders of modern physics. Bruno was tried by the inquisition; unlike Galileo, he did not recant and was burned at the stake in 1600.

12.  See Wilson (1992), particularly chapters 11 and 12, pp.215-280.

## References

Aeschylus. *Aeschylus I,* eds D. Grene and R. Lattimore. New York: Washington Square Press, 1967. (Original translation published in 1953)

Campbell, Joseph. *The Power of Myth.* New York: Doubleday, 1988.

Gimbutas, Marija. *The Civilization of the Goddess.* San Francisco, CA: HarperCollins, 1991.

Eliot, T.S. *Selected Poems.* London, UK: Penguin, 1948. (Originally published in 1922)

Frazer, J. *The Golden Bough: A Study in Comparative Religion.* London, UK: Macmillan, 1890.

Graves, R. *The White Goddess.* New York: Vintage Books, 1948.

Jones, A.J. *et al,* eds. *The New Testament of the Jerusalem Bible.* Garden City, NJ: Doubleday, 1966.

Joyce, James. *Ulysses.* New York: Vintage Books, 1961. (Originally published in 1922)

Juergens, S. *The New Marian Missal for Daily Mass.* New York: Regina Press, 1957.

Kirk, G.S. and J.E. Raven. *The Presocratic Philosophers.* Cambridge, UK: The University Press, 1957.

Lao Tzu. *The Complete Works of Lao Tzu,* ed. and transl. Hua-Ching Ni. Malibu, CA: The Shrine of the Eternal Breath of Tao, 1979.

Larsen, S. "The Making of a Zulu Sangoma, Vusumazulu Credo Mutwa," *Shaman's Drum,* 35 (1994):22-32.

Locke, R.F. *The Book of the Navajo.* Los Angeles, CA: Mankind Books, 1976.

Nei, M. and A.K. Roychoudhury. "Gene differences between Caucasian, Negro, and Japanese population," *Science,* 177 (1972):343-436.

Plato. "Phaedrus," *The Collected Dialogues of Plato,* eds. E. Hamilton and H. Cairns. New York: Bollingen Foundation, 1963, pp.475-525.

Seed, J., J. Macy, P. Fleming, and A. Naess. *Thinking Like a Mountain.* Philadelphia, PA: New Society Publishers, 1988.

Stevens, Wallace. "The life of the poet," *Wallace Stevens Reading His Poems.* New York: Caedmon, cassette recording, side 2, number 10, 1987. (Recording date not given).

Swimme, B. and T. Berry. *The Universe Story.* San Francisco, CA: HarperSan Francisco, 1992.

Weston, J. *From Ritual to Romance.* Garden City, NJ: Doubleday, 1957. (Originally published in 1921)

Wilhelm, R. and C. Baynes, trans. *The I Ching* or *Book of Changes.* Princeton, NJ: Princeton University Press, 1967.

Wilson, E.O. *The Diversity of Life.* New York: Norton, 1992.

Yates, F. "Bruno, Giordano," *The Encyclopedia of Philosophy,* vol.1, ed. P. Edwards. New York: Macmillan, 1967, pp.405-408.

_____ . Sociobiology, the Abridged Edition. Cambridge, MA: Harvard University Press, 1980.

# DISCUSSION

With Burleigh and Coffey

*Scott*: I want to express my sadness about what I have heard. The words really hurt my heart a lot. I want to concur with Dr. Kremer that, in fact, the Western medical, scientific paradigm, through its compartimentalization and reductionism, tends to reduce a lot of the mystery and magic of life, esp. for healers. Yet, at the same time, the same compartimentalization occurs within academic circles where we hole ourselves up in square boxes and allow our mental machinations to fly. Something gets lost. Male/female, indigenous/Euro-American tribe, mind/body/spirit, these are words which don't exist in indigenous languages. *Tunkasila Wakan Tanka,* there is no English correlate for that. It is both one and neither. The same separation is keeping us from embracing the common humanity. Indigenous people? I live and am an associate and apprentice of elders. They don't recognize me as something separate from them. They have a word in Lakota, *mitakuye oyasin,* that means, "all my relations," we are all connected. The same is true when they tell me that there is just one tribe—the human tribe. Until we come to that realization, we are continuing to be caught in the duality of our own minds, our own language. It's a trap. I am not trying to become a Native American, I am trying to become human. That means to recognize my relations with everyone, regardless of race, gender, social-economic background, nationality. Until we truly live with that realization, we are continuing to fragment this world and are divided within our internal landscapes. *Mitakuye oyasin.*

*Burleigh*: I agree with you and a great deal with what you have said. I cannot speak for Jürgen on that point, but, I think, he would also agree with me. This paper, and a lot of the work he is trying to address, concerns people who are approaching the concept of "all our relations" from the point of view of seeing this separation of all categories, people being out of their culture, out of their community, out of common humanity. It is a recognition. We just can't make a statement and step in there. There is a way that we need to go back and remember, who we are. Not going back and staying there, but bringing that knowing process forward.

*Coffey:* I don't think it is a contradiction to say both (and this is a little bit Hegel), that we are all one, not just one humanity, but one life, because it is also all of the animals and all the plants. We are also not all identical. To say we are all one is not blotting out all the differences. I think the diversity in being is for a reason. We need to experience what we are, the wholeness of what we are, while also allowing everything else to be. To emphasize one side of that equation, we lose somehow the unity. We have to be expansive and recognize the diversity.

*Rudiak-Gillard:* What you just said, reminded me of a concept I learned when I was studying with Rowena. She calls it "synarchy." It is honoring the cultural diversity of all beings, working in harmony that preserves all. A lot of my journey has been trying to understand how I can reach transcendence through my own embodiment and what it means to have a bloodline ancestry as well as an ancestry that formed in relationship to the spirit of the land. How do I balance that? I am still walking that path. I feel a lot of my desire for ceremony is formed by the land I grew up on, where I was conceived and evolved from, which is now California and the Western states, yet knowing that I am not an indigenous, tribal member, that I have bloodlines in Europe. So I am traveling a lot. Understanding the differences is a constant undertaking.

There are also pieces of information, I specifically would like to get. Rinda mentioned in Jürgen's paper something about navigation between Hawaii and Polynesia.

*Burleigh:* Tahiti.

*Rudiak-Gillard:* The people were all men. I don't think women did this. They would catch a swell and then travel on it. But what happened when they could not see? (A lot of this question has to do with my ability to navigate internally, e.g., when I can't see stars or I can't see the sun). The men used to lay their testicles on either side of the keel and the internal body sensing was so refined that they could feel when they would slide off the crest of the swell.

Part of the work I do when I am in areas where I don't know where I am going, when there is no training and no wisdom, is navigating by my own etherial senses. I am really happy to own this faculty when it comes to this masculine-feminine stuff. I would really like to know if anybody has any information about where this sense for navigation came from. We may not find out, although I know it is a real internal orienting mechanism I can trust.

*Ife:* Josephine, you claim that North Africa is part of Western thought. What is your basis, especially for the myth of Isis and Osiris?

*Coffey:* I am thinking of Egypt.

*Ife:* Isis and Osiris is the basis for the myth of my ancestors. African scholars found this myth to be the basis of our pantheon. I see the importance of knowing who you are. You are growing up here in this society while I had to live with two cultures, staying in touch with my own indigenous culture and working with my people while having to compete with the Western society. Then I hear statements you made and I am sure your intent was honorable, but you have to compete with this also. That is why I think it is important that people get in touch with who they are, because when you know who you are, you can bring something to the whole, i.e., contribute to the whole for everyone. But when you are in constant denial or you attach to something you find charming or unique or exotic or what appeals to you at that moment, it is not the same.

Rinda, when I hear you talking about in the essay you read for Jurgen, are you coming from that group and do you have something to give that's valid?

*Wimmer:* I had also a lot of mixed feelings about Jurgen's paper. Part of what I saw is rather sad. There is a certain assumption and the first part of the assumption is that there is a Euro-Western mind. In any society, at any particular time, there always has been an imbalance, a product of whatever culture or whatever place we have lived in. Part of it has to do with the fact that we have a lot of cookie crumbling going on. People who are born in cities have absolutely nothing to which they can turn to, especially, with a lot of broken families. They want to find out about their heritage or their background. I use the term Heinz 57, because I don't have another word for it. There is so much which is blended into almost the same. But basically, by trying to reach backwards and trying to say, I am going to adopt this particular type of ceremony or this particular type of venue because this is were my great aunt or my great uncle came from and because this particular society was looking a certain way, also tends to negate the aspects we live in. There are a lot of people who cannot get around trees because they happen to live in an area filled with cement. They had no experiences around trees during their whole life. It is really sad to hear this certain stance, pointing back and forth in Jurgen's essay, saying that this particular side is negative and this particular side is positive. If we take a look at where we are at the conference, unity and polarity, we could more or less say, it is transcendence. It is not looking backwards and forwards, but it is looking beyond. If we would look beyond, we would be able to take things from this standpoint. This is where I live, this is where my life is. How can I make myself whole, rather then saying that it comes from living in a particular community with a particular culture, with a particular set of ideas. I think, once it gets outside of the realm of the mind and we can get away from that perspective, maybe we can get beyond these cowboy and Indian ideas. People are trying to play Christians or whatever and it should be people trying to find the whole within themselves.

*Burleigh:* Mary, I agree with you. Though Heinz 57 is good, too. If all of my ancestors would get in one room together, none of them would come out alive. What Jurgen was looking for is not so much that there is a particular right, or a particular ceremony, or a particular group or tribe, he wants to go back to the concept of the whole mind which sees the whole universe. He wants to recognize that we are all one and it is not pulling it down to just either side. It is trying to find whatever personal roots we bring forward.

*Coffey:* I think it is happening to all of us here. I meant it seriously. I spoke of the myth of our people and "by our people" I meant, collectively, Europeans. I did not speak to Africans and I apologize, but I spoke of my part of the experience. Most of us are raised in a Western European tradition. It has not happened yet. It happened to me that I experienced my Irish moods. When it happened, I felt as if I were in a very repressive English environment. My myth as an American is still to come. This is not to leave out other people, by any means. The African experience is so profoundly important and continues to be, as much as the Native American and the Haitian experience.

*Fellows:* Jo, I wonder whether you read the *Mutant Message—Downunder* (Lees Summit, MO: MM Co., 1991)? It is about a woman who studied with the aborigines. She actually went on a walk about with them. She sees herself as a mutant because this was the way she was seen by the aborigines. The aboriginal tribe decided not to bring the next generation forward because of what they saw and they said, "it is really up to you mutants to decide what you want to do with this world now." This message was actually hopeful, but I was also thinking in terms of the indigenous mind.

The other question I have is looking at the myth of Gilgamesh, one of the first culture heroes we had in one of the first cities. The question is where is Enkidu now?

*Becker:* I am Michaela Irma Becker. I say this name because I took Jurgen's course, learning—transforming, learning—transforming. I spent time with it and read his paper over and over again. The first thing we had to do was going back to our own roots. Then we were supposed to go on and do all other papers, but I never got out of this going to my own roots business. Irma Becker is my grandmother, Michaela is my great grandmother on my other side. I am still doing it, I am communicating with them. The reason I am here right now is only because I am allowing them to live. They live really through me. I have to say, if it weren't for Jurgen's course and all this transforming and learning, I wouldn't have done it. It takes a little bit more than just hearing it, you have to really experience it. You learn and you transform. You look back and you look forward and you see where you are. I found out that I am one fourth French, which I did not know. I found that my grandmother, whom I did not know, committed suicide or was murdered. So I asked her directly, "Did you kill yourself or where you murdered?" She told me in a dream, "I killed myself, don't blame your grandfather!" Where is the rest of my family? In New Orleans? I call up Walter Johnsons in New Orleans, they were all black. Maybe I got a whole black family in New Orleans?

*Lamson:* I have two main thoughts. I was recently reading Elizabeth Thonas' book, *Tribe of the Tiger* (Englewood Cliffs, NJ: S. & S. Trade, 1994) and was struck by the concern about an endangered species that has been created in the last century through genetic biology. There was very great concern that this species is going to be extinct and it did not even exist two hundred years ago. This is one thought, another thought I had is there is constant change and sameness. The African Yoruba tradition, which I am very familiar with, was created through a blending of many different things. There is not just one source. Egypt is one source and there was an indigenous population in Nigeria, both created the Yoruba tradition. There was borrowing back and forth between many religions. What I am struck by, no matter what the changes are, there are certain universal archetypes which pop up all over the world. We might get away from them, because of certain events in our life, but they are in all of us; they are part of all of us. However, we might be a new creation. Americans might be an endangered species that just was created a few hundred years ago, but we have certain values. There are certain features in our culture which have been created from a mixture that is very special. It does not mean that we have totally lost everything; it still comes up in our dreams.

*Scott:* I like to share a prophecy from the Hopi people. There were some elders who had a vision. In this vision, the children of the oppressors of the native people are going to step forward to wear beads in their hair and learn the old ways from the ancestors, because all the children of the elders are leaving the reservations to find a good life. I and, I am certain, many of the people here, live the legacy of this vision. I was born on the continent of Turtle Island, indigenous to this place. I was indoctrinated into a Christian tradition which I could not relate to. It did not gel in the spiritual fabric of myself. When I was brought into ceremony through sun dance and sweat lodge, the ancestors spoke to me. Unless you are a first-generation person who came over from Europe or from wherever, we all are indigenous to here; we are, however, a heterogeneous mixture of many different cultures and backgrounds. So I think, it is imperative now that we each find within ourselves the ceremony and tradition which speaks deeply and resonates in our soul, then we will be able to find wholeness. Then we can come together in community, as a collective community of people from various traditions, from different backgrounds and cultures.

*Burleigh*: I want to answer because you are typifying what basically was talked about in Jurgen's essay. We are not taking a piece of a ceremony here and there, we are walking and living in a tradition which is real. You ARE in that tradition. There are people who are of an inner tradition which they have totally adopted and, at the point of adoption, they are. When stepping into the traditional mind, there is the feeling that it has been denied, which definitely is not the case. What this really will do, is inviting people who have not moved into a particular tradition to look at their own past and roots to find out what is there. Because it is only by looking through our past that we begin to move into what we are all creating together.

# A WALK THROUGH
# THE CRETAN LABYRINTH

Coquelicot Rudiak-Gillard
(with Dijeridu music by Phillip Scott)

The Cretan Labyrinth is one of the oldest known patterns which has been repeated in many cultures: Afghanistan, England (Glastonbury Tor Maze and on rocks at Tintagel), India, on pillars in Pompei, and on finger rings and timber of houses on Sumatra. It is also the Hopi symbol for the earth mother. In Finland and Sweden, variations of this pattern are used during spring rites. Baltic fishermen ran the maze to evoke protection and abundance before setting sail.

To walk the maze is to walk the sun's movement across the sky and the cycles of life, death, rebirth, reflected in seasonal changes.

The Cretan labyrinth is a unicursal labyrinth—one path in and one path out. It does not conceal the goal from view. It is not a cognitive puzzle, no false pathway or choice to confuse or challenge you like a maze. It represents a pilgrimage from imbalance to balance, balancing right and left hemi-spheres of the brain. It leads from off-centeredness to centeredness. It is a journey that reconnects us to spirit.

To enter the labyrinth, I invite participants to release themselves to the journey, to keep their spirits open, expansive, receptive, and centered.

Trying to fit eighty plus people into 16-inch pathways simultaneously is challenging. We didn't make it, but it was a study in co-operation. Some people gave way, when the group got stuck. They left the labyrinth so that the rest of the group could move. This was done in a general spirit of good will, laughter and patience. This experience was also an ice breaker. Everyone involved became very close at certain points during the journey when we were compressed, two people to every foot of space. I was also struck by how it served as a metaphor, reflecting of what it takes for a large group of high energy people to stay balanced and centered even when their toes were literally being stepped on.

Many people used the labyrinth before, during, and after the conference in a much more meditative fashion. I used the labyrinth to ground and balance my energy throughout the conference.

There are many ways to travel a labyrinth: run, crawl, skip, be led by another through the labyrinth with eyes closed, to walk slowly, meditatively, putting one foot directly in front of another or digging into the earth or sand.

Labyrinths are to he enjoyed and played in. During the sacred journey through the labyrinth we engage in whatever way spirit leads us.

### References

Ashe, Geoffrey. *The Glastonbury Tor Maze.* Published in England.

Fisher, Adrian and Jeff Saward. *The British Maze Guide.* Published in England, 1991.

____, and George Gerster. *The Art of the Maze.* Published in England, 1990.

Kraft, John. *The Goddess in the Labyrinth.* Published in Sweden.

# FROM MAIMONIDES TO HEURISTICS: AN INNOVATIVE RESEARCH MODEL FOR PARAPSYCHOLOGY

Mena E. Potts

I first developed this heuristic research model for my research with precognitive dreams based on early childhood experiences. I grew up in the Middle West and these concepts were not encouraged. I recently came out of the closet and worked on a model that can be applied to a wide range of parapsychological research questions. The research was really self research, based on my own experiences. Following my presentation, my husband, Attorney Dominic J. Potts, will demonstrate the application of the model to his published precognitive dream of January 31, 1986. In order to accommodate the allocated conference time frame, the model and dream are presented in an abbreviated form. Full references have been provided to enable a larger and complete exploration for those who wish to do so.

The research model I developed was achieved through the merger of Ullman and Krippner's Maimonides research findings (Ullman and Krippner, 1970; Ullman, Krippner with Vaughan, 1989), Ullman's Social and Psi Vigilance theories (1961, 1986), Ullman's Experiential Dream Group Process (Ullman and Zimmerman, 1985; Ullman, 1989) and Moustakas' Heuristic Research Model (1961, 1981, 1985, 1988, 1990) into a new psi-dream research model.

## Ullman and Krippner's Maimonides Psi Dream Research

My model is predicated upon Ullman and Krippner's (1970) Maimonides dream research findings that experiential meaning embodied in metaphors appears to be the key to understanding dream consciousness and the manifestation of psi. In Ullman and Krippner's (1970) research, linkage occurred at the juncture of experiential meaning for both subject and agent. The interactional psi model formulated by Montague Ullman and Stanley Krippner at Maimonides Dream Laboratory is the bridge to this new parapsychological research model.

Based upon their research findings, Ullman, Krippner, and Vaughan concluded that vigilance is the primary function of psi dreaming. While dreaming, the dreamer is alerted to novel intrusions entering into the conscious field. While involved in the vigilance operation, the dreamer sometimes accesses future life experiences which are meaningfully related to the dreamer's current concerns. The dreamer strives toward resolution of the present dilemma through an integration of all available information and extends the scanning process to the "psi field" in search of relevant external influences.

## Moustakas' Heuristic Research Model

The Heuristic Research Model encourages passionate self-involvement and self-exploration in inquiry. The focus is "upon the essential meanings connected with every day human experiences" (Douglass & Moustakas, 1985:39).

Heuristic research is a qualitative method which arrives at the themes and essences of experience. In heuristic research, "The question of validity is one of meaning: Does the ultimate depiction of the experience derived...present the meanings and essences of the experience?" (Moustakas, 1990:32).

Douglass and Moustakas (1985) explicated three phases of the design:

1. Immersion, the first phase, is comprised of indwelling, the internal frame of reference and self-search;

2. acquisition (collection of data), the second phase, consists of tacit knowing, intuition, inference, self-dialogue, self-disclosure, and signitive-symbolic-representations;

3. realization (synthesis), the third phase, is comprised of intentionality, verification and dissemination as processes essential to integration and communication of findings.

## Conclusion

This parapsychological research model enables the researcher to explore the qualities, meanings, associative processes and essences of psi-dream experiences and other psychological experiences. Each component in this model is a research tool which can be creatively employed by parapsychologists, Ullman and Krippner's Interactional Psi Model and Maimonides Findings, Ullman's Psi Vigilance Theory and Experiential Dream Group Process, and Moustakas' Heuristic Research Model can be individually or collectively applied to a wide range of parapsychological research questions.

# APPLICATION OF THE HEURISTIC RESEARCH MODEL TO A PRECOGNITIVE DREAM EXPERIENCE

Dominic J. Potts

## Dominic's Precognitive Dream

On January 31, 1986, I dreamed I was standing on an elevated porch looking down into the street below. There I saw one of my client's, Harry, trying to start the engine of his tractor trailer rig. Harry is an interstate truck driver. It appeared in the dream that he was starting out on one of his trips. Suddenly I became concerned because I saw a small fire below his truck begin to grow and creep up toward the engine compartment of his tractor trailer as Harry was oblivious of it while he was unsuccessfully attempting to start the engine. I shouted out to warn Harry about the fire because I realized he was unaware of it. I shouted because I feared the fire could cause an explosion if it reached the engine. I shouted and waved but Harry could neither see nor hear me. Finally, Harry got the truck started and it lumbered off slowly before the fire could erupt. Then the dream ended.

Upon awakening, I told Mena about the dream. We applied Ullman's Experiential Process. Mena asked me to write the dream down immediately and then to call Harry and report the dream. I wrote out the dream but I resisted calling Harry, believing he would think the dream was silly. Harry is a big burly truck driver—a macho type who could be a role model for a Marlboro cigarette ad. Mena continued to discuss the dream with me and kept prompting me to call Harry and tell him about it. "It couldn't hurt," she urged, "and it might be helpful to him. Even if it doesn't contain a warning, Harry will be pleased you were so concerned." Finally I relented and called Harry. I read my dream to him and Harry was actually complimented to get my call. He told me he was just leaving to pick up a load of steel at Weirton, West Virginia, and take it on to Maryland.

## Harry's Precognized Experience

Three days later, Harry called me back from the State of Maryland. He was excited. He told me my dream had helped him to avoid a serious fire. He related his experience to me and then agreed to write it out for my documentation. Here is what he wrote.

On Monday, I left the truck stop with my load. I had stopped for a bite to eat. Shortly after I left the truck stop, I was pulling up a hill when everything happened. There was a fire and a tremendous amount of smoke up under the hood. The alternator on my truck got hot and blew up. It was in the engine compartment. There was a little fire and a lot of smoke. As soon as it happened, I thought of the dream. That's basically because everything that happened brought back the dream to me. So evidently there are messages in dreams. It made me more cautious than normal. I would say from this that I now believe in dreams to that effect. The dream alerted me because as soon as I smelled the smoke, I killed the engine. Otherwise, I probably would have burned the truck up.

## Research Model Application and Essential Meaning

By applying Mena's precognitive dream research model to my dream, the following meaning emerged.

I feel this precognitive dream actually symbolizes my legal philosophy of client representation. I also believe it occurred because of my philosophy of client representation.

My practice of law is confined to the representation of injury victims.

Personal injury representation and litigation is not only an art and a science, it is also an intensely human relationship. I believe that an attorney cannot represent an injury victim effectively unless he is willing to relate to the client on an intimate basis. If an attorney feels intellectually superior to, or professionally aloof from, his client, he will compromise the client's interest during settlement negotiation or jury trial because the attorney's representation will be mechanical and sterile, even if he is technically proficient and litigationally masterful.

I believe if the attorney is incapable of entering into a close human relationship with his client, the attorney will not be able to reach the heart and mind of the jury because he will not have reached the heart and mind of his client.

In my practice of law, it is my philosophy that the client's concerns and struggles become my concerns and struggles. I respect the dignity and individuality of each client. I do not view a client impersonally or transiently. A client is not merely one of hundreds of clients in our office. Each client is an important individual. We take a personal interest in each client. We may have hundreds of cases in our office, but this is the only case the client has.

Therefore, I dignify my clients by involving them as "co-counsel" with me in the case. This respectful relationship makes us "equals." This makes both of us an indispensable part of a greater whole. I value the clients' perspective and the clients value my legal experience. No one understands the clients' injury conditions and how they have damaged the clients' lifestyle better than the clients, because clients must live daily in the body, mind, spirit, and soul that were damaged.

Therefore, in my representation of personal injury victims, I try to undergo the clients' total injury-experience vicariously, with all its concomitant physical pain, functional disability, and emotional anguish. Only in this way can I truly empathize with the clients' situation, fully appreciate it, and effectively represent it as legal counsel.

Accordingly, in my philosophy of client representation, I develop a close human relationship with each client. In representing a client, the impairment of the client's quality of life is the measure of damages I seek to be compensated. To the extent the client's injury conditions and complications have deprived him of the ability to enjoy the quality of life fully, and to pursue life's happiness and pleasures fully, to that extent the law requires, and I seek, full restitution from the tortfeasor or negligent wrongdoer.

Relating this to my precognitive dream about Harry, the dream symbolizes the close representation, empathy, concern, and merging of consciousness I share with each client I represent. At the time I had this dream, I was representing Harry in a personal injury case. Shortly before this dream, Harry had returned to work after recuperating from a serious and disabling injury he had suffered when another semi-truck crossed over the centerline and side-swiped Harry's rig in Pittsburgh.

On reflection, I feel the dream allowed me to perceive a potential peril to Harry and enabled me to warn and prepare him to intervene timely and effectively in order to stave off a potential disaster. The dream, therefore, metaphorically reflects my legal philosophy in representing injury victims. I feel I would not have had this dream, were it not for my philosophy of client representation.

By applying Mena's precognitive dream research model the essential meanings, associative processes and essences of my psi dream metaphors emerged. I was able to alert Harry and heighten his vigilance, enabling him to act with alacrity to abort potential peril in its incipient stage. As the research process disclosed, my precognitive dream was part of my active professional life and my meaningful interaction with clients. This finding is consistent with Ullman and Krippner's interactional psi model and their research findings (1970) that experiential meaning embodied in metaphors appears to be the key to understanding dream consciousness and the manifestation of psi.

## References

Douglass, B. and C. Moustakas. "Heuristic inquiry: The internal search to know," *Journal of Humanistic Psychology, 25* (1985):39-55.

Moustakas, C. *Heuristic Research.* Newbury Park, CA: Sage, 1990.

_____ . *Phenomenology, Science and Psychotherapy.* Cape Breton, Canada: University College, Family Life Institute, 1988.

_____ . *Rhythms, Rituals and Relationships.* Detroit, MI: Center for Humanistic Studies, 1981.

Ullman, M. "The experiential dream group," *The Variety of Dream Experience: Expanding Our Ways of Working With Dreams,* eds. Ullman and Limmer. New York: Continuum, 1989, pp.1-26. (Originally published in 1987)

_____ . "Vigilance theory and psi. Part II. Physiological, psychological, and parapsychological aspects," *Journal of the American Society for Psychical Research, 80* (1986):375-391.

_____ . "Dreaming, altered states of consciousness and the problem of vigilance," *Journal of Nervous and Mental Disease, 133* (1961):529-535.

_____ , and S. Krippner. *Dream Studies and Telepathy: An Experimental Approach.* New York: Parapsychology Foundation, Parapsychological Monographs No. 12, 1970.

_____ , S. Krippner, with A. Vaughan. *Dream Telepathy: Experiments in Nocturnal ESP.* Jefferson, NC: McFarland, 2nd ed., 1989.

_____ , and M. Zimmerman. *Working With Dreams.* Los Angeles, CA: J.P. Tarcher, 1985. (Originally published in 1979)

# EMOTIONAL COURAGE

Joanne and Ron Mied

Emotional courage is the ability to uncover what is most feared. It allows an individual to release a depth of unconscious emotions which are disturbing to re-experience. It relieves the individual from excruciating, painful body sensations from the past. It permits to let go of a destructive mental self image. The emergence of these factors to consciousness seems to threaten our survival and sanity, Their release exposes and heals irrational feelings that we have spent our whole adult lives concealing. Emotional courage penetrates denial, rationalization, and all previous superficial healing efforts. It is real risk. These buried emotions overwhelm any sense of controlling mind.

Emotional courage heals the core of our traumatized self. It is a self-authenticating act of courage which leads to other heroic acts. These bold and spirited actions add to our personal evolution and the fulfillment of our true potential as physical, emotional, intellectual, and spiritual beings.

*          *          *

Emotional courage is initiated after a painful recognition of an important and repeated life failure which may be a divorce, a succession of abusive partners, the death of a loved one, a career disappointment, or a tragic event involving our children. Recognition of our failure is the most compelling reason we begin self-inspection with earnest and in depth. We tire of blaming others. We run out of excuses, rationalizations, and the hope that our life will miraculously improve.

An event shatters the illusion that we can fix our deteriorating lives by manipulating people and objects. A depression follows when we realize our problem must be dealt with internally. We experience feelings of loneliness and alienation, which are the result of childhood traumata we have been running from our entire lives.

Simultaneously, we become aware of a deep unrelenting desire for something. It may be a fulfilling career, an intimate relationship, or a physical healing. It is a whisper that becomes a shout, drowning out our superficiality. We move to new action, real change. And we begin to understand *we* must change.

We are confused and uncertain about how to proceed. The emotional terrain is so life threatening that we cannot begin without sufficient support. And we must find a guide who can safely lead us through our difficulty.

If we are afraid of working at emotional depth, we will never affect a substantial life change. As children, we were afraid of the dark and as adults we are afraid of this shadow of our unconscious. As children we were convinced we are flawed, and as adults we are frightened that our imperfections are irreparable so we never review our childish conclusions.

Buried emotions, painful bodily sensations, and negative self-imagery are so overwhelming, we fixate on performance and achievement. We hope the next relationship, accomplishment, or purchase will relieve our internal distress. But it never does. What we need to do is to deal with our internalized stress directly. If we can relieve the internal tension caused by unconscious emotions, we can effectively deal with the external world by making better decisions. Stress leads to panic and panic decisions are always wrong.

We suppress and deny our deep feelings of panic by focusing on our "next" goal. "I'll be happy when I'm married," "when I'm financially successful," "when I'm famous." We concentrate so intently on the goal that we never feel the panic driving the impulse. We are so consumed by our idealized future, we never feel the present dissatisfaction that is the primary motivation.

Dealing with our internalized stress takes emotional courage because it requires us to re-experience and release past traumatic experiences. Although emotional courage is inspired by the recognition of a life failure, that recognition of failure re-occurs every six months. And we ignore it.

Why do we ignore the failure? Because we do not know how to fix it. Our attitude is" "My problem can't be solved! Maybe other people can be happy, I can't."

Anyone who is not passionately involved in his/her career, who is not experiencing deep emotional and physical intimacy in his/her marriage, or who is not developing friendships that inspire growth is saying to his/herself, "My problem can't be solver!"

"If my problem can't be solved, why should I even begin working on it? I will work around my imperfections. I will ignore my dissatisfactions and do the best I can. I will settle for the money in my career. I will settle for a civil roommate instead of a spouse and refrain from dwelling on my disappointments. I will complain to my friends and listen to them complain because change is impossible."

When we say, "My problem can't be solved," we are actually saying, "I'm too afraid to re-experience my childhood traumata because they threaten my survival and my sanity." We are saying our past was so painful, we are not sure we have the courage to endure re-examining it. We are subconsciously repeating this to ourselves every minute of every hour that we are denying the failures and denying ourselves the realization of our aspirations.

It is easier for us to initiate new action when we see living examples.

Therefore, I am presenting several cases of emotional courage to allow us to feel the ordeal of the process; and show that real people have survived and benefited from the ordeal. These stories are no composites, they are actual examples of emotional courage. Only the names have been changed.

*          *          *

Since Hilary divorced an abusive husband, she has had several unsatisfactory affairs with married men, and desperately wants more for herself and her children.

Hilary begins by explaining that her father committed suicide when she was twelve years old. As she tells of grieving her father's loss, she is matter-of-fact. When questioned about her cool emotional stance, she says she has already released her childhood feelings. She says that there is nothing more to tell or feel about the tragedy.

With more questioning about her father's suicide, she slips into confusion and disorientation which indicates that she is actually emotionally numb. Underneath that numbness are buried emotions so painful that the only way a twelve-year-old girl could persevere, was through suppression and denial.

Hilary remains confused and disoriented, until her buried grief and guilt surface. She involuntarily moves back in time to her father's death. And she bursts into tears frequently, without any ability to inhibit her emotional expression. Overwhelming emotions erupt without warning. Her body feels heavy. Her heart seems irreparably broken. A sense of doom pervades. Her thoughts and feelings are lost in the past. She cannot focus on the present. She concentrates one every detail of the weeks surrounding her father's death.

As a child, Hilary had little emotional connection with her mother, so her father is the light of her life. Even though he was a heavy drinker, he took the children places on weekends and spent precious time playing with Hilary.

When Hilary was twelve years old, her mother threw her father out of the house because of his drinking. A week later when he called and talked to Hilary on the phone about her upcoming birthday, her mother stood by anxiously, but did not speak to him. When Hilary got off the phone, her mother chastised her for not asking him to come home. Hilary felt devastated by her mother's comments. The next day her father committed suicide. Hilary blamed herself for her father's death, because she didn't ask him to come home.

Hilary's unconscious grief and guilt are releasing. After the powerful waves of emotions subside and the physical agony abates, Hilary's mind summarizes every detail in the sequence of tragic events. With her emotions cleared, she gains invaluable insight into how her response to her father's death shaped her relationships with men.

In the midst of her terrible grief, Hilary subconsciously made a decision, "Never marry anyone you love or they will die." She is afraid to be close to a man she really loves for fear he will die and again she will experience deep loss. If she marries someone she loves, she fears she will be sentencing him to death. These frozen childish feelings unconsciously guide her adult choices in relationships. Each loveless choice insures loneliness and failure. Slowly her mistaken choices become crystal clear.

She is freed from the pattern of negative behavior that caused her to be with men she didn't love. Her new found clarity about her past life makes the future seem bright. Today, Hilary's choices in men are inspired by hard won wisdom and love. She knows she will not repeat the same unconscious pattern. Hilary is really doing well and very happy.

*          *          *

Even though Bill was an athlete and an excellent student, his teachers and coaches often remarked that he never lived up to his potential. In college, his grades plummeted and he gave up his athletic scholarship in his senior year. As he grew older, he became more and more dysfunctional. An unconscious fear of men kept him at low paying jobs. He desperately wanted to find employment that was satisfying. At forty, he finally noticed that he was unreasonably afraid in reasonable situations. And he wanted to find out why.

His only memories of early childhood were isolated incidents with long, blank lapses. As Bill allowed childhood memories to surface, glimpses of tragic scenes began to penetrate his life long denial, but he assumed he was "imagining things." His first recollections were small, sudden, mental flashes which he quickly buried again. They were fragments of pictures accompanied by muscle spasms, and then a frozen millisecond of terror.

After two years of slipping in and out of denial, Bill accepts the truth that he has been sexually abused by his father. He is shocked and lost in a sea of overpowering emotions which he can no longer resist or control. He is propelled back to a time of unthinkable betrayal by a monster called "dad."

Horrible mental pictures and the self-destructive self-imagery flood his mind. He feels like he is a piece of meat with no soul. He feels powerless from being brutally overpowered repeatedly. He senses that sexual abuse is about domination, humiliation, and power rather than physical gratification.

The complex of emotions that shaped his personality surface. Shame, guilt, betrayal, and rage predominate. He blames himself as a five-year-old for causing his father's behavior. He forgives in spite of his rage. He understands that his confusion over pain and pleasure came from the sexual abuse. Finally, he re-experiences the searing pain of being sodomized as a young child. The bodily distress takes weeks to release. The physical torment surpasses the mental anguish, but it is the last place in a dreadful puzzle that puts the whole tragedy to rest.

After recovering his memories, he says, "Now, my whole life makes sense. I understand why I did what I did all those years." He sees that subconsciously he lived under the threat of being sexually abused by men. He was very uncomfortable meeting new men and being in a room alone with them. His business aspirations had been undermined by fear.

Today, Bill has a successful counseling practice working with both men and women. He cannot believe how fulfilled he is in his career. No obstacle seems to be overwhelming.

*          *          *

Thirty-nine year-old Dennise is re-experiencing being eight years old. Her heart is pounding and aching. Her mouth is dry, and her breathing is very deep. Her silent fear turns to breathless panic, then tears of terror. A buried feeling is tearing its way to her surface awareness, but she is being guided safely through her moment of crisis. She loses all her adult control of her feelings.

Dennise's father rarely hits her, but he is always distant and never shows his emotions. She fears him because she can never tell what is going on inside of him. He gives very stern looks when he is displeased. This frightens her more, and she tries harder to please him and gain his fatherly favors.

She is two years old emotionally. Childish terror of her father whispers from her lips. She repeats, "He scares me! He scares me!" She is shocked. This is a complex reversal of her conscious feelings toward him. Mom is always the cruel one and, now too, Dad is an overwhelming threat. This is unbearable.

Thirty-nine-year-old Dennise realizes that she tricked herself as a child into believing she was not afraid of him, but instead was attracted to him. This subversion led her to misjudge her intimate partners.

She thought it was her mother's constant criticism that created her low self-esteem and self-destructive behavior, but fear of her father completes the picture. She only can be attracted to men she is afraid of because that fear reminds her of her father. As a child, she hoped her father would rescue her from her mother's cruelty.

Dennise realizes abusive men hide their feelings, dominate with criticism, control with fear tactics and finally explode in rage. These emotional hooks drew Dennise to loveless partners. She is grateful to be free of this pattern. She is building self-esteem and making new choices regarding men.

*          *          *

As Jane prepares herself emotionally, terror sweeps across her face.

Tears drip from her swollen eyes. She begins to shake violently and uncontrollably. She is held and encouraged, while she sobs, "I'm afraid I'm going mad." She feels like she will break to millions of tiny pieces and turn to dust. Her face darkens as the energy drains from her expression. Her dreaded emotion is anger. Anger slowly transforms her from a normal, healthy looking woman to one who appears seriously ill. Her skin turns white and clammy. Her eyes look sunken. And her body appears lifeless although it continues to shake. She looks haggard and withered like someone bedridden for years. Her disintegrating transformation from health to sickness is dramatic.

While she is shaking, she repeats, "I'll go crazy? I'll go crazy?" Jane is guided to breathe more and more deeply. She is reminded that the emotion and the physical symptoms will pass. As Jane continues breathing deeply, she returns to her normal healthy looking self and regains her composure.

Jane courageously repeats this exercise of allowing her anger to surface. Each time she shakes less. Each time she is less fearful and becomes less physically ill. Each time she expresses more bottled rage at her father. Her fury is utterly shocking to her because she idealized her father who died when she was eighteen.

As a child, Jane is repeatedly tortured by her older brother who is favored by her mother. Her complaints fall on deaf ears. Every time she rocks the family boat or has a temper tantrum, her parents tell her she is acting crazy. And they say that "if you are crazy, you will be put away in an mental institution." The threat is repeated many times and is highly effective in forcing Jane to suppress her anger. Unfortunately, the anger finds its expression in illness.

Jane is very threatened when she allows her anger to surface, but she now realizes that she has buried emotions that need to be released. She sees the similarities between the physical symptoms that occur when she is expressing her anger and when she is bedridden. She now feels her health issue can be resolved, it is not an incurable disease. This knowledge is a great relief to her.

\*        \*        \*

The courage displayed in deep, behavior-changing emotional work is always a crisis. We are facing past unconscious emotions, mental images, and bodily sensations that are perceived as life threatening. A crisis occurs which manifests emotionally as terror, grief, or rage. There is temporary disorientation and dysfunction, followed by a feeling that all emotional control is lost.

As the crisis passes, life changing insights occur. The reasons for long standing negative behavior and self-destructive choices become obvious.

There is a shift from the victim perspective to personal responsibility. The most profound change occurs in the internal state. The constant interior panic lessens or fades. This is a great comfort as we realize what we were actually seeking is interior heart space from which we can attend to our life, the inner strength to meet challenges effectively. Creativity begins to flourish and very often lifetime goals are achieved. Emotional courage is the true source of change in our lives.

# BEYOND FORGIVENESS:
# A QUESTION OF INVENTING PEACE

Carolina Marks

The Seville Statement of 1986 on "Aggression and the Brain," written by a group of twenty scholars, states that violence and war are not biologically determined but culturally developed through the tools of obedience, idealism, suggestibility, information gathering, and budget analysis. The skillful use of these tools develops a culture that accepts violence as a solution to its problems and builds egos ready for war. The Seville Statement maintains that the same species that are capable of inventing war are also capable of inventing peace.

So the first question we should ask is could the very same tools that are used to invent war, i.e., suggestibility, idealism, information gathering, etc., also be used to invent peace? I think it is possible to use the very same tools. The premise on which I want to base this paper is what materials or substances should we use as tools. What should we work with to redirect our media and culture to develop or invent peace? We should also ask whether or not we have to use these obviously effective tools? Some substances are different from the substances and materials we use to invent war. Just as bombs, metal, fear and hate are used to invent war and develop a warlike, violence-prone culture, we also have substances necessary for the invention of peace such as food, clothing, shelter, community, trust, forgiveness, respect, affection, compassion and admiration. These proposed peace substances, already available, can be used in new and very different forms not to support war but to invent lasting peace. So we must look at how we use, interpret, combine and recombine, emphasize and de-emphasize these life-giving substances.

Since we are talking about culture, we can no longer talk only individually or psychologically, we have to include all of us. We have to talk about ourselves as interdependent and co-responsible. Any actions of one of us has an effect on everyone else. What qualities are necessary for inventing peace? How can we escalate peace so that it becomes manageable?

The WWFP (World Wall For Peace) is an invention that seeks to offer the opportunity for global and local cultures to invent peace. It is a format for humanity's capacity to focus on peace, develop the wisdom we already have in order to invent peace and prevent war. The artist in everyone is asked to paint the poetry of his/her heart, his/her vision of peace on ceramic tiles. As a preventive medicine wheel of love, it is designed to have the tiles work like herbs, vitamins and vaccine to prevent war. It includes now twenty-four walls in two different countries and three different states.

As founding director of this work, I have had the privilege of learning from it every day, now for ten years. It has created me as I created it. In so far, as this growth has taught me about peace, I would like to share this growth with you so that it may be useful also to your process.

Where did this work of art come from? A sign on a fence, "Yes and no" [shows slides] inspired me to reach out of my pain and despair. The work was born out of the darkest, desperate void which finally filled up and overflowed into a blessed anger. It said, "I can no longer tolerate this unacceptable situation, this loss, this abandonment of goodness. I can no longer tolerate this waste, neither in the world nor in my own life. Anger combined with hope produced determination.

I had lost a job I cherished at J.F.K. University. I had been teaching "Sculpture as a Media of Sacred Art, Creativity and Personal Process." There had been a lot of love and some strife with a few students which seemed totally manageable to me. My dean gave me a leave of absence because he could not handle my energy. I felt shut out of my beloved spiritual community. I felt abandoned and admonished without clarity. It was a divorce.

I cried every day. In order to move into peace, in order to live, I had to forgive. This was a substance that I knew and it had to be part of my peace. These drawings [slides] are called "Forgiving the Terrible Mother." Although the terrible mother was my male dean, I recognized that he was indeed my mother in another form. Ten years later, this monster grew again and I came to understand it finally as "the accomplishment monster." At this point in time, forgiveness was the only path to take. Living with a terrible monster inside was unbearable. Working through these drawings, with these methods of peace-making, I was able to get on, move out of it, let go and live to create again. After these drawings, the healing took place and it was then that I was able to begin to create the path that led me here today—The World Wall for Peace.

My ultimate peace method of choice became retreat, forgiveness, and self-protection. I chose a path where there was no competition. This is a life-long habit of transcendence, of rising above it. My motto is, "if life gave me lemons, I'll make lemonade."

As you can see, I rose above the situation and, in the end, was marching against the monster of nuclear war with my mother who was unmasked. The only answer that seemed to work was Stage One—forgiveness and transformation—the first peace solution.

Stage Two was patience. Persistence beats resistance. It was at the height of the Cold War, when the idea came to create the Peace Wall in order to discover peace inside myself and to recover a community that would not let me go, where no one would be cast out or abandoned. Maybe I would find out what real peace was. So the first Peace Wall (opposite City Hall in Berkeley) created me, as I created it. It saved and redeemed me in my own eyes, as a needed, valuable, worthwhile human being. Throughout the many obstacles to be overcome, I developed patience and persistence.

Most of all, I learned the eleventh commandment: Thou shalt not get stuck in insult. If I had allowed myself to be offended, insulted, hurt, I would never have gotten one tile on the wall. I learned not to pick up the insult, to let it lie there. If I would have picked it up, it would have become garbage to carry around with me. Then it would start to smell and drive people away. The rewards of the Peace Wall were great. I saw many miracles of the right person showing up at the right time to help.

My year in the Soviet Union especially brought this kind of right people at the right time—untold lessons and blessings. The Russians taught me a new kind of responsibility. They were true to their word, true to what they promised, and never failed to show up, because they didn't feel like it (unlike in Californian culture). As a culture, they are capable of great intimacy, because they are able to share their troubles, unlike American culture. They say if you ask an American how he feels, he will always say, "he is fine," because Americans love success.

1990 was a hard year. Upon my return from Russia where I had built a Peace Wall in Moscow, I felt again lonely, without the Russian consistency, kisses and sharing of troubles. There seemed to be a loss of innocence. First, there was the shock of the Persian Gulf War that shattered the ecstasy of the Berlin Wall coming down and my year of teaching the joys of democracy and non-violence to Russian youth. Then my personal life and health had an upheaval. My mother died, causing grief that resulted in a sibling's divorce, and subsequent patterns of family struggle, ending in another family cold war. Once again feelings of senseless abandonment of goodness, of waste and loss arose. One cold war ends and another begins.

To regain my balance, I consciously developed an emotional blueprint of peace choices, using the artist-as-healer to pull myself through. How is it possible to create vitality and peace in the world, peace in our culture, peace in our youth, most of all peace in myself? I developed a symbolic cross-cultural map of the elements—the Earth, Air, Fire and Water—leading to peace and I taught this map to children in the Fruitvale District of Oakland.

This was all very valuable work, working in East Oakland, in a multicultural situation with youth in crisis. I made a great deal of progress, working with three thousand youth and six hundred adults. The wall was completed and dedicated this spring (slides).

As my work took me deeper into the problem of how to create real peace, it became for me personally an increasingly illusive and desperate journey. Peace seemed less and less plausible in everyday life. At best there was a relative horizontal continuum of peace, the ability to give up guns, to give up gangs, to give up drugs, alcohol, plutonium, and polluting the earth.

Every time I thought I had the answer, the solution, it slipped away. Worst of all, I ran into a brick wall, the Peace Wall. The very thing I was trying to create seemed to bring me into conflict, pain, and ego problems. I perceived them as other people's ego problems, their attachment to competitiveness, macho domination or whatever. How could this be? A woman in Oakland summed it up by saying, "Does it have to be a Peace Wall? Be realistic. This is Oakland."

My window of hope on world peace, American peace and personal peace had shrunk down from a mountain vista view to a small chink in the wall, in a prison of despair. About a month ago, it reached a point of hopelessness when a personal friendship took an unexpected detour and my fear of abandonment clicked in, leaving me in a state of emotional bankruptcy. There was no pulling out of it, no rising above it left. Forgiveness even wasn't the answer. I felt like death warmed over on a low flame.

Luckily there was an opportunity to take a seminar with a French group called ACC, "At the Heart of Communication." This seminar was a great luxury to me, something I had been looking for a long time. It was a safe place to get out of the success oriented, "Have a nice day!" culture and explore in great depth the shadow side of ourselves.

This nine-day experience was taught by Claire Nuer, a French jew and holocaust survivor who had melanoma of the eye and only three months to live when she started this work nine years ago. This was just what I needed.

The first day I confronted head-on one of my worst anger/fear family patterns, the fear of abandonment, or the black sheep syndrome. As the process progressed, I found instead a safe guard, a process and a place that would protect against the negative experience. Everyone made a commitment to make each other, themselves, and the leaders good.

Another seed, that was planted the first day, held me when I had the impulse to cut and run. It was a reference to the driving need for recognition that propels us. I saw in myself the monster that had driven me for a very long time, especially since my diagnosis of "low vision."

The second day we did what is called a false start exercise, where we took a childhood experience of dramatic impact and examined our emotional responses. Most importantly, we examined our beliefs about that event. Then we rewrote the whole story, opening the door an inch or two, instead of looking through a keyhole. We took a recent conflict we had experienced prior to the seminar and looked at that event in regards to our emotions and our beliefs. We re-examined this conflict every other day and tried to find out how we could have acted differently. It was amazing how much the two seemingly unrelated conflicts lined up with one another, pointing to a pattern of response.

The pattern of response came to be understood as a sieve. We all have these sieves through which we filter all of our experience, our beliefs. I began to clearly see my sieve of abandonment pattern, the lost victim. In this brilliant creative breakthrough, Claire showed us how to take apart our ego, piece by piece.

We saw how the egos of the victim/victor, abuser/abused are essentially the same. We saw that they were held in place like a sieve to filter all of our experience, our beliefs, so that our minds would say "we are right." The sieve not only did that but often became also our driving idea, our expectation. We saw that we had a choice and could allow holes to emerge in the sieve. I saw how forgiveness can become part of the sieve, how it can be a self-righteous way out of feeling victimized, how it can be a reaction.

Forgiveness can be useful to reinforce the ego. Instead of experiencing something, it can also be used to separate us from others, and from co-responsibility. This is a real problem for Judeo-Christian culture. Does this mean that forgiveness is to be eliminated altogether? No, it only needs to be used as an element of wholeness, of love.

To eliminate forgiveness would be like eliminating good medicine. Take Tylenol, for example. Too much Tylenol can destroy your liver and you may die of cirrhosis. The healing power of pain killers is very important, yet it can become a mask for the valuable real experience of pain that teaches you what you need and don't need in order to live. Forgiveness can become a deadly drug for relationships.

Forgiveness only needs to be used with wisdom as a necessary healing element for wholeness. Forgiveness is a part of every single day, in very small doses, more like forgiveness in the Buddhist sense, the act of letting go. This can be a very powerful part of everyday life. So the healing power of forgiveness, when it is not attached to the ego, may become a destructive drug. It is, however, a powerful and useful medicine to create peace. In small doses, it can even prevent the illness of violence and war.

However, forgiveness is not something that you can live on. For health it is important to live beyond forgiveness. Look at the IRA laying down their arms. This is a time of forgiveness, of healing. It is the beginning of relief, and the ecstasy of leaving the fear and pain behind. As forgiveness works on the illness, it strips away guilt and disappointment. Layers of trust can be built. The prison of the ego is left behind. Look at how much trust we have built up in Russia over these last ten years. We are now beyond forgiveness.

Forgiveness doesn't work as a medicine without the choice of the self for healing. Will and desire have to say what they want and what they don't want. I want to live beyond the victor and the victim. Auschwitz, Rwanda and Bosnia are totally unacceptable. The guns in our streets are all totally unacceptable. I want to live beyond the prison of my ego. I don't want to be isolated any longer, I do want to love.

In the seminar we shared our pain (Buddhists, Jews, Palestinians, Christians) about bombs, holocaust, incest, homelessness, prejudice, rape, childhood abuse, and abandonment, Aids, cancer, disability, grief, loss, and death. This sharing of the pain together was the element, the substance beyond ego, beyond pain killers, beyond forgiveness. It was beyond hope. It was humanity altogether ready to say "war and violence, fear and hate are totally unacceptable." It was humanity ready to commit one hundred per cent to invent peace.

During the seminar, we did not experience the intimacy of shared anger and hate against "them," the terrible monsters, instead we experienced a breakthrough to change humanities' pattern, the weapons of the ego that all of us use to survive and to kill.

The culmination of this part was a film by a man named Bernard who had lost forty-eight members of his family in the genocide of the jews in Poland. The straight forward film of bare-bone truth was followed by the peace round-table where we had a sharing by two holocaust survivors, a homosexual with Aids, the daughter of an SS man and, in the process of the circle, a woman who had been four years old when the bomb was dropped in Hiroshima. She burst forth to share her pain and an American whose father had worked on the atomic bomb emerged also. The peace round-table revealed to all of us how completely unacceptable the suffering of the fear- and hate-oriented ego is and that there is definitely a way out of the prison of ego in all of us which will set each of us free.

We can commit to changing our culture, to making ourselves and each other good. We can commit to going beyond forgiveness and beyond hope. We can commit to going forward one hundred per cent.

For me personally, although I was growing and deeply touched, and stimulated by the incredible passage of learning and events that were happening during the nine days, it was not until the last day of the seminar that

I broke through and shifted beyond my ego. I woke up in the morning, hanging on to my resistance, as a dream of shame had woken me up. I saw myself weak and helpless and incapable of connecting at all with anything. I saw my mind carefully, artfully resist and withdraw, planning not to even show up the last day. I did drag myself to my feet when dawn came and found myself back there, still hanging on to my comfortable ego, my escape hatch.

Claire began the day summing things up and talking about when we had been babies and in a state of undifferentiation, that love was all around us and supporting us. We touched the hot stove. We were told not to touch that monster, it would hurt us and, out of that recognition, came the recognition of others and ourselves, the survival of the ego. We weren't told that it was our responsibility not to touch the stove, that the stove was doing the right thing by being a stove. Then she said the accomplishment monster only recognizes what it wants to reward. I was struck by this metaphor, realizing that the accomplishment monster in my mind was my mother and that the stove was my father.

Then Claire showed some more slides of Auschwitz where her father died and she read letters from her father to her mother who had hid her daughter. The letters were so simple, so straight forward, so undemanding. They were love in its simple, unpretentious form. They were the love that keeps us all here on the earth, the simple connection. "Thank you for the bread, your package arrived today. It was opened and the bread was missing. It was so good to get your letter. Say goodbye to my little one, a thousand kisses. They are coming for us tomorrow."

I saw myself so spoiled, so demanding, an ungrateful wretch, not only abused but an abuser, not only victim but controller. I was willing to own this. This set me free, released me from the prison of my ego.

We can go beyond forgiveness, beyond hope which is only fifty per cent. We can go to one hundred per cent and commit to peace.

Now we have a chance to re-invent peace because the very same thing that drove out creativity is bringing it back and with creativity we have a great deal more choices. We can go beyond obedience, beyond idealism and suggestibility. We can arrive at a place where we can say "I want peace. I don't want war. I choose peace, I choose to stay out of cultural and personal ego. I find war and violence absolutely unacceptable for the earth, for myself, for humanity." Then we can find the ground of our being. It is called love without contingency, without the fear monster, and without the accomplishment monster. This love is beyond the prison of the ego, beyond forgiveness, beyond hope. This love is one hundred per cent.

# DISCUSSION

## With Rudiak-Gillard, Marks, the Mieds, and the Potts

*Goodman:* My question is for Mena and Dominik. The dream you presented was certainly next to an ordinary one. As an anthropologist, I know what fun it is to create an elaborate theoretical superstructure for something that we experience. Many of us have cognitive dreams, for me, personally, it is like a stream that runs past my ordinary life. Some of the dreams are significant and perhaps the theories that were developed with the help of Stanley Krippner's structure may apply, but usually some dreams are quite common place and instead of putting this tremendous superstructure of theoretical interpretation on it, it is just fun.

The other day, I was expecting some Indian friends for supper in Cuyamunque, New Mexico, where I live in the summer. The night before, I had a dream that I was standing in front of a porch and was looking for some of my shoes. There were lots of shoes. but I just could not find mine. In the evening, Rosita, the grandmother of the family, was saying, "I can't walk on your path today because I have high-heel shoes on. I wonder where my other shoes are. I think they are in the truck. I think I should look for my shoes." Yes, this was right, I knew, there was somebody looking for shoes.

My question, after this long introduction, is "have you or has anybody thought of how to teach this ability?" I discovered it quite by accident, it just happened. It would be great if it could be taught. As a neurophysiologically interested anthropologist, I want to know what happens in our brain.

This was the way I happened to discover a great deal about the religious altered state and how I could teach it. Those of you who worked on this dream interpretation, may want to try teaching it. I am convinced that such methods in fact did exist or still exist. Maybe you know?

Just briefly: There is an anecdote in connection with Custer's last stand where one of the Indian chiefs was asked, "Are you not going out to fight this battle?" and he said, "No, I am going home to dream." Afterwards he was asked what he had dreamed and he said, "I dreamed that the white men were riding but they were riding upside down." He dreamed the outcome of the battle. So I am sure there were such traditions and I would like to submit to you that it would be great to discover how something like that could be taught. Or have you already? This is my question, after a long introduction. Maybe you are hiding something from us?

*Potts, Dominic:* I refer to Mena. I am an attorney, I know how to dodge an issue when I get a good question.

*Potts, Mena*: I am persuaded that it is an innate capacity that we all possess. It is not only a gifted medium who has this ability.

*Goodman*: Right.

*Potts, Mena:* It begins by paying attention to our dreams. When people begin to do this, they will notice sometimes precognitive events they would otherwise not even be aware of; but some of the dreams are quite trivial also.

*Goodman:* Exactly, and it is the trivial experiences we should pay attention to. They are the fun. They are the kind of companion to our ordinary reality.

*Potts, Mena:* Yes, instead of just the tragic elements.

*Vilenskaya*: I would like to thank all presenters, but especially Carolina Marks. Thank you very much for your honesty and sincerity with which you shared your work. I would like to give a testimonial. Two or three months ago, Carolina and I went to the Fruitvale Bart Station where her tiles are exhibited. At that time, I was in the middle of my own healing journey, after going down, going up, and going down again. These tiles have a magic capacity of bringing peace, as if people who painted these tiles put images into them to bring peace. Thank you for your work!

*O'Connell:* To Dominic, I want to introduce myself as another attorney. I want to stress the importance of what you are saying about your willingness to be at par with your clients, not putting yourself above them. Although in the dream you were looking down and, in a sense, were holding the situation as a protector of the process, yet, you did not hold yourself above it in relationship to your humanness. What I am doing is thinking about how your philosophy changes your effectiveness of being a lawyer. Let's look at what some doctors have been developing in the last five to ten years, it is called the partnership model. The language you used was that you were "co-council" with your clients, because, essentially, it is their process.

The other connection I made was with Jurgen Kremer's paper, stressing the indigenous mind as one way we can be participating in our own reality. This model is allowing ourselves to be co-council.

*Potts, Dominic:* Allowing the client to be co-council.

*O'Connell:* You are not displacing their participation in their own life process. This is one of the main features and differences in the two modalities we are talking about—the progress culture and the indigenous culture.

*Potts, Dominic:* It is extremely important if you want to reach the heart and the mind of the jury, you really have to reach the heart and mind of your client, too. You have to be able to understand what the client is going through, what he is currently experiencing, the uncertainty and fear about the future. You can only do this when you relate intimately with the client. If you stay aloof because you don't want your vulnerabilities to be exposed by the client, this should never happen.

*O'Connell:* On the other hand, you were also talking about how you keep yourself distant. It protects the mystique. In my experience, it also protects you from answering questions you don't want to respond to. Be accountable, but don't loose client control.

There is another part which has been typical for the mind set of attorneys, "We know better; we know what you need" We displace people again in their own life process. I wanted just reinforce what you are saying. There are a group of holistic legal practitioners at the East Coast. A new group has also formed during the last years here in California.

*Potts, Dominic:* We are very much interested in the holistic movement.

*Chase:* This is for Coquelicot. I am teaching "orientation and mobility." The science of orientation and mobility is teaching cane travel to blind people. So I did your circle, the maze out there, with my eyes closed. It would be a very enriching experience for blind people to participate. There was a lot of chaos I could hear. My whole process was very simple and also very exciting to imagine a sightless person to get a perspective of how many people were there when we moved together and when we separated. It was a great feedback, just orally. Thank you for that!

*Rudiak-Gillard:* I am concerned about balances and how non-sighted people can be brought back into balance with sighted people. I am more than willing to get together with you. Also, people who can neither hear nor see could feel their body with the earth as their level.

*Heinze:* I want to thank all the speakers, especially Coquelicot. She had difficulties, because she could not lay out the Cretan Labyrinth in a larger area. So we had to make shift but it still worked. Thank you for putting up with the restrictions!

*Rudiak-Gillard:* I would have been most pleased, if I could have had two-foot pathways, instead of one-foot ones. It really amazed me how much came out. People really stayed in the moment.

*Heinze:* I also want to thank Philip Scotts for his chanting and the playing of the didjeridu. I want to thank Joanne and Ron who shortened their oral presentation considerably. I should mention that they are giving workshops on psychogenics. You can approach them if you are interested. Thank you Carolina for your life's odyssey, and special thanks go to Mena and Dominik Potts, not only for their thought-provoking presentation but they are the ones who donated the air ticket for Pai Ely to join us from Recife, Brazil. This was a big present to the conference; the Potts deserve a special round of applause.

# THE SUMMER WHEEL OF JOY

Lillian Rhinehard and Paula Engelhorn

The Sun Wheel is an ancient circle of rainbow color. It is often represented on the Earth in the form of stone circles. Before there was written history, ancient peoples gathered in the desert of the Southwest and built these circles of forgotten wisdom. The early people celebrated the seasons of each passing year through the great Sun Wheel ceremonies. Every season, year after year, another Sun Wheel was built and another ceremony performed. So it happened, a long long time ago, that the people gathered for their summer sun wheel ceremony called the Wheel of Joy.

In an forgotten time, in a land of red earth and turquoise sky, the people waited patiently for their summer ceremony to begin. The Wheel of Joy ceremony celebrated the return of the summer sun, shinning brightly upon the land. The return of days filled with the joy of growing crops and children running free in the hot summer air.

When the Spring Ceremony is complete, the people begin to prepare for the Summer Ceremony. They spend three months working on small sun wheels made of reed or wood. Each wheel is covered with yarn, thread, beads, and feathers. The members of the tribe, from the youngest child to the oldest and wisest elder, make the small wheels in a meditative state. Many prayers are said as they bead and place feathers on their wheels. They ask for good crops and enough rain to bring the crops to harvest. They pray for good health and give thanks as their hands make the beautiful small wheels.

Now the tribe is gathered in a circle. As they wait for the summer ceremony to begin, each person is holding a small exquisite sun wheel. The same pattern for building the wheel is followed in all ceremonies. The ceremonial leader, the Keeper of the Rainbow, lays the center stone. The chosen elders place the directional stones; the tribal representatives complete the wheel with the stones that form the circumference. Yet each ceremonial wheel has its unique and special contribution to welcome the new season. The summer wheel gives the tribal members a greater verbal participation as the wheel is being built. It is a time of happiness, a time when the sun is closest to the Earth. The people are filled with joy, reflecting the return of the summer sun.

The Keeper of the Rainbow begins the ceremony by holding high a large, clear crystal. As the sun leaps into the crystal, he says, "Behold the Rainbow." A shout of joy goes up from the people and they say, "We behold the Rainbow." Then the Keeper holds both his arms up to the sun and says, "Behold the sun." The people respond by saying, "We behold the sun." The Keeper holds high the central stone and says, "The Great Spirit is in us and all around us."

As the Elders hold their stones up, they say, "May the people be filled with the joy of the sun." The tribal representatives hold their stones high and say, "May the sun fill this stone and bring life to the people." As the stepping stones are being placed, each representative says, "May the stepping stones be illuminated by the sun." When the wheel is finished, the Keeper returns to the center. Raising his arms, he says, "Children of the Rainbow, behold the sun!" The people respond, "We behold the sun."

The Keeper then says, "Let the sign of the sun be upon all the children of the rainbow." Backing out of the center, he joins the great circle of people, surrounding the Sun Wheel.

When the Keeper is at the edge of the circle, he says, "The Wheel of Joy is once again upon the Earth, let the people rejoice!" The drummers drum and the flute players pipe as the people sing a song of joy and circle to the left. When the wheel has been circled once and as the sound of the flute players continues to fill the air, the people sit down in a great circle surrounding the wheel. Turning to the person sitting to his left, the Keeper takes pollen from a sacred pot and places the sign of the sun upon the person's forehead. (The sign of the sun is an equal distance cross held within a circle.) As the Keeper places the sign of the person's forehead, he says, "You are a child of the light, blessed by the sun." The person sitting next to the Keeper takes the sacred pollen and, turning to his left says, the joyous words while placing the sign of the sun on the next person's forehead.

The last person to have his/her forehead blessed with the pollen is the Keeper of the Rainbow. After the sign is upon his forehead, he walks to the center of the circle, raises his arms and says once again, "Children of the

Sun, behold the Rainbow!" The people return his words by saying, "We behold the sun, the bringer of Light."

There is a wonderful equality in this ceremony. The circle is the magic space that allows this total equality. In a circle, there is no one place more important than any other. There is no one person more important than another. The circle holds everything, encompasses all life, all ways on a equal basis. In the Wheel of Joy ceremony everyone is sitting in the circle, no one is symbolically higher than another, and the leader is the last to have the sign of the sun placed on his forehead.

In an interview, a white medicine woman, Evelyn Eaton, referred to many early Indian tribes as accepting all paths. During the interview, she told a little story, illustrating the idea of circle equality. "If you say for you the Great Spirit can only be reached by standing on your head, then an Indian will gladly stand on his head to honor your way." Of course, the reverse often doesn't occur. A lot of people follow one way and never find another path acceptable or equal to their own. The early tribes had a unique and special relationship with many different paths because of circle teachings.

Circling back to the forgotten time of ancient Sun Wheel ceremonies, flying on the wings of spirit, the summer ceremony continues. The Wheel of Joy is built and the sign of the sun is on everyone's forehead. The leader and the elders walk into the center. The Keeper stretches his arms wide and says, "Children of the Rainbow, give of yourselves!" Then he places his meditation sun wheel on the central stone with these words, "I am a child of the Sun giving to the Light." When the gift of the little wheel is given, the Keeper says a prayer of thanksgiving for the Sun, for the Light upon the people and upon the Earth. He backs out of the circle and sits with his brothers and sisters. The elder of the East holds high his meditation wheel and places it on the stone representing the East, saying a prayer for the blessed Spirits of the East. Each elder in turn gives away his meditation wheel with a prayer for the Direction s/he represents.

One by one, tribe members enter the Sun Wheel and are joined by a person sitting directly across the wheel. As the pairs reach the center of the wheel, they embrace and give each other their sun wheel of light and love. These diminutive wheels are symbols of joining with all the Children of the Rainbow in the great circle. Each child of the Rainbow enters the Sun Wheel until all in the great circle have given away and received a beautiful meditation wheel.

When everyone has exchanged a meditation sun wheel, the ceremony ends. For an almost perfect moment, Earth, Sky and man came together in harmony. The people rejoice as they feel the singing of the Earth and the singing of the Sky. The electric blue sky fills with the brilliance of the sun and the earth receives the light with open arms. The Keeper of the Rainbow raises his arms to receive the gift of Light and the Children of the Rainbow raise their arms with him. The sun spirit flows through the people and they rejoice. Once more the Keeper raises his voice and says, "Children of the Rainbow behold the sun!" and the people answer with a shout of joy that echoes through the land, "We behold the sun."

It is a windy, blustery day. The air has the barest touch of summer. Lillian and I are in the old north, Qn Quebec. We are translating the ancient ceremonies into everyday realities as best as we can. We are in a room with a high ceiling, pale blue walls, and a bare wooden floor. Out on the street, cars go by, and children holler with the first promise of the end of another harsh, long winter. Our French is non-existent, but we are lucky, most of the people in the room speak English. It isn't the endless red desert and we are not covered by a turquoise sky, yet the Summer Wheel of Joy ceremony can be conducted in any land and an touch the hearts of many people.

The participants are comfortably sitting around the room. We have placed a simple colored representation of a Sun Wheel in the middle of the room. It is the focus point for the ceremony. Lillian drums and we begin to speak of the ancient summer ceremony. We tell the story of the meditation sun wheels and how the people gathered around their great stone sun wheels. We talk of the ancient rainbow tribe and tell how the people gave the meditation wheels to one another. Then we suggest the participants make a small give-away sun wheel.

There is yarn, reed, beads, and feathers available to make these woven wheels. People are encouraged to go outside and look for small stones, branches, feathers, and other wonderful small objects that seem to find their way into their hands. Even in the middle of large cities, these gifts of nature are available.

The drumming resumes as the participants gather their materials to make the meditation wheels. Black birds call through the window and the cold northern breeze becomes stronger and beats against the house. Everywhere and in every circumstance, birds, the wind, all of nature will interact with each of us if we are willing to listen to the rhythm of their song.

Everyone, having gathered material, finds a place to sit, and begins making the small sun wheels. The drumming continues and each of us, in our way, feels part of this wondrous circle, cycle of life. We are in a room, far away from the American Southeast, yet we are connecting back to the ancient ceremonies. Listening to the story of the forgotten people's summer ceremony, listening to the drum and working on the small sun wheels connects all of us to the distant past. We become part of the continuing cycle of never ending circles of light.

The meditation wheels are finished in that special time held in union with all. Everyone comes together and we form a circle around the Sun Wheel.

Individuals speak of their works, each covered with small, delicate objects. Then, two by two, the participants walk to the center of the wheel, embrace and give each other their small wheels created with love.

We finish this day of bright promise by sitting in a circle around the wheel. We have switched the order of the ceremony. Not because we felt this order would be better, it is how we remembered the ceremony. Lillian takes a bit of corn pollen from a shell and places it on the forehead of the person sitting next to her. Around the circle the ceremony continues and the words, "You are a Child of the Light, blessed by the Sun," are repeated over and over again, until the shell with pollen is past around the circle. When the ceremony is finished, the room takes on a glow, it appears lighter, like a sunny day when rains have washed everything to a sparkling glow.

At the end of the ceremony, the faces around the circle have a gentle look of contentment. Each of us realizes we have taken part in an ancient ceremony of healing. Each of us feels that somehow we have been changed for the better through the ceremony. As if the pollen blessing on our foreheads went deep into our being and altered our perspective of the world around us.

Ceremony can transcend our humanness, can bring us together in harmonic meeting that is not often achieved. We walk in suits of flesh and bone, doubt and greed. We are by our nature less than what we want to be. We often achieve far less then we hope, dream, or demand of ourselves. Ceremony binds us to the faults that we each encompass, and perhaps those very faults are the most magnificent part of each of us. We are acceptable in the great circle, not only acceptable but loved and cherished by the Great Spirit, and by all our relations. During ceremony we can become magnificent, transcending frailties and becoming part of the whole, the great circle of life.

The ancients who did the first sun wheel ceremonies must have been much like us. Most of the time bumbling along, saying "me" first, or at least "what about me." No more perfect, no less frail than any of us. What made them special, what makes us all special is our ability to overcome ourselves enough to sometimes see a crack in the darkness, to let in the Light. To celebrate together, searching for that illusive gift called healing: healing for ourselves, our brothers and sisters, for the Earth Mother, and for all our relations.

Let us come together in circles of ancient knowledge, translating and celebrating ceremonies older than recorded history. Knowing that what we are and who we are can make a difference. Let us put our critical self away for a while and join in circles of ceremony for the healing of all life.

# ALCHEMICAL HYPNOTHERAPY

Elaine Fellow

I will discuss the teachings and application of Alchemical Hypnotherapy as developed by David Quigley. I will also relate my own experiences during an Alchemical Hypnotherapy weekend.

Webster's dictionary defines alchemy as, "the process of transforming something common into something special....the inexplicable and mysterious power of transmuting" (1990:68). The symbol for Alchemical Hypnotherapy is, indeed, the phoenix, the bird who burns itself in a funeral pile only to rise afresh from its own ashes. Or we can compare this hypnotherapeutical process with an oyster creating a pearl from a grain of sand.

Hypnosis is an ancient technology for controlling mind and body. Through trance induction—music, fasting, drumming, dancing, psychoactive drugs, etc.—shamans, for example, contacted the spirit world in their search for healing powers and inner knowledge. In fact, many of us experience a *light* trance state when watching television, driving a car, or daydreaming. Massage, acupressure, and body work are other trance induction methods to achieve this state, in fact, any repetitive action can create this slightly relaxed, suggestible state. We find ourselves open to emotions and memories connected with the unconscious mind where thoughts and images occur spontaneously. As this state deepens, it bypasses the "analyzer" or critical factor of the conscious mind and moves into a partial regression or *medium* trance state. In this state, we are alert, aware of the past and present, but also in a highly suggestible condition that is ideal for the "interactive" process of Alchemical Hypnotherapy.

Alchemical Hypnotherapy focuses on a specific form of hypnosis aiming at the client's *own* unconscious mind and utilizing the *client's* inner powers in the form of inner guides and independent, inner personalities to transform unresolved mental, physical, emotional and spiritual issues so that the individual feels again healthy and empowered. It allows seekers to create their own mythology and experience of spiritual forces within their subconscious mind. David Quigley who developed Alchemical Hypnotherapy, defines it as "interactive trance work using archetypes/guides to empower clients in discovering, aligning with, and living out their life purposes" (1992:1). The client cannot be in the usual *deep*, totally regressed (sonambulistic) state that traditional hypnotherapists utilize for suggestive work. In this deep hypnotic state, the client feels no sensations from the body, is profoundly relaxed and unconscious. The client is also totally dependent on the hypnotherapist's suggestions.

In Alchemical Hypnotherapy, however, clients are alert enough to be interactive and come up with their own images, issues, and levels of awareness into the cause and cure of their problems. Contact with true inner guides empowers clients to heal and transform themselves by allowing these guides to take over the process instead of the hypnotherapist whose role is primarily the one of a facilitator. David Quigley created six techniques, based on Jung's teachings, to swiftly transform consciousness:

1. Etheral Plane Communication,
2. Running and Changing Incidents,
3. Nurturing the Inner Child/Inner Family Work,
4. Inner Guide Work (including the finding of the Inner Mate),
5. Advanced Forms of Past Life Regression, and
6. Conference Room Therapy (1992:7).

The first process, *Etheral Plane Communication,* allows clients to confront, clarify, and complete unfinished business with others without having a face-to-face situation. Going back and forth between the client and the person being addressed, the client is able to explore all feelings and thoughts safely without consequences, having an emotional experience of self and others, similar to the "empty chair" technique in hypnotherapy. Communication becomes completed when the client reports a "shift" in the body and in the original perspective. The technique is especially helpful in completing communication with someone who has died.

*Running and Changing Incidents* is the second technique which is used when a client has been holding a past emotional experience, albeit unconsciously, a traumatic memory in the body, manifesting as a body symptom. By going into the body part and accessing the memory in trance, the client relives the event and can change the circumstances and outcome, making it a positive, healing, and empowering event, thus alleviating the symptom by releasing the trauma. This technique is frequently used when working with the Inner Child who is the carrier of childhood traumata.

The third process, *Nurturing the Inner Child/Inner Family Work,* deals with the primary emotional and body needs of the client which are key factors in alchemical work. Without "emotional clearing" of childhood traumata, further alchemical work cannot proceed or effect significant change. The Inner Child is the little boy or girl within the client that depends on and needs care, protection and attention. This Inner Child needs emotional security and happiness by securing both Inner Mother and Inner Father figures who can provide role models of appropriate behaviors, and give the Inner Child unconditional love and support. These three inner figures constitute the "Sacred Trinity" of the Inner Family. Also, the Inner Child is a "guide to all other guides," often used to test the genuineness of other inner figures.

There are "false" guides. Each guide needs to be questioned and his/her purpose ascertained. The Inner Child's response to the guide determines its validity.

The fourth technique of *Inner Guide Work* is critical to finding the *Inner Mate* who sometimes becomes the carrier of the contrasexual parent of the Inner Child. This figure exemplifies compensatory and ideal qualities the client seeks in an external mate, similar to Jung's anima/animus concepts but broader in scope of roles. The Inner Mate is adept in teaching clients about relationships and helps attract potential mates; gay clients may have same sex Inner Mates. An Inner Mates may also function as "muse," inspiring creativity.

David Quigley states that there are many other types of "Spirit" Guides; the Wise Old Man/Woman who may be aspects of the Higher Self, the Inner Healer, Saints/Messiahs, Nature Spirits, Past Life Personalities, etc. These guides often have a gift, song or message for the client to heighten awareness, for protection or awakening healing and creative abilities. One category, Nature Spirits, is divided into:

a. devas: large universal beings controlling plant and animal kingdoms, and nature, they connect the client with the earth;

b. elementals: small beings, fairies, elves, trolls, who have special gifts for the client;

c. animal spirits: animal soul(s) of the client can be used in clairvoyance, power and healing or symbolic manifestations of unresolved emotional issues;

d. allies: beings that offer the client unusual power, awareness and insight (Quigley, 1989:48-50; see also Castaneda).

The fifth process is contacting *Past Life Personalities* to bring forth creative abilities, talents and knowledge acquired in a past life. These personalities are mostly used as guides for specific knowledge or talents on a consultation basis. They can be brought into the client's current life permanently and can be integrated into the client's present consciousness by the "Elixir of Immortality" (Quigley, 1992:65). This revolutionary technique has to be handled with care and foresight because the Past Life Personality can bring up unwanted traits as well. The Elixir method involves negotiation and reassignment of tasks and behavior and contracts when undesirable traits are present.

Finally, there is the *Conference Room* technique, used whenever a client needs to make a decision, but is experiencing inner conflict which prevents any resolution. The alchemical hypnotherapist helps the client first identify the different voices or "subpersonalities" within and then develops the positive aspects of each with the client. The goal is to negotiate a workable contract, agreeable to all subpersonalities. The client's identity and will become integrated in the process; similar techniques are used for multiple personality disorders. Common issues brought to the Conference Room are relationship issues, job or career choices, and addiction issues. Examples of subpersonalities are the Judge, Rebel, Artist, Critic, Scientist, Romantic, Tantrika, Clown, etc. Their positions at the Conference Room table indicate alliances, power, and changes occurring within the client.

I work with heroin addicts and this category of addiction disorders is divided into three different sub-personalities:

1. the addictive sub-personality likes the client and tries to make him/her feel better, or

2. hates the client because s/he has not been listening to him/her and tries to undermine him/her all the time, and there are also

3. entities which are not part of the client. They don't care about the client and just use his/her body as a vehicle to get substances. These have to be exercised or sent away.

For the past year, I have gone through intensive Alchemical Hypnotherapy training, utilizing all the techniques described in this paper with clients, other trainees, and therapists. It has made a qualitative difference in my life, increasing my awareness and resourcefulness, helping me feel integrated and grounded, and allowing me to be of service to others. Of special interest to this conference may be my recent experience during an empowerment weekend.

Prior to the weekend, I had been contacting and working on power animals with another alchemical hypnotherapist. I wanted group support during the intensive 3-day process to help me move through several issues of "letting go."

My particular journey became the ultimate letting go of a "death" experience. Other members of the group were beating drums as I went into trance, said goodbye to loved ones, prepared for death, experienced death, and then journeyed to the "upper world." Spontaneous inner figures appeared as guides, first an owl, then a polar bear, and finally a deer. All animals were associated with death in shamanic tradition. Each had a message for me. There also appeared an Indian called "I will fight no more forever." The animal guides gave me a golden heart before I returned to waking consciousness.

It was an intense experience. I felt noticeably lighter and the area around my heart and chest felt expanded and open. I felt I had released a lot of pain. Later my friends reported a difference in my appearance. I was more resolute and calm and able to complete transactions. I have brought back the wisdom of the animals and the Indian guide. The owl showed me how to silently observe others, alert to even the subtlest cues, and I find now myself frequently anticipating other's responses. The polar bear showed me how to "pace" myself and others emotionally, so that we can arrive at agreeable and understandable places in conversation and during therapy. My determination has been enhanced and sometimes I feel the power and strength of the polar bear. The deer showed me how to listen carefully, receiving other's messages. It reminded me of transformation, because the deer loses and regains its antlers every season. I felt connected with a circle of animals and other realities. Finally, the Indian "I will fight no more forever" helps me in relationship with others. I am learning to "let go" of attachments to others and things important to me in this world of appearance. I have been feeling an invisible connection with something, an essence beyond what I know that allows me to be more my self, more fully real.

## References

Quigley, David. *The Alchemical Hypnotherapy Workbook.* Self-published, 1992

_____ . *Alchemical Hypnotherapy.* Redway, CA: Lost Coast Press, 1989.

*Webster's Ninth New Collegiate Dictionary.* Springfield, MA: Merriam-Webster, Inc. Publishers, 1990.

# ALCHEMICAL HOMEOPATHY

Howard Teich

Shamanism is the backbone of alchemy and quantum physics. Shamans, alchemists and quantum physicists all know that matter is alive. Shamans found their matter in nature, alchemists in their laboratories and quantum physicists in their microscopes at a subatomic level.

We know light energy travels at 186,000 miles a second. Matter is light traveling at less than 186,000 miles a second. All beings and matter in the universe, from rocks, worms to psychologists, are beings of light. We are "trapped light."

The brain is essentially a clump of the same sort matter that makes up rocks and stars. The matter being studied by shamans, alchemists and quantum physicists is the psyche. Shamans have specialized in the psyche for probably hundreds of thousands of years. It may be possible to see that the shamans' discoveries are the foundation of alchemy and quantum physics.

Shamanism, alchemy and quantum physics have at least five principles in common.

1. Light is life,
2. the dual nature of the universe,
3. the separation of duality,
4. the union of duality,
5. the maintenance of the dual vision.

## Light is Life

Through trance shamans know how to transcend matter and transform themselves into "beings of light." In rituals, shamans ascend to the "sky," or some high, lofty place and find the name of the celestial god who often means "luminous, shining, light or White Light."

An Australian medicine man asks an apprentice to drink water with rock crystals placed inside a cup. These rock crystals are "solidified light," broken off parts of the throne of the Supreme Being. After drinking this crystal water, the apprentice succeeds in seeing spirits. In Venezuela, shamans use sacred rattles filled with quartz crystal to main communication with the supernatural. When shamans die, their soul merges with the quartz crystal spirits inside the rattle. As the rattle is shaken, the dead soul ascends to the center of the celestial dome in the form of light. Shamans in Borneo have "light stones" that tell about the patient's soul and where it has strayed. In Huichol shamanism, the ancestral shamans can return to the earth to dwell among their kin in rock crystal as solidified light and communicate with the sources of supernatural power for guidance. To become "light" connects shamans to the spirit world where they obtain the secrets of healing. One becomes a shaman when one is filled with light.

Shamans used trance and quartz crystals to change themselves to light. The alchemists call their stone the "Philosopher's Stone." The Philosopher's Stone is known as the "light of nature" or the "fiery light." In 1926, C.G. Jung rescued alchemy from the dust bins of the past, finding that alchemy was the historically underlying structure of his psychology of individuation. Jung once said that

> I had very soon seen that analytical psychology coincided in a most curious way with alchemy. The experiences of the alchemists were, in a sense, my experiences, and their world was my world. This was, of course, a momentous discovery. I had stumbled upon the historical counterpart of my psychology of the unconscious (1963:205).

The first step in alchemy to produce the Philosopher's Stone is to find the *prima materia*. Jung found that the *prima materia* was our greed, power, insecurities and addictions, the shadow in a thousand names. The shadow needs to be transformed from a fragment that possessed us unconsciously into part of our wholeness. The Philosopher's Stone is the end result of the alchemical change process. The Philosopher's Stone is now what we call the self, god, consciousness, evolution, the Divine Light. The experiences of the self or consciousness is generally accompanied by visions and light symbols like brilliance, illumination, shining and haloes.

Shamans, alchemists, and quantum physicists are all in search of the light of the self, the Divine Light, a principle of wholeness and consciousness. This light is the central organizing principle of life. Light is life. Love is light. In this spirit, alchemists say that whoever has this secret of light or knowledge of the Self would know the mysteries of creation and know that there was no death and knew how to regenerate life.

## The Dual Nature of the Universe

Shamans acknowledge the dual nature of light traveling down the moon ladders to the underworld to deal with spirits and powers of the earth that connect to sacrifice, blood, suffering, desires and ascend up the sun ladder to the celestial realms connecting to upperworld messages about establishing a primordial balance. Among modern people, dreams that refer to upward or downward movements like ladders, stairs, elevators, climbing, mountains, flying are symbols of this upward sun ladder and the descending moon ladder. Shamans know that light has a dual nature and see the sun and the moon ladders as their ways to reach this dual light.

The sun and the moon were the two primordial lights of the alchemical texts. In 1926, Jung wrote his first commentary on an ancient Chinese alchemical text, called *The Secret of the Golden Flower* (1962). The Golden Flower is a symbol of the light that is the Tao. This heavenly light of the Tao is consciousness or the Self. This light of the Tao is the light between the sun eye and the moon eye. The deepest and most wonderful secret of yoga is to maintain the circulation of this light between the sun and moon eye. It creates the Tao, the elixir of Life.

The great discovery that launched quantum physics was that light or energy has a dual nature. It appears as wave or particle. Light unobserved is in wave form. When light waves are observed by a human being, the waves are "popped" and become particles; matter is manifested. What determines whether it is a wave or a particle is the observer. This is called the observer effect. In many spiritual traditions, the right brain is called the moon brain and the left brain the sun brain. The waves of quantum physics are processed by the moon brain and correspond to the moon symbolism of shamans and alchemists. The left brain, the sun brain, manifests waves into particles of matter and corresponds to the sun symbolism of shamans and alchemists. As

Mircea Eliade states: "Clearly man's (our) integration into the cosmos can only take place if we can bring ourselves into harmony with the two astral rhythms 'unifying' sun and moon in our living bodies" (1958:179).

Our consciousness and mind set determines which waves will be "popped" and become solar particles of light and matter. The more expansive our consciousness, the more possibilities we can manifest.

## The Separation of Duality

Once the dual nature of the universe is acknowledged as having a lunar wave and solar particle nature, the next step for shamans, alchemists and quantum physicists is to separate this duality into opposites. Shamans separate themselves from their bodies through trance and travel to the upperworld via the sun ladder and the underworld via the moon ladder to learn the secrets of healing. Alchemists summarized their transformation formula as "dissolve and coagulate," which means separate and join. During this separation stage, sun and moon qualities are separated. This is necessary before there can be a union of opposites. In quantum physics, this separation is called the *principle of exclusion.* What occurs in this separation stage?

Let us look at the quantum *principle of exclusion* and what it means. Matter forms when light waves become light particles, thus forming atoms. Atoms are made up of electrons which carry a negative charge, neutrons have a neutral charge and protons have a positive charge. In 1925, the Nobel Prize-winning physicist Wolfgang Pauli proposed the *principle of exclusion.* Electrons are the negative charge in atoms. Electrons exclude each other from entering the same territory. This is called electron self-hatred (Wolf, 1984:141). "Each electron behaves like Greta Garbo, crying to all the other electrons surrounding it, 'I vant to be alone'" (Wolf, 1984:141). This aloneness makes atomic molecular structures different and forms an endless variety of complex life forms.

Our brain is filled with electrons. Electrons are responsible for all brain activity. The *principle of exclusion* keeps electrons from collapsing back into light. Electrons keep matter as "trapped light." They allow matter to assume its complex forms. Electron exclusion may be the quantum factor that gives each of us our unique ego identity.

In alchemy, the *prima materia* is composed of chaotic matter where the opposites are not separated from each other. A procedure of separation called *seperatio* is required to differentiate the matter into opposites. In creation myths, this is often seen as differentiation into two parts, light and dark, heaven and earth or male and female. When opposites are undifferentiated, one tends to identify with one of the opposites and projects the other on someone else. Consciousness is the space between the opposites and means that a conscious individual can endure the tension between the opposites. In dreams, swords, knives, sharp cutting edges, boundaries, lines, limits, measurements and images of death and killing are images of separation.

Shamans specialize in trance to separate themselves from the matter of the body by becoming light spirits to gain the knowledge of the sky or underworld. This separation helps them communicate with demons and spirits without becoming possessed. Even in the shamans' "election," they are separated from the community and have access to regions inaccessible to others.

Alchemy and shamanism are both founded on the initiation archetype of *rite of passage,* a death and rebirth ritual. Shamans and alchemists do not need to physically die to separate from the world of matter to explore the world of light and death. This stage of separating light from matter is the same as the *principle of exclusion* in quantum physics where electrons keep separate from each other and form the varieties of matter that make life possible.

## The Union of Duality

Once the dual nature of light is separated as lunar waves and solar particles, these solar-lunar qualities need to be joined in a union. Shamans call this love, for alchemists it is the joining stage, called *conunctio* or the "Royal Marriage." Quantum physicists call this the *principle of inclusion.*

When quantum waves are seen by a human observer, they change to particles. These particles are called photons (different from protons which are the positive charge in atoms). Photons have the ability to "include" each other in each other's territory. This is opposite of electrons which exclude each other from the same territory. Lasers beams operate on this photon principle.

Our psyche is made up of electrons. Photons, as particles of light, are the communication devices between the electrons in the psyche. As physicist Fred Alan Wolf says,

> ...ancient spiritual teachings were that light is love. Was this more than a metaphor? If so, then we could think of each subatomic photon or light particle that is transmitted through our brain and nervous system as containing a unit of love (1991:121).

When shamans return from trance, they bring photons of light back to their bodies. These solar light particles as "units of love" are transmitted to the electrons in the shamans' body and then communicated to themselves and their patients through sympathetic vibrations, e.g., song, dance, sacred sounds, chants, rattling, bells, and sometimes drugs. Healing is the union of these units of light love energy vibrations in the shamans' body with those of their patients. Life is the dance of the union of light and matter, or in quantum physics terms, between photons of light and the electrons of matter.

Alchemists and shamans have as their highest symbol the dual nature of the Divine Light, the sun and the moon. The marriage of the sun and the moon is a universal theme that emerges in many spiritual traditions. For example, the Chinese *yang* and *yin* were sun and moon before they were labeled male and female by European scholars. In India, the ultimate goal of *hatha yoga* is the union of the sun and moon; *ha* translates as sun and *tha* as moon and *yoga* is union. In the Kundalini tradition, the left nostril carries the moon current and the right nostril the sun breath. These two breaths need to be coordinated in each of the seven major chakras for enlightenment. In the Peyote ceremony, red bird rises in the morning where the sun hits the moon altar. In Egypt, the scarab is the symbol of rebirth which rises in the last chamber of the underworld where the sun and the moon would meet. Many cultures have their sacred celebration like the original Olympic games, timed around the union of the sun and the moon in the sky.

What are these dual sun particles and lunar wave energies that are the foundation of shamanism, alchemy and quantum physics? The qualities of solar particles are left brain functions, such as sequential thinking, goal directed behavior, clarity, willfulness, competitiveness, analysis and linguistics. In Western culture, these functions have been labeled masculine. Moon-wave, right-brain qualities are intuition, tenderness, receptivity, compassion, prayer, melodic speech, musical, emotional and visual availability; these attributes have been labeled feminine.

Jung took the idea that men needed to integrate their lunar feminine side and women their solar masculine side in the alchemical the union of the sun and moon.

I would like to share an alchemical secret that Jung wrote about at the end of his life, but did not use to revise his psychology of the feminine side of men and the masculine side of women. The "secret to be revealed" in alchemy is that before the Judeo-Christian era there were many male moon gods and female sun goddesses. This means that for men the necessary union is the male moon and male sun, not the feminine side of men. For women, the union is the female sun and the female moon, not their masculine side. Labeling the sun as masculine and the moon as feminine, disregards the knowledge of goddess culture that knew that the sun and moon could be labeled either gender. Taking off the gender restrictive labels opens the solar and lunar to be energy polarities within masculinity and femininity and the union to occur with the non-gender lunar waves and solar particles. This is consistent with quantum physics which never labelled energies by gender.

## The Maintenance of the Dual Vision

As we have seen, reality is light and has a dual or paradoxical nature. Shamans and alchemists use this dual nature of the Divine Light of the self, god or evolution, calling it the sun and moon, while quantum physicists call this dual nature waves and particles. The danger is if we limit our vision to only seeing one of these lights. This revisioning is a return to the ancient Chinese original dual powers of the *yin* and *yang* as the moon and the sun. The final image in Egyptian mythology, the hawk, which is the shaman's bird, has a sun and a moon eye. By seeing with a solar and a lunar eye, we would be in the position of creating and circulating the light of the Tao, self, god or evolution as the Divine Light.

Lao-tsu describes this double vision in the *Tao te Ching.*

When people see some things as beautiful,
other things become ugly.
When people see some things as good,
other things become bad.
Being and non-being create each other.
Difficult and easy support each other.
Long and short define each other.
High and low depend on each other.
Before and after follow each other
(Mitchell, 1988:2.)

The mysterium conjunctionis, the mystery of the union of opposites, is the highest mystery of the alchemical tradition. The alchemic formula to obtain the Philosopher's Stone is to add to the sun and the moon a quintessence substance called the Philosopher's Mercury. This entity is the breath, spirit, and soul which is the origin of all things. The Philosophers' Mercury is for us, the participant observer, the light of love searching for the "units of love," inside and outside of us. Homeopathic healing is that like heals like. The alchemical union of the solar and the lunar energies without our own genders and the quantum physicists' photons, lights as particles of love, enter the same territory of alchemical homeopathy.

Shamans and alchemists found that love heals and creates love. Let's hope that we take their lessons and develop our light bodies as participant observers and create and discover the light of the self, god, and evolution. By seeing with solar and lunar eyes, we live the kaleidoscope of life that, at every turn, reveals the sacred and opens us up to the deeper mysteries of transcendence.

Many of us here have suffered over much of our lives, surrendered and abandoned ourselves to a higher path. We had visions or experiences of the self, god, evolution, the Divine Light. However, illumination is not enlightenment. The challenge is to integrate the human illumination with divine enlightenment and live an enlightened human life.

## References

Eliade, Mircea. *Patterns in Comparative Religion.* New York: Sheed and Ward, 1958.

Jung, Carl Gustav. *Memories, Dreams, Reflections,* ed. A. Jaffe. New York: Pantheon, 1963.

_____ . "Foreword," *The Secret of the Golden Flower, A Chinese Book of Life,* transl. Richard Wilhelm. New York: Harvest/HBJ Book, 1962.

Mitchell, Stephen. *Tao Te Ching.* San Francisco, CA: Harper and Row, 1988.

Wolf, Fred Alan. *The Eagle's Quest.* New York: Simon and Schuster, 1991.

_____ . *Star Wave.* New York: Macmillan Publishing Co., 1984.

# SPIRITUAL ALCHEMY, DEVOTION AND THE SOUL

Robert Cogburn

Alchemy is known as a difficult subject, complex in the extreme, full of unexplained terms and symbolism, confusing if not confused and employing many devices intended to mislead all but the initiated. Few who have studied alchemy have gained any usable understanding of its mysteries, and yet "alchemy" is becoming almost a buzz word in our time, perhaps destined to the same fate as "shamanism." You probably know that there are several kinds of alchemy, as well as distinct developments of alchemy in China, India, and the West. In most cases, when people refer to the old alchemy, they mean the alchemy of metals. There is also an alchemy of medicines, aimed especially at prolonging life, and these two are lumped under the term "experimental" or "laboratory alchemy." Then there is spiritual alchemy, really an alchemy of body, soul and spirit, and this is my main interest. What follows is a brief essay based on my experience with alchemy and I will tell how I happened on this strange path of knowledge.

It began when I developed an early interest in chemistry. By the time I was nine I had begun to assemble a chemical laboratory in the basement of our home in Oakland. My father accompanied me on trips to local chemical supply houses and purchased glassware, Bunsen burners and many chemicals generally, considered too dangerous for a child to handle. He was naively trusting that I would do no harm and fortunately I managed not to blow myself or anything else of great importance up in the course of my experiments.

For five years this laboratory was my main interest, until a move and the traumas of adolescence intervened. In fact, while I read books describing standard chemical experiments and tried a number of them, I soon tired of this line of inquiry. The laboratory became a place where I would enter a rich fantasy life, a kind of waking dreaming, and the hours would fly away. At this time I knew nothing of alchemy, but I can now look back and realize that I had entered spontaneously into the world of dreams and images that pervade and characterize much alchemical thought. For the most part the chemistry had become incidental except as it served as a staging for psychological fermentation. This tenuous entry upon the *great work* remained unconscious during those years, as did its fruits, which nevertheless have emerged from time to time in my life, like plums materializing out of the void. For many years I did not recognize the true nature of these gifts and psychological crises would ensure. Curiously, these events led to life changes and transformations that were effective in bringing me step by step along a path of knowledge in spite of my lack of understanding. In fact, I am convinced that this naivete often facilitated the process, since my conscious attempts at control or evasion were shunted.

In the early 1970s, my wife Elizabeth and I began a regular series of pilgrimages into the canyon country of the high southwestern desert. We had become students of Qabalah and were seeking a way of making this path of knowledge more directly and viscerally real in our experience. These trips occurred in high summer when the danger of flash floods was maximum and, as a result, we had the country to ourselves. The inherent danger was a positive factor in an even more important way since it required us to maintain a special alertness to what was happening in both the outer and the inner worlds at all times.

We set up a magical circle in the sand and improvised directional altars, according to Qabalistic principles, and then lived in this site-made-sacred for a week. Or we did simple ceremonies, meditating, listening to our Inner Teachers and communing with nature in a way quite unaccustomed in our ordinary lives. These practices affected us deeply and provided some of the insights and inspiration that Elizabeth wove into dances upon the Qabalic Tree of Life which have inspired many companions.

In time, these dances became the centerpiece of our spiritual life, and I am deeply grateful to Elizabeth for creating this remarkable ceremonial practice that we have been able to celebrate and grow in together. Whether in the desert canyons or dancing around Tiphareth on the Tree of Life, we realized that these times in sacred space could result in significant changes in our personalities and our lives, *provided* we formulated clear images of the changes that we desired and then followed through in the months ahead doing the work necessary to make them a part of ordinary life. In alchemical terms these are the repeated distillations necessary to purify and refine our *matter*.

After many years we began to be aware of something else in the culmination of these dances besides the heightened awareness and visionary experiences. It was a kind of glow that pervaded all being, tingeing the world around us and our consciousness, especially wonderful in encounters with our beloved companions. There was no question that this was true *gold, philosophical gold,* as the alchemists called it, and we came to use another alchemical term, calling it the *dew of heaven*.

We had to learn that this state could be maintained only by a certain kind of attention, and that the dew would dry very quickly during such activities as driving in traffic or doing a lot of linear thinking. Worst of all was any lapse into an egotistic state. This would transmute the *gold* into *lead* in the twinkling of an eye, accompanied by a terrible sensation of falling into the abyss. In spite of such lapses, the dew would return and persist for many days, even weeks, after the dance, but gradually it lessened and finally disappeared. Of course, this provoked a deeply felt need to find a way to live in this state more fully.

As part of my Qabalistic studies, I had begun to read the writings of some of the spiritual alchemists by the early 1980s. Mostly what I read was very mysterious and confusing, but I was deeply intrigued by the mystery and my intuition said, "This is your path." The Qabalah provided essential keys to understanding what the alchemical masters were talking about, especially the writings of Paul Foster Case (1985) on this subject.[1] The writings of C.G. Jung on alchemy have also been very useful to me, for he was the first modern person to understand the central importance of the soul in Western spiritual alchemy. While the books continue to be of some interest, we have come to rely more and more on the prayer of silence and the Inner Teacher to show us the way.

Alchemists are constantly referring to the four elements, fire, water, air, and earth, the three principles, Mercury, Sulphur and Salt, the seven classical metals and their corresponding planets. It is important when reading alchemical writing to realize that none of these are what the names mean in common usage. Often the sages will indicate this in so many words in their writings, and they employ devices such as referring to "our gold," "our copper," etc. Here the modifier "our" indicates not only that these substances have a special meaning in alchemy but also that they have a particular reference to the personal sphere and even to the body. The terms are used symbolically, thus each has a variety of attributes and qualities and may be referred to in many ways. These references depend on context, and so they often seem contradictory. For example, *water* in its primary usage may signify the primal form-giving nature of mental intention and often it stands for the *first matter* out of which all things are made. Thus it may be said quite truly that this is no common water, that it is a water that does not wet the hand, is not out of dew, rain, springs, the sea, rivers, etc. and, at the same time, and with equal truth, it is the most common of things since everything we see, even ourselves, is a manifestation of it. It flies with the birds in the air and swims with the fish in the sea, etc. So the first key to alchemy is to understand that it often employs a multivalued, symbolic, right brain language.

This symbolic language is the native tongue of the soul, and our conscious experience of the soul is through the faculty of imagination. Giving serious attention to dreams, fantasies and the creative process opens a path into the world of the soul, and we cross its threshold when we begin to experience its images and events as having an absolute reality that transcends the at most conditional reality of the physical world. The feeling of meaningfulness in life and particular events derives from the soul, and it is in this realm that we may find a calling to a particular life work and our destiny. Work with the soul leads naturally to the development of a unique way of being, depending on inner sources for its shaping and validation, rather than finding ourselves by conforming to some collective ideal. The former is, of course, the process Jung called "individuation." The writings and especially the drawings of many of the alchemists can leave no doubt that they were engaged in this process.

It is said that the great work of alchemy consists of the union of the Sun and the Moon with the aid of Mercury. This conjunction and the union of the Sacred King and Queen are leading examples of the mystical or chemical marriage that was a central theme of alchemy. Jung wrote at length about this process in his *Mysterium Coniunctionis* (1963), and Howard Teich and Elizabeth Cogburn have added the realization that the conjunction can be accomplished through working with the same gender inner twins that have appeared in many mythologies and arise spontaneously in consciousness, as detailed in their presentations last year.

Besides the work with the soul there is the work of the spirit, and in this lies the highest goal of alchemy. In its culmination, the alchemist succeeds in producing the *Philosophers' Stone* and thereby realizes the *philosophical gold* in unlimited measure. The experimental alchemists consider the *stone* to be a mysterious physical substance, the tiniest grain of which could transmute common lead into gold. On the other hand, scholars of spiritual alchemy have speculated that it is a state that has been described as Christ Consciousness. In fact, both may have some part of the truth, for there are esoteric teachings that the making of the *stone* corresponds to subtle changes in the alchemist's body, changes in cell chemistry and in the function of certain glands. It should be noted that, while the language may suggest that the *stone* is manufactured, those who have succeeded point out that their success depended on an intervention of divine grace, and that the operation cannot be carried to completion by human consciousness unaided.

In ordinary human consciousness we perceive ourselves as separate, isolated beings, in principle free to do what we will. Careful observation of ourselves and our actions, particularly in a contemplative state, leads to the intellectual realization that this picture is not right. In particular, if we carefully observe the process of making a difficult decision we find that the actual volitional impulse that decides does not come from the personal level of consciousness but from somewhere beyond. It was clearly realized in Qabalah, as well as the great Eastern philosophies, that there is One Will and One Life Energy, and that we are particular manifestations of that One, like the leaves of a tree. The intellectual realization that this is the case, and the conviction (or faith in the old sense) that this is the truth, based on observation of our experience, is an essential preparation for realization of consciousness that transcends the personal or for the making of the *stone* in alchemical terms; but just as the menu is not the dinner so this conviction is not the experience.

Ordinary consciousness is bound in the subject-object manifold of awareness; it attempts to escape this condition but simply reinforces the experience of being imprisoned. In the East, many yogic practices were developed to overcome this impasse, but they seldom reach the desired result without the guidance and active intervention of a master. The process generally involves renouncing attachments of any kind and all objects of desire, and a Western person is likely to wonder why anyone would want to do that anyway.

Western alchemy offered a different approach based on the soul, involving the imagination and the desire nature. In the ancient world, these faculties were attributed to Venus, and Venus corresponds to the metal copper in alchemy. Venus is the ruler of the astrological sign Taurus, which in turn corresponds to the neck and throat in the body. In the *Turba Philosophorum,* one of the first alchemical texts to enter Europe, being a translation from Islamic sources into Latin, it is said.

> Know, all present, that no true tincture is made except from our copper. Do not, therefore, exhaust your brains and your money, lest ye fill your hearts with sorrow. I will give you a fundamental axiom, that unless you turn the aforesaid copper into white and make visible coins and then afterwards again turn it into redness until a tincture results, verily ye accomplish nothing. Burn therefore the copper, break it up, deprive it of its blackness by cooking, imbuing and wash it until the same becomes white. Then rule it.[2]

While this passage has been interpreted by some to refer to laboratory procedure, in fact, it provides a particularly lucid description of the process involved in spiritual alchemy. In this regard, note the first statement, that no true tincture is except from "our copper." Remember that "our copper" signifies the desire nature and associated faculty of imagination. The old sciences knew that desire, accompanied by strong imagery, acted as a channel for the One Will, the volitional aspect of the One Consciousness from which all things are made. The process of burning our desire nature, breaking it up and depriving it of its blackness by cooking, imbuing and washing until it becomes white, then ruling it, describes the purification of desire through our life in the world, learning by reflection on our experience what things are worthy of desire and what not. This leads naturally to desiring to bring good to others and above all to the desire to know and serve the Holy One, and this is the state of devotion.

When we enter deeply into a contemplative state of devotion, it is not uncommon to experience a feeling of swelling in the throat. In this state the gentle fire of Venus is at work in the glands of the throat and, on the energy level, in the throat chakra: in this event a tincture begins to be made from our copper. The passage about turning the copper into white and making visible coins refers to the white or silver stage of the alchemical work, ruled by the Moon. In this process we come to a clear understanding of the nature of creation and our place in it and are able to dwell in this awareness when in a contemplative state. Our experience with the *dew of heaven* is a part of this white Moon stage, but the Great Work is completed in the red or gold stage, ruled by the Sun, in which we take what we have learned from our contemplation out into action in the world. For this to work, we must accomplish the *mysterium coniunctionis* of contemplation and action, and it is in this process that the tincture results that signifies the making of the Philosopher's Stone and the mystic union of body, soul, and spirit.

## Notes

1. The writings of Case on alchemy are primarily contained in privileged communications available to members of the Builders of the Adytum.

2. The passages of the *Turba* are attributed to various Greek philosophers, they are a transparent device of its unknown author. The one quoted occurs in the Ninth Dictum, attributed to Eximenus. A 1914 edition of Waite's translation from the Latin is available in reprint, as indicated in the references.

## References

Case, Paul Foster. *The True and Invisible Rosicrucian Order.* York Beach, ME: Samuel Wiser, Inc., 1985.

Cogburn, Elizabeth. "The Alchemical Journey of Unifying the Sun and the Moon,"

*Proceedings of the Tenth International Conference on the Study of Shamanism and Alternate Modes of Healing,* ed. Ruth-Inge Heinze. Berkeley, CA: Independent Scholars of Asia, Inc., 1993, pp.111-122.

Eliade, Mircea. *The Forge and the Crucible, The Origins and Structures of Alchemy.* Chicago, IL: The University of Chicago Press, 2nd ed., 1956.

Haeffner, Mark. *The Dictionary of Alchemy, From Maria Prophetissa to Isaac Newton.* London: The Aquarian Press, 1991.

Holmyard, E.J. *Alchemy.* Middlesex, England: Penguin Books, 1957.

Jung, Carl Gustav. *Psychology and Alchemy.* Princeton, NJ: Princeton University Press, 2nd ed., 1968.

_____. *Alchemical Studies.* Princeton, NJ: Princeton University Press, 1967.

_____. *Mysterium Coniunctionis.* New York: Pantheon Books, 1963.

Teich, Howard. "The Sacred Marriage of Sun and Moon," *Proceedings of the Tenth International Conference on the Study of Shamanism and Alternate Modes of Healing,* ed. Ruth-Inge Heinze. Berkeley, CA: Independent Scholars of Asia, Inc., 1993, pp.107-111.

Waite, A.E., transl. *The Turba Philosophorum or Assembly of the Sages.* Kila, MT: Kessinger Publishing Co. (reprint of the 1914 edition).

# ADVENTURES IN CREATING AN ALCHEMICAL PARTNERSHIP BETWEEN SAME GENDER INNER SUN AND MOON

Elizabeth Cogburn

Qabalah is a map of consciousness and a method of spiritual unfoldment. Although not always called by this name. It is a modern expression of a mystical core tradition in Western culture. The body of teachings have been gathered, synthesized and adapted over several millennia from the wisdom of the Hebrews, Egyptians, Greeks, Babylonians, Assyrians, Hindus, early Christians, and others, in the syncretic traditions of Western Asia and Mediterranean cultures (see Fowden, 1986; the theme of syncretism is central to his work).

In essence, Qabalah never made the split between spirit and matter. Our teachings proclaim that all matter IS spirit in condensed form, that all matter is therefore conscious and can be engaged with. We are told "to know the One Life, study Nature." I regard Qabalah, as I know it, to be a Western shamanic tradition.

In our lineage, the Tarot is seen as the spiritual companion of the Tree of Life. Together they help us to discover who we really are, why we are here, how the universe works from a metaphysical perspective, how to live a worthy life, and how to prepare for death. The teachings, practices and rituals guide us along a "Path of Return" to *being* in the knowledge and practice of the non-separateness—the Unity, the Oneness—of all life.

This Unitive State, this experience of at-one-ment—atonement—or BE-ING in harmonious integration within and without, cannot be contrived or forced. As aspirants on the "Path of Return" we hold the intention of devoting our energy to preparing our physical, emotional and mental vehicles to be received into Wholeness or the Mystical Union, through the Grace of the Holy One Life, the Conscious Energy of the Universe.

"Naive" is one of my favorite words. Its Latin tap root is *natus,* meaning "to be born." It is a good key word to open this chapter of my story which is about a birth as well as a union. *Nativus* is a branch of the Latin root, meaning "native, natural, a natural simplicity, instinctive." I want to extend these meanings to indicate attitudes of Beginner's Mind, Open Attention and what I call "Conscious Innocence," generated by Inner Necessity, which I find are essential to the alchemical journey of effecting the "union of the Sun and the Moon with the aid of Mercury." To provide for origin and authentic experience, I take what I call the "naive approach" of happen first, reflect on our own experience second and later consult other sources in person and print for clarification and expansion, confirmation or contrast, always remembering that our own experience, and the meanings we distill through reflection, are our own primary truth.

In my talk last year, I introduced you to the explorations of our Qabalistic Tree of Life Ceremonial Theater in which we have sought, as free as possible of culturally imposed gender and value categories, to discover and profile the characteristics, faculties and styles of our own same gender inner Suns and Moons. We include inquiry into their Shadow or "unskillful" aspects, ask each person to consider whether they themselves have identified or having been "led" more with one twin than the other, and whether they can identify other people who have been important Suns or Moons in their lives (Cogburn, 1993). We presented some of these profiles in our Appendix of the Proceedings (Cogburn, 1993:116-122). I emphasized our felt need to reclaim the archetypes and ancient myths of the solar feminine and the lunar masculine in confirmation of the realities of women who know in themselves a solar energy that is part of their femininity, and the realities of men who seek to reinstate their lunar energy as an aspect of their masculinity.

Here let me relate the comments of a man in a group in Boulder where we introduced this work recently. He was a big man with sun-bursting energy and a big voice, a therapist who works a lot with men's groups. When his turn came to speak in our Council of Reflection on the sun/moon/mercury practices, we had enacted on our Tree Ground earlier, he boomed across the room to his wife words to the effect that, "This is going to change things between us. I thought you had a corner on all the moon stuff and I have resented this SO MUCH. But now I find out this moon of mine is a GUY! This is GREAT! I can stop hating you for holding all the moon energy and be in how I really love you while I get on with being my own moon man!" This is one bold response to the question we have posed, as to whether we can identify benefits from this paradigm and process in intimate relationships with others.

Let us turn now to our other questions. Are our Sun and Moon seeking this union? How can we recognize the process or know if it is happening? Can we consciously cultivate, assist or enhance it? Why should we want it? How would this inner union benefit us within ourselves?

With the attitudes of Beginner's Mind and Open Attention, I have personally repeated at all of our gatherings over three years, our Basic Three Pillars Tree of Life practice where we invite each of our Inner Twins to "live and move in me and be of my being" and then consider what aid we need toward their union, or harmonious interplay, as a way of discovering the character and function of our personal Mercury. I have found that, even though I try to start each practice from a "blank page," the "personalities" of my Sun and Moon Twins remain consistent and in each round reveal deeper layers and more subtleties of themselves.

Thus I felt that I was well enough acquainted with them by the spring of 1993 that, as part of my inner preparations for our Tree of Life Sun Dance coming up in June, I would sound each of them out on the possibility of forming a partnership. I was clear that in most areas of my adult life I have tended to identify with and meet the world from my sun side, that in my mid-life years my Moon Twin did not get much recognition or the quiet solitude that she enjoys and needs for her areas of creative expression. I had been increasingly aware of my hunger to bring her forward out of the Shadow and live more from her energy. I had noted that most of the strong Suns in my life have been other women, beginning with my mother, that my favorite Sun-men have also been men who work with the earth and with animals, and that I have had wonderful close relationships with men who lead from their masculine Moon energy—my husband of forty years being the most important.

To my surprise and consternation, my Twins each regarded the subject of union with repugnance and disdain. My Sun looked straight at me and grimaced with a wrinkled nose, popping eyes and curled lips and said, "You have got to be kidding. Me get together with that head tripping cold fish? That kill joy! I'd call her a wet blanket if she weren't so dry and chilly. Aloof, self-absorbed—contemplating she calls it, thinking, having visions, meditating. We mustn't disturb her precious solitude. Have you seen her annoyed looks and how she withdrew with that impatient air when I invited people in and we tended the temple and created the music and dance rituals for our ceremonials? Or when we got excited talking about our lives or we went off to do some garden project? I have to tell you that Moon woman is the damper in my stove pipe and the cork in my champagne. No way am I teaming up with her!"

My Moon drew herself up in her fringed veils and, looking off to the side and down her nose, said "My dear, one would hope that you speak in jest. All these years I have had to struggle just to preserve a small space of shady serenity and quiet in the midst of that creature's bumptious enthusiasm and pervasive intrusiveness. She is always either radiantly brilliant or raves biliously into every crevice and corner. Action, action, action, she's never still. She depends on me for energy and vision to inspire her in creating life and the ceremonials, but when I try to share thoughts with her while walking in those so called "strolling gardens," she says she creates for such purposes, do you know that she cannot even set out without her trowel and pruning shears. I can't string two sentences together, much less a thought, before she has stopped to poke and prune, tuck and trim. She says she's taking in everything I'm saying and that she can think better when she's moving, but being around her feels just too bright, busy and disjointed for me. No, I think any sort of liaison with her would be quite out of the question."

As you can imagine, I felt quite taken aback. When I discussed the situation with my friend, Dr. Howard Teich, whose original work on the same gender inner twins has been so encouraging for me, he chuckled and said that this is fairly typical—that when the twins are first coming into conscious awareness, they do tend to appear as antagonists. I was also helped by my husband who had noticed that our teachings on Qabalistic Alchemy use the word "union" sparingly, tending rather to circulate around ideas and images of the apprentice alchemist's developing skill in choosing "right combinations" to affect the situation at hand "suavely and with great ingenuity."

When our Sun Dance rolled around last year, I took the whole matter back to my inner Council of Guides, Teachers and Mentors, relating to them these responses from the Twins, my confusion about what to do and asking for their help. They threw back their heads and burst into big laughter. As I stared wide-eyed wondering what was so funny, they explained to me that the unitive process is well under way, is going on all the time, and is in some measure inevitable though I may enhance its progress in so far as to devote myself to holding this intention and attending my spiritual unfoldment. This made sense to me because I connected it to my understanding that all life is seeded with an impulse to grow and develop and that there are stages in the evolution of human consciousness which, for most of us, open up only with conscious desire and earnest attention. The best thing for me to do, the Teachers said, would be to open my attention and they would be pleased to nudge me into awareness of the many little things happening in my daily life that are signs of, and results of, the energies of the Twins coming into better balance.

Then later, during the Dance, we again repeated our Three Pillar practice on the Tree of Life with our individual Suns/Moons and Mercuries. This time, as I was walking the Middle Pillar, talking with Mercury about the help I needed, I received a very important teaching, in fact an initiation which has changed my whole sense of who I am and how I am in the world. I was told that it was now time for me to shift my point of identification away from either my sun or moon to the position of Mercury and to concentrate on BEING the one who effects the bringing together, the interweaving, the "right combinations" of the gifts of my Sun and Moon. This felt entirely right and comfortable, the natural next step. And though I had little notion of how to go about it or what it would lead to, still I knew something irrevocable had been laid down in my "soul bones" that would be revealed to me as I held in focus my new intention to identify with the reconciling position of my Mercury.

After that Sun Dance I wrote the paper on the Inner Twins that I presented last year. Writing for me is a way of tapping into layers of consciousness I am not aware of in my ordinary waking state. I put my hands over the keys and watch the screen to see that is going to appear. I had lots of journal pages to draw from in compiling descriptions of my Sun and Moon, very little on Mercury. However, as I invited Mercury to speak, she came through my fingers with a clear and elaborate profile as the holder of the vision and intention toward this mystical union as well as having the mediating skills needed to effect it. And further, she set right to work with the Sun and Moon, drawing up a list of items she saw as shared ground between them (Cogburn, 1993)—something that had not occurred to me to do. She even began then and there suggesting to the twins ways in which each of them might enhance their own fuller expression by appreciating and supporting the other.

I forgot all these details in the chaos of our lives at that time. This is important to mention for two reasons. For one, I want to show that the unitive process is indeed perking right along just under the surface of daily demands and hard work. And for another, I think that the stage of life I am in has everything to do with feeling called by, and to, these concerns at this time.

Robert and I have been in a life passage for the last two and a half years.

We have been completing the responsibilities and accomplishments of our mid-life years as we have been visioning and preparing for, stepping over the threshold into our apprentice elderhood. This has been a very turbulent time of final completions of big family affairs. We have viewed each of these as rituals in life—as the ultimate ceremonial, and have given our attention and energy as we would to any sacred endeavor. Supporting two daughters through their Ph.Ds in psychology, assisting our youngest to come out as a lesbian and then stage a big white-lace church wedding in Portland, attending my aged mother so she could pass through her final decline and graceful death at home in our loving arms, seeing Robert through the concluding of his academic career in mathematics where "retire" is closer in meaning to "retread" than to stopping an active life. The worst part for us was the enormous task of sorting through and moving our things out of our Albuquerque home and ceremonial center in the extreme heat of summer, cleaning and repairing it mostly ourselves, and suffering the crass materialism of the real estate mentality which could only think in terms of selling a commodity which we knew as a beautiful living being, a Place Spirit, we were passing on to new stewards.

Our October Tree of Life Ceremonial at our Taos home coincided with the conclusion of that last ordeal so that we had a huge harvest of thanksgiving, a much needed rest and a time in the Temple to regroup.

The outer details of the next phase have been about combining our households, and learning how to live under the same roof again after fifteen years of commuter marriage. We continue to plunge into our physical and mental projects with our customary drive and persistence—this year digging grand new garden areas and building a new ceremonial room onto the house. And for the first time we have been able to team up together to prepare the teachings for our ceremonials and our contributions to gatherings such as this one.

I feel that this time in my life is the pay off, the reward, for all the hard work, doubt and struggle of the mid-life years. I feel happier and more present to life than ever before. The possibilities of tomorrow are vastly more interesting to me than any memories of the past. And, it certainly does feel like what Jean Shinoda Bolen calls a "liminal" time. "Limen" is the Latin word for "threshold," Indicating in our context, to paraphrase Bolen, an "in-between" state in which we are neither who we used to be, nor who we are becoming, where ordinary perception and glimpses of eternity overlap, where intuited possibility is on the threshold of tangible manifestation (Bolen, 1994:7-8)

Even though I forgot the details of my Mercury character over the years, the shift to identification with Mercury did stay with me and took root. I noticed from time to time over the winter and into the spring that I seemed to automatically carrying an inner image of being in the middle with my Sun and Moon at either hand as I wove or braided them around me as if I were the staff of Caduceus and they the gold and silver serpents.

I realized that while we did swing out for periods into their special territories, attending their interests and projects, and that occasionally there was some annoyed growling and resistance, still the over all feeling was different. Each side knows now that we *will get* back to the center and to our own realm eventually, so neither is afraid of being eclipsed or of being absorbed so that identity is lost.

My Sun now admits to her bone deep relief to be freed from the pace and intensity of her ceremonial travel schedule, the burdens of leadership and of attending too large a garden of souls. She is absolutely delighted to turn some of that energy to tending her plant gardens with the companionship of the sky and clouds, wind, rain, snow, devas, fairies, birds and animals. She welcomes a few friends, a few students, retreatants, and consultees and a smaller, more intimate circle of Tree of Life companions who share her aspirations. She is happy to see, and occasionally assist, her Sun husband as he goes about his building projects. She even speaks with warm appreciation of the good company of both her Moon and his Moon who provide endless interesting and lively conversation, and who team up to keep a schedule of spiritual practices, encouraging her to take the lead in the singing and moving meditations. It pleases her so to find both the Moons strolling and sitting about her gardens. And she is able to join them in these quiet meditations, though she continues to carry her pruning shears, discreetly tucked in a pocket.

My introverted Moon has at last come into her own. The long cold quiet winter in Taos attending the inquiries of her inner life was utter bliss for her. She acknowledges her gratitude to Sun for those beautiful gardens and also for the interesting people Sun gathers to join the conversation and meditation. She is pleased to have helped Sun realize how much more deeply she can savor all that is going on about her, and how many more aspects of her inner gardens she can find and explore, when there are not so many other people and outer distractions to attend to.

Mercury slipped around the edges of Sun and Moon, quietly encouraging them in their new found mutual enhancement while she herself applied for a new passport, subscribed to new adventures and worked travel magazines that seemed to appear from nowhere, and made plans with her friends for trips abroad next year. Until I reviewed Mercury's profile in July in preparing this paper, I myself had wondered where the energy for all this was coming from since I was only aware of my relief and delight at being home with no travel plans.

When, on June 17th this year, we set aside our tools, unplugged the phones and locked the front gate to begin this year's Tree of Life Sun Dance in our temple garden, I made a stumbling approach like a weary and thirsty traveler finally finding the oasis. For about eight weeks we had been doing the heavy physical labor involved in the planting season and the building project and had not taken quiet time to recuperate and prepare ourselves. I so vividly felt the first of the Seven Gates we pass through on our way into the Dance as a major threshold in my life and was aware that my exhausted and unprepared state was actually a blessing in this instance as I was so open and, in a way, fresh for something new to happen.

The Sixth Gate consists of walking each of the Paths of the Tree of Life, inviting review and new teachings. In our lineage, each Path is assigned a Key of the major arcana of spiritual Tarot which is undertood to represent an aspect of both our own consciousness and the Universal Consciousness of which all things are made.

As I attempted to reconnect with, literally to remember, the relevance of each key to my own consciousness, a practice of twenty-four years, I felt vacant, empty, unknowing. So on the Path for Key 1, addressing the faculty of Attention, I said, "Yes, but attention to *what* now?" "Ask and ye shall receive" was the immediate answer. I am to "Learn to live in the garden and stay awake." I wanted to know, "awake to *what?*" As I made my way along the paths, each key showed me variations of the theme that it is all about balance, harmony, "right combination" as a dynamic process which I must attend with awareness every day." "Fine," I said as I got down to the Path of Key 20, and had in my mind the alchemical notion that all of this is supposed to lead to the creation of a new third of some kind. "So tell me what baby are we birthing with all of this?" "Oh," they said, "how about a BABY ELDER?!" Now it was my turn to burst into laughter at the obvious and delicious rightness of this response. I also breathed, deeply savoring a sense of being "on course," noticing the feelings of relief and release in my body.

Later along in the ceremonial on our Tree of Life dance ground which is meant to be an outward and visible symbol of an inward and spiritual reality, I experienced another level of initiation into identifying my Mercury with the True or Higher Self seated at the center of the Tree. I can allude to this mysterious experience as a shift in my beingness, felt literally in my body as a rushing infusion into my cells, imbuing me with a sense of being subtly but irreversibly changed and of coming from a new place. This True Self is the real actor in all the personality dramas of my daily life. In the realm of the Soul, she is the loving witness who observes, evaluates and equilibrates my expressions of the One Energy in daily life. And through her, there is a continual circulation of, and access to conscious connection with pure Spirit.

This experience is too new, too deep and too numinous to speak more about. So I will end by telling you the Tree's closing gesture of confirmation to me. At our Give Away blanket which ends the two-week Dance retreat, the first gift to each dancer is from the Tree itself in the form of a Tarot Key which is to be our guide, teacher, for the next year. My gift this year is Key 14, called "temperance," in the old meaning of imparting strength by skillful combining. This Path originates in the central sphere of the True Self and is the skillful alchemist presiding over the "right combinations" needed to manifest Spirit in daily life on earth, "suavely and with great ingenuity."

Recently I have discovered numerous images from 16th century alchemical texts of this equilibrating figure as a woman called Mercury.[1] And you will notice that she has fire in one hand and water in the other hand, bringing fire to the water and water to the fire. So I brought her here in my childlike attempt "to get there."

## Note

1.    See plates in Stanislas Klossiwski de Rosa, *The Secret Art of Alchemy*. London: Thames and Hudson, 1973, and Carl Gustav Jung, *Psychology and Alchemy*. Collected Works, vol.12. Princeton, NJ: Bollingen Foundation, 1968.

## References

Bolen, Jean Shinoda. *Crossing to Avalon.* New York: Harper Collins, 1994.

Cogburn, Elizabeth. "The Alchemical Journey of Unifying the Sun and the Moon," *Proceedings of the Tenth International Conference on the Study of Shamanism and Alternate Modes of Healing,* ed. Ruth-Inge Heinze. Berkeley, CA: Independent Scholars of Asia, Inc., 1993, pp.111-122.

*The Emerald Tablet of Hermes Trismagistus,* transl. by the Builders of the Adytum. Los Angeles, CA.: Adytum, undated.

Fowden, Garth. *The Egyptian Hermes, A Historical Approach to the Late Pagan Mind.* Princeton, NJ: Princeton University Press, 1986.

Neumann, Erich. *The Great Mother.* Princeton, NJ: Bollingen Foundation, 1963.

# DISCUSSION

With the Cogburns, Fellows, and Teich

Weiland: I am really excited not only by the weekend but by all the presentations this morning. They are right along the line where I am learning. They are a celebration of the differences between the Sun and the Moon or whatever we want to call it.

I want to share with you an experience I had a couple of month ago when I had to drive from New York to Illinois in thirteen hours straight, alone. After four, five hours, I was in unity, I was in the Oneness. It was terrific, except that the car was going off track in this Oneness. So I thought, "what shall I do, I have to get home." So I decided to create the Moon and the Sun and they were arguing until I was back on track. We learned a lot from each other. Therefore I want to honor the differences as well as the union between the two.

*Gersch*: I enjoyed the whole morning—the symbolism, the beautiful wording, and the explanations. It was very touching. My question is: I admire and honor the traditional terms being used but am also curious about new words and a new language for the 21st century. I really would like to know some sources where I can find some inspiration.

I also would like to mention that I was touched by Elizabeth's words. My wife is probably a Sun, much more powerful as a woman and I am more on the male Moon side. It was really interesting to hear your dialogue. It sounded familiar to me.

*Teich*: I don't know anything new, but if anybody is interested in alchemy, Edward Edinger's book, *The Anatomy of the Psyche* (La Salle, IL: Open Court, 1985) is really a must. Also, in my struggle with quantum physics, the only person I was able to grasp was Fred Alan Wolf. He wrote a book, *The Eagle's Quest* (New York: Summit Books, 1991) in which he describes mostly his journey to South America. The book is shamanic oriented and includes some great examples from quantum physics.

*Etcheverry:* We saw alchemy in action, one by Elizabeth reporting and one by Elaine's tears. The third one was so subtle that I had to come up and say something about it—the passing of the stone. When the stone came to you, Howard, I saw your heart open and I saw the blood coming in. You then announced that you were centered. I just wanted to record that.

*Teich:* I felt chills when you said that. It was exactly what had happened to me. I was so anxious and when Ruth gave me the stone, it was a totally different experience.

Elaine, with your tears, we saw this transformation, this alchemy working within you, from one experience to the experience where you are now.

*Winstedt:* I have a question for Howard about your interpretation of the observer effect which concerns the transition from wave into particle. My understanding of that has more to do with uncertainty. The unobserved object exists in a state of uncertainty and it depends on what type of observation occurs, whether it becomes either a wave or a particle. Maybe I misunderstood your interpretation of this function or, perhaps, something else is going on?

*Teich:* That something collapses into a wave or a particle is not what I was reading into it. Maybe, I am inaccurate. What I have felt is that the union of the Sun and the Moon is the magical transition point of the wave and the particle. You sound as if you are technically more knowledgeable than I.

*Winstedt:* I was just wondering how these two ideas translate. My understanding is that it moves from an uncertain state into either a wave or a particle, depending on the kind of observation and I like to work just with that.

*Teich:* This is the kind of question I had when I was wondering how the lunar is so much shamanic and artistic. At that level, it would even be more consistent in that form rather than splitting off, as I was describing it. It seems to be even more consistent with the energy that goes into the *psyche. I really thank you for the contribution.*

*Gersch:* It is probably true that this technical clarification is necessary, but actually, in the scientific field, the theory about light being a wave or a particle has not really been figured out. It might appear that scientists know what they are talking about, but, in a deeper sense, it is very uncertain. They don't know and I wish they would know better. In fact, it has not been satisfactorily explained or discovered. Scientists rather avoid to be definite. So it is better to say, in the name of science, we are really uncertain what happens.

*Scott:* Thank you, for all your synthesis. It is really marvelous to see all the synchronicities and parallels and disciplines. My question is directed to Elaine. You mentioned that the animal powers are reflections of your own unconscious. I am not conversant in alchemical hypnotherapy, more in shamanic viewpoints, so I wonder whether you could elaborate on what you mean by animal powers representing the unconscious?

*Fellows:* Sometimes they can be your own soul. We know that, in shamanic tradition, you may have an animal soul or souls but animals may also be unresolved emotional issues, as described in alchemical hypnotherapy.

*Heinze:* Felicitas will be talking tonight about the animal connection. Maybe you get an answer then?

*Fellows:* Quigley speaks in his book about these two connections, either the souls or unresolved emotional inner conflicts.

*Scott:* My own experience is that these spirits or energy forms manifest through animal energies, based on our own constructual concept of the universe. They appear this way and that's how we relate to them. They are actually external to ourselves. Many of the answers they provide are unbeknownst to us and that's why we evoke them. They may be a reflection, some sort of a mirror, but they still exist autonomously, as I understand it from a shamanic point of view.

*Teich*: I associate where some of this comes from with the reptilian brain. Phillip asked me a question at lunch where he pointed out that, in shamanism, the Sun and the Moon are really not the end. Yes, the sun ladder and the moon ladder are passage ways. I really did not get into that because I thought the issue was complicated enough.

# TRANSFORMATIVE EXPERIENCES AND PARAPSYCHOLOGICAL PHENOMENA: A CROSS-CULTURAL PERSPECTIVE

Larissa Vilenskaya

All that we do
Is touched with ocean, yet we remain
On the shore of what we know.
*Richard Purdy Wilbur (1969/1992:750)*

## Introduction

In the course of my activities in the field of parapsychology for over twenty-five years, I have been engaged in experimental as well as field research, and other phenomenological/experiential approaches. One of the issues that has been of great interest to me throughout these years was a search for psychological correlates of parapsychological (also called psi or psychic) abilities. This realm of phenomena includes extrasensory perception (ESP), also called remote viewing, i.e., perception of information which cannot be obtained through known senses or by other ordinary means (Targ and Harary, 1984; McMoneagle, 1993; Vilenskaya, 1993). I am against the term "paranormal," often used in literature in relation to these phenomena, because I believe they are normal human faculties, although seldom accessible on demand.

To be more specific, for me, the above issue of psychological correlates of psi includes three different aspects. If persons manifest psi abilities at such a level that they have been confirmed by reliable observers and/or by laboratory experiments involving the use of standard scientific methodologies, then I would like to pose the following questions: (1) Are there any personality characteristics common to these individuals? (2) Have these individuals had any specific or unusual events or experiences before they began to manifest such abilities? and (3) Are there any methods to train, develop, and/or facilitate such abilities?

Issues (1) and (3) have been considered by a number of researchers. Earlier approaches to the study of attitudes and personality traits in experimental parapsychology were reviewed by Palmer (1977). After having analyzed a large experimental database, he emphasized the low reliability of ESP scores in experimental attempts and concluded that the data seem to suggest that two kinds of people are most likely to perform best in laboratory tests of ESP: (a) people who are relatively well adjusted, and (b) people who believe in ESP. These conclusions seem obvious: If I say to myself that I am incapable of performing a certain task because I do not believe in my own capabilities, nor do I believe that anyone else can perform the task, then it is unlikely that I will be able to perform. Although the last fifteen years yielded some new insights (e.g., Lantz and Kiernan, 1986; Galperin, 1993), they did not move us much closer to understanding what kind of people would be more successful in laboratory ESP tests. Because of space limitations, I will focus here exclusively on item (2) of the above list, i.e., psi and unusual or transformative experiences.

My presentation is based on data accumulated during literature and field research in Russia and in the USA. I have found that there seems to be a cross-cultural tendency in individuals who have had a transformative experience to accept and embrace psi abilities as an inherent part of their lives. Less data are available concerning laboratory-confirmed manifestations of psi abilities, but a similar tendency seems to hold there as well. As I will show below, scholarly and shamanistic/transpersonal approaches, and ancient and modern views come together, yielding similar conclusions to illuminate the multiplicity and diversity of mental and spiritual capacities.

## Transformative Experiences

There is a vast literature about the mystical, spiritual, initiatory and otherwise transformative experiences of saints, sages, shamans, monks, visionaries, and ordinary people from all walks of life. The phenomenon has been known for centuries and does not constitute an outcome of New Age-type thinking. Transformative experiences broadly discussed in literature include near-death (Ring, 1980, 1984, 1992, 1993), meditative (Murphy and Donovan, 19889), psychedelic (Grof, 1988), Kundalini-awakening experiences (Sannella, 1992), unidentified flying object (UFO) encounters (Ring, 1992), and firewalking (Vilenskaya and Steffy, 1991). Some of these means for transformation (e.g., meditation) are deliberate, while others are spontaneous, unexpected occurrences in human life.

The after-effects of a transformative experience, which can be interpreted "as indicative of a generalized awakening of higher human potential" (Ring, 1993:198), are most clearly described in studies of near-death experiences (NDEs). They include changes in (1) self-concept and personal values, (2) religious or spiritual orientation, and (3) psychic awareness. Among personal changes, Ring (1980, 1884, 1993) notes a heightened appreciation of life, greater feelings of self-worth, an increased concern and a greater appreciation for the welfare of others. In the area of religious and spiritual changes, he emphasizes that NDEers acquire a more universalistic worldview. Finally, venturing into the realm of parapsychology, Ring indicates that psychic sensitivity and development increase in NDEers.

## Near-Death Experiences and Psi

My initial intention was to explore the interrelationship between near-death experiences and psi performance, in particular, remote viewing. This was prompted by my encounter with a person whose remote viewing ability was confirmed in laboratory studies and who had experienced an NDE two decades earlier. Specifically, the idea for this paper occurred to me after personal meetings with Joseph McMoneagle, author of *Mind Trek; Exploring Consciousness, Time and Space through Remote Viewing*. He repeatedly demonstrated excellent remote viewing abilities, both at SRI International and Science Application International Corporation (SAIC) Cognitive Sciences Laboratory, under strictly controlled laboratory conditions. Many of these experiments and their results are described in *Mind Trek*.

In his book, McMoneagle wrote about his near-death experience in 1970, providing a vivid and compelling description of his encounter with spiritual reality:

...I...was...engulfed in the most brilliant and softest white light imaginable....I knew immediately that I had been absorbed by a Being of Light, with unimaginable qualities and quantities of power, goods, strength, and beauty.

There is no comparable place in physical reality to experience such total awareness. The love, protection, joy, giving, sharing, and being that I experienced in the Light at that moment was absolutely overwhelming and pure in its essence....The voice of Light was crystal clear and embodied the purest form of warmth and love....The voice in the Light said within my mind, "Go back. You are not going to die."...I argued with it. I was so intensely comfortable and at ease in my new state of consciousness that I could quite easily have embedded myself within the light and just existed there for the rest of eternity. Right there, in the folds of the light, was where I wanted to be. But such wasn't to be the case (1993:32-33).

This event changed McMoneagle's life. Among other effects, it resulted in what he called "spontaneous knowledge." He described it in the following terms:

...[This is] knowing what someone is thinking when they are talking to you. Knowing things about people which they have not openly shared. I would later come to understand this new-found sensitivity is called psychic functioning. But at the time I didn't know what to call it. Without going into any detail, there were things I suddenly and quite spontaneously knew about people very close to me, that had been closely guarded secrets prior to my NDE. These thoughts would just come into my head when I least expected them. Most were shocks to me emotionally, especially the information relative to relationships....It was like suddenly tapping into a completely new information line, one over which you have no control (1993:37).

These and similar experiences prompted McMoneagle to participate in laboratory psi experiments—in which he succeeded remarkably. Without the results of laboratory tests, one could say that it was just his imagination, that he was "unstable," "paranoid," and "delusional." These are the words often used to explain away psychic functioning. But, he is one of the few who can present solid evidence.

Another is Peter Hurkos, a Dutchman who showed an extraordinary psychic talent and successfully participated in numerous ESP experiments after an NDE that had occurred when he was 30. A house painter at that time (in 1941), he fell down from a ladder, was unconscious in a hospital for four days, and returned to life with a gift to sense past and future events in people's lives:

...I remember the time I was falling and I didn't want to die. Then everything was black. And when I woke up I had no mind of my own. And then I got my gift. I was in somebody else's mind, and I was scared because I didn't know what was happening. My father and mother said it's not the same Peter anymore. They said he died and I came back with two minds...hearing the voice and seeing the pictures (Browning, 1970:13).

What he saw in his mind included his first vision of a fire in his house (which actually occurred five days later). It posed a danger to his son and turned out to be true in every detail (Browning, 1970:45).

Anecdotal accounts of psychic experiences following an NDE are widespread (e.g., Brinkley with Perry, 1994:108-123; Harris and Bascom, 1990:166-172), although they are usually treated with caution in scholarly literature. When individuals claim that they experienced psychic perception, a post hoc assessment of which of these cases may actually involve psi represents a fairly difficult endeavor.

Still, a possible interrelationship between NDE and psi was discussed and explored by, among others, Heaney (1984), Ring (1980, 1984, 1991, 1992), Greyson (1983), Kohr (1980, 1982, 1983), Rogers (1983), Schroter-Kunhardt (1993), and Sutherland (1990). Heaney, in his chapter entitled, "Transpersonal States and Near-Death Experiences," reviewed most of the major studies of NDEs through 1981 and offered the hypothesis that such experiences "may be archetypal and symbolic experiences, deep experiences of the individual and collective psyche, combined with some ESP phenomena" (1984:225).

Ring (1980, 1984, 1991, 1992) developed self-report scales and compared responses of those individuals who actually had experienced an NDE, with a control group of those who were interested in NDEs. In one of his studies, NDEers (26 individuals) were asked whether the frequency of their psi experiences (listed in Table 1) has increased since their NDE, while the control group was asked to report on changes since their interest in NDEs began.

## Table 1

### Psi Experiences of NDEers vs. Control Group

| Item | NDEers | Controls |
|---|---|---|
| general psi ability | 61% | 32% |
| telepathic experiences | 60% | 24% |
| precognitive experiences | 62% | 22% |
| psychic healing ability | 42% | 11% |

Kohr (1982, 1983) conducted a similar survey and compared three different groups. One included 358 individuals who had never come close to death, the second was comprised of 105 people who claimed to have had a close call with death but without an intense experience associated with it, and the third involved 84 individuals whose responses to a questionnaire indicated they had an NDE. Analysis revealed that the NDE group manifested a significantly greater incidence of self-reported psi and psi-related experiences, dreams, and, what the author calls, mystical states.

Greyson (1983) conducted a survey among 80 members of the International Association for Near-Death Studies (IANDS) who had experienced an NDE. Because they were specifically instructed to note whether they had psychic and/or psi-related (e.g., out-of-body, OBE) experiences before or after their NDEs, this added the following logical questions: (a) perhaps these individuals were psychically sensitive before an NDE, and (b) perhaps NDEs tend to occur in psychically sensitive individuals. The results of this survey showed that among near-death experiencers, psychic and psi-related experiences were reported to have occurred more frequently after than before the NDE; the difference turned out to be statistically significant (p 0.0001).

It should be emphasized again that in all of the above studies, we are dealing with self-report data and unverified accounts of psi experiences; while in the case of McMoneagle, we have laboratory-confirmed psi performances. One, however, reinforces the other, especially in the light of recent confirmed positive correlation (p 0.0015) between reported personal psi experiences and the results of laboratory ESP tests (Honorton, 1992).

## Transformative Experiences and Psi: Interview Findings

When traveling in Russia in November/December 1993, I conducted interviews with four individuals in Moscow who had had near-death experiences. I was interested in exploring whether the tendency observed in the above surveys would be found in a different culture. My first intention was to conduct a similar survey. However, due to the limited time of my trip, I found only a small number of individuals for the sample and, therefore, decided on a vertical, instead of horizontal, approach, i.e., to learn as much as possible from each of the interviewees. As I will describe below, this attempt did not work the way I had intended.

My first meeting was with Mzia Levashova (Solomonia), a famous healer and reputed psychic. An intense woman with penetrating eyes, she tended not to answer my questions but to talk about what she considered to be important to tell me and the world. Mzia (born in 1958) had a near-death experience in late 1991. She described her encounter with a Higher Being who appeared to her in the shape of a huge white and pink cloud, while she, herself, was in an "energy form":

> I found myself not having any shape, but being a golden-yellow energy field, spiritual field. I sensed myself to be enormous, my field covered tremendously large space. This state was like a deep, sweet meditation in total peace, kindness, happiness and joy of my energy being, my soul. When I moved close to the Higher Being, He gave me energy which sent me back to this world—it was too

early, it was premature for me to leave (personal communication, Moscow, October 1993).

Before her NDE, Mzia was already a well-known healer, the founder and director of a school in Moscow that taught "energy" healing, laying-on of hands, and distant healing to their numerous students and followers. During our meeting, Mzia remembered that, as a child, she was seeing auras. She had her first out-of-body experience when she was four or five. By 12 or 13, she was already reputed among her acquaintances to be a healer and a "witch," with extensive knowledge of "subtle energies" and non-ordinary realities, received on her "astral travels." (It should be noted that the root for the Russian word *ved'ma* ("witch") comes from the word *vedat'* which means "to know."

Later, I had a lengthy discussion with one of Mzia's former students, Natalia Sugrobova, a psychologist who is currently the head of her own school of healing through "energy work," "subtle field" interaction, meditation, and visualization. She studied with Mzia before Mzia's near-death experience. Natalia gave me several examples of Mzia performing successfully what seemed to be psychic diagnoses of the health problems of her clients, sometimes uncommon and often precisely described conditions. She emphasized, however, that although the apparent psychic statements were impressive, conventional means of receiving information were not excluded. Natalia also mentioned that, when she studied with Mzia, what she learned from her was primarily on a non-verbal level, the level of a direct experience, rather than through conventional ways of learning.

Next I met with Yulia F. Vorobyova from the Ukrainian town of Donetsk. She visited Moscow at that time, was in a hurry and could devote only less than twenty minutes to our meeting. Thus, an in-depth interview was not possible. Before her accident, Vorobyova worked in Donetsk as a crane operator and, as she said, did not have any "special" or "magic" powers. Although she became well-known in recent years and gave numerous press interviews, her manner of speech is still that of a simple, uneducated person. On March 3, 1978, Vorobyova (who was 37 at the time) endured an electric shock of 380 volts. She lost consciousness and was taken to a hospital. According to her, she was pronounced dead, and they were about to do a post-mortem on her, when they found signs of life. In Vorobyova's description of her experience, there were no "classical" NDE features, such as a meeting with a Being of Light or a life review. She spoke only about being in peace and not wanting to return. Yulia woke up in the hospital, and for six months afterwards she had trouble sleeping and experienced severe headaches. When these symptoms disappeared, she unexpectedly acquired an ability to see inside the human body and was able to describe people's internal organs. In 1987, she was examined at the Kiev Institute of Nuclear Physics. She was shown people with some internal organs surgically removed or having some health problems or anomalies in their bodies, and she was able to define these anomalies. She said that she also could find grey stones in a dark room and generally was able to find her bearings in the dark. She was even nicknamed "a live X-ray," and several articles in the Soviet press (e.g., *Moscow News,* 1991:15) discussed her abilities of psychic diagnosis and distant perception, including successful attempts to locate missing persons. Interestingly, Buryats, an ethnic group in Siberia, believe that being struck by lightning constitutes a shamanic initiation. They believe that the *nerjer utxatay,* the lightning shaman, who is imbued with the power of the lightning bolt, acquires the strongest divination and healing powers (Krader, 1975:118). At the end of our brief meeting, I asked Yulia whether she had heard of that tradition; she had not.

Another interviewee, Bella Davidova, told me that she survived three clinical deaths. She burned, was drowned, and was dying of leukemia, but survived and, as she said, started a totally new and different life. A housewife without the slightest interest in the spiritual or psychic dimension before her first NDE, she began to paint pictures of saints, angels, and other worlds. When I visited her apartment, Bella showed me dozens and dozens of large, vivid paintings. There were so many of them that, in her small place, little space was left for anything else. Over and over again she described her on-going interaction with Higher Beings and their insistence that she continue to paint the icons, thereby bringing more "spiritual energy" to the world. She related to me numerous incidences in which her paintings, which radiated that "life energy" had a healing effect on their viewers. The paintings were said to put viewers in a state of catharsis, spiritual purification, and the feeling of unity with the universe. As far as her psychic experiences are concerned, Bella talked about numerous predictions—in her personal life, for her friends, and even on a national/international scale. No independent verification was possible. During this interview (similar to my discussion with another artist, Igor, that I will describe below), I encountered the same problem as in my meeting with Mzia: instead of answering questions, Bella persistently talked about good and evil, about the importance of prayer, and asked me repeatedly to convey the message which spiritual beings implore her to give to the world: If we humans don't change our ways, don't turn to God, don't learn to love and to be kind and compassionate to each other, this civilization will perish in devastating earthquakes, floods, and the fire of destruction.

My last meeting, which was with Igor Anisiforov, I found to be the most interesting. A soft-spoken man with kind eyes, he is the creator of unique "bioenergetic paintings," depicting cosmic temples, the Virgin Mary, spiritual beings, and subtle energies. Igor believes that his pictures speak to the

True Self, the essence of every person, even if the person is not consciously aware. I found Igor's paintings truly fascinating, especially when I learned Igor had never studied art nor painted before his NDE. He was not inclined to talk about the NDE, implying that it was ineffable and sacred to him. I respected his attitude and immediately stopped probing, focusing instead on his psychic experiences. He described some instances of distant perception and precognitive dreams, as well as several out-of-body experiences. He related that during an OBE, he saw several people in his friend's apartment, several kilometers away. He had not met those people, did not know them, but when he later described what he had seen to his friend, the friend confirmed his impression in all details.

Although my initial approach to the interviews was somewhat unsuccessful, the tendency of individuals who had experienced an NDE to report more psychic and psi-related experiences, seems to be cross-culturally observable. For myself, many additional questions still remain unanswered.

## Continuing the Search

Ring's (1992) study indicates that his findings concerning personal transformation undergone by NDEers (including their apparent increase in psychic awareness) are also true with regard to those who have had UFO encounters—irrespective of what the UFO is believed to be. In particular, he found that persons who, as adults, report UFO encounters or NDEs were not as children especially inclined toward a world of fantasy, but "they are apparently already sensitive to nonordinary realities" (1992:129), i.e., they reported that, as children, they had premonitions, out-of-body, and other kinds of psychic experiences. Therefore, despite the above-cited findings by Greyson (1983) that NDEers had more psychic experiences after their NDEs than prior to them, the question whether both transformative and psychic experiences occur more often in particular kinds of people or have an underlying common cause/phenomenon/process remains unanswered.

Both Ring (1984, 1992) and Greyson (1993a, 1993b) drew research attention to a possible association between NDE and an awakening of a biological or psychophysical process known in Eastern tradition as kundalini. While discussion of the concept of kundalini and kundalini-awakening experiences is beyond the scope of this paper (see Sannella, 1992), it should be pointed out that Ring (1984) proposed two possible explanations of the similarities between after-affects of NDEs and kundalini-awakening experiences: either that kundalini is the energy underlying the near-death experience, and thus every NDE is an indication of an aroused kundalini; or that the near-death experience is one of many possible triggers that can stimulate a kundalini awakening, but does not necessarily do so in every case.

Seeking more objective evidence of kundalini among NDEers, Ring (1984, 1992) included nine kundalini items in a 60-item inventory administered to 74 individuals who had experienced NDEs and to a control group of 54 subjects who expressed interest in NDEs but never had one themselves. The NDEers were roughly three times more likely to acknowledge these nine physical manifestations typical of kundalini activation than were the control subjects. Greyson (1993a) then administered a simplified 19-item index of the Bentov-Sannella physio-kundalini syndrome (Sannella, 1992) to 153 NDEers and 55 subjects who came close to death but did not have an NDE. Statistical evaluation of the results showed a significant difference between the two groups (p 0.0001).

The above studies and some findings from both literature and field research drew my attention to the significance of exploring another issue in relation to both transformative experiences and psychic functioning: the involvement of altered states of consciousness.

## Alternate States of Consciousness and Psi

In his study of NDEers, Ring (1991) emphasized that, apparently as the result of the experience, NDEers become more susceptible to altered (or non-ordinary) states of consciousness (ASCs).[1] Ring (1991) pointed out that NDE involves experiencing an ASC, and that those individuals who had experienced it are most likely to enter it again and remember it and the visions and/or events which happened in that state. Greyson (1983) found that after an NDE individuals reported significantly more occurrences of apparent psi-conducive states (e.g., unusually vivid dreams) than prior to the experience (p 0.0001).

It should be noted that the issue of psi-conducive states is still controversial in experimental parapsychology. On one hand, it was experimentally demonstrated that REM sleep (Ullman and Krippner, 1970; Ullman, Krippner, and Vaughan, 1973). lucid dreaming (LaBerge, 1993), hypnosis (Schechter, 1984), meditative states (Honorton, 1977), and the states induced by a *Ganzfeld* ("total field") procedure that creates a homogeneous perceptual environment (Bem and Honorton, 1994) are apparently conducive to psi. On the other hand, an attempted meta-analysis of ESP studies contrasting hypnosis and a comparison condition (Stanford and Stein, 1993) produced mixed results. Nevertheless, if we step outside the laboratory and examine anthropological data, apparent psi perception of information inaccessible by ordinary means is reported to occur in an ASC in virtually all cultures that employ shamanic practices (e.g., Kalweit, 1992). In describing a "hierarchy of levels running from normal to higher consciousness," Kalweit emphasized that "the principle that binds the various levels is an increasing feeling of unity" (1992:218) and that "...telepathy and clairvoyance arise through a strong feeling of unity between oneself and the environment" (1992:219).

In his writings, Stanislav Grof, a well-known researcher of ASCs, has expressed a similar view:

> There exists one interesting subcategory of transpersonal phenomena that can be frequently validated and even researched experimentally. Here belong telepathy, psychic diagnosis, clairvoyance, clairaudience, and other instances of extrasensory perception....From a broader perspective, there is no reason to sort out the so-called paranormal phenomena as a special category. Since many other types of transpersonal experiences quite typically involve access to new information about the universe through extrasensory channels, the clear boundary between psychology and parapsychology disappears, or becomes rather arbitrary, when the existence of the transpersonal domain is recognized and acknowledged....The transpersonal phenomena reveal connections between the individual and the cosmos which are at present beyond comprehension. All we can say is that somewhere in the process of...[individual] unfolding, a strange qualitative Moebius-like leap seems to occur, in which deep self-exploration of the individual unconscious turns into a process of experiential adventure in the universe-at-large, which involves what can best be described as cosmic consciousness or the superconscious mind.

> While the nature of transpersonal experiences is clearly fundamentally incompatible with mechanistic science, it...is of critical importance for any serious approach to such phenomena as psychedelic states, shamanism, religion, rites of passage, mythology, [and] parapsychology...(1988:162-164).

Thus, the issue of how to reconcile anthropological/experiential and laboratory findings regarding psi-conducive states remains open.

## NDE and Shamanic Initiation

In the course of inquiry, my attention was drawn to an opinion of psychologist Dr. Charles Tart who, in his introduction to McMoneagle's book, wrote:

> A crucial element in some...mystery religions was initiation. Not a mere formal ritual, as we have come to think of initiations, but trials, vision quests, undertaken only by the most serious seekers and aided by prolonged periods of fasting, purification, isolation, and drama. The highest kind of initiation involved inducing an NDE, such that the seeker knew from personal experience that the human mind was more than the body and would survive death.

> While the details of these procedures have been lost to us, a strange historical development has occurred. Modern medicine, not generally known for its spiritual bent has developed resuscitation technology that has effectively "initiated" many people into the Mysteries (1993:12).

This conclusion becomes clearer in light of Doore's description of simi-

larities between shamanic initiation journeys, yogic samadhi states and reports of NDEs:

> Whether through yogic meditation, shamanic drumming, or the use of sacred
> mind-altering plants, the candidate for knowledge is brought face-to-face with
> the experience of death and the states of consciousness that appear immediately
> after death. Sometimes this experience may be an actual close encounter with
> death, as in those cases in which a man or woman becomes a shaman after a
> serious illness; in other cases, the initiatory experience may be controlled by an
> experienced elder shaman or guru who may use any of a variety of techniques
> to bring about a non-life-threatening visionary "simulation" of the death
> experience (1990:267-268).

I find it very important to emphasize the above conclusion that symbolic
death/rebirth experience, ego-death in shamanic initiations, does not necessarily involve "an actual close encounter with death." I believe that popular
interpretations of legitimate attempts of researchers to study transformative
after-effects of NDEs present a danger. Some of the individuals who are
interested in psychological and spiritual transformation may, consciously or
unconsciously, become involved in a dangerous game of seeking situations
which bring them close to death—actually not to die but to be transformed.
This danger may be enforced by our Western culture which does not offer
accepted and easily accessible paths to ASCs and shamanic initiations. In
this connection. I would like to remind all of us of a relevant quote of Dag
Hammarskjold: "Do not seek death. Death will find you. But seek the road
which makes death a fulfillment" (1993).

## Conclusion

In my research, I found that all types of experiences which, similarly to
NDEs, seem to enhance a person's psychic awareness, do involve ASCs. In
particular, a shamanic initiation that involves an ASC appears to bestow psi
abilities as an inherent part of the newly acquired spectrum of abilities.
Therefore, a natural question arose: What if not a particular type of experience, but rather an ASC, is the common denominator of psi?

Researchers who conduct experimental studies of psi often emphasize
unreliability and elusiveness of psychic functioning (e.g., Schouten,
1993:313-314). Perhaps, the actual problem is not unreliability of psychic
functioning per se, but that many of those who attempt to bring psi into
laboratories do not understand nor accept the premise that psi manifests itself in an ASC.

Thus, in the course of my inquiry into correlates of psychic functioning,
I made a circle and returned to the beginning of my search, to shamanic
practices, initiations, and rites of passage. This circle, however, is a spiral
that, like a sacred spiral of a Native-American fire dance (Vilenskaya,

1992:137), takes us to our own center and to a new level of understanding of ourselves and the world. Again, as often happens, each end is a new beginning.

## Acknowledgements

I am grateful to all my friends and colleagues in Russia and in this country who generously shared with me their knowledge. My special thanks are to Dr. Ruth-Inge Heinze for her continuing support, Dr. Edwin C. May for kindly providing me with the time to complete this study, and to Charlotte Berney and Christine James for their editorial comments.

## *Note*

1. Heinze (1993) proposed the term "alternate states of consciousness," since ASCs have distinct state-specific qualities and don't "coexist" with other states. Some ASCs can be induced by various means, e.g., meditation, drumming, dancing, as well as hypnotic induction used in our Western culture. The NDE state, however, is caused by a natural, internal, not currently understood process.

## *References*

Bem, D.J., and C. Honorton. "Does psi exist? Replicable evidence for an anomalous process of information transfer," *Psychological Bulletin,* 115:1 (1994):4-18.

Brinkley, D. with P. Perry. *Saved by the Light.* New York: Villard Books, 1994.

Doore, G. "Journeys to the land of the dead: Shamanism and samadhi," *What Survives? Contemporary Explorations of Life after Death,* ed. G. Doore. Los Angeles, CA: Jeremy P. Tarcher, 1990, pp.265-272.

Galperin, Ya. G., ed. *Psikhologicheskiye Aspekty Otsenki Lichnosti Tselitelya* [Psychological Aspects of Personality Assessment of Healers]. Moscow: ENIOM, 1933. (In Russian)

Greyson, B. "Near-death experiences and the physio-kundalini syndrome," *Journal of Religion and Health,* 32:4 (1993a):277-290.

____ . "The physio-kundalini syndrome and mental illness," *Journal of Transpersonal Psychology,* 25:1 (1993b):43-58.

____ . "Increase in psychic phenomena following near-death experiences," *Theta,* 11:2 (1983):26-29.

Grof, S. *The Adventure of Self-Discovery.* Albany, NY: State University of New York Press, 1988.

Hammarskjold, Dag. "Verse," *The Unknown Region, Inspirations on Living and Dying,* ed. Eileen Campbell. Hammersmith, England: The Aquarian Press, 1993.

Harris, B. and L.C. Bascom. *Full Circle.* New York: Pocket Books.

Heaney, J.J. "Transpersonal states and near-death experiences," *Psyche and Spirit,* ed. J.J. Heaney. Ramsey, NJ: Paulist Press, 1984.

Heinze, R.-I. "Alternate states of consciousness," *Silver Threads: 25 Years of Parapsychology Research,* eds B. Kane, J. Millay, and D. Brown. Westport, CT: Praeger, 1993, pp.201-209.

Honorton, C. "The Ganzfeld novice: Four predictors of initial ESP performance," *Proceedings of the 35th Annual Convention of the Parapsychological Association.* Las Vegas, NV: August 9-13, 1992. Charlottesville, VA: The Parapsychological Association, Inc., 1992, pp.51-58.

_____ . "Psi and internal attention states," *Handbook of Parapsychology,* ed. B.B. Wolman. New York: Van Nostrand Reinhold, 1977, pp.435-472.

Kalweit, H. *Shamans, Healers and Medicine Men.* Boston, MA: Shambhala, 1992.

Kohr, R.L. "Near-death experiences, altered states, and psi sensitivity," *Anabiosis—The Journal for Near-Death Studies,* 3:2 (1983):15-176.

_____ . "Near-death experience and its relationship to psi and various altered states" *Journal of the American Society for Psychical Research,* 74 (1980):397-411.

Krader, L. "The shamanistic tradition of the Buryats (Siberia)," *Anthropos,* 7 0 (1975:105-144.

LaBerge, S. "A preliminary study of anomalous perception during lucid dreaming," *Phenomenological Research and Analysis* E.C. May, W.L.W. Luke, and N.D. Lantz, Final Report, SAIC Subcontract No.29-92-0085-71. Menlo Park, CA: SAC Cognitive Sciences Laboratory, 3 February 1993, Appendix E, pp.1-7.

Lantz, N.D. and R.J. Kiernan. *Neuropsychological Assessment of Participants in Psychoenergetic Tasks,* Final Report—Objective C, Task 5. Menlo Park, CA: SRI International, December 1986.

McMoneagle, J. *Mind Trek: Exploring Consciousness, Time and Space Through Remote Viewing.* Norfolk, VA: Hampton Roads Publishing, 1993.

*Moscow News,* "Yulia Vorobyova's 'blind' eyes," 17 (April 28-May 5, 1991):15.

Murphy, M. and S. Donovan. *The Physical and Psychological Effects of Meditation.* San Rafael, CA: Esalen Institute, 1989.

Palmer, J.A. "Attitudes and personality traits in experimental ESP research," *Handbook of Parapsychology,* ed. B.B. Wolman. New York: Van Nostrand Reinhold, 1977, pp.175-201.

Ring, K. "The near-death experience," *Path Beyond Ego: The Transpersonal Vision,* eds R. Walsh and F. Vaughan. Los Angeles, CA: Jeremy P. Tarcher/Perigee, 1993, pp.195-205.

_____ . *The Omega Project: Near-Death Experiences, UFO Encounters, and Mind at Large.* New York: William Morrow/Quill, 1992.

_____ . "Paranormal antecedents and aftereffects of near-death experiences: Findings from new research," *ASPR Newsletter,* 17:3 (1991:47-49.

_____ . *Life at Death*. New York: Coward, McCann and Geoghegan, 1980.

Rogers, H.H. "Conference report: Parapsychology and the near-death experience," *Applied Psi Newsletter*, 2:1-2 (1983):11-12.

Sannella, L. *The Kundalini Experience*. Lower Lake, CA: Integral Publishing, rev.ed., 1992. (Originally published in 1976)

Schechter, E.I. "Hypnotic induction vs. control conditions: Illustrating an approach to the evaluation of replicability in parapsychology," *Journal of the American Society for Psychical Research*, 78 (1984)1-27.

Schouten, S.A. "Are we making progress?" *Psi Research Methodology: A Re-Examination. Proceedings of an International Conference held in Chapel Hill, NC, October 29-30 1988 eds. L. Coly and J.D.S. McMahon. New York: Parapsychology Foundation, 1993 pp.295-322.*

Schroter-Kunhardt,M. "A review of near-death experiences," *Journal of Scientific Exploration*, 7:3 (1993):219-239.

Stanford, R.G. and A. Stein, "A meta-analysis of ESP studies contrasting hypnosis and a comparison condition," *Proceedings of the 36th Annual Convention of the Parapsychological Association*, Toronto, Canada, August 15-19, 1993. Charlottesville, VA: The Parapsychological Association, Inc., pp.105-125.

Sutherland, C. "Psychic phenomena following near-death experiences, *Journal of Near-Death Studies*, 9 (1990):93-102.

Targ, R. and K. Harary. *The Mind Race: Understanding and Using Psychic Abilities*. New York: Villard Books, 1984.

Ullman, M. and S. Krippner. *Dream Studies and Telepathy: An Experimental Approach*. New York: Parapsychology Foundation, 1970.

Ullman, M., S.Krippner, and A. Vaughan. *Dream Telepathy*. New York: Macmillan, 1973.

Vilenskaya, L. "Where Science and Spirit Intersect: Parapsychological Research in the Former Soviet Union," *Proceedings of the Tenth International Conference on the Study of Shamanism and Alternate Modes of Healing*, ed. R.-I. Heinze. Berkeley, CA: Independent Scholars of Asia, Inc., 1993, pp.158-172.

_____ . "The Sacred Fire: Healing among Cherokee Indians—A Personal Perspective," *Proceedings of the Ninth International Conference on the Study of Shamanism and Alternate Modes of Healing*, ed. R.-I. Heinze. Berkeley, CA: Independent Scholars of Asia, Inc., 1992, pp.133-143.

_____ , and J. Steffy. *Firewalking: A New Look at an Old Enigma*. Falls Village, CT: The Bramble Company, 1991.

Wilbur, Richard Purdy. "For Wilbur" (1969, reproduced in a Xeroxed anthology of poems, 1992), p.750.

# RITUALISTIC SMOKING AS FOOD FOR THOUGHT: ESOTERIC PRACTICE IN NATIVE NORTHWESTERN CALIFORNIA

Jack Norton (Hupa-Cherokee) and Jana Rivers Norton

## Part I: Significance of the Act

Two years ago my four-year-old granddaughter and I were driving along a ridge road when she saw a dead deer lying near the edge. Deer are a relatively common sight on the Hoopa Indian Reservation in northwestern California, but this was the first dead deer she had seen so close. "Perhaps we should stop and offer it tobacco to help its spirit pass to the next world," I suggested. As we sprinkled tobacco on the carcass, we said aloud, "May your spirit journey to help you make payment along the way."

In the following months and years we have generally followed this procedure for many animals slain along the roads that intrude into their territories and threaten their lives. Once we made payment to a hazel bush before cutting a branch to form a hockey stick in her imaginary competition on ice, and it seemed she had grasped a genuine insight into this ontological universality because in several instances she initiated rituals or had suggested that her daddy might follow her example when hunting in the fall.

Last year, however, as we were driving, she looked up and quietly said, "Poppa, my teacher's aid said that giving tobacco to dead animals is silly and does not do any good. Tobacco is dirty and we must not handle it." For a trusting kindergartner, teachers and their helpers are paramount and in the excitement of learning and developing relationships to their classmates, the value and truth of their world is fragile. Who is Tasha, my granddaughter, to believe? By what right does a institutionalized system have to assault another culture? What epistemological stance will she take in the coming years? Will she and her children's children live graciously and beautifully within this earth? Will they honor all life and liveliness?

Perhaps I am overreacting because of my love for Tasha and all young children. Children are gifts of beauty from the creation and each is special. Each is unique. There is no one that is the same, yet all children are given a universal love of their parents. They ask for nothing but a reciprocation of that truth. However, few are accorded this love, and most will end up suppressing the abuse and assaults from their loved ones or an uncaring, arbitrary, profane society. Thus the reciprocated hurt to others by the criminal lies in these early patterns of denial to spiritual integrity. As adults they will have the size and strength to release the unconscious forces from a paradoxical and inimical situation of receiving hurt from a fundamental condition of love. It is frightening to now hear that some fourteen-year olds and younger have murdered adults or beaten even younger children to death. Every criminal act and resultant pain has here its genesis. Yet, fortunately, not all children are abused nor do all abused children become criminals.

It is in this grace that my hope for Tasha and all children resides. If I continue demonstrations of responsibility and respect to all things: rocks, trees, animals, humans, and spirits, for example, then Tasha will have a foundation that contramands the lifelessness and exploitative views of present values. When she is an adult, she will have choices that content against the pain and darkness. But, perhaps, she and I are fortunate because we still inhabit a world where these lessons are viable. We still have original ceremonies and supporting legends that clearly demonstrate patterns of experiencing the marvelous mystery of life and the attendant paths within it.

Recently our spiritual leader, we call them doctors, stated succinctly:

> ...this physical is a battleground and it's within the dark and that we individually existed before we entered into the physical. We are here at Creator's desires. We each, individually, were given purposes for our existence here. We were not sent into this darkness unarmed. We were given three weapons: the prayer pipe, the spiritual dance grounds, and the spiritual places up on the mountains for guidance and protection and security—to show us the way—to guide us (McClellan, (1985:64).

This paper discusses the role of the pipe as one of the three weapons or gifts Creator gave us to make choices that enhance life and contest against darkness and discord. The pipe, and of course, tobacco is a sentient being and the responsible person ritually smoking stands between the sacred and the profane, the mystical and practical, the unknown and known. While standing within the center, upon this threshold, we are guided by the truths of spiritual realities through legends, myths and direct leadership of spiritual doctors.

## Part II: Mythic Constructs

Myths, perceived within an epistemological dimension, can thus be identified as sources of human consciousness and transformative insights. Such an interpretation acknowledges the necessity of psychic wholeneSs found in mythic images and primordial gestures as well as embraces the importance of place, purpose and performance. The spiritual efficacy of various verbal instructions intrinsic to native northwestern California, for example, is paramount to the continuance and well-being of the individual and the community. Vital to cultural well-being, a native northwestern mythological perspective expresses the wisdom and creative imagination of an individual, a society, a Creator.

Native northwestern California mythos is seen by many indigenous peoples as both practical and spiritual, acting as gentle guides, which teach ancient truths as they relate to a specific environment as well as a universal reality.

Myths speak of balance, how to live in harmony with the earth, with the cosmos and with each other. Myths unfold meaning, stimulate awareness and psychological growth. Most importantly, myths render an epistemological image of the universe, a perception of creation, which allows a vision of one's place within the sacred circumference of the world. These mythic constructs, when applied to the esoteric practice of ritual smoking, reveal a complex weave, a pattern of significance and spiritual fortitude, woven from integral fibers to create the fabric of native northwestern cosmology. For example, the Yurok story, "Pulekukwerek Travels and Makes the Sky," begins as the Sky Possessor journeys across the Yurok world to weave a gigantic sky net before the Yurok people came to be.

### Pulekukwerek Travels and Makes the Sky

Pulekukwerek took out his pipe and prepared to smoke. There was nothing there, no fire, and the floor [of the house] was smooth. Pulekukwerek took out his fire drill and turned it. It burned. He lit the pipe and gave it to [Sky Possessor] to draw at.

[Sky Possessor] took it, sucked once, and spoke, "You are the kind of man I like to see."

Pulekukwerek said, "I shall live with you if you will do what I wish."

"Yes, it is well," said the man, "whatever you say I shall do."

"I will tell you,' said Pulekukwerek. "I have gone halfway [over the world]. I want to make all this world good. Then I thought and looked up, but could see nothing. I wish we had fog close by [above]. It would look well."

[Sky Possessor] replied, "Well, light another [pipe]. Then we shall go out and you will tell me what it is you wish to have."

Pulekukwerek gave him another pipeful, for Pulekukwerek had grown with his hand full of tobacco. It was never gone. He always had it with him....They went out. Pulekukwerek said, "If you can make it that, it will be called sky, Wes'ona. If you can make it that in the evening we see something good. We shall call that stars."

Pulekukwerek set his fire drill. He tried [to light his pipe] but it was too windy. Then he went inside the coil [of strings out of which they were to make the sky]. There he got fire and lit his pipe....He took the pipe, drew it well, went to the middle [of the strings], put its opening over the cross of the strings, blew, and it spread out. Then he went to the right end, put the end of the string into the pipe, blew and fog came out and spread. Some are black and some are white. They are clouds....

Then the man said, "Now, what are we going to do?"

Pulekukwerek said, "Now, we will raise [the sky net]. But wait. I shall make the stars." Then Pulekukwerek lit his pipe to make the stars. He drew long, blew the smoke into his...hand, threw it down, blew into his hand again, threw the smoke downward, again and again, and made the stars (Lame Willy of Weitspun, 1907/1976:116-130).

Pulekukwerek, as a spiritual being, brings beauty into existence for the benefit of those who will follow him into this world. As a vital force of creation, Pulekukwerek demonstrates the importance and purpose of ritualistic tobacco use. That is, as a method for obtaining sincere, heart-felt endeavors of personal or cosmological magnitude. As a creative element, Pulekukwerek signifies the importance of balance and the proper utilization of esoteric practice—to establish a relationship with the spiritual forces residing in the physical landscape. For a participant to be successful, an active relationship with the sky is essential, since the sky within a native northwestern epistemological framework, is a part of everything that exists. *Ki wes'onah* is, as anthropologist Thomas Buckley writes, "energy which moves against itself and creates waves and these waves go through everything" (1989:37). Hence, as my teachers indicate, and I understand it, curing, redemptive power comes from the sky—from the source of all things—and this energy can be utilized and transformed in significant ways, creating a diversity of healing potential by those who, through years of aesthetic training, *hohkep* (purification), which smoking is an inherent part of, have earned the ability and responsibility of being *teno:ek* (well-versed) in matters of spirit.

The ritualistic use of tobacco is, however, a serious process, which requires austerity and a focused resolve. It is a form of religious contemplation and communication with the forces of nature, and as such, should only be practiced with the utmost care.

## Pulekukwerek and Tobacco

At first, tobacco was not used. People took pepperwood leaves, dried them, and smoked them as tobacco. Many were killed by that, it is so strong.

Then Pulekukwerek came to smoke it and did not like it. He is the one who threw it away. He used [true] tobacco, he said,

"I will give you seeds as you can raise it for yourselves." Then they planted it, grew it, and smoked it after it was dry.

But some tobacco was still too strong. People smoking it fell over and died. Pulekukwerek...heard that this tobacco was even worse than the pepperwood tobacco and killed more people. So he came upriver. All along they were raising tobacco. He came to Rekwoi. There he began to smoke. He said, "No one will be killed by this," and he blew tobacco out from his hand. Then he went up along the river to other places.

At Kenek, he heard, the Earthquakes lived, ten of them, and it was a bad place to smoke. That is why he went to Kenek, because the ten Earthquake brothers killed people there with their tobacco....

Pulekukwerek came into the sweat house. He saw much tobacco hanging in baskets in the sweat house, drying. He said, "That is what I want: I like to smoke." Then he smoked [with them]. He smoked seven pipes. He was talking as if he did not feel anything: they saw him act like this. When he had smoked nine pipes, they saw that he was feeling it. When he had smoked ten, he fell over. They carried him out and threw him in the brush.

One day the children there said, "There is a little boy up here on the rocks. He is sliding down them." That was Pulekukwerek come to life again....He came back to the sweat house.

Pulekukwerek said, "This tobacco will kill no one anymore. Anyone can smoke it." So it is that no one is killed by tobacco, because Pulekukwerek stopped them from killing people there (Jack of Murek, 1907/1976:367-368).

Pulekukwerek restores the proper balance and helps people learn the appropriateness of their action. As a force of balance, Pulekukwerek embodies the importance of discovering and maintaining equilibrium through esoteric means. Ritualized smoking is one method for obtaining these ends by way of earning a dialogical relationship with universal forces through spiritually enacted reciprocity. For the act of smoking is said to feed the spirituals that which they are always thankful for. This is keenly illustrated within the Yurok story "Water-Monster Helper" wherein the spiritual initiate must pay ten baskets of tobacco to a mythic, liminal entity called a Kames or water monster. It lived near the initiate's village of Wespen along the Klamath River and had helped the initiate to recover his stolen child. Similar to the Thunder Brothers, in the preceding story, the Kames can be described as the manifestation of *woge* (spiritual) energy. The initiate who is on a journey for spiritual insights into the nature of reality and the nature of his own reality in conjunction with the natural realm, seeks medicine making abilities to heal his sick child within the watery depths of the Klamath. Water's potential here as "the reservoir of all potentialities of existence," as Mircea Eliade (1969:151) contends, is an essential aspect of native northwestern metaphysics since to make medicine takes the ability to overcome one's most inner fear in order to discover who one really is. The story depicts the initiates efforts to do so through direct contact with a water monster, or that which is seen as highly dangerous, yet that which possesses extreme transformative, life-giving potential. The initiate, through his earnest quest, earns the pity of the Kames who helps rescue the child and gives him the formula for the proper medicine.

...So he carried the tobacco there, [where the Kames was] ten baskets, and he put it on top of the rock. So he crawled up, that Kames to get his tobacco. It was his pay, that tobacco, for having helped him. And [the Kames] said to the one who grew at Wespen, "Take marrow and rub it on him; that is how he will have his flesh again, that child. He will be well from that." And the child became wholly well (Jim of Pekwan, 1907/1976:398).

The Yurok story "The Water Monster Helper" clearly demonstrates not only the healing potential of ritualized tobacco if used correctly and for the benefit of creation, but reveals the very special relationship that may develop between the spiritual practitioner and spiritual entities which inhabit the native northwestern California landscape. Personalized, esoteric practice has a pragmatic as well as a highly sacred nature, which may help those practitioners individually and collectively as a people.

...The woge said, "If a person wants to tell me something, let him [or her] come up [into the hills] in the evening and stay all night. Let [them] bring tobacco...and angelica root, only those two. And he [or she] must be careful [beforehand]: [they] must get sweat house wood, and drink no water, and go with no women [or men]. Then I shall answer [them] if [they call] my name; but if [they] do not do that I shall not answer; and if I answer, [they] will have what [they] want (Mack of Weitspus, 1907/1976:291).

This I and thou exchange between human beings and the beingness of the natural realm, which develops from proper esoteric means, is the real potential elicited within the mythic constructs of native northwestern metaphysics. Tobacco as a transformative, reciprocal agent of healing strength, as an agent which may lead to individual wellness and community continuance, is deeply rooted in the spiritual tenets and lessons taught. The pity and guidance of creation as it is embodied within the spirituality infused landscape of native northwestern California is a viable and necessary part of achieving balance in the cosmos as well as maintaining both psychological and physiological wellness.

Yet the ritualized use of tobacco is not only a means for achieving a relationship to the physical world of matter. It involves learning the ability to transform one's own being in such a way that the true nature of the universe is revealed. The sacred prayer pipe, as a weapon against the darkness or unknown aspects of one's own being, is considered not only a vehicle of such transformation, it is a living entity which becomes infused with the spiritual strength of the practitioner, as well as a passage way for the healing strength of the universe to enter one's heart during the ritual process. According to several myths, the pipe is indeed alive with spirit.

> The pipes were called pegwolau orowos. I think the house in which they are kept is called pegwolau because the pipes are made of pegwol [soapstone). They were a pair or mates. Therefore they were called "married" (wohpema). They were kept in the house, buried in a stone box or cyst with a cover. I do not know whether the male or the female pipe or both were used in the [first salmon] ceremony. Anciently, the man who kept them, the head of the house, opened the cyst every month and threw angelica root into it. When white people were first seen on the coast, one or two at a time appearing along the beach a few days apart (about 1850), the house was burned by some of them and one of the pipes was broken across in two places. The man who then kept them...was afraid that the unbroken pipe might leave its cyst and the house because its mate was broken. Hence he made it a new mate. This like the original one made completely of stone and one foot long....In the old days, pipes made completely of stone were not smoked or allowed to be used otherwise; and later on, when Indians began to make them to sell to whites, my father was against it (Spott, 1942:171-172).

Hence, a belief in the integrity and purpose of creation, whatever the manifestation of form, and the ritualized demonstration of that belief is paramount before one even begins to live a spiritually enacted life.

The mythic examples shared give us as listeners an opportunity to look within our own hearts, within our own lives, to address the wounds of modern existence. We have the choice to either divine the natural rhythms of the universe through our own authentic, esoteric means and in return be blessed by the beauty and compassion of the universe, which the *woge* represent, or to turn our backs to our own beauty and hence the beauty of creation and become, as a traditional doctor of native northwestern California suggests, "lost to Creator" (McClellan, 1985:64), misplaced and alienated from each other and the world. Yet always there is a price—a responsibility implicit in the choices one makes to integrate the energies of creation. Our choice as Indo-Europeans who now dwell upon the ancient soil, still held sacred by the original people of this continent, may very well be to face our own fears that have arisen out of actions such as disturbing or destroying objects of sacred significance or embodied acts of ignorance that assault cultural differences. We must remember that even the most earnest attempt to restore our own sense of oneness to place, may be an intrusion, even an offense to the integrity of certain sacred areas if we do not fully grasp the specific, ordained function that place serves within an indigenous cosmological perspective. In addition, we may be required to once again embrace European lands we left behind in order to open to the ancestral, spiritual entities of our own racial memories, and finally, to live our lives with humility and grace, knowing that we may be required to seek beauty in all things.

## References

Buckley, T. "Doing your thinking," *I Become Part of It: Sacred Dimensions in Native American Life,* eds D.M. Dooling and P.J. Smith. San Francisco, CA: Harper and Row, 1989.

Eliade, M. *Images and Symbols: Studies in Religious Symbolism.* New York: Sheed & Ward, 1969.

Jack of Murek. "Pulekukwerek and tobacco" (1907), *Yurok Myths,* ed, A.L. Kroeber. Berkeley, CA: University of California Press, 1976.

Jim of Pekwan. 'The Water-Monster Helper" (1907), *Yurok Myths,* ed. A.L. Kroeber. Berkeley, CA: University of California Press, 1976.

Lame Willy of Weitspun. "Pulekukwerek travels and makes the Sky" (1907), *Yurok Myths*, ed. A.L. Kroeber. Berkeley, CA: University of California Press, 1976.

Mack of Weitspus. "Origin of death" (1907), *Yurok Myths,* ed. A.L. Kroeber. Berkeley, CA: University of California Press, 1976.

McClellan, R. Set her for you. Video transcripts. Arcata, CA: Shanandoah Films, Inc., 1985.

Spott, R. "First salmon rite at Welkway," *Yurok Narratives.* Berkeley, CA: University of California Press, 1942.

# TWO WAYS TO DIE: APOPTOSIS AND NECROSIS

Cheri Quincy

*As above, so below*
*As within, so without.*

The mechanisms of biology offer profound insights into the behavior of the complete organisms. Ontogeny recapitulates phylogeny. For example, when the mechanisms of nerve transmission at the molecular level are examined, insight into possible types of perception, thought and behavior are illuminated. Metaphors from immunology are applied to cultural pathologies and processes. Social cancers are "cut out," children are "vaccinated" against violence. I propose that the specific molecular processes of dying, of the termination and recycling of our intracellular parts, are not simply disintegration events at the end of life, but also a model for the transfer of consciousness that occurs in the process of "natural" death. Apoptosis is the name of this process in biology. This survival of information, of our essence, beyond death, may be parallel to descriptions of *Phowa,* the transfer of consciousness at the moment of death in Tibetan spiritual practice. In the words of Padmasambhava,

> Human beings face two causes of death: untimely death and death due to the exhaustion of their natural lifespan....like a lamp which has run out of oil. There is no way of averting death...; you have to get ready to go (Sogyal Rinpoche, 1992:244).

The process of individual cell death (irreversible loss of vital structure and function) has recently been examined by molecular biologists. It is now apparent that there are two types and mechanisms of cell death, *apoptosis* (apo-tosis) and *necrosis.* Apoptosis, first noticed and named in 1972 (Kerr *et al,* 1972:239-257), is also known as "programmed" or "physiologic" cell death (or PCD) and is an active, natural form of cell death (or suicide) that occurs in many cells throughout the body. It is complementary, but opposite, to *mitosis* (cell reproduction) in normal, healthy homeostasis. Apoptosis is the major process responsible for normal cell death in embryological remodeling, brain development, adult cell turnover and differentiation, and prior to healing after some diseases. The apoptosis process includes an activation step, production of specific proteins, activation of an internal endonuclease (an enzyme that deconstructs nucleic acids—DNA, RNA) and then an orderly contraction and resorption of the nucleic material, *before the cell membrane integrity is lost.* The cell shrinks, and no inflammation occurs. All this happens very quickly, within a few minutes, and seems to occur in individual cells in an organ or tissue essentially at random. For example, nine out of ten thymus cells will die by this method, but we cannot tell which will die or which will survive, prior to the event. Liver cells, skin cells, brain cells, white blood cells, all cells are potentially subject to apoptosis, and all cells contain the genetic instructions to do so. Millions of cells die every hour. In fact, parts of us are dying all the time. Our health depends on it.

Necrosis, on the other hand, occurs when cells die instantaneously in response to an overwhelming insult, toxin or trauma (accidental or violent death). Cells are broken, or swell and burst, and contents are released all at once, usually damaging or killing other cells nearby. In necrosis, the cell membrane is irreparably damaged, proteins and nucleotides coagulate and leak into the surrounding tissue. These released fluids result in the classical medical signs of tissue damage: heat, pain, swelling, redness, and loss of function. These effects do *not* occur in apoptosis (PCD). In response to the perception of free fluids, substance P, one of the mediators of inflammation causing pain (capsicum is an analogue of substance P, and causes "pure" pain when applied to a mucus membrane), the immune system is activated to send repair cells, fibroblasts, to make a scab and then a scar, white cells to phagocytose cell fragments and invading bacteria or dirt, and a variety of other messages to begin and complete repairs of the injured tissue. These repair events do not occur in apoptosis. Apoptosis, therefore, is not damage.

## Human Dying

Can the discovery of these two very different processes generate insight into the process of human conscious dying? Can human beings die in two different ways? Is this something over which we have conscious control or choice? Individual cell death can be triggered by stress (Fischman, 1993:1211); so can organism death. Cells die when they age, as do we, and by as many different time-tables. Apparently, some cells die to limit the adverse effects of an area of necrosis, or severe injury, and thereby enhance the survival of their neighbors ("cytologic altruism"!). Such self-sacrifice occurs at the human level also. Cells isolated from their targets invoke suicide programs; so do we. What is the mechanism? What are the signals? What is the message?

In apoptosis, cells go through specific steps. First, there is a reversible, pre-commitment stage, then an irreversible commitment to die, and then an active process of specific protein production and preparation, prior to actual activation of the terminal events. I believe these stages profoundly clarify some of the questions about the timing and stages of "natural" human death, the triggers and influences associated with the end of life, and the prospect for personal survival after death, including the mechanisms by which it may occur. Apoptosis may help us understand our intuitive antipathy to violent, or accidental death, which does not empower the transfer of information, and a natural death which is not painful and includes a pre-terminal transfer of information "code," the DNA, our physiologic memories, an essence of ourselves.

## Cell Survival

NEW Research published in *Science* just last year revealed that

During the development of the vertebrate nervous system, up to 50 percent or more of many types of neurons die soon after they form synaptic connections with their target cells. This is thought to reflect the failure of these neurons to obtain adequate amounts of specific neurotrophic factors...signals from other cells required for survival. These survival signals seem to act by suppressing an intrinsic cell suicide program (Raff, *et al*, 1993:695-700).

Apparently all of our cells require specific electro-chemical communication in order to survive. Cell persistence is directly related to the amount and quality of a cell's connection to other cells in the organism. For individual human beings it has been demonstrated that isolated individuals have decreased survival, and that people in relationship, even with a pet, live longer than those living alone. For our cells, both the quality and the quantity of communication is important, but in some situations one may compensate for scarcity of the other.

These trophic factors, the mediators of survival, include varieties of NGF (nerve growth factors) and transmitters that *de-activate* intrinsic death processes. Natural death is mediated by genetic information. Some of the specific genes responsible for apoptosis are known (e.g., *bcl-2, bax, bcl-x*). They are the same in all mammals and are in fact evolutionarily conserved from worms to man, suggesting their fundamental value to all types of life. Programmed cell death has been observed in nematodes, insects, plants, amphibians, fish, birds and mammals (Schwartzman and Cidlowski, 1993). This process occurs inside the cocoon, deleting juvenile tissues, during the metamorphosis of insects. The process is described evocatively in *The Secret Life of Plants:*

> ...worm-like rootlets, which Darwin likened to a brain, burrow constantly downward with thin white threads, crowding themselves firmly into the soil, tasting it as they go....As the special burrowing cells are worn out by contact with stones...they are replaced, but when they reach a source of nourishment *they die,* and are replaced by cells designed to collect the mineral salts (Tompkins, 1989:x).

The *timely* invocation of natural death is vitally important to normal growth and health maintenance. What would happen if we "turned off" the death genes? For example, when one of the genes (bcl-2) that prevents death is overactive and cells don't die "on time," a specific kind of cancer results. Our bodies continually produce new white blood cells, and, if they do not die within a few days, follicular b-cell lymphoma, a kind of leukemia occurs. And our protective "killer T cells" presumably kill target organisms by inducing PCD. PCD also eliminates T-cells that malfunction and/or become self-reactive (auto-immune). Suggestions that HIV infection predisposes T cells to premature apoptosis have led to exciting new approaches for research against AIDS. (For example, immunosuppressive drugs can stop white cell apoptosis, but to use them to treat an immunodeficiency disease will take some study.)

Cell suicide has been shown to be involved in cellular effects resulting from irradiation, chemotherapy, ischemia, trauma, ATP (energy) depletion, neuronal injury, low blood sugar, excessive excitation, free radical damage and even genetic errors. In our bodies, for a cell, it is "better to be dead than damaged," or in error. In fact, the accumulation of cellular damage and the toleration of error may be responsible for some of the deterioration effects we ascribe to aging. In the PCD scenario, *aging is actually a failure of physiologic death and replacement processes.* Only by resisting death can a cell accumulate damage and stay alive or "age." A human fibroblast can double 60 to 70 times, then it stops. The last cell is as healthy as the first. Timing is everything: gestation, birth, growth, and death may be in one line, damage, deterioration and aging seem to occur on separate time lines; they may not be causally linked, and they interact in complicated ways.

What are the messengers that regulate this process? Interleukins, NGF, proteins, free radicals, neurotransmitters, stress hormones, minerals and antibodies, sometimes in specific sequences. Prostate cells die by apoptosis when deprived of testosterone. Adrenal cells die without ACTH. When given barbiturates or progesterone, *fewer* liver cells die, and the liver enlarges. Size reverts to normal when the drugs are removed. The genes of PCD and their protein products are being investigated as oncogenes (cancer causing genes), tumor suppressors, anti-infective agents, growth re-modulators, and antiaging agents. But it seems that the boundary between growing and dying is a narrow one and that neither is unregulated. In fact, the principle of "checks and balances" is well utilized by our physiology. The maintenance of a balance between cell death and cell rebirth (reincarnation?) is complicated. "I create a new body every year," (Chopra, Winter 1993:19).

## Cell Death

The genes controlling cell suicide exist in all living cells. At least two genes trigger it, and are normally repressed by outside messengers. At least one gene represses it and can be turned off, to initiate the process. Once the conditions occur that predispose or commit a cell to suicide, what is the process from there? How does this occur, and what happens to the information (DNA, RNA,...) contained in the cell?

The memory of each cell is represented by the sum of its contents, but primarily by its DNA, RNA, and associated nuclear matrix ("I would like to propose that what we call our physical body is just a place that our memories call home for the time being" [Chopra, 1993]). Apoptosis begins with the activation of specific endonucleases (enzymes) that clip the nucleic acids into small, 200 base-pair sections, condensing them. Apoptosis will not occur if the endonuclease is inactivated or blocked. There is no apparent proteolysis of histones or other nuclear proteins. Organelle, like mitochondria, seem to stay intact to the last. Finally, the cell membrane shrinks around the pieces and the cell is phagocytosed (actively absorbed) by its neighbors, even by cells not normally phagocytic, like skin cells. The cellular information is transferred to these neighbors and a new cell is created.

## Questions/Hypotheses

Does death via apoptosis, a "natural death," continue a complete reso-nance of the "death-ed" cell or the "deathed" individual? Does artificial or accidental death destroy (all/part of) the crystal coherence of the chemical energy state; terminating instead of de-resolution. In accidental death, recy-cling of the components takes place after complete digestion only. (How does morphologic resonance [Sheldrake] apply to this model?)

Generational continuity of formation may depend on the uninterrupted sequential natural deaths received by subsequent generations. On a cellular level, do the re-absorbed genetic fragments somehow enrich or enhance or modify (or educate) the surrounding cells in the organism-through-time? A bootstrapping to immortality—like the eternal amoeba—splitting into two over and over again—unless terminated by accident.

*What is the possibility of the persistence of personal consciousness?* Like the nuclear matrix in our cells, and our personal memory, personal consciousness is continually modified by its own experience and enlarged by the experiences of others (information) it receives on its path in time and in-carnation. Resist change, stay the same, or be changed and re-arranged, "your" choice! When is change growth? When is change damage? Choose to die (activate apoptosis) at the right time and be absorbed by the surround-ing "other"? This "Luminous Ground"? Or stay alive, acquire error, "age," and die in pain. If all souls survive, could those practiced in the *painless* transfer of consciousness be less likely to acquire karma in the process of dying itself?

*And where did these genes come from?* A gift from the Green? Or per-haps a viral gene, misapplied? The redundancy built into the process of apoptosis (i.e., two genes that activate, one to suppress, each with a fail-safe switching system), suggests the "we" are still tinkering with the balance between growth and decay, transformation and boredom...apoptosis and mi-tosis.

Additionally, since there is no inflammation, the process of physiologic cell death is painless. Pain is a message amplified by the neuro-immune system, calling for repair responses. Natural cell dying and subsequent re-placement does not cause pain; it is a natural process, of no threat to the organism, no repair is required, no scars are formed. Perhaps one of the messages from our biology is that there is no pain if the transfer of memory occurs before the external envelope ruptures. A description of this process be the advice I heard years ago from Jean Millay, "...as every good witch knows, your soul must leave your body before the flames hit your feet."

One part of dying is to release attachments and dissociate from identifi-cation with the body. Pain is a powerful attachment. If death is accidental and occurs in a state of pain, then the opportunity to acquire karma due to the persons's reaction to pain (fear, anger, confusion, denial, etc.) may be increased. Or, if death is not done via apoptosis, perhaps the transfer of information is chaotic or incomplete. That is, if death is not an active process, there may not be survival of coherent information. Do not pass! Go!

Models that may apply to the transfer of genetic/nucleic information have recently been published, e.g., "Liquid-crystalline mesophases of ...DNA...."

> If our cognitive knowledge is viewed as a "crystal" of digitized data surrounded by a "solution" of analogically coded information, including emotions and instincts, then there is a dynamic interaction between the solution and the crystal. The crystal tends to dissolve when our emotional state is elevated, and to "recrystallize" when the emotions/energy subsides....When we develop a sufficiently high pitch of emotion, we can realign our whole conceptual set; this in fact is one function of religious ritual and revivals (Greyson, 1991).

# Phowa

*The Tibetan Book of Living and Dying* says,

> The Phowa practice that is most commonly used is known as the "phowa of three recognitions": recognition of our central channel as the path; recognition of our consciousness as the traveler; and recognition of a buddha realm as the destination.

> The painful bardo of dying lasts from the beginning of the process of dying right up until the end of what is known as the "inner respiration"; this, in turn, culminates in the dawning of the nature of mind, what we call the "Ground Luminosity," at the moment of death (Sogyal Rinpoche, 1992).

## Further,

> Now that the bardo of dying dawns upon me,
> I will abandon all grasping, yearning and attachment,
> Enter undistracted into clear awareness of the teaching,
> *And eject my consciousness into the space of unborn Rigpa.*
> As I leave this compound body of flesh and blood,
> I will know it to be a transitory illusion *(ibid).*

## From the Stages of Dissolution,

> At the time of death, the five inner elements gradually dissolve into one another....At the time when consciousness dissolves into space, which is like fainting, if we have had good realization of the emptiness of the Dharmakaya while meditating in our previous life and have confidence in this understanding, then we will recognize this state and will be liberated into the Dharmakaya (Norbu, 1991).

> At present our mind is encased in a net, the net of the "wind of karma." And the "wind of karma" is encased itself in a net, the net of our physical body...as soon as our body has separated into mind and matter, in the gap before it is

encased once again in the net of a future body, the mind...is independent, free... and we can recognize the nature of mind (Sogyal Rinpoche, 1992).

## References

Chopra, Deepak. " Timeless Mind, Ageless Body," *Noetic Bulletin* (Winter 1993):19.

Fischman, J. "This is your brain on stress," *Science, 262* (November 19, 1993):1211.

Greyson, Bruce. "Near-Death Experiences and Systems Theories: A Biosociological Approach to Mystical States," *The Journal of Mind and Behavior* (1991).

Kerr, J.F.R., A.H. Wylie, and A.R. Currie. "Apoptosis: a basic biological phenomenon with wide-ranging implications in tissue kinetics" *Br.J. Cancer, 26* (1972):239-257.

Norbu, Thinley. "The Stages of Dissolving [Tibet: Thim-rim)," *The Small Golden Key.* New York: Jewell Publishing, 1991.

Raff, M.C. *et al.* "Programmed Cell Death and the Control of Cell Survival: Lessons from the Nervous System," *Science, 262* (October 29, 1993):695-700.

Schwartzman, R.A. and J.A. Cidlowski. "Apoptosis: The Biochemistry and Molecular Biology of Programmed Cell Death," *Endocrine Reviews, 14:2* (1993).

Sogyal Rinpoche, *The Tibetan Book of Living and Dying.* New York: Harper, Collins, 1992.

# A SHAMANIC EXPLORATION IN HEALING
# PART III: THE JOURNEY HOME

C. Jess Groesbeck

This presentation is the last of a three-part series. It began, three years ago, with an essay entitled, "Psychotherapy and Demonic Possession." Two years ago, I made a second presentation, "When a Healer Dies."

This year I want to continue an unusual case report on a woman named Eurydice. Thirty-eight years old and Caucasian, she had been, for a number of years, in intense Jungian psychoanalysis for her dissociative, multiple personality disorder.

There had been an integration or fusion of many personalities in the mid-1980s. Most of the personalities had been fused by 1990, when a very angry personality named Ava appeared. It was around the time of Eurydice's divorce which went on for two and a half years. During this time, she had a mild stroke from which she eventually recovered. She also had an episode of breast cancer.

The initial paper in this series focused on the etiology of cancer and it was suggested that the shamanic illness of spirit intrusion may have contributed to this condition.

In the second paper, I explored the unusual development during which Eurydice's cancer, as it progressed, intimately involved her main healing personality—my wife. Sharon Groesbeck was a nurse and a psychotherapist. Eurydice asked Sharon to be with her when she would be dying (she had been pronounced terminal in the mid-part of 1991). Sharon said "yes," but tragically died herself in November of 1991. What ensued was an incredible shamanic journey, with many healing forces operating, to keep Eurydice alive.

The second paper addressed the question what seems to take place when a healer dies. What are the effects? My answer was that the healer returns in shamanic fashion from the other world to complete her job in the spirit of healing for the dying patient. It is my opinion that my wife Sharon Groesbeck did keep her promise in being with the patient. What's more, my wife appeared to me in a vision in the summer of 1992 on my trip to Africa and facilitated my own healing during the mourning process. It was only after this visionary experience that my own resolution of her death to some degree came about. The patient also began to accept the loss.

In this, the third paper, I will attempt to complete the transition in treatment and healing that took place from the summer of 1992 to the present time. I have called it, "The Journey Home," as it reflects the whole issue of death and crossing over to the other side.

In March of 1992, Eurydice was very pale and yellow from chemotherapy and radiation. Nevertheless, she dressed herself in an attractive fashion in an attempt to move on with her life.

Interestingly, during this period, she was able to engage in some reflections about her early years. She recalled that the old man who molested her when she was young (when she lived in the country) was exposed by a school counselor who then called her parents. The parents were shocked, but nothing was done and the abusive relationship continued.

Later, after the old man had died, Eurydice's mother continued to meet with his wife, in an attempt to keep the relationship with this man.

As previously presented, it was during this time, after Sharon's death, that Eurydice's dreams and visions primarily focused on a tunnel experience. She would be at the entrance of a long tunnel. At the other end of the deep and dark tunnel, there would be a light and Sharon would be there waiting for her, beckoning her, initially very gently. These dreams and visions repeated themselves on a daily basis for weeks and months. It was only after several months that they began to lessen. There even was a time when I was with Sharon at the other end of the tunnel, thus raising some questions about my mortality, i.e., passing on to the next world. In addition, it has to be remembered that the patient also had a premonitory experience of Sharon's and a friend's death.

So, in the spring of 1992, Eurydice struggled. It was a great temptation for her to give up and go down the tunnel to join Sharon. It was hard to say "no." Yet, she would never quite get down there. She described a repetitive dream in which she would be with Sharon on a road near a cliff. Sharon would get too close and then fall over. Eurydice would reach out to grab Sharon's hand. Sharon would scream, ask for help, and would want to come back. At times, Eurydice could not hang on and Sharon would actually fall. Before her fall, Sharon would be frightened and pleading for help. It was in these dreams that Eurydice finally began to accept the reality that Sharon was really gone. She also began to feel guilty that the stress she caused Sharon was the reason for the latter's death.

It was during this time that I pointed out that this may have played some part, however, Sharon had a serious heart disease and there were many other events going on in her life.

On March 24, 1992, then, a striking session took place. Eurydice underwent chemotherapy and a number of tests were taken together with other evaluations. Questions were raised as to whether her cancer was regressing as a result of the treatment. It was an anxious time. During this period, I spoke to her alter personality who was a "helper" and healing personality and she had the following series of dreams:

> Dream One: "Sharon is now in the tunnel, calling. Jess sometimes is calling me, too. He is with Sharon. He isn't always there."

Comment: She felt confused about the dream and whether it was encouraging her to go with Sharon. She did not understand it.

> Dream Two: "I am walking down the road with Sharon. She slips and falls off the cliff. I try to hang on to her. She screams. I can't hang onto her. She lets go and is lost. And then she really dies, because I can't take care of her.

Comment: Again, there was no understanding of this dream. There was only confusion and anxiety.

> Dream Three: "I am at the ocean, swimming and I can't get back because the waves are overcoming me. Sharon is on the shore. She says I am not worth saving. In diving, I am trying to catch her, and she says, 'I'm not worth the energy.'"

Comment: Here again there was no understanding. Certainly it appeared that she was devaluating herself. It also meant she was trying to reconcile the actual loss of Sharon.

*Dream Four:* "I see an automobile accident. Sharon is in the car, I try to go and get her out. She asks for help. I can't get her out. She is pinned in the car."

*Comment:* Here again was an obstacle between her and her healer who was supposed to save and help her. There was a weariness—a diminution of energy.

By the 28th of March, 1992, Ned, her alter personality, was basically out and Eurydice was gone for thirty-six hours, the longest time she had ever been gone. Ava, the demonic spirit, was clapping with joy. It was a grave situation. Eurydice had been informed that she had only six months to live because the doctors didn't get all the cancer, and it was spreading to her neck and breast. The spinal fluid was clear, but the liver was deteriorating. It was totally devastating that she had to leave. Clearly, Eurydice was contemplating suicide. I felt an urgency to get her back from this terrible long journey. Eurydice had already said goodbye to several people and Ned was now taking over.

Finally, after almost forty-eight hours, Eurydice came back. She said she did not want to live because she had only six more months anyway. There was a challenge that she needed to start eating, and she reluctantly agreed. She almost wanted to be convinced. Ned was very fatigued.

By May 2, 1992, she moved into an apartment with the support system of her friend who was a doctor. She seemed to be having fewer dreams of Sharon. Sharon was not so insistent anymore that Eurydice go so far down into the tunnel. She felt more tired and filled with pain.

One of the child personalities, Jeannie, emerged and asked Eurydice to stay with her and work things out. She was very cooperative, as she was fearful of losing Sharon. I had given her a copy of my paper on the "Wounded Healer," and she took great comfort in reading it for the first time. (This is something I seldom do with patients.)

By May 18, 1992, she was a little better, and even went to her daughter's graduation ceremony. She felt somewhat healed. Her son didn't want to live with her because he was afraid she was going to die and leave him. It was hard for all concerned.

Since she had gone to Hawaii, she began to see another therapist with a Jungian background.

She was taking so much medication that she could not drive a car. This was a great crisis for her, because Eurydice loved to drive.

By the middle of June, while I was visiting Africa, Eurydice was having a very difficult time. There was a conflict in my wanting to come back earlier on account of this patient. In fact, I did end up coming home four days sooner than expected. According to Ned, she made a suicidal attempt at this time, taking a drug overdose.

By the 16th of June, 1992, she indicated she was very tired and wanted to "go and rest." This sounded like a suicidal preoccupation. Over the next week, things were very tense and difficult. She was taking a lot of medication, but it was hard for her to talk much because she was sedated.

On the 20th day of June, 1992, she had a death dream in which all her healers died. Eurydice was again able to drive her car, but doing very poorly. She was "alone and cold" and could not connect with her mother. She then presented a very curious dream:

> I'm going to a contest where they have sort of a public awards presentation somewhere in the forest under trees near a river city. There are bears being given recognition. I go and enjoy it very much. On my way is someone helping me—a person who has two names: Sharon and Carol. While I am distracted by enjoying the contest, I come back and find that they both are dead. I don't know how they died. It happened rather suddenly. I then feel very sheepish, very sad and very upset with myself that I did not attend to and did not pay any attention to them. It is unclear how they died.

She then became very remorseful, feeling that anyone she gets close to her dies. This happened to her former therapist who died, Sharon, and now a friend who also had been told she had ovarian cancer. There was an attempt to mourn the loss of these people, yet she was terrified in dying alone, and was overwhelmed. She also had a dream where she was drowning. She wanted quality time with her children and wanted to go on to die. She cried and sobbed a great deal.

It was noted by Ned that the dream of Carol and Sharon which had occurred several years ago, was now repeated. It was seemingly predictive of Sharon's death. During this session, Eurydice was quite tearful. She wasn't able to focus on anyone in Hawaii. She felt very lonely and isolated. She also felt terrified.

Ava came regularly, but she was not making too much of an impact, even though she was pressing Eurydice to destroy herself. Eurydice was in terror, between life and death. She went into the tunnel toward the other side, almost crossing over into the next life.

During the session on the next day, she was feeling very sad, cold and alone again. She was doing poorly later that night. Her body wasn't responding and it was hard for her to talk. Her breathing was difficult in the early hours of the morning. I made a night home visit to her because I felt she could die almost any time. When I obtained some medication for her, Ava came out and indicated she was glad that Eurydice at last was dying. Ned was very cooperative, realizing now that she experienced all her guilt. She was taking high doses of narcotics.

The day after, however, she was doing somewhat better, even dealing more directly with anger toward Sharon for the first time, Sharon had died and left her. This was an unexpected turn of events. On one hand, it meant she was still mourning Sharon, on the other hand, she felt Sharon had broken through the wall, got to Eurydice and then took part of her soul with her.

On the 28th of June 1992, Eurydice was preoccupied with earthquakes. There was an earthquake warning in California in a town near San Bernardino. It was recommended that people should not drive. This brought back earlier memories of tornadoes when she had lived in Kansas and Missouri. She talked about cousins and herself, sitting and touching each other, staying together and being secure at a frightening time.

At this point, there was a natural evolution of the therapeutic work between us. She asked for a religious blessing which my friend and I gave her. It was a remarkable experience. Most importantly, I surprised myself by commanding that the evil spirit Ava leave. Indeed, after that session, there was a great commotion and an emotional shift. After that I was informed by Ned that the spirit had gone! This was, indeed, the case and Ava never came back.

I also promised Eurydice that she would be able to get the rest she needed to finish her mission in life, whatever that was. She would complete all her assignments.

The next day, there was another meeting and I thought it would be my last face to face session I would ever have with her. I really felt that she would die before I had a chance to see her again. I indicated that I would be having a memorial for my wife and would let her know when that was to be. (Although a funeral had already been held, this was to be a special memorial for Sharon.)

At that point, I informed Ned, for the first time, of the original vision I had about the diagnosis of Eurydice and her multiple personality disorder. I told him many other things about her and about her family connections. It was very difficult to say goodbye, but I felt in many ways, this was going to be. I even indicated to her that if she saw Sharon again to send her my love, that I would always be there with her and for her. I acknowledged that my wife Sharon had come to me in a vision while I had been in Africa and I thanked her. Eurydice even gave me permission to write her life story, which I intend to do. In fact, this presentation is part of it.

There was one other session before she left, as she didn't have to leave as early as she thought, and again some of the same issues were discussed. She again wanted a promise that she would not die alone.

Finally, a day after that, she wanted another session, but could not come, because she had difficulties breathing. However, things were going well enough to travel to Hawaii.

A week later she called from Hawaii. She had made the trip but it was very difficult. She was now working out the relationship with her daughter who was with her.

Two weeks later she was still moving ahead, but now in an intense furor with her daughter. I attempted, over the telephone, to conduct a makeshift session with Eurydice and her daughter to help them talk more objectively about one another. There was an amazing reminder that Ava, the evil demonic spirit, had now gone. Eurydice's anger toward Sharon was now coming out very strongly—it was unresolved anger.

In early August, another session took place concerning her relationship with her daughter. Unexpectedly, they were working out many deep feelings and I urged her not to write her daughter off but to stay with her and try to work things through. In fact, I felt a deep sense of satisfaction as much as I had ever felt in working with patients, because she was working this out and did not avoid it.

Finally, by the end of August (August 29, 1992), after a lot of struggles between Eurydice and her daughter, she displayed an amazing amount of strength. She tended to dissociate, but then she had a dream:

> I go through various apartments to get to my apartment, through the balcony, stairs and so forth. Then I get into my apartment and find that it needs to be protected. I have some white owls there, but I can't take care of or feed them. They are getting sick and I am sick. [The white owl is the Acura, the protecting spirit of Hawaii.]

Eurydice went now to the Jungian therapist on Hawaii who noted that the dream indicated she needed protection and that her daughter had to leave her home.

I did not hear from her for several weeks. Then, about October 12, 1992, she again was feeling tired and defeated and wanted another session with me. Miraculously, she was still hanging on. She had many dreams about Sharon. In some dreams, she was upset that Sharon was there and she did not want to let Sharon in. She seemed to be screening Sharon out. However, Sharon was there in many private places, supporting her. Sharon then said to Eurydice that she was sorry she left her for a while—she knew she had left Eurydice dangling. Eurydice was bonding with her new therapist and the white owls were coming often.

At this time, a man pursued her and wanted to date her. This had happened for a long time. In one of her dreams she was being rolled up and suffocated. However, she seemed to hang on, miraculously so. Yet, she was feeling tired and defeated. She seemed to be doing better while she was working with another therapist and I did not hear so much from her during the ensuing weeks. However, when I did speak with her again, she suffered a great deal of pain.

Finally, on October 18, 1992, she felt abandoned by her family, her daughter and others. In fact, she tried to jump off the balcony the previous night to commit suicide. I had been called by Ned a couple of times. Eurydice sounded self-destructive. I spent a session with her over the telephone. She had cut herself off from her parents and her children. She avoided dealing with issues surrounding her children. Ned was trying to control her medication and again she began having more dreams of Sharon. Sharon was telling her that soon she would be there with her. She would be able to stay on the other side and need not have to come back. There was a quality change now. Eurydice was alienating herself from people as she seemed to be approaching an impending death, particularly with the ongoing drug addiction.

By October 21, 1992, she still appeared to be suicidal. She then had a dream in which a *sunami* (tidal wave) was coming. In this dream, she looked out and saw trees uprooted and everything turned over. "I look and suddenly see the water rising. It comes up into the bedroom. It's rising above the roofs and there is no way to get out."

This appeared to me truly a death dream and I felt the beginning of the end. I didn't discuss it much with Eurydice or even Ned. As the pain hit, I felt this would be the natural way she would go. She seemed to be accepting the idea of dying and was not afraid of it.

On October 25, 1992, she continued to take her medication. She had two other horrifying dreams, in one the new therapist in Hawaii came and one of the white owls was picking this therapist up and took her to the ocean, dropping her there. In the dream, she never saw the therapist again. In the second dream, she was swimming near the beach and the tidal wave came. It sucked up the water and the therapist was thrown into the tidal wave. When the wave came and rushed by, her therapist was gone. This was sobering, because the healer was being destroyed again.

Medication was continued and Ned was holding his own, handling the pain, but feeling it more and more.

By October 27, 1992, she was still very lonely and sad, and I recommended hospice care. At this time, her cousin said she was coming over to give her a blood transfusion.

By November 16, 1992, Eurydice had gone to a Kahuna who had said she was too far gone to really be helped. This discouraged her a great deal. She continued involvement with the Jungian therapist. Finally, on a Friday, a Catholic priest gave her the last rites when she had trouble breathing. A friend even offered to put her out of her misery to end it all. Eurydice did not agree to that, although she was tempted. The therapist was angry with her for calling her so much. I urged her to talk with her. I would also talk to her as much as possible. Meanwhile, she was continuing with her medications.

Finally, Ned spoke with the therapist and indicated Eurydice was angry at me. She had another dream in which I was there. The white male owl took me out to the sea and never came back with me. Four days later, he came back, but Dr. Groesbeck was gone. The male and the female white owl were there again, and both flew away and neither came back. This seemed to be true journeys to the other side.

The dream of Sharon beckoning Eurydice down the tunnel continued also in renewed fashion. Interestingly, Eurydice took a trip with her cousin to the volcano on a helicopter. She later had a dream in which red lava was covering her. By then, Ned said he was feeling the pain of the cancer more and more, something he never felt before. He thought it was time for hospice care.

There was no word from her within the next few weeks and I finally called her. She was distraught because someone had broken into her apartment. They stole her journals and jewelry, but nothing else. This was very peculiar. Some questions about her daughter having done this were raised.

In the next few days, she continued taking pain medication and was "hanging on." Now the dreams of the male and female white owl came back and they were in her bedroom. She cemented the door to keep them in. The female tried to fly out the door, with her wings flapping. She also had again dreams of the tunnel. She continued working with the native healer and talked about the white owls as being her protectors.

Pain was a problem at this point: it was more intense, Eurydice decided to wait two more months before returning to the mainland. Things were stabilizing. However, by November 19, 1992, she was weakening. She could not spend a full session to discuss issues due to her weakness.

However, Eurydice had a remarkable experience two nights previous to our next session. She had visited the Mormon Tabernacle Choir and had seen several people. She thought she had seen Sharon's ghost-like face. This was very eerie. She even had trouble believing Sharon had really died.

Medications continued and her state was about the same in December 1992. She was paying $1,500 a month for narcotics and her liver was enlarged and more distended.

Then, on December 30, 1992, she had an incredible death and rebirth experience. I had made seven or eight telephone calls to her during the holidays and couldn't reach her. I wasn't even certain whether she had gone to the hospital or had died. Then she finally called, she had returned to the mainland.

She had gotten ill and started to swell. She stayed at her doctor-friend's home for six hours and then went into a medical crisis. They took her to a hospital in Honolulu and then flew her back to River City, California, where she got treatment. She was in the hospital, getting ready to return to Hawaii. The medical staff found that her liver was functioning and that she was miraculously improving and working more efficiently. She had a confrontation with her parents, her daughter and son, who all accused her of faking and lying, as if she did not have cancer. She told them they could believe what they wanted but gradually the parents calmed down. Her son wouldn't talk to her, but her daughter did. Communication opened up. She felt homesick for Hawaii and wanted to go back. For the first time in a long time she had a feeling that she wanted to live.

I felt so distant from her, because I did not know what was happening. Somehow I felt guilty about what had happened to her. She asked me about my Christmas and I indicated how hard it had been and how badly I felt about the loss of Sharon. She then administered some aid and comfort by giving me a kleenex during the session.

She then indicated she was a new woman, even her helper, Ned, would be leaving because he wasn't needed anymore.

Thereafter, she slept for two days and gained the will to live. Things turned around. Ned indicated a strange event. She had gone through a miraculous experience and attributed it to the blessing and anointing I and my friend had given her in the summer before she left. She received a new spark of life, went off the medication and didn't even look back. She took the leaves and herbs the Kahuna had given her to relieve the pain. She was even able to tolerate the pain. Then she reported the following series of visionary experiences:

> My children and I are in a room in a house together. We are playing games. The children lose at every game. Then suddenly I am falling asleep. And as I sleep, I feel someone tug on my arm and my chest and even my gums. Then I wake up and realize that I am in a strange place. I am in a place with candles. Chinese music is playing, and I am in a tent. My kids are there and they are on either side. They are using tweezers to take of the layers of skin. Then I see my owls: the male and female owl come and try to pull my children off and away. In the next visionary flash, I see the owls come and carry Jess off. I next come and see them carry Rhoda (the Hawaiian therapist) away.

Then, a few day's later, she had this dream:

> I was born, living in an apartment in Hawaii. I was a baby, but I am doing adult things. When I needed things in the kitchen, I would climb up on a stool. It was very hard to do, but I was up to doing things by moving around. I had to do it, because life was moving on. I crawled; otherwise, I would have fallen. Then I suddenly felt a pulling sensation. I woke up as though I had been in space.

> I feel these dreams mean different things. My children picking up my skin means that I decided to live. Maybe it was like there was a burning away of old attitudes, by peeling the skin off. I was going through a death process to be reborn.

> Next, the baby dream, being born like a baby, is the stage where I am at now.

Then she said, "Oh, Jess, you have given me a second chance. How did you feel when the anointing took place?" I indicated that it had been very powerful.

The chest pain and swelling were intense now, although her liver was better. A great change had taken place. She was passing clots. She was having allergic reactions where her thighs had been injected.

As she slept for those two days, a powerful change occurred in the functioning of her liver. There was almost a new person coming forth. The dreams of Sharon in the tunnel had stopped during the days previous, and she didn't have any more at the time. Daily dreams seemed important. She went through withdrawals from the drugs and did reasonably well. Things were quiet for several days.

She had further dreams, one about the male white owl putting water back into the ocean. And she had another dream in which she was trapped in a two-story house, but it was not clear what was going on. She then had recurrences of dreams about the barn where she had been raped as a child by the old man.

In January of 1993, she had minor emergency surgery.

This was a remarkable time, and for nearly a month, things seemed to be settling. I was in total amazement that perhaps a major change had really occurred. In fact, it appeared like a miracle.

By February 1993, she called and we had a session. During this session, she told about a dream where she had been in her bed in her condominium in Hawaii and a screen had opened. She saw a man (with no face) coming over the balcony into her apartment. He was carrying out all of her books, dishes, paintings—everything—even the stereo. He didn't say anything. He didn't have any weapons; he just communicated to her that she better shut up and not interfere. He went around the apartment, taking her food, then he locked everything and she couldn't get out. He then lifted everything out, going down the ropes from the balcony and jumping off the eighth-floor balcony. She then woke up.

At this time, she was preoccupied with whether she should move back to the mainland or not. She had no idea who the stranger was. The day before she had seen a man and carried guilt about this relationship, as it was sexual. He was still living with his wife and children. However, their relationship had apparently ended, though divorce had not occurred. She now felt she loved this man. It was a great struggle. In working on this dream, it appeared that if she was going to stay with this man, it might cost her everything. She indicated that, without the love and relationship she had with him, she would rather die.

It was as though Eurydice was back in life, having to face the same temptations she had always faced.

There was little discussion or interpretation by me, as I was not as involved with her. She went on working with the other therapist, but when she came back to the United States, she would eventually call me for an appointment.

She came to me because her mother was having an operation. When I saw her, I couldn't believe it. She was a new woman, dressed very nicely in slacks. She looked a little bit older. Her hair was well combed. She appeared healthy. She had been to her doctor who announced that her cancer was in remission. She was checked out in two different ways. The lymph glands and the spots on the liver had receded. She was doing much better. She truly began talking about a new life. She and her daughter were back together. They were going on a trip, trying to work on their relationship. She also had worked out a reasonably good relationship with a man she had been involved with. She was now finding Hawaii her true home and was working on forgiveness toward her mother. It felt very good.

Some review of her family history was carried out. Financial issues, privately and for her therapy, were also getting settled.

She had a few experiences in the previous two months in which she would go to the tunnel and Sharon would be there, but she could not go beyond the entrance. She would see Sharon far off. Sharon would be saying something, but Eurydice could not hear what she was saying. She just simply could not get there.

In other dreams of Sharon, she was walking above our house and sitting where we used to live. She was talking and Sharon would say, "It's not time yet." Sharon appeared relaxed, sitting there in nature. It was as though Eurydice would see her waiting, and this would comfort her. She would have an occasional crying spell about Sharon, but not so often anymore. She mistakenly even got a gift for Sharon at Christmas.

She also described a dream in which the white owls (the male and the female) were in her home protecting her. They would flap at people who came in, at times, to bother her. Others wouldn't be welcome. I confirmed with her that in the future there would be Sharon's memorial service. For the first time, it appeared to he an end of a treatment that had gone on for many years.

Two weeks after that, Eurydice called me and indicated that somebody had raped her. He didn't threaten her life, but he had a knife. She went on with her therapy and resolved that quite well. She described one dream, in which she was at a grave site, being lowered down. She looked up and there stood I and Sharon, looking down on her. However, this did not go very far. She linked some of this to the barn experience of earlier years, but she got through that very well, and it never really bothered her that much. Her present status was, indeed, one of the most remarkable healing experiences I've ever had.

This brings to a close the series of experiences with this woman who is someone I would never have predicted to be now alive. In summary, I would say when a healer dies, it's as though she will come back in shamanic fashion and carry out her promises to the patients who have been ill. Thus we see, if anything happened in this treatment, it was my wife who died so that this patient could live.

# DISCUSSION

## With Groesbeck, the Nortons, Quincy, and Vilenskaya

*Krippner:* I was moved by all the talks and just want to comment on Jess' presentation in case he intends to do some work with these dreams. In some Native American traditions, owls mean death. That she had two white owls might mean that she had one death and later on she will have another death.

Symbols are understood differently in different parts of the world. In Greece, the owl appears with Athena—to indicate wisdom. There could be a double meaning but I think the death symbol would be more appropriate to this dream.

I also want to comment on the beautiful and provocative presentation on tobacco. The American official position on drugs is quite hypocritical. Grade schoolers are told, recreational use of tobacco is bad. If sacred use of tobacco would be okay, they would have to say that sacred use of Peyote is okay, too.

*Rubik:* I am really impressed and deeply touched by the depth of all speakers. Cheri, your talk went very far in addressing the denial of death and showing that death is natural. I wanted to make three points. You seem to leave necrosis out of the picture. I would like to offer the possibility that necrosis too is natural. From a more Eastern point of view, perhaps, death by apoptosis could be seen as excess yin and necrosis could be seen as contracted yang. From discussions with many people, I learned that some people would prefer to go the quick, light-bulb going out way while others would prefer a more extended, gentler death. I think there are options.

With that I would also like to encourage you to continue your research. Genetics are now moving into an interplay of epigenetic factors. It would be very valuable to bring in an interactive approach of the environment of consciousness into your theory of death as you continue to expand it. I know from experience that interaction with loved ones seems to keep people alive who otherwise, physiologically, very well should be dead.

Thirdly, I would like to encourage you and your colleagues to analyze the *lacrimae mortis* (the tears of death). People have studied tears shed under different emotional states. The tears of emotional release are very different from allergic tears when cutting an onion. No one, to my knowledge, has ever analyzed the *lacrimae mortis*. About thirty per cent of people have this phenomenon at the moment of their death. It would be valuable to make a biochemical study of these tears, to understand more the emotional state at the point of death.

*Olsen:* I picked up the *Mutant Message—Downunder* (Lees Summit, MO: MM Co., 1991) which has a couple of paragraphs on this topic.

> ...The Real People saw nothing savage in paying a debt, or showing your gratitude to the earth by letting some of your own blood spill onto the sand. Also they believe in honoring the individual desire of a person who wishes to stop nourishment and sit in the open to end their worldly existence. They do not believe that death by disease or accident is natural. After all, they said, you can't really kill something eternal. You did not create it, and you can't kill it. They believe in free will; freely the soul chooses to come; so how can rules be just that say he cannot go home? It is not a personality decision made in this manifested reality. It is an eternal level decision that made the all-knowing SELF.

> They believe the natural way to exit the human experience is by exercising one's freewill and choice. At about age one hundred and twenty or thirty, when a person gets excited about returning forever, and after asking ONENESS if it is in the highest good, they call for a party, a celebration of their life.

> The Real People nation have for centuries had a practice at birth to speak the same first phrase to all newborns. Each person hears the exact first human words: "WE LOVE YOU AND SUPPORT YOU ON THE JOURNEY." At their final celebration, everyone hugs them and repeats this phrase again. What you heard when you came, is what you hear when you leave. Then the departing person sits down in the sand and shuts down the body system. In less than two minutes they are gone. There is no sorrow or mourning (1991:155-156).

*Heinze:* What Cheri presented is immensely important. The message is that our fear of death causes pain. If you are not afraid of death and actually know that you are dying from the moment of birth on, you live much better.

*Hall:* I want to briefly address Dr. Groesbeck and also Cheri. For five years, off and on, I had the great fortune to work with a fifty-patient hospice unit in Denver. I was not working with home death, we were processing death and dying. As volunteers, we used to reflect on the two processes of dying we could not explain. One was that we would see physical symptoms heal before the moment of death. Individuals would be clear and lucid. Swelling would be down. They no longer required neither pain medication nor fluid and they were not unanesthetized. They were in peace and off they went.

The other one is that I talked to a nurse in Sebastopol who works with birthing, but her first experience was with death and dying and I asked her why she was going back and forth between disciplines. She looked at me and said, " My dear, it is all portal work, you know." Jess, perhaps your wife found the other side of the portal, too.

*Groesbeck:* In my experience, there were times I could feel the presence of my wife as well as Eurydice's connection to the tunnel and the other side. Eurydice was, indeed, close to the other side and through her I felt the connection to my wife.

*Coffey:* Jeff, that is a beautiful memorial for your wife, but I have a question for Jana and Jack. You mentioned the sacred pipes that were male and female. Were they of different kinds of wood? Or different other material?

*Rivers:* Those particular pipes were made of stone, soapstone. Other pipes may be made out of wood, but for healing purposes, e.g., the first salmon rites, the pipes are made out of stone.

*Norton:* A lot of times the pipes made out of stone are used when we approach death. All of this ties together, they may be taken to the mountains and that part of you can be left in the mountains, too.

*Alwyn:* I want to address Cheri. What you said, gladdened my heart. I had an experience that allowed me to see a genetic transfer through generations. My mother's mother passed away voluntarily, drifting and closing down. And I was part of my mother's transfer. She willingly gave up her time and knew that was part of it. I am watching my father now. He resists and I see the dichotomy. It is very encouraging to hear that the scientific background is now coming out for what I spiritually experienced. I found it healing, for my work in healing other, too. Thank you.

*Quincy:* What you are talking about is the reason that I got into this study. My intuition has been that there had been choices that we are called to make. Death is not a termination but a healing. We can look for the mechanism through which it would occur. Culturally, it is our phobia of the concept that prevents us from experiencing things like spontaneous remission. It prevents us from leaving our body, even in non-death situations, with confidence.

*Scott:* I would like to thank Jack and Jana for their presentation on the sacred pipe. I would also like to address the concept of death. First of all, thank you, for your elucidations on the molecular level. This essentially for me is the project in shamanism, we can, molecularly, reorganize our spiritual and our physical being, so that we can pass through the portal completely conscious and then embrace other worlds. However, something that is not quite gelling with me is the recognition that we are somehow in control. There are certainly cases in medical records that people who are apparently healthy go. There has to be a recognition that there are forces and there are spirits and intentions that are far greater than ourselves and that it is the Source or the Great Spirit, if you will, who ultimately determines when we have learned the lessons, as we are walking this life path, and when it is time we must gladly accept death. For me, death is my shadow and my ally. When I can make death my ally and embrace it then I can truly live.

*Etcheverry:* I work a lot with people who are really ill, also people who are dying. In Chinese traditional medicine we can often tell about three to five days before somebody dies. The pulse becomes normal and everything normalizes. I just thought this was really important. Also, I had a near death experience and found that I had a much easier connection with spirit and an easier way of being in both realms. It helped me a lot.

*Heinze:* Just as a side remark, you cannot be in two worlds at the same time, but you can alternate, of course. I want to thank all panelists for their profound remarks. I strongly recommend the book Cheri mentioned, Sogyal Rinpoches's *Tibetan Book of Living and Dying* (San Francisco, CA: Harper, 1992). It will be useful in preparing for your own death and also for assisting loved one's in their death.

# THE EMERALD RIVER
# OF COMPASSION

Rowena Pattee Kryder

The purpose of this rite is to invoke the intelligences that will enable us to select the correct "reading" for our collective shamanic group at this time.

I have arranged a large circle of the *Gaia Matrix Oracle Old Earth Symbols* on the grass, from eternity to freedom (through all 64 symbols).

Everyone participating is to select a symbol card from the *Gaia Matrix Oracle* (1990) and let that be a reading for each person individually. As we gather around the large colored cloth symbols on the grass, let us attune to our individual central question.

Now, as I pass in front of you, I invite each of you to sing a different melody to one basic rhythm. Everyone's "song" will be different and yet it will have a strong collective rhythm. Continue to repeat your melody and the basic rhythm over and over, each person adding a new one. When I have gone around the whole circle, we will begin moving in rhythm to our chant and the drum. At a certain point, I will stop drumming and you are to stop where you are and cease singing. When anyone holds in his/her hand the same symbol that is on the ground in front of you, that will indicate the corresponding story we are to read from the *Emerald River of Compassion.*

The symbol was *Freedom,* the very last symbol. The following reading is excerpted from my book, *The Emerald River of Compassion* (1994:458-461).

*The Dirge for the Death of the Old Earth*

Freedom
White of white within white

Facing
one's shadow
brings
freedom.

While ominous expectancy ripples from pole to pole at the dying of an age, strife-weary dragons hold together a tremulous maze of brooding seas and oppressed continents. Scattered about the planet are those called to the depths where the crushed emerald waters rise in vortices of hope. With the joy of intrinsic knowing running through their channels, they live their vow amid the tumult of the decaying world. The poetic fountain of divine imagination can flow within the heart of anyone, but only these courageous ones feel it and use it.

Lomo travels the land, drumming in the hills where people meet in sacred trust. He knows the loneliness of humankind, except for those whose drums beat to the pulse of the Fifth World. Starlie, who left Tokyo reeling in confusion, at last has surrendered to the inner music that tells him, *The prophecies will be fulfilled.* Now his games reconstruct the world from the prophetic traditions of his people. He meets Lomo in New York, where they pour old Hopi stories into a cup of revelation and drink the new vision.

At a concert a few blocks away, Pete's Holocaust Rock band is blasting through the imprisoning thought forms of urban automatism. The uniform, repressive monotony of the first movement, "Entropy," builds into the blaring tones of "Holocaust" in which drums, marimbas, and synthesizers explode in a crescendo of spirit. Thousands, feeling the ancient beat resound through the concrete beneath their feet, begin to dance, touched by a tincture of God. The music falls like shrapnel upon the hip crowd that responds in hallucinogenic abandon.

Allen and Martha cling to their seats, trying to reconcile the heretical visions of a New Age son with their own crumbling fundamentalism. Allen gapes at the dizzying scene, which reminds him of the fertile bramble of junk at the dump back home. But the noise presses him back into life.

The band, in a thundering cry for liberty, turns metal into music and sound-waves into light. The electronic vibrancy is lifted by the white dissonance that shatters the shadows of the Old Earth. Starlie laughs as he and Lomo walk toward the flashing lights of the concert hall. They arrive just in time for the apocalyptic surge of heavy metal. Pete calls out over the microphone, "We shall no longer believe in purity while living in hell! This monstrous system of contradictions calls for the final movement, the 'Cosmic Dirge.' Let's go!"

Within the drumming and strumming rises the voice of the River, crushing the casement of meaningless lives and spinning them back to renewed purpose. Sonics become the "Word" that ripples at one with the River. The babel of human speech merges with the inarticulate muttering of matter and seethes in the quaking Old Earth.

A storm brews all over the world. Visionaries behold Satan rising up toward Christos. Some behold the kachinas dancing with demons, others the conflict between devas and asuras. A phoenix cries. Dragons hiss and roll through the electrified air. Crowds in cities everywhere assemble and dissipate in an uneasy melding of hope and trepidation.

"The eternal return is returning!" shouts Starlie, dancing amid the throngs around the band.

The dirge resounds with the pain inflicted in the past: The lamentations of not living one's life, and of succumbing to hatred and anger; the lamentations of neglected children; the lamentations of crime and warfare; the lamentations of the amnesia of paradise, the golden age, and love. The dirge billows with the death of racism, genocide, complacency, and apathy.

In the music is the eternally pathless path, the face of the unknown. The scourge of history, nations, and races brings the end of messiahship and of clinging to false hope. The demise of the Old Earth brings destruction to the caves of Plato and the Paleolithic tribes. It topples Teotihuacan and the tableland of Anahua, and it pulverizes the Sumerian cuneiforms at Napput.

Crowds wander down the River, chanting and mourning through the ruins of New York, Paris, Bombay, Beijing, San Salvador, Jerusalem, and

Calcutta. Homeless people roam the streets or huddle in taverns and the caverns of condemned buildings. Lomo and Starlie add their drums to the flutes, whistles, sticks, and bells that sound the living dirge. In Berlin, Bangkok, Budapest, and Moscow, thousands join the procession swelling with the pulse of life.

Intensity builds as the clouds condense into tightening spirals. Rain torrents down, creating a sea of mud. Lifetimes of pain are released in the wailing, which rises and spreads like the concentric circles of Atlantis. Okeanos, the god of the ocean, rises into a hurricane that swirls in violence from Earth to heaven.

"Come, mysteries of chaos!" call out the Primal Waters. "Reveal the harmonies in your deep order! The island of New Earth rises from the sea! My waters are in your bones and the salt of your blood."

"Holy Europe, holy Asia, holy Africa," sings a chorus of angels amidst hallelujahs. "Holy Polynesia? Holy Australia! Holy Atlantic Ocean! Whole Earth holy! Holy! Holy, we call Kukuklan! Atum! Zeus!"

"None but the Sun," Pravin calls as he feels Savitri within him.

Languages pulsate with new meaning. Forms reveal their hidden beauty. In the quickening energy of life and love, the fall of rain is felt as a kiss, the darkness as a blessing.

Throngs migrate across the Earth. The Mother of the World, invisible to all, churns the poisons of the planet into a roiling brew, cast into storms over the face of the waters: The Atlantic, the Pacific, the Indian, the Arctic. The Trickster in nature hurls cyclones, mud slides and volcanic eruptions.

The burning waters rage inside the human spine. The Mother-Creatrix-Sophia is everywhere, offering not even a hell for a refuge! Every pain and experience is transformable in the metamorphic soup of the River of Compassion. The turbulence stirs the memory of millennia, releasing the addictions of the ages, and separating seed from weed, wheat from chaff, and life from sin. The end of the River meets the source, turning and churning pollutants toward purity.

The veil is rent. Some see the turbulence, some the hand of the Mother, and others the vortex—the projection of denied desire flashing in the darkness. Unbelievers believe, and false believers believe no longer. The holographic screens of the universe have shattered.

The geometry of the Earth reveals its unkempt lines beyond the continents of dirt and stone. Old dragons—having long held the Earth together—return rejoicing to the whirling heavens as the energy of the ley lines is restored. Poisonous hatred and blame—long hurled at the dragons by an ignorant humanity—are now stirred by the Mother of the World into an oceanic swell.

Rolling tidal waves level the villages of the Pacific islands in a watery baptism. As palm trees twist beneath the sea, Zoa, Mujaji, and Nummo take refuge in underwater island caves. Convening there is the council of ancient scribes, retainers of the esoteric wisdom, who speak in the silence of the deep: "The blood of the Earth shall soon run pure. Brimstone, ashes, deluge, death! Let us dance all night to honor the return of the snake goddesses!" Wild, passionate, and ecstatic, the islanders revive the archaic tribal dance, driving out the madness that poses as sanity, so that the true human dance can begin.

As the storms rage above, the iridescent obelisk of Zar rises from the lapis lazuli door on the floor of the Pacific, invisible to all but those who have held the loving vision for humanity. Some already live in the divine imagination of the Land of Zar, where the dolphins dance, the diatoms delight, and the whales circle clockwise around the base of the obelisk.

At home in Malta, Channon enters the massive stone ruin where he hears the music of Zar sailing above the swells of a perishing world. "I see titans raising an obelisk, like those of Egypt, only more clear and translucent!" he cries out in his visionary state. "I see now! I have been intoxicated by my desires—addicted to having and holding. The titans are our benefactors!" Yes, he reflects, *the titans in humanity rise to fall once again. The titans have been unloosed from the mountain tops where the sacred fire of the Immortals flames within reach. It was the titans who lifted the stones of the megaliths and pyramids to align the energy with dragon veins and ley lines. Now they return to raise the obelisk.*

Many die to the Old Earth on this night of nights. In Madrid, Manila, Bucharest, Baghdad, and Dublin, voices rise in chorus to the sweeping Zarian music. Some dance in orgy. Some dance in mystery. Some dance in love. Angels and demons bear witness to the acceleration and chaos of events on Earth as the multidimensional light casts the divine imagination into the confusion of cultures in total transformation. The courageous ones defy time and the laws of a perishing world, for the colors of the robe of the Creatrix vibrate within their awakened flesh. The archetypal forces weave through the migration of souls and press vibrations of new social forms into their bodies.

East and West meet in the Chinese countryside, where Christa, enfolded in Karl's arms, hears the rhythms and tones of Zar rising from the distant shore and beyond, in the swells of the Pacific. She realizes the story she is to tell is unfinished, for a new humanity is coming. It is a story she knows cannot be told with words. Dancing and whirling in sound and color, it surges forth as she hears a song:

*The Virgin/Child's Song of the River*

I am the waters springing from wells where hearts are true.
I bring ecstasy whenever you summon deep powers.
I am the rising up of purity when you call for truth.
I am the mother of creativity when my womb is honored.
Well, womb, and wonder are the ever-flowing sources of my service.
I am the reservoir within all sentient beings.
I am yourself when you express from the source.
I serve everyone alike though I am silent and unseen.
I am the freedom of not-knowing.
You can find me in life and pristine forests.
I am the sea that births all beings.
The Sun is my lover who brings bliss to the pure at heart.
You can find me when you bask in the light of the Moon.
I am the limit of dominion and render each being the freedom to be.

How can one know one's being?
All that is, floats, all that is not, sinks.

## References

Kryder, Rowena Pattee. *The Emerald River of Compassion*. Santa Fe, NM: Bear Books, 1994.

_____ . *Gaia Matric Oracle*. Mount Shasta, CA: Golden Point Productions, 1990.

# MISUSE OF PSYCHIC POWER

Madrina Denig

For ten years I have been going to Peru, but not every year. In 1980, I was studying to become a religious science minister. I had also a part-time job with Alberto Villoldo who took groups to Brazil and Peru to study with healers. So I began making trips with him even though I did not know whether this was something I ever wanted to do. My thesis in ministerial school was Native American Healing and Spiritual Practices as they relate to the science of mind. Because I am part Cherokee, I had grown up with ideas that seem to conform with religious science.

The next thing I knew was that I am in Peru, becoming apprentice to don

Eduardo Calderon, El Tuno. Alberto worked with him for a few years and I was the first female apprentice of don Eduardo.

What I want to talk about today is what I learned about the misuse of psychic power, as it happened during my work with Eduardo, with Villoldo, and with other *curanderos* I met down there.

Eduardo, at the time I met him, was a very simple man. He lived in a fishing village and went out to fish everyday for his fourteen children. He had a lot of power as a shaman but did not use it in a materialistic way. By the time my association with Villoldo ended, Eduardo was supposed to go to Switzerland to be part of a conference on shamanism. He took a bus from Tullo (which is north of Lima) to the airport, got to the foot of the steps going up to the plane and then said, "I am not going," turned around and went back. Meanwhile, in Switzerland, they were waiting for him. From that point to about four years later when he was spending half a year annually in Europe with his students, Alberto Villoldo was instrumental in bringing him out. As I worked with Villoldo over the years and still am, I saw some misuse of power. Eduardo was corrupted, not intentionally but as he wanted to share his teachings with so many people, he allowed things to happen that he did not oversee as closely as he should have.

Some of you may have seen the video on "Healing States." I was asked to be part of the filming done with Eduardo's advanced students. The film crew came from Austria and was prepared for three weeks of shooting. A group of about twenty people was told that we were the advanced students. It turned out that there were many people in the group simply to fill in because they were charging $3,000 to be able to do this. They had to take people who were just interested but had not done any of the work which turned out to be really disastrous. In the process of filming they wanted to get all the phenomena, the advancement through the various initiations that Eduardo took his students through and condensed it into three weeks. Eduardo had always said that taking the *remedio,* the San Pedro cactus, we should do it no more than twice a year. He had to do it every day in the process of the filming. We found out later, not only that we were taking a *remedio* every other day, there were also other substances that had been added about which we did not know. It was very irresponsible and, for me, it was definitely a misuse of power. Debra Carroll who used to be an editor of *Shaman's Drum,* was one who had a very bad reaction. She was taken off the plane when she got back to San Francisco, unconscious. I had a very bad episode from it too, because the San Pedro, as far as I understand it, is Mescaline which will stay in your liver. You can have flashbacks for years, like you do when you take LSD. Giving that to people who were not prepared for it was a misuse of power.

I have observed changes in Eduardo over the years. The last time I saw him, he confessed to me, "I have lost my power, I am trying to get it back, but I don't know if I ever will be able to." That's is very sad for a shaman as powerful as Eduardo had been. Part of that, was for money. However, what Eduardo received on that three-week trip was only $500. I happened to know because I was Villoldo's administrative assistant and knew that the Foundation made $30,000. I did not know whether I should use names but in this case there was a very irresponsible person who now is changing somewhat. He is now taking groups into parts of Peru near Colleriti where the spiritual practices are very pure. I found out about four months ago that there are now groups taken in to the Qu'ros. That upsets me. Do we have the right to say, "you have to keep your purity, at all costs." It is part of the promotion what disturbs me. But when they reach out and seek their knowledge, there will be people who will respond. The people who are taking these groups down need to really maintain their integrity, because you will be dealing with people who are not prepared for the high level of work. The Qu'ros are practicing a very high level of Andean mysticism and that needs to be addressed. I think there is a flyer of somebody here who is taking groups to Brazil which has a very high level of integrity, I am addressing the groups that Villoldo takes. If you participate in one of these groups, go prepared, be very prepared. You will get something wonderful from it because the people there really want to share their teachings and, I think, we have to help them too. There is innocence.

Also, last year Elizabeth Jenkins spoke about an initiation in Andean mysticism. I had that initiation. I was approached by a man who was an anthropologist and also a charismatic Catholic. He was one of the Andean masters. He came to me and said that the Master Jesus had said he should initiate me. I did not know the man and was to be given this initiation as the first non-Peruvian and as the first woman. It was as Elizabeth described it, a wonderful experience. I took it as complete initiation. Three days after I had this initiation, Juan came to me and said, "You have been initiated now, Madrina, you can now initiate other people and each time you initiate someone, I have a contract, you will give me $300." So it is not only our people from who are misusing their power. They have seen all these people coming down, making lots of money. When you take a group, you make lots of money and they had not been given their share for what they have been doing in the case of Eduardo. Now they are saying, "Give it to us! Let us share!"

I spoke at a conference in August of 1992 that there was a movement which turned into a big fight. The Peruvians are now saying they don't want any group coming and doing their ceremonies at their sacred sites, only Indian ceremonies should be conducted there. It is a very powerful movement. They just might win because they are working at the level of the tourist bureau and it might very well happen. I am the only voice pleading with them not to do that. But how can I really plead? Talking against the misuse of power by the people coming from America, I cannot really do that with the clearest of conscience.

Furthermore, because I was Eduardo's apprentice and choose to live in Cuzco, he would come and I would always participate in the work which was done there. One night, we were out in a remote area where there were two caves, one we call the Cave of the Monkeys. It is also the Cave of the Moon. We did some work in the circle and then each of us had to go alone into each of the two caves. I have a problem with that but I did it. And then we had to find a spot alone out in the darkness on this hillside. I have a problem with that too, going back to a childhood experience, when I had been locked up in a little log cabin church all night in the Missouri Ozarks, as punishment for telling on my daddy. I was alone and kept wanting to go back to Eduardo. It was my fear, but finally I gave in and, as I started back toward him, suddenly, he was not whistling or rattling anymore. It was very dark, but I found my way to him. He had collapsed on the ground and was calling me. He had been attacked by the *brujos*, the other shamans in the area. He should have known that. If he had gone to these people and had asked permission to work there, it would have been given. If you go to *curanderos* and *brujos* in Peru and ask for permission, they will give it. Because he had come so many times, doing his work without permission, they decided that's enough. They attacked him and he almost died. Everything he had taught me about healing, just completely disappeared. The only thing I could do was I knelt behind him, put my left hand over his heart, pressed my chest against his back and began to circulate energy from my heart to his. He recovered and it was a great lesson for both of us. However, afterwards I became the brunt of the attacks of these people, because Eduardo went away and I stayed.

Very strange things began to happen. I am a religious science minister and part of the science of mind philosophy is, we don't recognize evil. But what I have found out personally in the last couple of years, I have to recognize that there is a dark side and I happen to believe that my power is greater than that, but I have to be aware. I have to be very aware. One thing that happens is that I do most of my work in the daytime, before it was not that way. Around Cuzco, I do my work mainly during the day. At Tambomachai, which are the fountains, I do initiations. I was there with a group that had only one man. We were sixteen. Eduardo had told me because of the problems I was having that I should go to that place and use one of my power tools, an original digging stick from Australia. I was to drive the stick forcefully into the ground and declare my right to be there. So I did. Here was my circle and I am kneeling. I drove the stick into the ground and it came right back, almost put out my light. The eyes are the lights. I had a goose egg, an

Ostrich egg, for about three weeks and I suddenly knew, I had to humbly kneel and ask permission to be there. Then I looked up and there was a young man and a boy sitting across the stream watching me. I continued to work for three more hours. They came up to me afterwards and did not say a word. They just took my hands and nodded. And I knew they had been sent from the village. There is a village of just *brujos*. They don't call themselves *curanderos* there, they call themselves *brujos*. They were giving me permission as long as I work in the light. At Machu Picchu I can work at night and that's where I do my most effective work. But in Cuzco, I have to work at day time and I have to tell them that. Their domain is at night and now I have permission. I feel okay now doing it.

In the time left, I want to tell about another attack from another shaman. I came home one day to find a note at my door that just said, "El Senor de Checlado estaba aqui para conversar con ti." The Lord of Checlado had been there from a town in the north where San Pedro shamanism is practiced (what Eduardo is doing, too). In Cuzco it is the coca and in the jungle it is the ayavasca. So I got in touch with him. He wanted me to come and see how he worked because he wanted to get an invitation to come to this conference, to some of the universities, and then bring groups down to study with him. After a five-day course, costing $5,000, he would give you a certificate that you are now a San Pedro shaman. I did not want to do that, especially not knowing how he worked. He got me on that one, saying, "how can you say that when you do not know how I work." So I went to one of his meetings one night. I understood that he would be working with a group of people. When I got there, he began cooking his *remedio* an hour and a half before the ceremony was about to start. It needs to be cooked a minimum of seven hours. When I tasted the *remedio* there were other things in it that should not been in it. I knew that war had been declared so I did not know why. He was giving me massive doses, using a bull horn, Eduardo uses a shell. You pour it into your nose and swallow. If you can keep it down, you really feel you are a warrior. I was keeping all of that down, and he kept sending me more and more. He put me outside the circle, you don't do that. He put me into an unprotected area and, at one point, he had one of his assistants tell me, "You really ought to know that there is a powerful green serpent and it is going to consume you." That's my ally and I knew it was not going to consume me. He threw at me everything he could. And then, at the end, they told me, they wanted a thousand dollars. I refused. He followed me home, very angry. Not only had he called some musicians, he sent them to my place and they wanted their money, too. I said, "Money, for what? I did not make a contract with you." So there were three very angry people sending angry thoughts to me. He had been told that I was a wealthy widow with money in Swiss banks, lots of property in the United States and lots of money in each of the banks in Cuzco. So I picked up my phone and said, "Do you believe that the dead can talk. I am going to call my husband, my ex-husband." He was very angry.

We can also misuse power by not using it. I had not been using it to protect myself and have suffered from it. So now I am awake and learning. I have to be even better trained if I want to continue with this work. You don't know into what kind of situation you may run. The blind religious scientist that I had been has to know how to integrate, how not to misuse it and how to use it for healing. I certainly have found out how it can be used very destructively.

# DISABILITIES AND EMPOWERMENT: EXPLORATION INTO DISABILITIES AND THE NEED FOR PSYCHO-CULTURAL DEVELOPMENT

Mary A. Wimmer and Raymond B. Miller

## Introduction

The purpose of this paper is to explore identity problems of the disabled. We want to examine the need for distinction between differing sectors of this population commonly grouped together under one single modality term "disabled." We want to establish the need for individualized psychological models corresponding to these different sectors; and lastly, we want to show how shamanistic techniques could assist therapists so that those referred to as "disabled" can gain valuable insights into their identity and can become self-empowered.

The term "disabled" (or "handicapped" or earlier "crippled," "lame," or "frail") has been used to define a population as varied as those whose health was considered fragile. The distinction between the population led to several identifying titles, i.e., "blind" (sight impaired), "deaf," "mute," "deaf and dumb" (hearing impaired), "spastic," "palsy" (cerebral palsy, also thought to be mentally retarded), "slow," "stupid," "dumb", "queer in the head," "mentally retarded" (mentally impaired), mongoloid (Down's syndrome), "limp," "lame," etc., relating those who have a wide range of physical disabilities such as paraplegics, quadriplegics, "club feet," elephantiasis, Siamese twins to individuals with cleft palette. With the development of AIDS and HIV, any immune system disease has also fallen under the umbrella term "disabled."

In using the term "disabled," society has lumped together all individuals ranging from those with deteriorating diseases to those who have a sustained functional lifetime difference. This group is treated the same—"disabled." The problem with stereotyping presents the impression that all persons who are disabled are "fragile" or deteriorating from their "condition." It also creates a view that this population is composed of mere "survivalists," much the same as early anthropologists drew similar conclusions about black slave folklore (see Herskovits' *Myth of the Negro Past*, 1941).

## Historical Background

Little is known about the role of the disabled historically. According to George DeVos:

> ...little is known about the lives of the disabled in Europe. I do remember hearing in my travels to Europe, that the disabled were often court jesters and clowns during the renaissance period. They were also often the ones which we now refer to as "mimes," and, of course, beggars in the streets. There was also the idea that those born disabled had the "mark of the devil" on them. They were often times stoned to death or put into work houses as children by their parents in fear for their own lives (1993).

If historical information is hazy at best, current history goes to show that as late as the early 1970s, individuals with "different" disabilities were still institutionalized.

> (They) were taught basic survival skills such as: bathing, combing their hair, brushing their teeth, dressing themselves, doing basic chores such as washing dishes and making beds (Lighthouse of the Blind, 1978).

The director of *Lighthouse of the Blind* which housed as many as 250 students in one county (King County) stereotyped his students as blind, deaf, mentally retarded, and some handicapped (children). A job listing in the *Post Intelligencer*, Seattle, Washington, November 1978, read: "Job position available for 'teachers' [quotation marks mine] interested in working with handicapped people." I inquired as to whether this job required a teacher's certificate and was told "no." (The above description of "basic skills" would have been my "job duties" if I had been hired for the position.)

In 1974, Education Code 504 and Legislation 94-96 were passed to "open classrooms to children with disabilities, giving them access to an equal education in the regular school district." This ruling opened up the gambit of media attention to stories about the disabled, books for children discussing different disabilities and classes in education on the pathological needs of children entering the classroom. Currently, the United States have adopted a "Bill of Rights" for the disabled, known as Americans with Disabilities Act (1990) which allows this population equal access to public transportation, public buildings and establishments, as well as equal opportunity in the job market (exactly 26 years after Title IV which gave equal opportunities to "All Races, Religions, and Creeds" at the work place (Section 2000e, Federal Code, pp.1984-1987).

## Methodology

Reviewing the emotional and psychological needs of the disabled, this paper is based on conversations with other disabled individuals and observations of (or the lack of) data available on their emotional needs. Due to the fact of limited (or non-existent) forms of "healthy mental models of the blind, deaf, cerebral palsic, dyslexic, paraplegic, quadriplegic, etc. in society, current psychological models of observation can only be based on "normal, non-disabled" models of society which may not prove to be relevant to this population. In the process of trying to find alternative means of coping with disabilities, I have found, in my discussions with other disabled individuals a similar technique of "out of body journeying" which they use to deal with physical pain, emotional stress, mental confusion, similar to those used in shamanistic journeying.

In "Shamanistic Counseling and the Disabled," I will discuss briefly correlational findings among the disabled as predisposition to shamanistic methodologies of "mind travel."

The eleven subjects we used were:

*blind* - 1 person, female; age 26; uses guide dog; black

*cerebral palsy* - 4 persons, 3 female, 1 male; ages 19-26; 3 wheelchaired, 1 ambulatory; 1 hispanic, 3 Caucasians

*deaf* - 1 person, female; age 21; uses ASL; Caucasian

*dyslexic* - 2 persons, female; age 26-34; n/a; Caucasian

*MS* - 1 person, female; age 27; wheelchair; Caucasian

*anxiety disorder* - 1 person, female; age 34; medicated; Caucasian

*fibermyalgia* - 1 person, female; age 22; sometimes uses wheelchair; Caucasian

We talked with these individuals and recorded their comments about how they relax and if they do anything (e.g., close the drapes, turn on some kind of music) to help them relax. The last question was why they did what they had done and whether it had any effect on their lives. Their answers are listed in the section on "Shamanistic Counseling and the Disabled."

## Discussion

While the rights, discussed earlier, have opened opportunities to the disabled, little has been done to understand the disabled population. Employers are taught about how to accommodate their environment for disabled workers. Teachers are taught about the different physical conditions of the disabled, and rehabilitation workers are taught how to "sell" a disabled worker to an employer. All these facts are physically based.

Socially and psychologically, little has been done to clarify the needs of the disabled population. The tasks of psychologists is to observe the "abnormal" based on the theoretical construct model of a "healthy male human mind." This does not include what may be "normal" or "healthy" for an individual with a disability. For example, if a disabled person is angry, perhaps anger is healthy for that individual. Lack of anger would then signify "apathy" or depression. Again, the problem is that the "norm" is based on a different population and different cultural understanding. How can employers, teachers, students, etc., comprehend a disability, when they fail to understand the respective individual's emotions?

To restate: Children with disabilities (once identified) are tracked to check their needs and their progress. The stages are based on psychological models of Anna Freud and Jean Piaget. These foremost psychologists founded their theories of development on "normally functioning children based on age and development." The mean age development of a disabled child (again, differentiating the type of disability) may actually contain healthy norms of its own, in terms of physical development, but also psychological maturation.

As a child progresses toward adolescence, less observation and work is provided by a social worker or therapist. As an adult, an individual would then be transferred to a social worker specializing in assisting the disabled toward independent living and employment. The focus again is on the physical need of the disabled, not the emotional or psychological needs.

## Shamanistic Counseling and the Disabled

In the process of shamanistic journeying with the use of drums, rattles, etc, individuals are guided to look for an entry into the earth (or a "ladder," depending on which world they decide to go) to come in contact with guides that can assist with particular questions, a problem or information. At some point, individuals are guided (by the shaman) to their power ally (usually an animal or a person) who will then help them and give a sense of self-esteem or empowerment.

To parallel this process, interviews were conducted. Individuals with different disabilities told stories about leaving their body to cope with bodily pain, exhaustion, emotional upheaval, and societal pressures.

1. A female, blind African-American, a methodist in Ohio, confided in me that she often gets exhausted at the end of the day and feels "beat up." I asked her what she did to release the tension and her response was that

> I simply lay down on my bed, put on some music and drift to this field of flowers. There I can run and sit on a rock, looking at this nearby mountain. I usually come back with some answers to my problems and, at least, be refreshed.

Being blind since birth, she has adapted to her environment through journey work.

2. A male Caucasian, cerebral palsy client in Ohio expressed that he began to visualize a place outside his environment as early at seven years old. "Because life was so painful, I could take my troubles there (a mining camp at a mountain side that I identified as Monte Christo in Washington)." He has never travelled further than going on a fishing trip to Toronto, Canada.

3. A female, hispanic, cerebral palsy client from California, identified as a Catholic, admitted in conversation on March 12, 1992, that to be present in her body was hard, because it is so painful. She explained that she liked to day-dream about visiting Christ and talking with him about her troubles. She also mentioned that is the place from where she writes her short stories and creates a sense of understanding for herself.

4. A female, Caucasian, cerebral palsy client in California told me in a telephone conversation that she could not get by without "traveling in her mind." She explained that her cerebral palsy causes her body to cramp uncontrollably and leaves her, at times, crying when she is in her bed, unable to move. She explained that she allows herself to follow her breath. She is monitoring her breathing and slows it down so that she can breathe freely. From this point on, she lets her mind drift. "I have this place I go to, it's a real pretty lake and I throw stones into it, watching the ripples. I stay there as long as I can. There I can run, walk, and there is no pain."

5. A female, Caucasian, cerebral palsy client in New York used mostly a talking board to communicate. Being a quadriplegic cerebral palsy patient, she was confined to a wheelchair. As Raymond was counseling her on the phone on December 4, 1992, about school and family matters, she expressed desperation about her limitations. A picture of a hillside with a rock to sit on, flowers, green grass, sun shine, etc., came into Raymond's mind. He asked her if this was a place where she felt happy, strong and positive. She gasped, surprised that he knew about her secret place. He later admitted that he had a place like that, too.

6. A deaf, female Caucasian in California identified herself as a Wiccan.

Using sign language, she told me what happens to her in a drumming circle or during a guided meditation. She can't hear what's being said, as for the music she signed the equivalent to "who cares" (not translatable). She likes the drumming because she can feel the beat in her body. She expressed to me that she likes to leave her body because she feels free and it allows her to be in her own world that accepts her for herself and not because she is deaf.

7. I met a dyslexic Caucasian woman in California at a Michael Harner workshop. She claimed that

> drumming helps me understand myself. For once, I feel that I am okay as I am. In my lower world journeying, I find support that I cannot find anywhere else. Also drumming seems to have an effect on my physical condition, making it easer for me to connect to things.

8. A dyslexic Caucasian woman in California was confused about many issues. I asked her what made her happy and her response was:

> God, I don't know but when I put my daughter to bed, sometimes, instead of watching TV, I lie down and just let my mind wander until I come to this place where it is all warm and (this is gonna sound strange, but) I don't have a body. I just feel free. After I open my eyes, my mind seems to focus so much easier.

9. A Caucasian woman with multiple sclerosis in North Carolina, who Raymond was counseling on November 8, 1993, was concerned about her pending SSI case as well as her living with her parents and the condition of her health. Because of the "down and out" emotional and physical condition of the woman, Raymond asked her whether she prayed. She related that she meditates and leaves her body to deal with her Mom who comes down hard on her.

10. Raymond was counseling a Caucasian woman with anxiety attacks in Georgia on May 17, 1994, about her financial difficulties. He felt the fear tighten in his chest and stomach and asked her if she had a lot of anxious feelings. She then confided that she was being treated for acute anxiety attacks. He asked if she was still on medication and she admitted," yes, I am." He then suggested that she should try to meditate and relax. She relayed to him that her doctor had already taught her how and that she saw pastel colors in her landscapes which seem to calm her down.

11. When I talked with a Caucasian woman with fibermyalgia, in Ohio, about this paper, I explained how I found that many individuals gave accounts about "journeying" and how it helped them escape their pain. Some had described a release from some bodily trauma and all experienced beneficial results psychologically. Her response was,

> Oh, yes! I started using methods similar to those of the shamans we were studying in my anthropology class, mostly out of curiosity. I found it worked. Especially since I have a rare case of fibermyalgia (in my organs) and I take a

lot of medication to stay out of pain. When I remember to do this, it helps me to stay much clearer and I tend to need less medication.

In tribal societies, shamans were the mediators and, as wounded warriors, knew of dismemberment. Shamans themselves may have been effected by different "disabilities." (I put "disabilities" in quotation marks because what may be considered a disability in one society may not be seen the same way in another.) The practice of shamanism also includes the idea that individuals must be able to use, adapt or adopt whatever works within their framework. In other words, individuals can be eclectic. Using shamanistic techniques like journeying, individuals will be able to find their own answers to their (and often also their communities') questions.

How can this benefit the disabled when society seems to withhold psychological support? Perhaps, by assisting disabled individuals in journey work, they can find their own answers to their questions, especially since identity among the disabled has shown to be twice as low than in the average society (Vogel, 1988, and California State University, 1990).

I am suggesting here that the above small study, conducted in Ohio and California, seems to have something in common.

1. All experienced pain and fatigue when dealing with their disabilities.

2. They want to use visual mind travel as means of escape or release from their mental or physical pain.

3. Some of those questioned found answers to their own questions or new hope in their lives by using mind travel.

4. Some experienced a change in their physical condition using mind travel.

5. All felt some relief by using mind travel.

6. Not always expressed in words, but mostly expressed was a change in emotional behavior through mind travel.

This study was exploratory and extremely limited in demographic size of population and random selection. The focus was mostly on whether other disabled individuals were using "mind travel" as a means of support and, if so, how closely does it mirror journey work done consciously. It would be interesting to investigate this behavior on a larger population with formal questionnaires and more representation of different disabilities.

## Conclusion

This paper has explored the need toward a cultural and psychological understanding of those who are considered disabled. Understanding the different conditions of the various sectors will allow emotional and psychological needs to be addressed. Until society establishes a clear picture of each sector, no understanding of what can assist that particular population can be developed.

In this limited study, which needs further evaluation and investigation, it was found that shamanistic techniques can be helpful, even to people who, at the time they began using these techniques, were not aware of the type of technique in which they were engaging. Even with this limited research, it has been observed that members of different sectors of disabilities found self-empowerment and their own answers to their problems. The techniques could, therefore, also be beneficial to others within this group as well.

## References

California State University. *Report on Disabled Student Reporting System. Selected 1988 Demographics.* Long Beach, CA: California State University, Analytic Studies, 1990.

DeVos, George. Telephone conversation, August 9, 1993.

_____ , and Lola Romanucci-Ross, eds. *Ethnic Identity, Cultural Continuities and Change.* Chicago, IL: University of Chicago Press, 1975.

Herskovits, Melvin. *Myth of the Negro Past.* New York/London: Harper, 1941.

Lighthouse of the Blind (director). Telephone conversation, November 1978.

*Post Intelligencer.* "Job Listing" (Seattle, WA, November 1978).

Vogel, Susan A. *Some Preliminary Findings on Predicting Success for LD College Students.* Barat College Report, 1988.

# TOUCHING THE UNTOUCHABLES

Panna Flower

How Do You Touch the Untouchables?

It almost sounds like a Zen koan. Mother Theresa, God bless her, went, with an open heart, to live with and heal the untouchables—those with leprosy. In this instance, it was a visible condition and it was external society which dubbed this population "untouchables," i.e., *we* (the clean ones) don't want to touch *them* (the unclean ones). However, in the case of human souls who have experienced abuse in early childhood and shut down to avoid the pain, it is their own wounded psyche which, from the inside, has donned the label "untouchable," i.e., *we* don't want *them* (anyone) to touch us every again, because it hurts too much. And so that label, with its implied request, settles down deep in the unconscious where it is safe and the invisible barricades are secured tightly.

How do you touch the untouchables?

A zen koan, for sure, because the answer doesn't come from the mind any more than "the sound of one hand clapping," because Webster's dictionary definition of "clap" doesn't fit one hand; and similarly Webster's dictionary definition of "touch" is confusing, when a person's experiential association is closer to the word "batter." And in many cases more so, when they've been battered using the voice as a vehicle of touch or using the environment as a vehicle of touch.

But I want to focus on people who have been abused using the more physical sense of the word "touch." For a massage therapist, our discipline is known as a "hands-on" profession.

So what do we do?

Let me add to the dilemma a bit before we get into the response. Most people who have been abused early on and have not moved very far into their recovery, through whatever therapy of choice might work for them, most people which have been battered will never tell you what they are feeling: they can't! They didn't have words then; they can't find them now. There wasn't a safe place then; they can't find one now. They developed a way of surviving without talking. They are determined to survive now. And for many of these people, even a gentle touch is horrible in its spontaneous associations. Massage thus can become a container for horror.

So what do we do?

Well, I got my inkling of the dilemma first hand when I began studying massage fifteen years ago. At that time, I had no sense of my own early childhood history. I can remember the lecture part and the demonstration part and that was wonderful (i.e., safe). I can remember the exchange part which was fine as long as I was the giver. And I remember the feeling when I lay down on the table and gritted my teeth politely and waited until it was over. A shoulder, an arm, a foot, it didn't matter. It had nothing to do with the quality of touch of my partner. This was just something I had to get through in order to be qualified to do what I felt called to do professionally.

It never occurred to me that someone else might be silently feeling the same thing and that this someone might someday be a client of mine. It never occurred until I met "Janet." On the surface, she seemed no different than any other client. A bit shy, perhaps; I honored the shyness. No, she'd never had a massage before. She was a nurse, accustomed to giving to others, but unaccustomed to receiving. (Does this sound familiar?) She was currently under a lot of stress, and someone had suggested she might benefit from a massage. Her medical history was unremarkable, no particular defined areas of stress or discomfort in the body. She had no preference for music or silence during the massage; whatever I liked was fine with her.

Something was missing, but it wasn't clear what. It wasn't until I put my hands on her that I realized that it was "Janet" who was missing. Her joints were more than flexible. Her muscles were flaccid and yielding, almost without definition. Everything about her body was willing to move in whatever way my hands requested. The subtle message was, "This is good for me: that's why I'm here. Let's do it and get it over with."

"Janet" returned every two weeks faithfully, and then one week she cancelled, "I won't be able to make it Friday." I didn't hear from her again. After a couple of follow-up attempts to find out whether she was alright, I let it go, although the memory of her haunted me from time to time. There was something very different, very compelling, very familiar. Early in our sessions, the thought had occurred to me that she might be a battered child, but having no template to compare against, I had dismissed the thought.

About a year later, for no apparent reason, I was moved to call "Janet" just to say, "Hi! How are you doing! I was thinking of you." God bless answering machines: she called back that night to say her mother was in the hospital critically ill and could she come to see me.

It was sheer grace that guided those first few sessions and since then she has been one of my best teachers. That first session she just sat and wrung her hands. Her body said clearly, "Fragile! Don't touch!" and I didn't. Over time, over many sessions, her story came out and in her own time she asked for a shoulder to rest her head on, a safe place with no strings. It was months before she got on the table again, but when she did, her body was very different. It had definition now. She had found a place where it was okay to say "yes" and it was okay to say "no." Sometimes she would say, "I need to go now" and we would end without question. Sometimes she would want to talk, sometimes she wouldn't. She was learning to listen to her own agenda at last, and I was learning the delicacy of listening with no agenda. I still see her occasionally now. She was the first who taught me, and since then many others have come; in fact, the majority of my practice now is people with a history (known or unknown at the start) of early childhood trauma.

So, how can I touch the untouchables, you ask yourself?

It is still a Zen koan. The answer still doesn't come from the mind—the elements—safety—permission—awareness—acceptance—agenda-less-ness—infinite patience! The ability to listen—and trust: above all trust your quiet inner voice. When you sense discomfort on the part of the client and ask "How are you doing?" and the answer quickly (and often without expression) comes back "fine," it is time to slow down. Be gentle but firm, and listen. Ask yourself, "Is this *my* discomfort?" Ask quietly of the body part you are in contact with "What do you need? What do you want? What is happening?" and let the body itself answer directly—and it will. Sometimes an anecdote or imagery will help, sometimes silence.

But most of all, listen and trust. This is a dance with the client as leader;

and as long as you are very clear about your own boundaries within which the client can lead, it will work. If your comfort zone is crossed, you let them know; an honest non-judgmental negotiation can be very healing. You may need to refer and that's okay too. We all have our forte, and my wish for you is to find yours and to blossom.

# THE USE OF ECSTATIC TRANCE IN THE TREATMENT OF ADDICTIVE AND ABUSED INDIVIDUALS

Jean-Michel Fitremann

## Introduction

With addictive or abused patients, we usually face difficulties in dealing with the body and with emotions which tend to be pre-emotional reactions rather than fully embodied emotions. Even if these unfortunate people cannot be fully categorized as psychotic in the psychiatric nosography, I usually call them pre-psychotics or socialized-psychotics because they can have very specific psychotic-like episodes although they function seemingly in a normal fashion the rest of the time. Reconnecting their body to the higher-level functions of language and imagination produces healing.

I found that the deep trance state used in possession rituals is particularly useful to help these patients, both with improving the recovery of their body functions, possibly going into their psychotic functioning without going through the usual emotional barrier which is very strong in this type of persons.

## Psychoses and Prepsychoses

The conventional DSM-III-R and DSM-IV classification of disturbances uses the categorical approach based on symptoms. A more fruitful and insightful approach would be a dimensional or multifactorial strategy, based on a more global behavior-traits observation or a deeper evaluation of the personality. It allows clearer ideas about the inner structure of the psychic system and supports more correct and successful therapeutic schemes. The more detailed we discriminate symptoms, the more categories we get which prove to be less useful. If we chose to characterize an individual in broader and more meaningful dimensions, the closer we get to deep inner structures.

I have told elsewhere how we can empirically and heuristically use our clinical knowledge to classify the major disturbances (1994) and to understand the mechanisms of addictive disorders. In this essay, I have chosen to use a three-dimensional approach for the assessment of major psychological diseases. It is mainly based on the interpretation of the psychotic behavior which seems to involve the rupture of the links between major functions of the psyche or the faulty functioning of one of them. The three basic functions I have chosen are the body function (which effects reactions, pre-emotions and basic drives, it also represents the reality for our psyche),[1] the rational function (which pertains to logical order and time-space causal analyses) and the global function (which produces analogies, associations, evocations and syntheses, and interprets reactions into emotions and feelings). They roughly correspond in the CNS respectively to the brain stem, the left and the right cortex hemispheres. The rupture of one link between these major functions or the faulty functioning of one produces addictive disorders or psychoses.

For the moment, I have chosen to name three canonical psychoses: essential autism, essential hysteria,[2] and essential schizophrenia. A combination, to various degrees, of these three components produces the whole spectrum of psychoses.

With a lesser damage of the psychic system, the ability to meet daily requirements increases and those clients have lesser although severe difficulties which are variously named addictions, abused-children neuroses or psychoses, manic-depressive or borderline disorders. We can imagine in this case that the damage to the major links has been less crippling than in the former cases and/or that the basic functions have been more developed so that a certain amount of social adjustment has been possible. Using a similar three-dimensional reference evolved from the essential psychoses chart, we now get: anorexia, psychopathy, and schizoid-paranoid as basic ailments on that level of severity. Various forms of bulimia and anorexia, gambling and excessive obesity, alcoholism, sexomania and other drug addictions (the latter being more or less related to the release of endogenic morphine-like compounds in the brain or their direct ingestion) can then be located on the chart as a combination of these major psychopathologies (see also, Fitremann, 1994).

So we see that, in essence, the major psychopathologies reflect fundamental defects of our psychic system, not as an inadequate content or learning as in the lesser disorders (neuroses and affective disorders), but as essentially a damage of the quality or the strength of the links between major structural functions. So, our therapeutic approach has to look for a restoration or a substitution of these damaged links. In the following, I will show how trance work can help reconnect major functions and improve overall functioning.

## The Need for a Body (emotions-feelings) and a Linkage (body-language) Healing

It is well known that a possible "repair" of these damaged links can be obtained through a clinical approach involving

1. the rebuilding of body-sensations, especially proprioceptive, and the reclaiming of body reactions (Reichian work),
2. the repeated mirroring and naming of body experiences (analytic work),
3. experiencing in the body the implications of words (gestalt work),
4. using a psychotherapist and/or group support as a structuring device (transference and group dynamic work).

The combined approach of all four (which I call structured therapy) gives a maximized chance of recovery. We see here that all four strategies favor the creation and the implementation of one or more of the missing links between the major functions.

In the transference work, the crippled psyche uses another psyche to activate the links. It functions better with an outside "linker" or "editor" for a while, the latter is needed for social stability, during which the inner linker can regenerate itself and eventually lead progressively to autonomous functioning. In this view of the clinical work, it is essential to be reminded that we work on the basic structure of the psyche, i.e., on the quality and capacity of the inner linkage and consequently on the aptitude of the major functions, not so much on their content. The content of the psyche is of course the material produced in the therapeutical work itself, but mostly it is irrelevant and only a means of access to the deeper structure.

I will show now that the ecstatic trance phenomena are a great road to the discovery of the structure of the psyche and its defects, a means to bypass the innumerable obstacles to the deeper unconscious (the deep unconscious being basically a reflection of our structural aspects), and a case of magnified transference phenomena which can be used to great profit.

## Setting and Method

In this essay, I shall use the concept of trance as used in ecstatic or possession trance. It is much deeper and, therefore, different from the hypnotic, the journeying, the meditation, or the lucid dreaming trance. It is characterized by a temporary evacuation of the "ego," the personal conscious and unconscious thoughts, feelings, memories and associated emotions and drives. The body is thus left with a somewhat blank psychic system, able to sustain raw energy patterns or other, borrowed or related, psychic systems. The impression from inside is a remnant of self-observation (a kind of consciousness) and an inability to control what is manifested in the body, the motion, sometimes the sound or the speech, and what is perceived as being received from external sources.

The term "ecstatic" or "ex-static" seems appropriate since *ex stasis* means literally "gone out, having left our body," referring to the personal mind-emotion set.

*The Circle*—I use most of the time group effects to produce and sustain trance states. As trance is highly contagious, the use of two or three patients in trance in specific locations helps. The unconscious affective bond between patients produces a sort of network of the trance effect, of which I am aware. It helps others to take time to soften and acquaint themselves with the peculiar feelings of a loose and autonomous body and assists them to come closer to that state of being.

At the beginning of a session, I would use free dancing and specific let-go exercises to help being more in the body, paying less attention to thoughts and external stimuli and feeling more in a so-called group "energy," that is participating to the *egregor* effect.[3] Drumming would also synchronize bodies and tune the people, inducing change in the sympathic-parasympathic balance characteristic of trance states (see, Lex, 1979).

*The Induction of Trance*—At first, most of the induction would come from the beat and rhythm, then it comes from the body motion. The strong rhythmic body motion is one of the best inductor of trance states, since it is both active (motor activation) and passive or retroactive (proprioceptive sensory stimulation) and thus concerns most of our CNS functioning and takes us into the so-called trophotropic balance. Normally, I would also use specific rhythmic movements such as those used in the *zikhr* ceremonies of the Sufis or the *katzugen-kai* settings of the Shintoists, for instance. These movements work on mainly three important points for trance induction: the sacrum, the diaphragm, the medulla-pons locus. Rhythmic and fast breathing would normally follow. It has to be increased and diaphragm-based to the extent of what is normally obtained in deep Reichian work. It is essentially non-regressive and non-imagination stimulating, this point is important. When the trance state starts to happen, panting associated with a burst of sweat or sometimes a sudden coldness is usual. This phenomenon, together with the disappearance of thoughts and the onset of strong vibrations, involuntary shaking of the body, marks the beginning of the transformation of the physiological state.

The group is trained to dance and breathe throughout the session. I would, as a rule, go myself into the trance state first, as deeply as possible using the various exercises and group motion. I would then be able to perceive the connections within the group and the states clients are in. I would probably pick the most ready of the dancing group members and lead them into the trance proper one by one. This will be done in two steps. First, being in a trance state myself, I would induce a trance state in them by simple projecting my intent or touching their body. Second, I would move their body in such a way as to induce a strong let-go and a vanishing of the last control signs. Specific touching and mobilization would do the rest. When they are in deep trance, their body moves freely.

In some settings, I would use whirling, as the dervishes, the Umbanda, the Tibetans, or those using the TTT method (Morgan, 1990). But to me, it is not merely the whirling technique that works, but the fact that I am in the other plane and take them there by contact (Villoldo, 1991). Also, in that state, time and touch are changed and I am able to see and feel them in a very different way. I touch right where it would work, rock them in a gentle manner as in an etheric dance and ask them internally to come with me and have no fear. This is due to a profound distortion of time, space and touch. Therefore, externally, in ordinary space-time where what really happens cannot be decoded, this delicate merging of two often appears as a fierce struggle!

*The Work on the Patient*—As he goes into a deeper trance, he also deepens my own state by induction and we are then in a dual, out of control, psychically merged, relationship. I would pick up whatever his problems or state or suffering appear, either as feelings in my own body or as spontaneous reactions. In that state, everything is as it comes, as if interaction has its own course. It cannot be interpreted at that time. Flashes of meaning seep through from time to time; in faint thoughts, in shouts or moans, or attitudes or postures, sometimes in words. The energetic body would be apparent and palpable and responding, as an enlarged body, and the body motions would seem amplified and slowed down and more wave-like as in a slow-motion picture. The defective organs, the residual inhibiting tensions, the places of energetic or affective suffering are displayed and can be worked on, through awareness, acceptance, release and soothing.

It has to be understood that the connection between me and the patient is very strong and very close in this state. I would act out a number of responses he cannot himself manifest and, in reflection, he will respond to my attitudes and inductions without even a word or touch on my part. So healing takes place. In this primitive, direct body-to-body interaction and merging of the two unconscious an exchange of a large amount of information which could have taken many months of therapy does happen.

*The Preparation for Trance Work*—Going into deep trance states takes some preparation. First, the ability to loosen the body has to be worked through. One should be able to entirely focus, investing uniquely in the body for long periods of time. Also, for ease and safety, the emotional issues should have been worked over and over. If not, they probably will show up when the fluidization of the body happens at the beginning of the induction and emotional discharge will happen instead of going into trance. It is not uncommon that in benevolent but misinformed trance settings, the expected trance does not appear and transforms into a collective hysterical crisis, especially if the leader is not aware of the discrimination between the emotional plane manifestation and the trance manifestations. One can easily mistake one for the other. Ecstacy can only been assessed when in the trance state. So being in an ecstatic trance state as a leader is a necessary condition.

The major benefit of trance work is to bypass, or go directly beyond the emotional level and its fears and pains. Great care must be taken to go into trance to avoid difficulties. If menacing emotions are repressed by anxiety, this will block the access to the trance state. If, on the contrary, emotions are sought as a way of discharge, a hysterical crisis will follow and the trance effect is lost.

There are certain precautions to take when going in and out of trance. In the highly fluidized body condition, little or no repression is possible. That the personal psyche is absent is no problem, but when some personal, mental and emotional material is present, without the repression mechanism of the body, decompensation may happen with borderline individuals. A special manoeuver can avoid the crisis, as described below, but nonetheless, care must be taken to have people work on their emotional issues before they use this technique or it is better to avoid it. So I advise that deep emotional and analytical work or character analysis be undertaken as a preparation for the trance work.

Second, a positive relationship with the leader-therapist is needed. In trance, the highly susceptible reactions and merging of the unconscious patterns will be obstacles if any unforeseen resentments or rejections of the therapist are present. In that state, he is first a guide to a certain plane and an actor/receptor at very subtle levels of the psyche, and it is best that an alliance is formed before this type of work is undertaken.

No magic will heal anyone with this type of technique, even if it can be a shortcut and if new material can be obtained and directly worked on during the setting, trance work results have to be fully analyzed and given meaning. So, a talking session is a minimum requirement, otherwise, patients have to replace the experience in their personal history, using conventional therapy or any personal help they need.

# What Happens in the Body during Trance

*Deep Unconscious Structure*—What is especially remarkable in the ecstatic trance work is the progressive and temporary disposal of the personal conscious-unconscious set. What remains to activate the body and its relationship to the patient and to the leader-therapist is somewhat mysterious. At first glance, there appear what seems to be deep unconscious patterns, they are the primitive or archaic patterns of the psyche. Very high energy discharges of the body are likely in the beginning, similar to epileptic seizures or convulsions. Some fetal, birth, neonate, or baby material appears sometimes, but not very often, showing remnants of personal activation during the work. Some raw, animal-like, instinctual reaction may show up, seemingly manifesting the most elementary patterns which can activate our bodies. In any case, they do not coincide with the Freudian id of pure sexual and irrepressive impulses. They and associated behavior have never occurred in my settings.[4] The deep unconscious, devoid of the ego and superego, to use Freudian concepts, seems rather sensible and wise, albeit primitive. Most of the time though, what comes out is surprising and, while many primary patterns and primitive organizations show up, they have always an intense and purposeful aspect, even when they are fierce or violent, as if an unknown, underlying, meaningful set is activating them.

My personal guess is that having gotten rid of the personal stuff, we are left with the bare deep structure of our psyche which is not totally incapable or monstrous but a substrate system organized in specific ways, corresponding to our personal history and our own idiosyncratic needs and purpose. This system shows up in trance with its various attributes and defects and produces characteristic patterns of motion in the body, interacting with the leader-therapist and group members. Without the cover of emotional and mental processes, the deep support of our psyche is acting naked and can be worked upon and used for healing.

*Low and High Archetypes and Their Degree of Completion*—We can, of course, readily think of Jung's Shadow archetype or the Anima archetype (Hopcke, 1992). As a matter of fact, some of the material produced in the trance state can readily be interpreted along these lines. In actuality, in a number of settings, the personal history is not totally vacated and a beautiful display of the Shadow archetype can be found. Looking at these patterns in a more naive and unprejudiced way, we would be able to see the Lion, the Snake, or the Spider; in another line, the Crippled Old Woman, the Magnificent, or the Trickster. Identified can also be the King, the Witch, or the Perfect Beauty. I have also witnessed or experienced the Adventurer, the Worm, the Horrid Beast, the Brute, and the Slave, Joy and Desire, You'll Never Get

Away With This, and Nero. I have been Eyes and a patient has been the Mother of All Beings, another the Whole Strength of the Jewish People.

There is, of course, the question of degree. We can play with Would be Kings or with Emperors, or with Sneaking Tom or Master of Perversion. With recognizable forms of the structured psyche, some degree of maturity of the patterns seems to be displayed, as if the "archetypal" structure, the substrate, the support of our personal psyche, as I call it, were susceptible to growth, improvement, learning and completion. There will also be combinations so that the displayed is never or rarely pure. This strongly supports Jung's views, though a Jungian analyst would probably be able to reduce to no more than ten to twenty basic types the combinations of the hundreds of characters we meet.

*Meeting the Deep Unconscious: Animals, Freaks, and Demons; the Evolved Self; the Archetypal Structure*—Meeting the deep unconscious levels requires time and strategy. The Shadow does not show itself easily. Some level of acceptance of the most rejected aspects of ourselves must be built up before our unconscious comes to light during the trance work. Acceptance builds up slowly and the patterns appear in due time when the meeting of oneself and the associated fears has occurred.

We have to remind ourselves that illness and ailments, psychopathological disorders are produced by strong adverse forces, which try to erase life from our bodies and kill happiness, the joy of and the lust for life. These forces may be collective but, for us, they are pervading in our psyche, coming also from our parents and educators. In the deep trance state, I have met these forces and this encounter is not to be minimized, either for the therapeutic path of my patients nor for my own preparations as a therapist.

One major feature, I discovered in trance work, is that the healing forces needed to help a disordered individual, i.e., the life forces that I have to sustain and put to work, must be of like nature and comparable strength to the adverse forces producing the illness.

I remember once I had to treat a patient whose life was a havoc. He was the trickiest person I had ever seen, a master of all perversions. During the trance work, he kept for a long time pretending, producing nothing although the trance state of the group was quite deep. I deepened my state until I reached a tremendous strength and certainty. My body started to whirl him about, to move him very strongly, while he was incredibly resisting and escaping in his pretense, until he fell to the ground. I had another surge of energy and epileptic-like fit, feeling a strange compulsion. The words "that one is a deadly beast" came to me. As my body went into a frantic fight, a new level of strength came int me and I hurled, rolled and twisted him as if he was a puppet. (He was 6 feet tall and weighed 180 pounds.) Suddenly I let go and stood up, while he wriggled and twisted on the floor like a hyena, wounded to death and let out an incredible guttural moan like an animal, shot in the bush. He finally let himself go. The wounded beast had emerged. After the session, he said reluctantly that he had never produced such a sound in his life. He had been authentic for the first time.

To drive out, i.e., to exorcise a deadly factor that we have born for a long time and which has produced so much harm already, we apparently need to oppose and match it. We need another life force, a healing force of similar nature and of equal strength, acting on the same plane. To heal a patient who is possessed by a wounded beast, we need another beast, wounded but healed who has the force to overcome the malevolent force.

One may meet also higher levels of evolution in trance. We may incarnate apparently highly evolved beings, which can be interpreted as the most evolved parts of ourselves, not to speak of spirits. The production in itself is very beneficial, since it makes us experience that we are not all bad. After some time, we may even have a sort of experiential map of who we are in terms of type and degree of maturation of our archetypal functions.

*Energies, Entities, and Spirits*—Because all interpretative work has to be postponed and looked at later in our ordinary state of consciousness, it is difficult to evaluate and conceptualize what has actually been lived through during the trance session. From an inner point of view, the motions, attitudes, crises and interactions are numerous messages of the ordinarily unconscious patterns, structures, and forms that activate and motivate our ordinary life. They can manifest in our bodies as anything from pure energy patterns to very evolved beings. So what are they? In any case, I pretend that whatever, or should we say, whoever manifests has a direct relationship to the respective individual. The meaning of this relationship may not appear at first glance but it will in the course of the therapy or on a later occasion. They may be felt to be purely external activators who took over the body, they are, in my experience, however, never without a connection to that individual. They can be manifestations of old history, entities acting like a shadow, a spiritual drive or an unconscious twin. They can be seen as whole psychic organizations, called to help on this life path. They can be seen as manifestations of an unseen world or, as I call it, an adjoined world or space, we can refer to or even act out through our body under certain conditions. They are always related to who we really are.

Now there are questions of degree, I think, from what I have seen and what I have experienced, that we are able, during these deep trance conditions, to incarnate or incorporate a great many patterns from our neighbors and other people available in the adjoining space, whether they are our basic patterns of primary drives, our species specific programs, or our collective social patterns, trance work proves that we are able to change them for a moment. We can incorporate other patterns, even patterns of other species, they are available as interchangeable programs to our psychic substrata. The patterns and programs that fit best our own substrate, however, have more chance and are easier to incorporate than other, non-related ones.

Here we come, of course, to the work with spirits. Incorporating patterns entirely external to us and manifesting them in our body during trance is an experience that tends to become easier with time. Important for the purpose of healing ourselves are personal history patterns. The manifestation of guiding spirits or beneficial old souls is possible along those lines, but it is a different type of approach when healing disturbed patients. It is spiritual healing and I will not deal with the spiritual aspects of trance work here because it is another strategy for healing and guidance, although these aspects are prominent in many traditions. I have to stress that personal history healing has to take place if one feels unable to meet the daily requirements and no spiritual healing can be substituted for that purpose.

## What Helps Healing

*Fluidizing the Body*—Many factors of this technique help the healing process. Using the strong induction and change in the physiology of the body, particularly the temporary reduction or vanishing of the tension is in itself very beneficial. It leaves a model of good health, without the restraint or suppression of active drives, and a model of spontaneous reaction that produces a lot of hope for a possible better condition. It brings an exceptional ease of bodily motion, an increase of the feeling of self-dimension, a great increase of sensitivity and perception, associated with the safety of expression, and, in the end, a great sensation of joy in the body itself which leaves the person with feelings of elation, bliss or ecstasy and inner peace. Of course, as the thoughts slowly come back after the session, tensions come back also and reduce spontaneity as well. But the temporary effect has had its imprint and sets a goal for improvement. Also, the effect of fluidization lasts more than a few hours, up to a few days and I have observed very different expressions and a lot of release of new material during the therapeutic hour following the trance session. Thus, trance work also strongly affects the analytical work during the following week.

*Learning to Let Go*—One would certainly know that to let go is not an obvious thing "to do." Reichian work is to some extent a fight between the good feeling of being more spontaneous and the fear of being antisocial. In trance work, the repressing thoughts and the good self-image are not present and the muscles cannot hold back the natural reactions or produce self-deceptive behavior. So let go is merely a matter of accepting the body limits and working through them with the aid of the guide who is himself in trance and supports the process.

This learning of letting go has numerous consequences in life. I have found an increase of self-confidence, self-affirmation and enterprise and a truer and better relationship with others. I have also noted an increase of bodily pleasure in all activities and more reliance on the sensations for evaluating what is happening. Of course, as one would expect, there may be a great improvement also of pleasurable sexual activities, an easier reached orgasm for women and often the discovery that orgasm is not merely ejaculation for men. The access to extended orgasmic states (Brauer, 1983) is much easier attained through trance work than through any other type of work I know of.

*Going Through Fears*—There are many steps to negotiate entry into ecstatic trance states. It is a path of losing the identification with the (Freudian) ego and the will to obtain and to control, usually associated with consciousness as we know it. We have to cross the fear of "nothing is going to happen," the fear of exposure, the fear of not performing, the fear of dizziness and puking, the fear of falling and hurting oneself, the fear of hurting others, the fear of getting crazy, the fear that the group will not be able to provide safety, the fear that the therapist is not able to contain our violence, the fear of losing consciousness, of the pitch dark space to cross, the fear of acting free and leaving our body, also the fear of having only one body. In all, we really meet constantly with the fear of dying.

When all these fears have been met and accepted, we have to face the fear of our own unconscious, our hidden patterns, our freak sides, and not being sound or good or acceptable. We face the hidden dark forces of life, the so-called evil forces, both in ourselves, as actors and producers of evil, and in the external world as challenges to meet and fight for survival and good health.

We may meet also the fear of allowing some foreign pattern or entity or spirit, as one wishes to call them, to use our body for their own sake and purpose. We all have in the past internalized our parents without our awareness or consent, but, during trance, it can happen by choice and with consciousness of what is happening.

*Going Beyond Emotions*—One interesting aspect of trance is the absence of emotions. Trance work is a demonstration that emotions stem from a learning process and are connected with our memories. When thoughts go, emotions go. Thoughts and personal history patterns produce muscle tension and prevent spontaneity. When thoughts go, tensions go. This tends to support some of the Freudian views to a limited extent, it supports completely the Reichian theory about the body. It is also an indirect confirmation of the James-Lange theory of emotions. Emotions are body reactions interpreted by the superior CNS cortical functions. Depending on the degree of the depth of trance, we can work on the emotional plane or on the deeper structure of the psyche and the pre-emotional levels. I would suggest that hypnotic states where only the rational-function (left brain) is blocked (Watzlawick, 1978) can be used to tackle emotional and affective difficulties and that ecstatic trance states, as I call them to remind that the "ego" is not there, can be used to meet the structural psyche, the support or substrata of the personal history contents. From my work, it is apparent that, among psychoses and borderline-psychoses and addictions, the prepsychoses are ailments of the structure and have to be treated on that level. To my knowledge, only strategies of the transference mechanism, psychodrama and mask-techniques, ultraregressive work, and the ecstatic trance can go directly to that level.

*Crisis Without Repression, Psychotic Symptoms Without Decompensation: A Way to Explore the Core of the Psychotic State*—As I have already said, beyond affective sets, emotional disease and personal history difficulties, we meet or rather display our innermost structure, raw and uncovered. This is the state where the defects which normally entrain psychotic reactions can readily be observed. A left-out body, a defect in sensory ability, a major distortion of perception, the lack of linkage between action or speech and needs or desires, the lack of meaning of attitudes, all of this shows itself rather in a unobtrusive display in trance. I don't want to give here any directions how to view those defects and how to remedy them, but an experienced therapist will know of what value a direct access to these structural idiosyncrasies is. To use a metaphor, in trance a patient is acting purely psychotic, without extra paraphernalia, in his real suffering, cut-off, unable to do anything, crippled, blocked in archaic forms of behavior, in mechanical or stereotyped activities, in pervert or freak attitudes, or vanished into dream space. Dealing directly with this psychotic core of the psyche is a very promising process for efficient clinical work.

*The Merging of Two Unconsciousnesses, Becoming Conscious, the Pinnacle of Transference, the Beginning of a Bond*—As I have said, in the deep trance state, the two psychic structures may merge easily and act as one structure with two bodies. Elements of the patient will appear into the therapist's consciousness and, in this state, are likely to be acted out since talking is not obvious in such a state. In this case, the therapist also manifests what cannot be produced in the patient's body, as if he is the patient himself.

Conversely, even slight motions or inductions from the therapist will act, on a very subliminal level, on the patient in trance and help the release or the manifestation of aspects of the deeper structure. Overtly, it may take the form of a body exchange, ranging from loving touch and dancing together to genuine struggling or healing using the hands.

It can also be a provocation to externalize deeply imprinted patterns of the patient. This is the mechanism of exorcism where previously incorporated patterns, presumably during childhood through parents, residing either in the psyche as an intrusive/obtrusive content or even "molded" into structural form will then become apparent, active and alive in the patient's body. Then, the work of meeting those patterns, accepting, re-owning and releasing them can proceed. It may take many sessions and many hours of trance work, but those manifestations move into the direction of healing in whatever way they occur.

There may be some difficulties with schizophrenic or schizoid patients, individuals who have cut the link to their body and its expression in particular for too long. They may be living in an imaginary space,[6] or they may be lost in a word space where words are acted upon as a child would do with cubes—pure formal items without meaning. Those patients would not readily go into trance until they have regained some body awareness and some connection between body and higher functions, since the body experience is what constitutes for our psyche the base of our inner reality.[1] The ecstatic trance is another state of being closely related to the adjoining space. Schizophrenics are not really connected to the adjoining space, but are in a state so close to it so that they can draw some information from it. However, they are not able to put it into a language intelligible to us nor can they talk of their inner structure (except in cryptic form) since their language function is disconnected from their bodies and the reality we live in and share. So they have to return first to more actuality to be "able" to go into trance. Once they have achieved a sufficient degree of being in their body, they become incomparable trancers, because they already know the way to those states, have little repression to work through and also little fear of becoming crazy.

Of course, being merged with the patient, acting out or mirroring his patterns, actualizing new links and new ways of behavior, going into deep psychic touch and receding to become a more realized self to interact with, confronting two psyches directly, using one psyche to help the other either to read itself or to act out its patterns, or to reinforce its structure for a while, all of this is what transference is about. So in trance work, the transference and counter-transference effects are at their height, somehow devoid of too embarrassing and difficult to assess affective motions, but nonetheless effective on the deepest level. Then we can allow to play or let play out the truest or most elementary underlying patterns of the relationship between patient and therapist and work through its aspects and meaning. In this fashion, we can really design a clinical strategy and get valuable clinical material to help difficult patients on their way to improvement.

During the trance work, a tentative bond between patient and therapist is solicited. It is created, deepened or exposed according to the advancement of the therapy itself. The crippling due to a weak linkage of functions in the patient's psyche is temporarily reduced while it uses the therapist's psyche to connect his own and become more functional. This can readily be observed as the patient reveals patterns he could not reveal in his normal state. He even moves or acts as a more complete individual which he could not do in his usual state. Hopefully, this beginning of a better functioning will increase over time until autonomy from the therapist and from the setting is achieved.

## Necessities and Cautions

*Analytical Setting*—I hope I have shown how trance work can help the therapist to get information and to act upon the deepest patterns of a disturbed individual. To my understanding, the deepest levels are related in some way to the arrangement of the system and actual structure of the psyche, as a support of the numerous content patterns learned through experience. However, work on that level cannot be of any use if two conditions are not met. First, the trance experience has to be expressed in words and told to significant individuals—the group members and the therapist. Second, the relationship between the patient and the therapist has to be worked through and be given meaning. Not necessarily at once, but in the course of time, the experiences have to make sense in the therapeutic relationship. This will ensure a progressive integration of the new experiences with the rest of the personality. Otherwise, the events experienced during the trance session will not be related in the patient's mind to his personal archaic history. They will remain new events in life and the trend to personal consistency will be lost. So I advise that this type of work should not be considered a singular event of stepping out, but rather an event among many during a correct therapy or analysis. Also, the emergence of deep unconscious material can be disastrous to one's sanity if proper therapeutic care is not provided to meet and integrate the revealed patterns.

As mentioned before, I do not want to talk about spiritual healing, where the therapist acts as a medium for some spirit guide who knows better and makes moves that the ordinary healer cannot make. This would be a different topic. What I advocate is that the therapist makes clear that spirit healing or magic are not going to happen during this type of trance work. It is only a strong technique to reinforce or accelerate the process of ordinary therapy. Healing on another level does not deal with the same psychological difficulties we have to work with.

*The Therapist in Trance*—Another necessity of this type of work is that the therapist should lead the session when in trance himself. This, of course, presents a number of technical difficulties, but it guarantees the expected success. One reason is that patients or group members will not go into deep trance states unless the therapist is safely anchored there himself. In the very sensitive state reached during induction, confidence and bond will be felt only if the therapist is already there. His actions will be felt as consistent and in tune with what is experienced. If the therapist is not in trance, patients will feel lonely, frightened, and not guided. The actions of the therapist will appear clumsy, out of place, incongruent, and even threatening. I had this experienced and it was difficult and lonely although I had previous trance experiences.

Another reason is that the members will have little chance of going into trance but more chance of showing emotional patterns, hysteric fits, violent crises, seduction games or the like when trance induction movements and beats are used by a therapist who is not in trance. When they stay more or less in normal space, all the usual therapist-patient or group-patient transference games will show up and will not be decoded until one is ready to accept that this was not a trance phenomenon.

*The Safety of the Setting*—All precautions for a therapeutic or ritual setting should be observed. The most important of all for me is the intention of the group and the intention of the therapist. No matter what good reasons the therapist may have, his unconscious repressed motives will be magnified in trance and acted out without even his will or notice. The same applies to the participants, but their position is different since they come to work precisely on those patterns and use the therapist's support to that effect. It should, however, be clear to them that this is a working place and a sensitive one so that any other intentions but producing and meeting oneself will compromise the work and should be discouraged.

*In and Out of Trance Without Decompensation*—The strong induction of trance—the drumming, the dance, the let-go exercises—have the effect of reducing the tensions in the body. The pressure of repressed emotions or the flooding by such emotions may happen, and, in extreme cases, actual decompensation may occur. Rigorous technique should then be used to avoid it. Regressive techniques and breathing patterns should be avoided and going in and out of trance should follow certain rules.

When going into trance, I look for the most susceptible individuals and be careful not to let them go into a crisis before we actually go into trance. I also would take care of going directly into trance and not encourage emotional discharge, especially with hysterical characters.

Learning how to go out of trance is important. One can chose to leave the trance state abruptly, as a shock, or let it fade out gradually. In the former case, the rapid transit between states is a process of learning. In the latter case, individuals will benefit from that state much longer and this is beneficial. When someone is bordering decompensation, I always take him out of trance abruptly, so that no personal pre-emotional material is working through the then liquidized body. The "defenses" return at once together with the memories.

*Trance as a New Addiction*—Treating addicted patients is by no means a simple task because trance, as many other things, is highly addictive. It can replace, in practical no time, drug habits, drinking or bulimia. I surmise that in the trance state we produce a lot of endorphines and other anxiety and pain reducing substances. To give only one proof of that I shall mention the drastic physiological change of the body in deep trance: no pain response to blows, cuts or scalds, very little bleeding in case of even a deep cut, no blisters in case of scalds. In a great number of addictions, what individuals look for is precisely the modification or the secretion of endorphines, either through sexual activities or through direct or indirect ingestion of a product containing morphine-like chemicals.[7] Addicted personalities can then displace their addiction and become dependant on trance for the reduction of their anxiety or psychological suffering. Of course, it may not be bad in itself, but it has to be worked through as with any other type of addiction.

## Notes

1. In this context, reality is defined as the residues of the body experience.

2. This is not to be confused with the more common repression or conversion hysteria. I use hysteria here in the sense of the hysterical side of psychosis, according to Jacques Lacan and Ginette Michaud (1992).

3. The word "egregor" comes from the Greek word for "to be awakened." The egregor effect, in Latin countries, refers usually to the build-up of so-called "group energy." In group psychoanalysis, it would be preferable to speak of the progressive or sudden condensation of a group unconscious where the unconscious of the members merges into a common course of action, emotion, thought, etc.

4. This is, of course, a theoretical problem: the monstrous id and its avid and pervert greed does not show up in ecstatic trance when the ego is not present, so if it appears in "normal" neurotic individuals, it must have been acquired.

5. The imaginary can be seen as a major function, akin to or included in what we have called "the global function."

6. The symbolic function which uses language is part of the rational function.

7. In alcohol abuse, the secretion of endorphines and enkephalines is produced secondary to the reaction of ethanol in the brain.

## References

Brauer, Alan and Donna. *Extended Sexual Orgasm.* New York: Warner Books, 1983.

Fitremann, Jean-Michel. *Alcolisme et Psychose.* Paris: University of Paris, VII, memo, 1994.

Hopcke, Robert H. *A Guided Tour of the Collected Works of Jung.* New York: A.C.G. Jung Foundation Books, 1992.

Lex, Barbara W. "The Neurobiology of Ritual Trance," *The Spectrum of Ritual,* ed. E.G. d'Aquili *et al.* New York: Columbia University Press, 1979.

Michaud, Ginette. *Corps et Psychose.* Paris: University of Paris VII, 1992.

Morgan, Douglas. *TTT, An Introduction to Trance Dancing.* Lantzville, B.C., Canada: Ship Cottage Press, 1990.

Villoldo, Alberto. "The Medical Doctor Turned Psychic Surgeon" [interview with Dr. Edson de Quieros], *Healing States,* eds. Alberto Villoldo and Stanley Krippner. New York: Fireside Book, Simon & Schuster, Inc., 1987, pp.27-38

Watzlawick, Paul. *The Language of Change, Elements of Therapeutic Communication.* New York: Basic Books, 1978.

# DISCUSSION

## With Denig, Flower, Miller, and Wimmer

*Krippner:* Madrina, I want to compliment you on your discussion of the great tragedy of the shaman you spoke of. I am happy to have an insight view of that situation. I also hope that you will share privately with the group the story of your own self-healing and also the remarkable tale you told me.

I am taking groups to Brazil for the Institute of Noetic Sciences. Two years ago I vowed it would be the last time. I am not well paid. I am getting about $170/day. It is the least remunerative work I do but people enjoy it. I push the Noetic Science people to give money to the healers in Brazil and tell participants to buy something from the native people. I am outraged when the native people get nothing. I must say that Pai Ely never takes money for himself but gives it right to the temple. I have seen the people at the temple using this money well.

The question I have for anybody on the panel who wants to respond is: all of you have used shamanistic or indigenous techniques in the amelioration of the suffering of the people and you have done this more or less on your own, how do you get this into medical schools and occupational therapy schools? How do you get this into the establishment? What you are doing is so valuable, have you had any success in getting it into places where other people could learn from it?

*Heinze:* I want to answer this very briefly. Jean Achterberg is working with a national granting agency on alternative methods of healing, together with Larry Dossey. So there are already granting agencies willing to give money for alternative research. And there are single physicians who invite shamans into their clinic. A student at Saybrook wrote her dissertation about a *curandera* at a Denver clinic. Stanford University hospital is also calling the Brazilian shaman Antonio Costa de Silva for certain cases. So single physicians are already inviting shamans, and granting agencies are willing to fund research. The establishment itself, however, is very inflexible. If patients would start to avoid the establishment and seek alternative healers, then the establishment may begin to learn. If they lose patients, they have to listen.

*Wimmer:* It is not just the physical aspects of showing other people what to do or even going in and working with other people, the sad part is that if somebody like myself is approaching universities, to bring the issues into their arena, physically disabled people often have a very tough time. Universities can pick from the top ten per cent and, unfortunately, at this time, disabled people are black-balled and prevented from getting Ph.Ds. We can get our master's degree but as soon as we try to apply for Ph.D. studies, universities are just not inviting us. Some of the work is being done but not amongst those who are disabled themselves.

*Denig:* Stanley, thank you. I will later, at some point, tell about the healing I experienced, but, just briefly, the part that applies now: I had a complete breakdown of my endocrine system and ended up with hepatitis. I was told at four o'clock on a Wednesday that the only thing which could save my life was probably a liver transplant. That night, a Religious Science minister who is my partner (she is from San Diego) and I had a short conversation and the next morning, at seven o'clock, I woke up knowing that I had been healed. I called my doctor immediately and she insisted on tests because she wanted to prove this to her colleagues. She believed it herself, without even seeing me. She did the tests and is now submitting the results to the Peruvian Medical Society. She knows about my work in shamanism and the work I am doing as a Religious Science minister. In that small way, it had a very powerful impact on medicine in Cuzco. Some minds have been opened and the people of the medical profession and academia look now at shamanism and the power of the mind in a very different way. I think my illness served a purpose.

*Wimmer:* Just a brief comment from my point of view. We are dealing with a very wounded society as a whole. It may not only require infinite patience, it implies infinite time and a great deal of patience.

*Heinze:* The announced Brazilian trip is organized by the interpreter of Pai Ely. She is Brazilian herself. It will be an extraordinary trip we can talk about later.

*Marks:* I really loved all presentations. They spoke to me on many levels. Madrina's presentation brought up a part of my paper I had not been able to get to—going beyond forgiveness. There are certain behaviors that are totally unacceptable. One of the shadows we can get into with our ego is non-conflict, not confronting the shadow we see in other people. Something like forgiveness can become part of the ego, can attach itself to the ego in a certain self-righteous sense and can become very difficult. We have to go beyond forgiveness and not allow behaviors that are totally unacceptable. We all need help to change these patterns of our ego. I still have compassion for the person who is behaving this way.

Through my disability (I just became legally blind), I had to get beyond forgiveness with that also. I found myself just forgiving, forgiving, forgiving a lot of injustice and ended up in a victim place with forgiveness. This is a real danger and a trap. I was taking care of people's feelings and their reactions towards me and was not taking care of myself.

*Wimmer:* One of the roles of the disabled is that when they come to terms with their disability, they have to become the specialists on their disability. They have to go out and explain to the world, what is going on and how it is going on and why it is going on. It is not the easiest process, for example, when you are just trying to get a telephone hook-up, or somebody helps you to clean the house because you cannot. With Raymond and me, groceries are at high premium. We have to carry packs around his neck in order to get groceries. You have to explain this to people and it is very tough.

*Chase:* I want to thank all of you but particularly Mary and Raymond, having been a special education teacher for many years in the field of visually impairment. What brought me to this conference is something I was thinking of doing for years. You have motivated and stimulated me in so many ways. One of the things I want to say about the field I am working in is maybe different from the education going on in the school for the handicapped. We have the good fortune that a visually impaired child has two kinds of specialists. They have occupational orientation and now they have the orientation in mobility with which I am assisting. I jumped into that and the reason was that, under this title, I can do much what is needed for the kids. One of the things is to be advocates for themselves. There are many more things. As teacher of the academic part, I was frustrated for years. I can't tell you how I was yanked back into the academic part. This year I made a commitment to stand my ground and take fewer hours and lesser pay so that I can stay with that phase of teaching living skills, coping skills for every possible arena.

Another thing, when you were talking about how the world views handicapped people, it is really an atrocity that the rest of the so-called normal world thinks disabled people are asexual. Fortunately, it has been addressed and I have seen on television special documentaries. I really like to see that coming to light and being solved.

*Miller*: You were speaking about being your own advocate. Sometimes it feels as if you are taking on educating the whole world. I like to share with those around us here, you take care of your small part, the ones that you touch directly first and you advocate for yourself and them first and then it spreads.

*Wimmer*: The second part is that you choose your battles very wisely. You fight those you can fight. When you spoke about the misconception that disabled people are asexual, one of the areas of interest I have is also trying to find out what is happening in the disabled community with respect to AIDS. I don't know if AIDS education is even going on, because sex is not taught. This is definitely something I am interested in.

*Becker*: I am wearing this mask and people ask me why I am wearing it. When I end up talking about it, I noticed, a lot of people turn off and walk away. They don't want to listen. That rejection is very hard, because people have asked me in the first place. I think educating people is more important than my feeling of rejection.

I was a masseuse for many years and found the same thing. Panna, you are the first one who ever brought it up. When people had been abused and I touched them, they were soft, almost like someone who was totally relaxed. How could it be? Is it dissociation? If I would get these individuals into another state of consciousness, would the feeling of their body be different?

*Flower*: I don't know. If I would say anything, I would be hypothesizing and come up with a head theory. I reported on my experience. What is important is to be able to recognize and respond to the experience.

*Grey*: To me it is obvious, this person has submitted so completely, like a dog rolling over, thinking "the masseuse won't hurt me as much if I give up." That is how I interpret the lax muscle tone.

*Flower*: That would be my hypothetical response. It is dangerous to resist, therefore, I don't resist. Touch is so horrible that I need to leave my body and it is left there flat. I am abandoning my body. That's my guess, but this is speaking for somebody else. I hesitate even to put out the vibration of speaking for another person. This is my personal way.

*Bray:* What Stanley was saying about waking up the medical community, I fell into my line of work because one patient was mistreated by the medical community. I wrote letters and, after I sort of educated them, they started to refer more and more patients to me. Doctors are so frustrated with chronic pain patients. They feel inadequate, so they take it out on the patients in a very hostile way, blaming the patients, accusing them of things that are not true. I am getting referrals from all over the city, doctors I don't even know. Doctors, on one hand, have a distrust of these patients, thinking they are pulling something on them or they are just so uncooperative. On the other hand, they are begging for help and they begin to understand the situation. Workmen's Compensation is paying for my work and this is a very medical system. Sometimes doctors refer patients to me and say they want biofeedback, that's as far as they can go, but, of course, I am doing more than that. Doctors are beginning to become aware that someone else can help.

*DuPraw Anderson:* I appreciate your presence, Madrina. What you have said and what you brought up is extremely important for me. My presentation tomorrow will be on work with the Incas and especially work with don Juan Munes del Prado. Working with those people, it has been an incredible exercise in how does the process of reciprocity work. It is a continued issue for me that helps me to focus on the present as much as possible. I also want to say that I had the great privilege of being brought to those contacts by Villoldo and don Juan now working with the Qu'ro people. There is also, Americo Yabar who comes in dreams and meditations. I consider him a true teacher. As I struggled with some of these issues, working in a Latin country with all the differences, I felt that part of the reciprocity between North and South America has to do with the presence of the feminine.

*Bray:* Mary and Raymond, thank you. I am also dyslexic. Fifty years ago nobody even knew about it or, at least, it was not spoken about very much. We were not led to believe that we were intelligent people. I work as a music therapist for the Santa Rosa Junior College. I work with elderly people in seven hospitals a week. In response to Stanley's suggestion, what I finally found was that I could not come in overtly. I had to place it under the guise of music, of therapy. I was very careful how I presented alternative modes of healing. All my therapy work and interest in dreams with my patients is done quietly, because this is the only way I could bring in what I have and stay acceptable. I am doing this for twenty years. Now, I am very much accepted and have the freedom to do it more overtly. That's probably the only way anybody of us will be able to do. It means going into the structure and just doing it.

# Entering the Silence

ellenHelga Weiland

A number of years ago, I attended a workshop led by Jean Houston. We spent the morning learning about the "Hero/Heroine's Journey" (Campbell, 1973).[1] On that particular Sunday afternoon, Jean was asking us to dance "The Journey." The oversized hotel room, transformed into "The Odyssey's" sphere, was divided into sections representing the various aspects of the impending expedition.

In undertaking the "Journey" (from which, by the way, none of us were exempt), one started at "The Call," moved through "Finding Allies," tricked one's way past the "Guardians of the Gate," gestated in the "Belly of the Whale," was challenged through the "Road of Trials," ecstatically rejoiced at receiving "The Gift," took "Magical Flight" home, again tricked one's way past the "Guardians," and returned to share the "Grace" with Community. At least, that was the general design of the journey.

A participant in this particular workshop brought an immense and beautiful African drum. That instrument was positioned just past the place of gifting, right in the middle of the territory of "Magical Flight." The drum had a deep sound. Its beat and rhythm were hard to miss, even over the amplified music.

I danced with ease through the various phases of the journey. When I came to that drum, I was enchanted, entranced. I lost awareness of my consciousness and I became the drum's rhythm. My beat and its beat sounded one heart. I fell asleep into that heartbeat. I do not know what awakened me, but suddenly I remembered my "Call." I remembered just in time to hear Jean announce the two-minute mark to finish.

Falling asleep into the drum was quite a lesson. In my slumber, I strayed from the path and fell in love with love. As a result of the shift of focus, I was failing to complete my "Call."

With difficulty, I tore myself out of the ecstasy of that heartbeat, that drumbeat, that drum. I struggled to regain my center; to find my path, and to bring my gift to matter.

I raced back across my life and counted how many times I had fallen in love with love and lost my way. I traced how many times I strayed from my journey in the darkness of the long and lonely night.

Loosing one's way may well be the most frequent event in each person's response to his/her "Call." I suspect that we spend more time randomly attaching to almost anything in the twilight of our semi-consciousness than we actually spend traveling our path.

The trick seems to be to reclaim ourselves, to reclaim awareness of our consciousness from life's incessant and multiple diversions. But in the outer and inner noise of modern day life, the hustle and bustle of everyday activity, in the sphere of the 20th century Odyssey, how do we reclaim our stream of consciousness?

Silence, for me, has been and is the tunnel through which I flow into the extended reality. In silence, I suspend the usual inner dialogue and noise, as well as my involvement in external diversions. During this suspension of busy work, I refrequence within "the Source." Silence allows my awakening into consciousness, into awareness of my immersion in, and unification with the universal flow. Silence facilitates the exquisite assimilation of that experience, and my ultimate creative reorganization.

Thinking of Jean's workshop reminds me of the many weekends and weeks which I have spent in the middle of a cornucopia of learning, of experiencing, of playing with masters who teach me the melodies of their song and the patterns of their dance. How often do I loose my own song and cavort along paths remote from my own while swimming in the waves of such learning?

I delight in excess and avail myself to the muchness of life, yet I also yearn to consciously choose the nourishment which I provide for my soul's growth: to note each element as it vibrates my senses into creative activation. I long to sit luxuriantly and to consume one palatable teaching after the other, so slowly, so deliciously, that my senses can distinguish every single essential learning molecule.

But the world, or the workshop does not stop flowing. It evolves rapidly and I find myself gulping and swallowing whole, and failing to savor the essential character of any of its budding flowers. Often I find myself full, bloated, even suffering psychic indigestion and mental flatulence with no subtle digestive aid in sight. At such times, I yearn for silence and a moment of resourcing.

All disciplines with which I am acquainted invite us to "come to center," "come home," "relax" and "focus." A good number of available techniques simulate silence. Yet when I examine the result closely, I find my surface activity calming, and my subconscious dialogues and images still in a turbulent race.

I have tried many suggestions. A single one, which has repeatedly allowed me to reclaim myself, was offered by my teacher Robert Masters during the Human Capacities Program.

Dr. Masters call his process "Entering the Silence."[1] He states:

> It is the aim of many kinds of meditation to empty the mind to cease the babble and all the noise from the unconscious that comes up into the conscious mind and to empty the mind of words, images and sensations.
>
> Emptying the mind is a very good thing to do.
>
> If you can empty the mind and keep it empty for a significant period of time, you break up many of the patterns of static and you achieve levels of tranquility and serenity that are difficult to achieve any other way. The person's mental and emotional as well as physical health is likely to improve with that kind of meditation practice.
>
> It is very easy to tell people to sit and try to not think, not have images, to empty the mind. But there are very few techniques that are taught for doing it that are adequate at all.
>
> One is able, however, to create a situation where one can have the experience of what it really means to be at peace within yourself and to have a mind that is empty of words and images, a mind just totally at rest. The possibility of achieving this rests upon two facts primarily.
>
> One is that it is impossible to think with words without moving the vocal apparatus to some extent. Whenever you think in words there are at least tiny movements that accompany that which, if made larger, would result in actual verbal speech.
>
> And in the same way it is impossible to have images without using the muscles of the eye, and having some, at least minuscule eye movements.
>
> There, if one is able to relax sufficiently, the vocal apparatus and the visual apparatus, then one will have neither words nor images. And the mind will be empty. There is no quicker way, or easier way to do it.

Today, in the interest of slowing just for a moment, the psychic ingestive process at this conference, of providing some time for mental digestion and absorption of the abundance of rich material already presented, and allocating some space for assimilation and creative refrequencing, I offer to you my variation of Bob's process.1 I trust that the experience will give our psychic digestive organs a brief rest and prepare us for an evening of further feasting.

*          *          *

To begin, spend some time breathing gently and deeply. Breathe all the way in, and all the way out. continue this breathing as I speak to you.

Through this exercise I ask you to focus only on my instructions. The ability to enter the silence is greatly increased by your ability to focus.

I invite you to honor the bountiful material which has already flowed into your field during this conference. Trust that none of this material will be lost.

Still breathing gently and completely, notice your mental state. Be aware of the thoughts moving about within you, and the nature and quality of those thoughts. Are you thinking in images, in words, or in a combination thereof?

Notice the tension and movement in the muscles of your eyes as they scan any images.

If your thoughts manifest in words, be aware of any inner dialogue. Is the dialogue a whisper or a shout? Notice what is occurring in your throat as you hear the words spoken.

It is impossible to think in words without moving the vocal apparatus to some extent. And, in the same way, it is impossible to have images without using the muscles of the eyes, and having some, at least minuscule eye movements. Therefore, if you were able to relax the vocal apparatus and the visual apparatus sufficiently, then you will have neither words nor images. and the mind will be empty.

Now attend your physical state of being. Are you comfortable, relaxed and at ease?

Shift and move around in your seats just a bit, adjusting again your posture.

Come to stillness.

Beginning with your feet, scan your entire body for any physical tensions. Just be aware of any tension and release it as much as possible.

We will proceed, for a short time, with a progressive relaxation exercise. As I ask you to create tension in various parts of your body, I don't invite you to introduce tension to the point of pain. At no time should these movements be painful, that is, pain in excess of what you normally experience.

Contract the arches and toes of your feet. Hold that tension a moment. Then, direct the arches and toes to sub-vocalize. Command "Toes release! Arches release!" Relax and let all tension flow from your feet.

Repeat that movement several times.

Notice the tension flowing from your feet.

Now flex and hold tension in your ankles.

Instruct your ankles to release.

Contract the calf muscles. Hold. Release.

With each of the movements, I suggest to you, direct the movement with your own sub-vocal instructions.

Flex and hold the tension in your knees.

Knees release and relax.

Continue to breathe gently and deeply.

Contract the muscles in your thighs and hold that tension. "Thighs relax and release."

Tighten all the muscles and joints in your legs. Hold. Release.

Now contract the muscles of your buttocks. Hold. Release.

Contract your abdominal and pelvic muscles. Hold that tension. Instruct your muscles to release.

Again contract. Hold. Release.

Contract and hold the muscles in your chest and upper abdomen. Hold. Release.

Contract and hold the muscles in your back. Hold. Release.

Contract the muscles in your entire torso. Hold that tension. Instruct your muscles to release.

Flex the joints in your fingers. Hold. Loosen and release.

Tighten your hands. Hold. Release.

Flex your wrists. Hold. Release.

Tighten your arms and elbows. Hold. Release.

In whatever way you can, introduce tension in your shoulders and shoulder blades. Hold that tension. Release.

Now tense your entire body. Hold that tension. Release and relax.

Sense all tension flowing from your body.

Now inhale, expanding your lower belly with the breath. Hold that breath for a moment and bounce that pressure from the lower belly into your chest and back into the belly. Just bounce that pocket of air back and forth between your belly and your chest for as long as you comfortably can. Exhale and feel the tension flow from you.

Repeat that process.

Now create some tension in your neck. Hold. Instruct your neck to release.

To the best of your ability tighten the muscles in the back of your head. Hold that tension. Release.

Sequentially tighten and release the muscles oN the side of your head; the jaw, the tongue, the lips, and cheeks. And release completely.

Tighten the entire face, the eyes, the ears, and upper head. Hold. Release.

Again tighten the entire body including all the parts of the head. Hold that tension. Instruct all of your muscles and joints to relax and release.

Sense every last bit of tension leaving your body.

Now attend to your eyes and eye muscles.

Image a golden eagle flying across a blue sky, dotted with fluffy white clouds. See that eagle circling way over to the left, high above the lake. See the eagle diving into the waters. See it emerging from the water, fish in talons, flying towards the distant cliffs on your right.

Let that image fade.

Image a genie emerging from a bottle. He towers over you. Then see him standing, arms folded, on the magic carpet which is carrying him into the distance out of your view. The carpet and the genie return circling in a wide counterclockwise motion around you. He circles wide to your right side, carrying a treasure chest in his arms.

Image that genie opening the treasure chest and showering its precious rainbow colored gems over the side of his magic carpet. The jewels fall in front of your feet. With your eyes you explore the bounty. Pick up a pearl and focus into its shimmering depth.

Let that image fade.

Image yourself sitting on a hill, seeing below you a very large, oval bicycle track with colorfully dressed racers peddling round and round at ever increasing speeds. First one racer leads, then another. The fastest of the racers passes the checkered flag, as the crowd cheers.

And let that image go.

Image now a winding road filling your field of vision. From the distance, a car drives the roads' hairpin turns in your direction. As it comes closer, you recognize the car. It stops not too far from you. Out of the car steps a person whom you casually know. She greets you with a smile.

Notice what your eye muscles do.

Let that image go.

Image a three-ring circus with a flying trapeze troop to the left, a juggler to the right, and a highly trained tiger act in the center. Your eyes move rapidly back and forth as you try to catch all of these activities.

The trapeze artist triple-somersaults through the air then is caught by her partner, while the juggler simultaneously spins numerous plates, one tiger lunges through the ring of fire, then leaps from his platform and bolts out of the left side of the tent.

Now let that image fade.

Be aware of any areas in which tension is increasing and give the instruction to release, relax and release. Particularly instruct the entire head, the face, the eyes, the jaw and lips, the tongue and the throat to release all tension.

Now recite, inaudibly, a nursery rhyme which you recall from your childhood. Just recite quietly any familiar childhood rhyme or poem.

Note what occurs in our throat.

Instruct all parts of your body, especially the eyes, throat, jaw, and tongue to relax and release. Release also any emotions or ideas you may be holding.

Recall and silently sing to yourself a hymn that you learned as a child.

Again instruct your jaw, tongue, throat, neck, face and eyes to release any tension.

Sing a national anthem or some patriotic song of the country of your birth.

Observe what tensions arise, and instruct all body parts involved to release the tensions.

Now recite or sing some popular poem or song which occurs to you.

Once again scan your body and instruct all body parts in which tension is arising, to release. Release the throat, tongue, jaw, eyes, and face.

Come to silence.

You experience no movement, no effort, no tension in your throat, jaw, tongue, mouth, eyes, or face. You are thinking about nothing, sitting as completely relaxed as possible. If a thought arises either as an image or a sub-vocalization, just release the muscles of your eyes, throat, jaw, and tongue.

Observe the emptiness when your eyes do nothing and your throat does nothing and your tongue does nothing. Just remain in that emptiness until I will direct you again.

Note the quality and content of any images which may arise from time to time. Do not invite or entertain these images. Just let them go. Empty the mind again and again and keep it as empty and silent as possible for as long as possible.

*[If you want to tape this exercise, leave as much time as is available to remain in the silence. You might want to fast-forward the tape for about five or ten minutes, or longer. Then complete the process with the following directions.]*

Slowly come back to this room, into this space, this time. I will count backwards from 10 to 1: 10, 9, 8, slowly returning, 7, 6, 5, all tensions released, 4, 3, 2, feeling refreshed and relaxed, 1. Eye lids open easily, you are fully awake and alert, looking around and stretching, sensing colors and shapes and their depth, around this room, seeing your neighbors, fully present, fully alert.

## Note
1. Based on the process, "Entering the Silence," by Dr. Robert E. Masters, Human Capacities Program, January 1987.

## Reference
Campbell, Joseph. "The Hero's Journey," *The Hero with a Thousand Faces.* Princeton, NJ: Princeton University Press, Bollingen Series XVII, 1973.

# LOVE IS THE KI:
# LET THE MEDICINE DO ME

Tomas Pinkson

I know it is September because two things happen with consistency. Ruth-Inge has her hoe-down and get together and it is always the time I come back from my vision quest in the mountains. It was an interesting experience

I had and I want to say a few words about it, leading to another experience I had a year and a half ago. Hopefully there will be a few minutes left to do some drumming.

This summer was my twenty-second year of going up to this place in the high sierra to fast and be with the goddess and be with the mystery. It is a measurement of my year, from one year to the next. I usually take a group of folks up there. It is about a two-day backpack over an eleven thousand-foot high mountain into the Cathedral Range in Yosemite.

This year, the Wilderness Permit they gave us was not good until the next day. It was about 5 o'clock p.m. when we got there and needed to get going. I was a little bit distracted when we got started because we were going in illegally. Our permit was not good until the next day, but I wanted to get going. There was a guy sitting by the trail head, he didn't have a ranger uniform on, but he was sitting there in a chair and he had a walkie-talkie. I was a little bit concerned of going ten steps down the trail and getting busted. We prayed and listened for guidance. It was now getting darker. I said, "let's go for it" and we took of, and started hiking up.

After a couple of hours, it was dark and we stopped for dinner. I had a nagging feeling in my head. I couldn't remember taking my car keys and putting them into my backpack. I always deliberately do this. I looked at my memory bank and could not find that memory. I checked my backpack, no keys. I checked all my pockets, no keys. I was not a happy camper. I had lost my keys. It was already dark, it was 9:30 p.m. and we had to make a decision. We will be up here for a week, what to do? One of the things about me is that I am basically very lazy, and I don't like the prospect of losing altitude I have already gained and worked really hard to achieve. We had already gained some altitude and could see far back down there where we had started. So I was not really happy about going back there and some of the people said, "Oh, it will be alright. Somebody will find the keys and give them to a ranger, and you can go to the ranger station when we come back and the keys will be there." I tried to figure out in my head what to do. The rational stuff, back and forth, and I could not get a clear answer.

So finally, I let it go but left the radar set on. I went ahead with the chores that were present—cleaning up from dinner and discussing with the group what lay ahead. My older daughter was there and I told her, "You can take them up to the lake and I can go back. I would leave my backpack here and go back, sleep out and meet you there in the morning." But I wasn't sure what to do and was still listening to inner guidance.

Fifteen minutes later I felt a tug in my abdomen, on my *hara,* like an energy line going back down the mountain to the parking lot and a voice from the keys saying, "We are here now but we won't be here much longer." It felt really clear. It did not feel like a head trip, it was solid. So I told the others, "I got that call, I am going back down, to get my keys." And I realized that I had to accept that the keys might not be there, just because I felt it strongly. "You may go all the way down there and have to come all the way up and it will be midnight by then. You will be exhausted. And you still have to go another couple of miles to the lake, without your keys." I didn't want to do that, but my listening said, "Yes," that's what I needed to do. "We won't be here much longer," said the voice. So I went for it.

Starting down the trail, I watched myself creating an intense pain state through negative judgments about myself. How could I be such a shmuck and forget my keys? How could I do that? I could see this production I was creating, every step down, one more piece of misery. And then, all of the sudden, like a doorway opening, like the Huichol say, the *nierika*, I saw the metaphor of it all. I had forgotten my keys and had to go back down the mountain to find my keys. I had lost my "ki". The Japanese word *ki* means energy. I was all bound up in knots. Ten feet down the trail, I got that the first key to restore my balance was to let go of the judgments and to forgive myself. I said, "Alright, okay. That's what it is about. This is the opening to the quest. To recognize how in our lives we have forgotten our keys and what mountains we have to go back down to find them."

The next realization, after I had forgiven myself and had let go of the judgments, was that I still was not happy about losing all this altitude and losing a couple of hours of time. I still was not a happy camper about that. What came out with that one was: "This is your life, right now. This is it. You got no guarantees about anything else. It is happening right here now. You have chosen to go back the mountain. You can do it in misery or you can find a way to transform it, so you can get off on it and you can enjoy it. Because if you are not enjoying it, who is creating it? You dreamed it up. So turn it around from a nightmare into a good dream." I said, "Okay, that is my life. So I need to be present with each step, going down the mountain. It is already dark." Just to show you how thorough I was in my preparations, when I left the backpack, I took a couple of extra batteries from my pack which I had brought from home and I congratulated myself. And then, half way down the trail, my flashlight went out. I lost my keys, I lost my light, but I said, "No problem, I got two extra batteries, boy, aren't you together!" Congratulating myself, I took out the batteries, oh shit, this was a three-battery flashlight! Fortunately, another man who wanted to spend some time with me, had a flashlight that worked.

On the way down, I was thinking to myself about my car alarm. I had two cars stolen recently while visiting my other daughter in L.A. and my insurance company said, "No insurance, if you don't get a car alarm," so I got one. I knew that if I would open the car without the key release, the alarms blast off in a wilderness parking lot. Since I don't know anything about cars, one of the other people in our group would have to figure out, how to disconnect it and that would take a while. I shuddered at that thought.

As we were getting closer to the parking lot, another doorway opened in my mind and helped me see what this was all about. The Great Mystery works in all things. It is easy in nature, to be in "second attention" because you are interacting directly with what Spirit created. You are not interacting with what two-legged created. So coming back from the mountain is coming back into a different world, a world where it is more difficult to be in "second attention." Here we are apprised to be in "first attention," defining our being in terms of our ego identity and all the rest of that rigmarole. So it is harder to stay open to the Goddess and what she gives us, through dreaming and feelings and intuition.

I had some very interesting experiences, coming back from the mountains and going over the bridge from one world into the other, including stopping at the Central Valley town to buy a water melon, then backing the van up, inadvertently bumping into some Hell's Angeles motor cycles, parked behind me, knocking them over and dealing with that energy which was interesting, as if I had run over their penises.

Approaching the parking lot, I saw that losing my keys and having the alarm go off for about ten or fifteen minutes, was a *poca de gracia*, a piece of grace from Spirit, saying, "I want you to be really attentive, going over a bridge here. I want you to be really aware that you go from one world to another. All that medicine I gave you in the mountains, I want you to bring it back with you. I don't want you to loose any of it. So I sat up this little scenario with your help. In fifteen minutes you will be there, with the alarm going blast, blast, blast! That's so you get it and are really present."

This is all lead-in to what I really want to talk about. How this experience speaks to me as a male in a culture which is so dominated by the masculine control trip. It's gotten way out of balance and as a result we are in deep trouble. We have lost our *ki;* collectively, we have lost *ki.*

I want to talk about an experience with a woman named dona Julietta, a Mazateca shamaness from Oaxaca, with whom I was connected a while back. One night, she took the people I was working with through a *Velada* with the sacred mushrooms, their communion sacrament. She set up her altar with candles and flowers, just beautiful and started the ceremony with prayers and singing. About an hour into it, all of the sudden, there on the altar was a card and I can't see what the card is about. It was about a three-inch card, and this card opened up and this energy just poured out of this card and just bowled me over. It hit me right in the chest and took me into ecstasy. I was in total bliss. I looked over to dona Julietta and her apprentice. I was just beaming. The next day they said, "You were just radiant." It was pure love, just incredible love.

Being a radical extremist, I thought, "If it is this good from fifteen feet away, I am going to, walk up and stick my head into it, stick my face into it." So I asked for permission from dona Julietta. She is my spiritual grandmother, my elder. She said, "go for it." I walked up and the closer I got, the more I was transformed. I saw what was on the other side of the card. It was the love of the mother for her children, the mother who never sleeps. It was a feminine, goddess energy. It was that loving mother, for whom there is absolutely nothing we can do in this life to make her stop loving us. She never even nods out, she is always there, sending out this love. I bent down to experience her love and tears poured down my cheeks. Pure love and appreciation. After a while, I came back to the other side and looked at the altar to see what was on the card. To my complete and utter surprise, it was a picture of the Virgin of Guadelupe.

Six months later, I was flying to Dublin, Ireland, to a conference with Ralph Metzner and I said, "Ralph, let me tell you what happened to me recently." I told him about my experience with dona Julietta and Ralph said, "Take a look at this." He brought out a magazine and there was a whole article about Guadalupe coming through in different ways to people around the world.

For me, shamanism is very much about opening to the feminine. From that feminine, intuitive, receptive place, we connect with the Great Mystery. She gives us guidance through our dreams, our bodies, our feelings, and our intuition how to be in right relationship with everything and everyone. Then we need to connect with the male energy to bring that out, to bring that through in our lives and to the world. It is a sacred marriage, working together in that way, in respectful partnership. So that's I wanted to share with relatives about the goddess, the Virgin of Guadalupe and her love for us. How beautiful she is and how we need, each in our own way, to open our hearts to her love and bring that through. Now I would like to drum just for a few moments.

I want to ask my nine-year-old nephew Kyle to come up here. He is from L.A., visiting. Kyle has a lot of good medicine. Friday night we were at a drumming circle and yesterday we were at a memorial service. A good friend of mine had been killed about six month ago. He was tree-trimming at Muir Beach and the power hit him and took him right out, just like that. I wanted to know where that tree was where he had been taken out, to perform a ceremony. Kyle came up shortly there after to visit and we went down to Muir Beach and spent a day out there. Then Kyle got bitten by a dog and we went up to the nearest house to get help and find out about who owned the dog. And, to my shock, there were the people who had found my friend. They were carpenters, working on the house. So they bandaged Kyle up and said, "The person who owns that dog lives up the street." So I went up there and, on the way, went right by that tree where my friend had died. And the dog who bit Kyle was named Kyle. This young man has a lot of medicine here.

I just want to invite you to bring your awareness down into your heart and, if the words and the images I am saying don't work for you, just translate them into whatever works for your integrity. What I's like to do, is invite us to open our hearts to the love of the Virgin of Guadelupe. All of us have equal access to be channelled into her love in this world.

[Drumming]

Virgin of Guadalupe! Thank you for your light and your love and your healing guidance, and your beauty, and your power and your magnificence! Dona Julietta, thank you! Thank you Mother Earth! Thank you, Mazatecan people! Thank you, Ruth-Inge, for bringing us together, for all the relations to make this happen, to make this a good *nierika,* that we get the medicine we need to strengthen ourselves to go forward in a good way. May it be so, ho!

# THE ANIMAL CONNECTION

Felicitas D. Goodman

One of the nuns who were my teachers at the Hungarian convent school in the 1920s once made the angry remark, "Some people might actually be descended from monkeys, but I certainly am not." The roots of her anger were clearly at the spot where so much modern environmentalism also runs against a brick wall, namely the claim that humans are certainly different from and absolutely superior to animals. Taking the larger view, this attitude is of relatively late derivation. Instead of considering it directly here, it is useful for this analysis rather to take a glance first at the oldest of human mythological traditions, that of the hunter-gatherers. As we hear the Navajo singers recite in the Emergence Story:

> In those times all the animals were like people. The four-footed beasts, the flying birds, the coiling snakes, and the crawling insects behaved the way that earth-surface people who occupy the world today behave.

> They built houses and lived as neighbors the way people do today. As people do today they married and increased their numbers. As people do today they worked and tended to their affairs. In those times the difference between human and nonhuman was not nearly as great as it is now (Zolbrod, (1984:98).

While in this narration the emphasis is on similarities between nonhuman and human, other mythological accounts make an additional, very important point. Humans and animals were not merely similar, they were, at the old time of all beginnings, as one. Take the story told by the Inupiaq (Inuit) shaman of the Tikigaq people of North Alaska.

> In the beginning there was an old woman.
> The old woman was an *aana*, a grandmother.
> The *aana* lived with her grandson in an iglu
> at the edge of a village.
> They were *aanagiik*, grandmother and another.
> No one knows where they lived.
> South of Tikigaq, maybe, on high ground.
> Perhaps further south, near Qikiqtagruk.
> It was dark in those days.
> The sun didn't shine.
> At night there was no moon.
> And things were opposite to how they are today.
> People walked on their hands.
> Snow was sea oil, sea oil was caribou fat.
> Now this *aana* spent her days on the iglu sleeping bench.
> She kept her lamp there.
> In those days people chewed their lamp-oil sediment.
> They chewed it with down from their murre-skin parkas.
> It turned into gum. The *aana* did this too.
> She chewed *puiya*, burnt lamp oil,
> and made gum from it with murres' down.
> This lamp oil was black.
> It turned white when she chewed it.
> Then one day the *aana* made the figure of a man with lamp-oil gum.
> She put a bird's bill on the forehead, the bill of a *tuluqaq*, a raven.
> Then she stood it on the bench and went to sleep.
> When the *aana* woke up, the figure was gone.
> She looked around her.
> There on the floor a young man sat.
> He had a raven's bill on his forehead.
> "Where have you come from?" the old woman asked him.
> She named all the villages she knew.
> But he didn't come from any of them.
> Then she remembered what she'd made before she slept.
> She said, "You must be my *puiya*."
> "Yes," said the man. And this was Tulunigraq (Asatchaq, 1992:5-6)

First of all, we need to understand the setting. The grandmother is legitimized as a being of the alternate reality, where everything is the opposite to what it is in the ordinary one. The myth is told with superb sparseness, but this point is elaborated: people walk on their hands, the snow is seal oil, the seal oil caribou fat. However, we are not allowed to dwell on that image, for as a first faint allusion to the miracle of transformation to come, we are told that when the *aana* chews the black-lamp oil, it turns white. The *aana,* in an almost off-hand act of creation, produces a lamp-oil figurine and then goes to sleep. Her sleep bridges the realities: her lamp-oil figurine, created in the alternate reality, becomes a young man in the ordinary reality, a human, but a human who is not from any of the surrounding villages, he rather bears the mark of his alternate-reality origin on his forehead in the form of a raven's bill. And while the *aana* as a spirit being is nameless, he has a name. With profound awe, the myth in its final sentence proclaims, "And this was Tulunigraq." Tulunigraq is a man but also "something like a raven," which is the translation of his name; he is the culture hero of the Tikigaq people. He conquers a woman who does not want to marry and thus wastefully hoards her sexuality, he harpoons a whale, whose body becomes the land for the people, and he steals the daylight, thus ensuring the balance of light and darkness for the newly emerging world.

All culture heroes of myth share this quality: they are humans, but their animal being anchors them in the alternate reality, that is their power base. That is the ease with which the legends told by hunters and gatherers, be they the !Kung San of Africa, the Indian Koyukon of our northern forests or the aborigines of Australia, slip in and out between animal and human identity. It testifies to the fact that in that venerable ancient tradition "humans and animals were as one."

A break in this fluidity begins to occur when, in some ecologically suitable areas, humans begin to add the cultivation of gardens to their subsistence strategy. Forcing the earth to yield a harvest instead of relying on what she yields voluntarily also starts to drive a wedge between humans and animals. There is a distance now, instead of easy identity, the animals are a thing apart, although still of the alternate reality, and so endowed with power which makes them take on the role of helpers. A Tewa Indian story starts out:

> At Ikeowings koochute'e, were living Olivella Flower and Yellow Corn Girl. Olivella Flower would go hunting everyday and bring a deer. He is a good boy, he never thinks of anything bad. He gives meat to every one, he leaves out nobody. To Old Spider Woman, to Buffalo and Deer, Olivella Flower took downy feathers, to all these he took them, to ask them to help him to do whatever he wants. He asks them every morning for help. So they help him (Parsons, 1994:19).

In fact, as the myth points out later, once such a relationship is established between humans and animals, the animal spirits are obliged to give aid to their human friends, just as humans in return need to carry out a ritual upon killing an animal that will free its spirit so it can be reincarnated once more. It is an obligatory gift exchange. As Vine Deloria, the author of the well-known *God Is Red*, himself a Lakota Sioux Indian, points out:

> In the religious world of most tribes, birds, animals and plants compose the "other peoples" of creation and, depending on the ceremony, various of these

peoples participate in human activities. If Jews and Christians see the action of a single deity at sacred places and in churches and synagogues, traditional Indian people see considerably more activity as the whole of creation becomes an active participant in ceremonial life (1994:78-79).

In other words, holding ceremonials for "all our relatives" includes "birds, animals, and plants." Given the historically antagonistic and uncomprehending attitude toward Indian ritual life by the dominant society in this country, it is understandable that nothing is divulged of the sacred rituals involving "birds, animals, and plants." However, in exploring ritual postures and the ecstatic trance experience, which utilize postures represented in the art of the hunters and the horticulturalists (Goodman, 1990), we were surprised to find a preponderance of metamorphosis postures represented by horticulturalist artists. These are postures where the trancers turn principally into animals including birds and insects, and also occasionally into plants, and thus they partake of the latter's power, their wisdom, and their kindness.

With the advent of agriculture, about 17,000 years ago, humankind experienced the dawn of a world qualitatively different from anything humans had inhabited before (Goodman, 1988:21-27). Instead of the ethics of appropriateness, moral judgement was cleaved into good and evil, social organization in both parts of reality reflected hierarchy, rather than egalitarianism. An omnipotent god and an equally omnipotent ruler occupied the peak, and in Aristotle's formulation, "beasts and stupid people" were relegated to the bottom rung, suitable only to be slaves, or, let us add, to be exterminated. The picture has not materially changed in the ensuing centuries. In the middle of the 19th century, e.g., the Federal Government of the United States paid bounty hunters $1 per wolf pelt, exterminating more than a million of these animals, and in California, $5 for an Indian man's scalp, $4 for a woman's, and $3 for a child's, disbursing well over a million dollars to settlers and Indian fighters (see, PBS TV series, *The American Experience,* "Ishi, the last Yahi," also Heizer, 1974:268-269).

The effect of agriculturalist attitudes toward animals is still extant in the city, the last of the adaptations to the habitat humans have evolved. But there, finally, it has come under attack, although with mixed results and often murky motivation. Foremost among the attackers are the animal rights groups. As is well known (see the review of a number of recent publications on their movement in *Science,* 262 (1993):1906-1908), the principal attack is directed against biomedical and behavioral research, which in the United States uses an estimated 20 to 30 million vertebrate animals annually. Polemics aside, one of these authors (Orlans, 1993) brings up the important ethical issue:

[while understanding the relationship between animal research and biomedical progress] she acknowledges the ethical paradox that confronts animal researches—we use animals because they are similar to us in behavior or psychology, but similarity in behavior and biology implies similarity of mental experience, thus the more justified the use of a species on scientific grounds, the less justified is its use on ethical grounds (*Science,* 1993:1908).

The same point is brought into even sharper focus by a book coauthored by Dale Peterson and Jane Goodall (1993), in which Goodall argues that whatever you would not do to a human being to gain knowledge, refrain likewise from doing to a chimpanzee. But when her coauthor suggests that given the human-like quality of chimps, researchers should switch to rhesus monkeys instead, we are back at the "beast as slave" argument all over again.

The exercise demonstrates strikingly into what a cul-de-sac modern thinking has taken us when beginning with agriculture, it emasculated the alternate reality until, in the city, it obfuscated its existence altogether. The question is not how to be more humane to slaves, but how to find our way back to what we might call the shaman's premise and then let social action follow from that, namely that humans and animals are "as one," that each animal as everything else in the visible world has its non-visible alternate, and that each animal being is in a more direct sense than humans a representative of that immense, glowing, powerful part of reality we call the alternate one and in this sense, sacred.

## References

Asatchaq. *The Things That Were Said Of Them: Shaman Stories and Oral Histories of the Tigigac Peoples,* transl. Tukummig and Tome Lowenstein. Berkeley, CA: University of California Press, 1992.

Deloria, Vine. "Sacred Lands and Religious Freedom," *American Indian Religion,* 1 (1994):73-84.

Goodman, Felicitas D. *Where the Spirits Ride the Wind.* Bloomington, IN: Indiana University Press, 1990.

_____ . *Ecstasy, Ritual, and Alternate Reality: Religion in a Pluralistic World.* Bloomington, IN: Indiana University Press, 1988.

Heizer, Robert F. *The Destruction of California Indians.* Lincoln, NB: University of Nebraska Press, 1974.

Orlans, F. Barbara. *In the Name of Science: Issues in Responsible Animal Experimentation.* New York: Oxford University Press, 1993.

Parsons, Elsie Clews, "Olivella Flower Escapes," *Tewa Tales.* Tucson, AZ: University of Arizona Press, 1994.

Peterson, Dale and Jane Goodall. *Visions of Caliban: On Chimpanzees and People.* Boston, MA: Houghton Mifflin, 1993.

Zolbrod, Paul G. *Dine bahane: The Navajo Creation Story.* Albuquerque, NM: University of New Mexico Press, 1984.

# DISCUSSION

## With Goodman, Pinkson and Weiland

*Stone:* Thank you all for your wonderful presentations.

I can tell how you were effected by this epiphany of Guadalupe, Tom, but there were other things you said. Before you got to this part—the imbalance of male power in the world—you used the term "goddess." I wonder if you could share with us more of your considerations about the meaning of the goddess for men.

*Pinkson:* I don't know of any more important work for me as a man. It has literally been a life saver to open to the energy, the presence of the goddess. And so, in all my work with men when I go out and speak, or in the spiritual community I am involved with, working with men, I speak about the goddess. On every level, the macro and the micro, there is opportunity for the sacred marriage. Without the sacred marriage we are lost in our relationships. As men we cannot heal ourselves until we find the feminine within ourselves and bring her out of the shadow. To develop in life, we need to develop a conscious relationship with her in order to do a better job with the women in our lives, with our grandmother and daughters and the babies, and Mother Earth herself. As we initiate to sacralize the marriage with the feminine inside of us, we open the door to deeper healing.

*Wimmer:* Felicitas, I want to make a comment about what you said about the denaturalization of humans, away from our own roots, and the whole process that animals are not part of the sapiens society altogether. I want to comment on what you said about "animals" and "stupidity," because it refers also to what I was talking about. Many disabled people are still being used for experimental purposes because they are not considered to be human beings. I know Ruth can talk about this to; about 150,000 persons were disabled in Germany and they lost their lives to euthanasia because they were not considered to be human.

*Bray:* I want to know more about the Black Virgin. There is a book by China Galant which came out a few years ago, *Longing for Darkness* (New York:

Penguin, 1991). She conducted a ten-year search to find the connection between the Black Madonna and the Green Tara.

*Pinkson:* China is an old friend of mine and I have read her book. When I was in Santa Fe, the women considered the Virgin of Guadalupe to be a black madonna. When I asked the Latino women in my healing group, they said, "No, no, Guadalupe is not a black madonna, she is brown."

*Bray:* There is one in Poland and there are some in South America.

*Denig:* Felicitas, I have been doing some work in Peru with one of your books about the positions. I have been living there for eleven years and did not have the advantage of twelve-step groups and a lot of therapies that are available in the USA. One time, I had a problem I was trying to work through. I was down on the floor in a very strange position. I began to cry and to sob in the voice of a little girl, about four years old, because I was remembering what had happened the night when I was left locked up in that church. The memories were coming back but the pain was so great, that I began to howl. Suddenly there was a ferocious black wolf in the room with me and I had locked the door to my bedroom. The black wolf, which appeared to be male, went to the door and was guarding it. Nobody was going to come through that door. So I continued with that process.

The story had been told in the family that my father was a country preacher, a charismatic healer, an evangelist and he and my mother had gone to conduct a mid-week revival service in this church. Driving home they thought they had me in the back seat of the car but they discovered they hadn't. So they drove back to get me. That night I recalled what really had happened. My father was driving just me and had asked my mother to stay home. He stopped in the woods to sexually abuse me again and the four-year-old girl said, "No, Daddy, I am going to tell on you." So to punish me and make sure that I never told anyone, he left me locked up in that church. When I had gone into one of these positions, I want you to know that healing took place, I stood beside that wolf and I screamed out into the night in the woods in that little church, "I am not a bad girl, you are a bad man." When I said that, the wolf turned white, went to the floor and was lying on his back. He wanted to play and have his belly rubbed. So anytime I hear those stories about the wolves, they are serving me, they are serving so many of us. Whatever that force was in me, my own shamanic studies came forth in that moment, also what I had learned from you. Without help of anybody else, with the position and the wolf I had healing. I want to acknowledge that.

*Goodman:* The wolf has such bad press. That always happens on the threshold when cultures change. What is sacred in the past, becomes frightful or sometimes despicable at a different state of development. The wolf used to be a power animal, a very strong one, a protector. I could go on with details. There were still traditions in the 15th and 16th century in Europe which considered the wolf to be a protector. But then came the Big Bad Wolf stories which led to almost total extermination of the species. This is terrible because we are losing and have lost another protector, another friend, which stood on that line of ordinary and nonordinary reality as your story demonstrates.

*Rising Star:* I enjoyed both of your presentations very much. Tom, it was good to see you again. You speak of Guadalupe appearing more and more over the planet, mother essence, the mother energy. She has come to me also. As you and some of you know, I have gone through a healing journey with breast cancer over the last few years. In that process, I had some profound experiences. I won't go into them but simply say that, in my massage, my healing work, I have this angel who works with me now. She looks like the one I saw on TV, and at the Harmonic Convergence on Mt.Shasta. I don't know whether anyone of you saw it.

I was working one day on a dear friend who is a fine healer herself, in Marine County a number of months ago. Total magic happened in that healing, because I got out of the way and Spirit came through. My angel was working, and I told her, "Our angels are really getting it on today." So there was an alchemical reaction between the two of us. At the end of the session, she said, "I see your angel now, too." And I said, "No, that is not my angel. What does she look like?" I could feel her presence and could, psychically, see her. When she described what she saw, I said, "No, that's the Mother." And she said, "Yeah!" The next day, I worked on another dear friend who is also a fine healer, and there was another synchronistic connection, working on her for a few hours. She had been to Egypt and said, "I see this Egyptian goddess coming." And I asked, "What does she look like?" "She is dressed in white." And, just as the day before, I said, "I know who that is. You may have another name for her but she is the Mother Essence again." It was a very powerful feeling and I know she is here. I feel her often, though I don't see her quite that clearly.

*Becker:* Thank you for making me feel comfortable and allowing to bring my baby (bird) today. I want to share with you, there is a wonderful book by Theodor Barber, *The Human Nature of Birds* (New York: Penguin, 1993). I have a mother who has a heart condition and I am not too well either. The birds have really helped to heal us. They are such wonderful creatures and so easy to take care of, especially living in a city apartment.

*Heinze*: Thank you. Much has been left unsaid and, I think, we will continue to explore these mysteries.

# VISITING A "PAI DO SANTOS" IN RECIFE, BRAZIL

Stanley Krippner

African slaves first were brought to Brazil in about 1550 to work on plantations in the northeastern part of the Portuguese colony. It has been estimated that the total number of slaves who eventually arrived in Brazil exceeded four million. Many of them were expropriated, often with the complicity of avaricious people from their own tribes, from the West African Coast, home of a variety of native cultures, such as the Yoruba, Male, Jeje, Fula, Fons, Fanti, and Ashanti (Barbosa, 1989). Permeating their belief systems were stories about spiritual deities or *orixas,* the primordial forces of nature. Powerful and terrifying, but so human that they could be talked to, pleaded with, and cajoled through special offerings, the *orixas* were part of the cultures the slaves brought to Brazil. The Yoruba belief in two realities—one visible (the *aye*) and one invisible (the *orum*) was common to other African beliefs, but any number of Yoruba perspectives on how to connect the two realms (through *axe* or spiritual energy) had influenced the spiritual practices of its neighbors (Barbosa, 1989).

## The "White Masks"

Upon their arrival the slaves' customs and languages were forbidden; they were baptized as Christians and forced to attend Roman Catholic church services. Slaves were allowed to hold their own religious meetings as long as they were Christian in nature; evidenced by the presence of pictures of Jesus, Mary, and the saints upon their altars. In this manner, the slaves gave their *orixas* the "white masks" of the Christian saints (Bastide, 1960). Olorum, god of creation, became God the Father or Jehovah. In the Yoruba culture, Olorum (as well as the other "Sky Gods" of West African cultures) was believed to be benevolent but aloof from human affairs. It was Olorum's children who interceded in people's daily lives, and who, for the slaves, corresponded to Jesus and the Catholic saints. Olorum's son, Obatala, the god of heavens and of purity, became Jesus Christ. Obatala's daughter, Yemanja, became the Virgin Mary, and her children Ogum,

Oxossi and Oxum became St.George (Jorge), St.Sebastian (Sebastiao), and St.Catherine (Caterina).

There was no direct counterpart for Satan in Yoruba mythology. However, the Christian devil shared some characteristics of the *exus* and the *pombajiras* (or *exas*), the messengers of the gods. These messengers often were mischievous, mixing up people's prayers and granting them someone else's request. They were regarded as extremely clever and needed to be appeased, usually at the beginning or the end of a ceremony.

At the same time, an ordered relationship with the forces of nature, as personified by the *orixas,* was essential for maintaining the well-being of the individual and the community. Africans knew that illness had natural causes but believed that these causes were brought on by discordant relations between people and their social and natural environment. Long before Western medicine recognized the fact, Africa's traditional healers had taken the position that the ecology and interpersonal relations affected people's health (Raboteau, 1986).

African religious practitioners gained access to supernatural power in three ways: by making offerings to the *orixas;* by "divining" or foretelling the future with the help of an *orixa;* and by being taken over by an *orixa,* ancestor, or other entity who—when benevolent—would warn the community about possible calamities, diagnose illness, and prescribe cures. The medium or person through whom these spirits speak and move, performed this task voluntarily, usually claiming not to remember the experience once it ended. The "trance" or altered state of consciousness required for the voluntary gift of the medium's mind and body to the *orixa,* was brought about by dancing, singing, and drumming. Preventive medicine consisted of using charms and rituals, as well as of living within the social constraints of one's culture. Treatment for afflicted people included herbal preparations, prayers, and sacrifices. Of these practices, letting the *orixa* "inhabit" one's body best survived the transition from Africa to Brazil.

With a few exceptions (e.g., Shango in Trinidad, Santeria in Cuba, Voudon in Haiti, Candomble and other African oriented movements in Brazil, the African religious traditions eventually disappeared among the slaves who were brought to the European colonies in the New World. However, the black "shouting churches" that grew out of the Protestant revival movement resembled some aspects of the West African rituals, but rather than letting the *orixas* "inhabit" their bodies, these slaves were "filled by the Holy Spirit" during their ecstatic experiences. These shifts in conscious experience were triggered by the church service's emotionally arousing sermons, songs, and prayers (Raboteau, 1986).

# The Emergence of Candomble

Of all the Brazilian spiritist movements, Candomble is said to be the one that most closely resembles the "pure" Yoruba religion of Africa, retaining the original names of many West African *orixas*. The name "Candomble" seems to have derived from *candombe*, a community dance held by the slaves who worked on coffee plantations. Later, such groups as Kardecismo and Umbanda emerged; the former drew heavily upon the teachings of Allen Kardec, a French spiritualist, while the later gave a greater emphasis to Brazil's Christian heritage than to the African *orixas*. If these three groups were to be placed on a continuum, Candomble would be closest to Brazil's African roots, Umbanda would be in the middle, and Kardecismo at the far end— although it does retain the spirits of slaves (i.e., *os pretos velhos* and descendants of escaped slaves who mated with Indians (i.e., *os caboclos*).

In 1830, three black freed women in Salvador bought an abandoned mill house to set up Brazil's first permanent Candomble temple. The three former slaves became *iyalorixas* (or *mae do santos,* the "mother of the saints"), and their apprentices became *iaos* (or *filha do santos,* "the daughters of the saints"). Today the "daughters" still learn how to sing, beat the drums, and dance in order to alter their consciousness and "falling" when their various spirit guides wanted to work through them. They also learn about the herbs and special teas and potions often needed by the indisposed members of their congregation (McGregor, 1962). The oldest of the temples or *terreiros,* the Casa Bianca or White House in Salvador, has been brought under the protection of the government's historic preservation law.

Brazil declared its independence in 1822 and the slaves were freed in 1888. Between the mid-1550s and the late 1800s, some fifteen generations of Brazilians had heard the stories of the *orixas,* of death by the evil eye, of illnesses cured by spirit counsel, and of marriages saved by spirit intervention. With the freeing of the slaves, Candomble and other Afro-Brazilian movements gained visibility as well as new adherents.

In 1818, a group of mediumistic practitioners was organized around the principles of homeopathy. Later, this group eagerly translated a book by Allan Kardec, a French spiritualist (or "spiritist," as he preferred to be called) that had been brought to Brazil from Europe in 1858. In it, they found a faith more sophisticated than Candomble, it circumvented the drum beating and most of the *orixas*. Yet, Kardecismo upheld the importance of incorporating spirit guides in healing services and religious ceremonies.

Umbanda was initiated about 1904 but did not congeal until a 1941 convocation of its members where Umbanda's founders claimed to be in contact with an American Indian spirit guide who taught them how to "purify" the African rites. Some Umbandistas use drums and make sacrifices, but others do not. All, however, emphasize the importance of spirit incorporation, and all venerate Jesus Christ. There are several other mediumistic (or "spiritistic") movements as well (e.g., Piji, Batuque), but Candomble, Kardecismo, and Umbanda are the three major syncretic groupings.

The practice of Candomble varies from region to region; for example, there are three main branches of Candomble and some 700 Candomble temples in the city of Salvador and other parts of the state of Bahia. In some Candomble temples, male mediums (the "fathers" and "brothers of the saints," i.e., *pai do santos* and *filho do santos*) participate in the ceremonies. The names of the *orixas* also vary, e.g., Obatala is referred to as Oxala in several parts of Brazil; Yemanja is often spelled Iemanja and is depicted variously as a stunning matron, a sea nymph, or a mermaid. In some regions, Odudua is venerated as the great Mother Goddess, the *orixa* of the earth, in other places, she has been forgotten.

Nago-gege Candomble is considered the purest form of the African religion to have taken roots in Brazil. Giesler (personal communication, March 23, 1994) emphasizes that the Nago-Gege Candomble's *orixa* is not the same as an Umbanda *orixa* in its nature or attributes, nor in its conceptualization, symbology, function, ritual obligation, ritual manifestation, ritual initiations, cosmology, and depth, nor in the nature of the associated altered conscious state. Thus, Ogum, the warrior *orixa* who carries a sword, can be a very different entity from group to group, although an outsider would not realize these differences.

I had an opportunity to apply Giesler' distinctions in 1991 when I visited a temple in Belem, Brazil, where "Amazonian Umbanda" was practiced. Statues of the major Candomble *orixas* were in place, but the basic ceremonies and beliefs were Umbandista.

## Pai Ely's Model of the Human Energy System

This report will focus on Pai Ely (Manuel Rabelo Pereira), a prominent *pai do santo* in Recife. It will present his system of "energy centers" or *chakras,* and several incidents that occurred during my three visits to his *terreiro* (temple) *O Centro Espirita,* in 1990, 1991, and 1993. On all three occasions, I was accompanied by members of the Institute of Noetic Sciences, the sponsor of the trips.

Pai Ely is a former bank executive. When he was in his early 40s, he began to see and hear spirits and *orixas.* He was uncomfortable with these entities and fought them, especially when they told him that he was being "called" to become a healer. But they made a series of dire predictions, each of which became true. Reluctantly, Pai Ely began the "laying-on of hands"; his friends and clients reported feeling "positive energy" and many of them reported an improvement in their condition. His bank was dismayed with these activities until the daughter of the bank president became seriously ill. She was scheduled to fly to the United States for an operation until Pai Ely saw her. After one session with him, her condition improved so remarkably that the trip and the operation were reportedly canceled.

Pai Ely told us that his teacher, Master Oascati, a man in his 70s at the time of our visit, lives in Benin, Africa. Master Oascati once told Pai Ely that he must constantly work on himself, trying to obtain clearer and purer information from the *orixas* during the time of submission to the spirits; it is extremely easy for one's own biases, experiences, and fantasies to contaminate the spiritual message. In his words, "The *orixa* paints only one small part of the picture; the medium must paint the rest." As a result, the client receives no "pure" information; it is unusual for more than 25 per cent of the *orixa's* message to get through. Further, many of the messages are from *exus, pombajiras,* or ancestral spirits, not *orixas;* these entities are not "illuminated beings" and may unknowingly distort information or deliberately play tricks on the mediums and their clients.

Pai Ely conceptualizes the human being as an "energy system"; in addition to the "solar plexus" and the "nerve plexus," there are ten major "spiritual energy centers" or *chakras,* and many minor centers, most notably those in the internal organs. This network is said to reflect the presence of the Candomble *orixas,* the forces of nature who reside both inside and outside human beings. In Pai Ely's model, some chakras are *exaustores,* funneling internal "energy" to places outside the body, as in healing. Other chakras are *ventiladores,* funneling "energy" into the body from outside sources, i.e., when spirits are contacted and "enter" the body. It is this *axe* or "spiritual energy" that connects the physical world or *axe* with the spiritual world or *orum.*

Table 1 presents the name and location of each chakra as well as whether it is an *exaustor* or *ventilador,* its function, its color, its respective *orixa* (both the primary or "'owner" *orixa* and the secondary or "adjunct" *orixa),* as well as the "domain" of the primary *orixa.* (The final two chakras are exceptions, as they are associated with the *pombajiras* and *exus.)* Each *orixa* has his or her own sacred day, food, and costume, allowing adepts to enhance their "spiritual energy" through a closer association with the spirit world. Although this is Pai Ely's model and is not characteristic of traditional Candomble, it represents an innovative attempt to elaborate the Afro-Brazilian viewpoints and syncretizes additional concepts, in this case the notion of chakras.

## Table 1: The Ten Major Energy Centers as Described by Pai Ely

The Peace Chakra *(exhaustor):*
Head
Intuition
White
Obatala (i.e., Oxala); Yemanja
Creation and dedication

The Love Chakra *(exhaustor* and *ventilador):*
Eyes
Perception
Pink
Ianca; Xango
Compassion and affection

The Purification Chakra *(exhaustor):*
Throat
Vocalization
Blue
Yemanja; Obatala (i.e., Oxala)
The oceans

The Movement Chakra *(ventilador):*
Back of neck
Coping
White and red
Ogum; Oxum
Iron and weapons

The Aspiration Chakra (exhaustor):
Heart
Spiritual Guidance
Gold
Oxum; Ogum
Fresh water rivers

The Vitality Chakra *(exhaustor):*
Liver
Endurance
Green
Oxossi; Oba
Hunting and the forest

The Transformation Chakra *(ventilador):*
Lower back
Death and rebirth
Violet
Nana; Ibeji twins
Still water and lakes

The Survival Chakra *(exhaustor):*
Base of spine, coccyx
Existence
Red
Xango; Ianca
Thunder, lightning, and justice

The Sensitivity Chakras *(ventiladores):*
Hands
Psychic development
Gray
The *pombajitas* (or *exas*)
Messengers of the *orixas*; arts and crafts

The Sexual Chakras *(exhaustores):*
Feet
Grounding
Black
The *exus*
Messengers of the *orixas;* luck and humor

There are between fourteen and twenty-three major *orixa* (depending on the group that keeps count) and dozens of minor *orixa*. They represent various domains of human behavior and nature, and some groups have one for each day of the year (Villarubbia, 1993). For example, the domain of Baayani is humility; of Dada, patience; of Ewa, war; of Itoko, time; of Erinle, transformation; of Logum Ede, fishing; Nana, death. Oba's domain is fighting; Obe's is professional work, Ossain's is medical plants; Oko's is the fields; Oranjan's is passages; Orunmila's is divination; Omoly's is healing; Oropu's is weather; and the Ibeji twins' domain is innocence (e.g., Verger, 1985). Among some groups, the major *orixa* appear in two or three forms; for example, Obatala can appear as a child or adolescent, an adult or an elder. Pai Ely's major *orixa* is Omolu while his minor *orixas* are Nana and Ogum; as a result, he believes that he is in constant contact with healing, death and power.

## A Son of the Temple

In order to obtain another perspective on *O Centro "Espirita,* I interviewed Jose Jairo da Silva. Jairo was 22 years of age at the time of my 1993 conversation with him, and he told me that his visions of spirits had originated when he was four. Jairo's parents took him to a physician who found no physical problem, and to a Mesa Branca temple that followed the teachings of Allen Kardec, a revered French Spiritist, even though his parents were Roman Catholic at the time. Jairo was first taken to a Candomble temple by his mother shortly after his seventh birthday. He had reported experiencing a "vision" which was followed by a headache. Pai Ely "closed off" Jairo's "sensitivity" so that he would have an orderly childhood.

Jairo's "sensitivity" emerged again at the age of ten when he was taken over by an *exu* for the first time. This event occurred shortly before his parents separated and his father left home. Jairo's mother was alarmed by this incident and called upon Jesus Christ for assistance. Jairo, however, recognized this *exu* as the spirit he had originally seen at the age of four. The *exu* was shirtless, muscular, had dark brown skin, thick black hair, and was wearing black trousers. Four days later he saw another spirit, a *pombajira* or *exa* who was wearing a simple print dress and was smoking a cigar. She had roses in her hand and in her black hair.

At the age of 12 he saw and heard a major *orixa*, Oxum, and gave his mind and body to her. This led to his initiation as a "son of the temple" shortly before his thirteenth birthday. In preparation for this ritual, he cleaned his body very thoroughly (i.e., an *amaci* ceremony), dressed himself completely in white, and sang all the temple songs. Pai Ely decided that Jairo was ready for this induction and shaved Jairo's hair, painting small white circles on his head and face. Palm leaves were tied to Jairo's forehead, and he walked around *O Centro Espirita* for thirty minutes. He then gave his body to Oxum again. In retrospect, Jairo finds it difficult to describe the "inhabiting" experience, but he recalls feeling cool and light. More important, he knew that the experience of "falling" was authentic.

Two of Jairo's friends, Silvana and Flavio, were initiated the same night. They were taken over by Ianca and Xango, the deities of lightning and of thunder, respectively. All three initiates were given small objects to hold in their hands for purposes of focusing. For example, Jairo was given a mirror because grooming was a favored activity for Oxum. For several hours afterwards, Jairo's hands felt cold and he experienced "waves of energy" all over his body. This was a remarkable experience for him and a major event in his spiritual life.

After three months, Jairo participated in another initiation ceremony. This time, he wore a bracelet of buzio shells, a collar of beads, and an elaborate gown that he had sewn himself. After the ceremony, he wore a necklace of buzios, and heard the voices of several benevolent entities who instructed him on various cleanup tasks. As a "son of the temple," Jairo must undertake various jobs at *O Centro Espirita*, show respect for the *pai do santos,* demonstrate care and compassion for all people, learn the names and functions of the *orixa,* and attend the temple meetings and spiritual functions.

## Initiating a "Daughter of the Saints"

In 1991, the Institute of Noetic Sciences group and I attended a Candomble ceremony in Pai Ely's temple, finding ourselves immersed in candle-light, incense, and drumming. Pai Ely had invited us to witness an initiation: A "daughter of the temple" was about to become an iao, a *filha do santos,* or "daughter of the saints," following a three-week period of solitude in an isolated room (the *ronco*) where her only visitor had been Pai Ely who had brought food, water, and counsel. As she emerged from the *ronco,* we noticed that her head had been shaved (the *raspagem da cabeca*), except for a thin tuft of hair in the middle of the head. We were told that this represented a modification of the original ceremony where the skin on top of the head was cut so that the *orixas* could receive a blood offering.

For several hours, we observed the initiate dance around *O Centro Espirita,* accompanied by other mediums who were letting various entities "inhabit" their bodies. Some of them had been initiated years earlier. They continued to venerate the *orixas* who guided the initiates. For some, it was Oxum, the *orixa* of the "sweet water" lakes and rivers; for others, it was Oxossi, the *orixa* of the forest. Having been silent for so long, the initiate's first words would be her *problamazao de nome,* the proclamation that would confirm the *orixa* who had served as her benefactor. Later that evening, the young woman gave us the name, "Oxumare," the *orixa* of the rainbow. She was then welcomed as the temple's newest "daughter of the saints."

Later, I discovered that Oxumare is a man for six months, a woman for the other six months of the year. She serves as the liaison between heaven and earth. I also was told that we had witnessed a *saida de iao,* ceremony in which the "daughter comes out" of her seclusion. It cumulates when the *orixa* whispers a special name (i.e., *dar o nome*). It was my understanding that the *iao* we observed already knew that she was a member of the Oxumare lineage. However, there were many Oxumares; old ones, young ones, female versions, male versions, in other words, Oxumares comes in all the colors of the rainbow. The particular identity of the initiate's Oxumare is a vital part of this ceremony and the spiritual growth of the new *iao.*

## An "At-a-Distance Depossession"

The diagnosis of "possession" is a serious matter. In these instances, the possessing spirit has taken over a person's body for various amounts of time. If it is an offending spirit, it has to be expelled and considerable follow-up is warranted to protect the client against possession by other spirit entities. Special foods, herbs, and purgatives may be accompanied by rituals, prayers, and/or imagery exercises.

Mimi, one of the members of our group asked Pai Ely if there was anything unusual about her daughter's diabetes, and he responded that she was a daughter of Yemanja, but was suffering from "spirit possession." Agreeing to attempt an "at-a-distance depossession," Pai Ely asked Mimi to write the name, address, and birth date of her daughter on a card and to change into white clothes.

The two of them knelt on the floor, and Mimi, in an all-white pants suit, closed her eyes in order to concentrate. Pai Ely took Mimi's hand and told her to grasp it tightly. He then shook Mimi's hand several times to facilitate a close connection between the two of them. Mimi opened her eyes and observed that Pai Ely's benign countenance had been replaced by a haughty sneer. Pai Ely had given his mind and body to the intruding spirit!

The spirit introduced himself as a count who had lived in France in the 1780s. Mimi's daughter had been his sister in that life, but they had violent political disagreements, Mimi's daughter telling her brother that he was oppressing the servants and peasants who worked for him. The count had been a royalist and was sent to the guillotine by the revolutionaries. Mimi's daughter spread his internal organs on the earth to demonstrate to his oppressed workers that he was dead. To drive home the point, she wrote the count's name on his liver!

The count refused to proceed "toward the light" to purify his soul. Instead, he stayed on the earthly plane, bent on revenge. He polluted a piece of white chocolate that a friend had given his sister, and she developed diabetes. The count laughed wickedly, because he had hounded his sister from one incarnation to the next, always inflicting illness upon her.

After this disclosure, Pai Ely regained control over his body and the spirit of the count disappeared. We were told that he finally had decided to undertake a journey "to the light" to begin his purification and spiritual development. In the meantime, Mimi was astonished. She recalled that her daughter had always felt that the trigger for the onset of her diabetes was a chocolate-eating binge while vacationing on a French beach.

Pai Ely gave Mimi's daughter specific directions, e.g., no smoking, no drinking, nor eating meat, nor having sex for 21 days, daily showers or baths, followed by a quick shower in water in which white rose petals have been steeped over night, daily cups of graviola tea, daily lighting of a candle in honor of Yemanja. Six months later I had the opportunity to question Mimi about the procedure. She told me that her daughter had followed the directions precisely. Her diabetic condition showed no change but her mood had improved, her energy level had increased, and she felt the regimen had been worth the effort.

## Unanswered Questions

After three visits to O Centro Espirita, several questions remained. Candomble and other Afro-Brazilian religious initiations are often bloody affairs (Wafer, 1993) and we speculated as to whether the Recife group sacrifices small birds and animals during some of their ceremonies. We also realized that in attaining and maintaining altered states of consciousness, drumming and dancing are the primary technologies, but mused whether mind-altering herbal brews are used during rituals, and/or during the three-week period of an initiate's seclusion, to intensify the experience (Barbosa, 1989)? Several *orixas* like to smoke cigars, and some Afro-Brazilian groups use strong tobacco for mind-altering purposes during their ceremonies (Villoldo & Krippner, 1988).

Giesler (personal communication, March 23, 1994) has emphasized the intricacy of Afro-Brazilian belief systems and the complexity of their derivations from African systems. My brief experiences in Recife would underscore his cautions and his conclusions. For instance, Giesler argues that some Brazilian groups purportedly carry on the Candomble tradition, but close inspection reveals that there has been an infusion of beliefs and practices from Umbanda, a 20th century syncretic religion. Giesler has found, for example, that Umbanda leaders often attend Candomble centers, undergo the *bori*—an introductory ritual obligation—and learn songs, dances, and even the *jica*, "possession tremble." Their practices becomes a mix, Giesler called them an "Umbandomble" sect that separates them from the Candomble practitioners who have attempted to remain faithful to their African roots. Leaders of such "Umbandomble": groups, Giesler argued, are not really *pais do santos* from the Candomble perspective, but *abias,* novices who have learned a minimum of Candomble lore and then combined it with Umbanda and/or Kardecismo rituals and beliefs.

Does Pai Ely qualify as a "shaman" because of his utilization of altered states of consciousness to assist members of his community? Does he meet the definition of "medium" because of his incorporation of spirits? Or could he be considered a "priest" because he officiates at religious rituals held regularly at a specific location. Heinze (1982) has pointed out that some practitioners perform as shamans on some occasions and as mediums on others. She also discussed the degree of control that shamans typically exhibit over the spirits they "channel," a trait not so characteristic of mediums (1992). In the meantime, perhaps it is appropriate to refer to him simply as a *pai do santos*, because that is his appellation in his own community.

There are few places on earth today where performance ritual is both available and accessible. Pai Ely impressed our group as a sincere practitioner of his faith. His congregation appeared to have tapped into a source both inspiring and exciting, both aesthetic and therapeutic, formulating a worldview that give Pai Ely opportunities both to serve his community and to use his *axe* (or spiritual energy) to pass from the every day world of *aye* to *orum*, the invisible dimension of existence. Sass observed that Western psychotherapists have taken a superior attitude toward Brazilian and similar practitioners who minister to similar sets of ailments throughout much of the world. Both offer their clients "not so much truth as a set of effective symbols, a language by which the chaos of life can be cloaked in a reassuring myth-like structure" (1986:300). Frank and Frank (1991:44-51) have identified the roles played by the implicit myths of Western psychotherapy in combating demoralization, inspiring expectations of help, providing new learning experiences, arousing the clients emotionally, enhancing a sense of self-efficacy, and affording opportunities for rehearsal and practice—precisely the same activities our group observed in Pai Ely's temple.

Sass recalled talking with a Brazilian actress who told him:

> You must not think we accept all this uncritically. For me the Orisha are like forces of the universe, psychological forces perhaps....But I would much rather think of myself as being in the presence of an Orisha than "getting in touch with my feelings" (1986:301).

## References

Barbosa, E. "The presence of the gods: Afro-Brazilian trance rituals, *Shaman's Drum* (Mid-Summer 1989):41-49.

Bastide, R. *Les religions africaines au Bresil.* Paris: Press Universitaires de France, 1960.

Frank, J.D. and J.B. Frank. *Persuasion and Healing: A Comparative Study of Psychotherapy.* Baltimore, MD: Johns Hopkins University Press, 3rd ed, 1991.

Giesler, P.V. "Brazilian Cult Classification," *Magico-Religious Healers of Brazil.* Tokyo: Arechi Publishing, in press.

Heinze, R.-I. "The role and functions of contemporary shamans in Southeast Asia," *Diogenes* (Summer 1992):133-144.

_____ . "Shamanism or mediumship: Toward a definition of different states of consciousness," *Phoenix: Journal of Transpersonal Anthropology,* 6:1-2 (1982):25-44.

McGregor, P. *The Moon and Two Mountains.* London: Souvenir Press, 1962.

Raboteau, A.J. "The Afro-American traditions," *Caring and Curing: Health and Medicine in Western Religious Traditions,* eds R.L. Numbers and D.W. Amundsen. New York: Macmillan, 1986, pp.539-562.

Sass, L. "Voodoo therapy," *Vogue* (September 1986):300-301.

Verger, P. *Orixas.* Salvador, Brazil: Editora Corrupio, 1985.

Villarubia, P. "Poseidos por los dioses," *Ano Cero, 39* (1993):34-40.

Villoldo, A. and S. Krippner. *Healing States.* New York: Fireside/Simon and Schuster, 1988.

Wafer, J. *The Taste of Blood: Spirit Possession in Brazilian Candomble.* Philadelphia, PA: University of Pennsylvania Press, 1993.

# THE DESTRUCTION OF SPIRIT MOUNTAIN: AN OBSERVATION OF CONFLICTING VALUES

William C. Leikam

The traditional sacred sites of the Assiniboine and the Gros Ventre are located on Spirit Mountain in the Little Rocky Mountains of northeastern Montana. Spirit Mountain is under attack by the world's largest mining corporation, Canadian based Pegasus. They are destroying the mountain for gold. In the process, the cyanide-based mining operations pollute the aquifers and streams, the people's only water supply which now has toxic levels of lead, zinc, and other contaminants. This toxicity has resulted in birth defects in both the human and animal population on the reservation. Recently, the Montana Water Control Board has brought a suit against Pegasus Mines for this pollution. However, even if they clean up the water supply, the problem of the destruction of sacred sites, the people's ancestral, spiritual roots, remains.

## My Role in the Struggle

In July of 1993, Muruga Booker and I were in contract negotiations with Latin Percussion, Inc., the world's largest manufacturer of percussion instruments. The Fort Belknap Industries, a branch of the Montana Indian Manufacturer's Network, was involved because we had made arrangements for the people of Fort Belknap to manufacture Muruga's *nada* drum to create additional jobs on the reservation. In the process of these business arrangements, we were invited to Fort Belknap by several tribal leaders to attend their Milk River Indian Days Pow Wow, one of the largest and most traditional pow wows still held in the United States.

The tribal elders present at the contract-signing ceremony already knew that we had helped other indigenous people globally to save the rain forests, e.g., through the highly successful album "Blues from the Rain Forest." A percentage of that album went to The Rain Forest Action Network. Immediately after signing the contract with Latin Percussion, we were asked by the traditional tribal elders, among them Medicine Man George Black Crow, to help stop Pegasus Mines from mining Spirit Mountain. In the conversation that ensued, elder Catherine Halver said,

What's happening up there on Spirit Mountain is not different from you sitting one Sunday morning in church and having a bulldozer come through the front door in search of gold....We have been fighting this for fourteen years and have gotten nowhere....We need your help (personal communication, 1993).

We were concerned about what we heard and offered to record an album with the proceeds going to their legal defense fund, Red Thunder, Inc., and to medical support. Consequently, the album "Spirit Mountain" was recorded and one hundred per cent of the proceeds went to the defense of Spirit Mountain.

## Background of the Region

As early as the 1860s, gold has been mined in the Little Rocky Mountains. It was a time when much of the native plains cultures were in disarray. They had to face the influx of white settlers, disagreement between their religious leaders, and with miners, hunters, loggers and the U.S.Army. It was at this time that the Ghost Dance movement arose on the plains to combat the white influence and maintain tradition. The Dream Cult of the Plains Indians came into existence out of older traditions and gained power, especially among the Nez Perce. Chief Joseph's father was one of their leaders. Culturally, the Indian people were in a state of transition, trying to accommodate and live with the white people and their new value system.

There were those Indian people who honored and worked to sustain their native traditions like Warrior Chief Yellow Knife and Chief Joseph, while others found the white man's ways irresistible. Some of the latter traveled east just so that they could learn more about Christianity, the white man's ways and have their own bible. This schism resulted in inter- and intratribal conflicts because the tribal elders who adapted the white man's ways, tended to sell their land for profit, and willingly moved onto reservations in direct opposition to the traditionalists.

This battle continues today on the Fort Belknap Reservation and many other reservations across the land. For a relative few people, the mining operations create jobs so sorely needed because the unemployment rate is estimated by tribal elders to be anywhere from 50-80 per cent, depending upon with whom you talk. However, for those like Medicine Man George Black Crow who works to maintain their traditions, the presence of Pegasus Mines is the source of destruction of their sacred land. So these traditionalists are in direct conflict with members of their own tribe. For some, such as Gary Niles Kimble, Executive Director of the Association of American Indian Affairs in New York and nephew of Elder Ms Catherine Haver, Spirit Mountain could well become a symbol of the battle against the widespread destruction of sacred sites within many traditional American Indian communities. This conflict even extends outside the reservation and includes those sites that New Agers plunder like Mount Shasta where well-meaning but "blind" people are destroying the sacred hot springs through their overzealous needs to "get back to the land."

## The Larger Picture

This extended visit to Fort Belknap was not the first time that I had observed what was taking place on reservations. I had the opportunity to talk with the people, both those who maintain traditions and those opposed to the traditions. Given these experiences and observations, the key problems that emerged from my perspective are unemployment, i.e., poverty sustained by racism. From this, I have come to the conclusion that, (1) racism is the social control mechanism of a dominant society who sustains its power by conquering people; and (2) this racism is furthered and deepened, albeit in most cases subconsciously, by the obliteration of traditions and the destruction of sacred sites. The people's self-esteem is undermined and, with that, their connection with their ancestral roots which is critical to maintain their strength as a culture.

This pattern can be seen around the world where such conflicts between traditions and economics exist. When sacred traditions and sites are destroyed, the elders and the shamans, the carriers of the sacred traditions, cannot maintain their direct link with their ancestors and the people suffer a personal and cultural malaise. Only those who can maintain traditions, and this necessitates the preservation of their sacred sites, feel a clear sense of self-esteem, self-respect and power. People become the agents of change in their drive to either keep or to reestablish their cultural roots and to oppose racism and injustice inflicted by the culture with opposing values. It is for this reason that the American Indian Movement (AIM) was feared by the United States Government during the late 1960s and 1970s, so that the siege of Wounded Knee occurred (see, "Incident at Oglala," song produced by Robert Redford, for the AIM movement).

It is the same reason why the aboriginal people of Australia are fighting against Japanese timber companies to maintain their sacred lands. That means, we find this conflict not only in the U.S. but also in Tibet, Africa, Australia, South America, and almost everywhere else where cultures are in collision; where the conquered people are continually subdued by their conquerors. The destruction of Spirit Mountain, the racism and poverty that are inflicted on the people, the continued presence of Pegasus Mines has established the battle lines for the traditional Assiniboine and the Gros Ventre. They are a culture fighting for their self-esteem through maintaining their heritage and sacred sites, their connection with their ancestors means living on Spirit Mountain.

If the conditions are not rectified and Pegasus Mines does not abandon Spirit Mountain, not only will these social and psychological conditions continue to exist but the people will continue to die from the pollution of their water supply. The further destruction of sacred sites elsewhere in the world also means that the native peoples of the earth are being stripped of their power and self-esteem as human beings and that racist wars are occurring in many parts of the world. Fort Belknap is but one example of the destruction of a culture engaged in its quest for survival through return to its spiritual roots.

# HARPIES: THE SEERESS, THE MAP MAKER, THE FIRE TENDER, AND THE DEATH STALKER

Siona Elvira Alwyn

I want to start with an announcement. A white buffalo calf has been born in Jamesville, Wisconsin. This event is very sacred to the Sioux who remember the prophecy of White-Buffalo-Woman that she would come back to unite the four tribes—the white, the black, the brown and the yellow tribes. The last white buffalo calf had been born in 1959 but it was not very healthy and died shortly after. This latest event is very important.

           \*            \*            \*

Darkness descends upon you and, as of this moment, you are dead.
What was your first feeling? Your last feeling?
What was you first thought? Your last thought?
What was your first fear? Your last fear?

No one is too high or too low, knows too much or too little at death. It is the Great Balancer. All enter and surrender everything to re-emerge in oneness.

The Ancients have called them Harpies—archetypes of the aspects of the Death Labyrinth, of fear and peace. Through encountering these archetypes in ritualistic ceremony, initiates were transformed and healing took place.

The Sisterhood of the Red Cauldron, an ancient Kelti Order of Earth priestesses,[1] with their accompanying priests of the Red Deer Klan, are corresponding archetypes of the Harpies.

The techniques used by these wise ones was, and is, for the transformational healing of the Sacred Trinity of mind, body, and spirit.

The Seeress, Kundry, visions the path in and out of the labyrinth of Death and Life.

The Map Maker, Ragnall, walks the path of the Death-in-life and Life-in-death.

The Fire Tender, Dindraine, enlivens the flame of death and rekindles the flame of rebirth.

The Death Stalker (the individual him- or herself) follows questors on their journey.

This is the East-West spirit walk manifesting in the North-South soul walk.

In the ancient tradition, the cauldron is the grail and the grail is the womb. Those priestess that focus their work on using the cauldron are doing a dark-to-light mirror transformation of the Underworld.

These are the Grail Maidens of the Holy Grail in myth and lore.

The Kelti tradition works with the three worlds: the Upper World, the Middle World, and the Underworld. This last, the Underworld, is the Earth's womb, her cauldron, and it is guarded by these priestesses, thus becoming a direct link and carrying on the tradition as teachers of Earth's wisdom. Through this deep connection they can lead you to discover the inner gifts and strengths to live more effectively in the Middle World; the "moment of the now."

Known as the "Dark Women of Knowledge," they are the active principle of the Kelti Goddess of Wisdom, Cerridwen. Each of us has a male counterpart in the Priesthood of the Red Deer Klan. These men hold the energies that each of us tap into and utilize in our healing work. Though one-unto-ourselves, this external polarity balance is essential to our work with the fire energy of transformation and is a mirror of our inner polarity balance.

Each priestess functions separately, physically, but all are constantly connected spiritually. Once a year we meet physically for high ceremony to renew our connection to each other as well as to our Mother Goddess. At this time we vision together and the next year's work is brought forth.

The Seeress Kundry guards tradition and is the voice of the Goddess. She has the status of Sibyl or Earth Speaker, and when she descends within she becomes one with the Earth itself and the wisdom carried within. Kundry brings forth esoteric knowledge needed for realignment of spirit energies of individuals as well as the Earth. Her task is the re-assembling of the fragmentary pieces of sacred knowledge of the land, as well as the ancient Kelti tradition of the Sisterhood. She weaves this knowledge of esoterica, into both earthly and transcendent lore. It is the Seeress, who, as direct communicator with spirit, establishes a clear channel for the way of Spirit. As does Galahad, the Trail Quest Knight, the male counterpart.

The Fire Tender, Dindraine, is the priestess whose relationship with the questor is that of the sacred marriage. She represents Danu, the Earth itself, and is thus the holder of earth energies. The pristine purity of fertility and its potential is poured into the healing process through her interaction. It is she who watches and stands apart as the way of grace expresses itself through her tending the sacred fire; the life spark, Kundalini. Bors was the Grail Knight who compliments this in the Grail process.

The Map Maker, Ragnall, is the agent of transformation who guides the individual to view what is despised—the shadow self—as worthwhile. For Ragnall represents both beauty and ugliness, light and shadow as the Loathly Lady who transforms into the Flower Bride. The Map Maker guides the individual to answer the questions: "What does one want most?" and "whom does the Grail serve?" They represent both the feminine and masculine principles of the Grail Quest. The balancing and unifying of the polarities within brings true freedom to grow into oneself by loving the shadow into oneness, to shine from within, restoring the internal wasteland to beauty and bounty. The priestess that walks the path of Map Maker walks the way of dedication of the heart also, often associated with Percival, the innocent fool.

My role is that of Map Maker, weaver of all the threads of the path of Wyrd, the web of life energies.

My work deals with connecting to the energies of an individual, unlocking and awakening their internal code stored in the DNA. This takes place through a process of dealing with the shadow self and the Underworld. The Underworld mirrors our own world, the Middle World, as a reflected reversal, i.e., the world of the unconscious. The use of consciousness and energy are the means to get there by bringing the individual to a point of sacrificing the ego personality, plunging through the abyss, and thus walking the She-labyrinth.

The planetary mind is the Underworld and the womb of the Earth is her magma cauldron of transformation.

In ancient times, underground formal chambers, caves, and labyrinths were the sites used, but now it is the ritual use of symbolic and inner labyrinths, combined with alchemical works that help spiritually and midwife the transformation to the clearing of the patterns of Earth connections to persons, relationships, and situations.

As Map Maker, my task is to create safe space; a womb, so to speak, for this transformation through the energy of fire, in the age-old tradition of alchemy. The connecting of the heart and belly, using energy diagrams or patterns, rebalances the individual.

The ancient technique of ritual death and rebirth is a quest accomplished in many ways throughout all cultures. The Kelti technique requires the threads of the web of life energy to be rewoven and enlivened. To walk the She-labyrinth, awakens the sleeper within, the life energy, for it is the giving over of the ritual death and chaos and going into one's depth to cross the abyss/void so as to regain life and structure in a new form. It is required to be stripped bare, surrendering to the moment; for at THIS moment one dies and at THIS moment one lives again. Embracing, merging, and melting to this is so difficult, but by clinging to the past wounds of separations and constrictions one cannot empty to be filled again, as woman does each moon time.

Only through the fires of unconditional love and complete compassion can this transformation take place. The She-labyrinth becomes a sanctuary only by walking it with mindfulness and being conscious of the moment. It is in being with one's self that this can take place. Though even in this, the comfort of the closeness of another known energy in the form of another person to balance the unknown energy of the abyss/void of death is required. As priestess, my duty at this time becomes the bearing witness and being a part of the energy flow; conscious of actively receiving and passively doing. Through the fire of compassion, the fire of the heart, the heart-belly caul-drons are transformed and reconnected.

As an exercise, put the palm of your right hand on your belly/womb and the palm of your left hand on your heart. In a figure eight pattern, begin to move energy from the heart to the belly and back up to the heart, all the while breathing in air/energy to the area and releasing air and sending energy to the other area. This brings the feminine and masculine aspects of nurturing and sustaining into balance.

The Death Stalker is the questor, whose task it is to integrate all into the moment, thus to experience/see the Grail, the divine within the moment.

The priestesses are the initiators in the Kelti Tradition of these aspects that are part of Western Tantra, the practice of identification of oneself with a fully enlightened divinity.

Nothing is viable unless we apply it to the present moment. To walk the old ways is to bring this wisdom to bear in the now.

Will you die to be re-born?

## Note

1.   Ancient order in Ireland, Scotland, and Wales, whose knowledge is based on oral tradition. The order later merged with the Celts.

# SACRED PLACES OF JAPAN: SACRED GEOGRAPHY IN THE VICINITY OF THE CITIES OF SENDAI AND NARA1

James A. Swan

In the misty rain
Mount Fuji is veiled all day—
How intriguing!
*Matsuo Basho (Ueda, 1991:102)*

## Introduction

The Japanese word *shi-zen* is the equivalent of the English word "nature" and yet the two words have different meanings that reveal important insights into the psychology of mind and nature in Japan. *Webster's Ninth New Collegiate Dictionary* offers several definitions of "nature" in English. They include the creative and controlling force in the universe, the external world, and natural scenery. Common among all the offered definitions is the concept that nature is something which is separate from oneself. In contrast, the Japanese word *shi-zen* has a different meaning. *Shi* is derived from two root words, *onozukara* and *mizukara*. *Onozukara* means "of itself" and "objectivity" and refers to a state that exists without any help from man. *Mizukara* is a balancing concept which means "self, subjectivity" and the "product of the human will." *Zen,* the second half of the word *shi-zen* refers to a state of mind. (It is not the same as the *zen* of Zen Buddhism.)

From this analysis, one can deduce that *onozukara* means nature as we conceptualize nature in the West and *mizukara* is similar to the Western concept of self. In the Japanese mind then one can say that the concept of *shi-zen* refers to a state of mind which arises from the unity of the human self with the natural world, being at their root one and the same. In the words of the Japanese author Isamu Kurita:

> ...The Japanese tend not to look at nature from a human point of view. They look at humans from the point of view of nature and try to abandon their individual selves and integrate themselves into nature. This attitude is made possible by viewing nature not as a disorderly chaos, but a higher level of harmony. Thus, grasping the natural order as the moment of the highest moral perfection, by observing it, and integrating oneself into it, one serves to discover the truth of life and make it sufficient (1992:123).

As opposed to Western natural sciences which seek to dissect and name natural objects, describe phenomena, discover the chemical and physical properties of nature, and study how natural objects may be used to meet human needs, they all use research methods that call for objective measurement. A traditional approach to nature study in Japan, China or Korea, would be to contemplate nature subjectively, seeking to understand natural phenomena as part of a dynamic, organic, ever-changing whole so as to bring human life and thought into harmony with nature. Once this state of mind, *satori,* is attained, then both nature and human society may prosper, as in the words of Tohoku University Biology Professor Yoshitaka Shimizu, "real wisdom comes from contact with nature" (quote from his speech in 1991).

The goal of harmony with nature is cultivated in many ways in Japanese culture. One example of the many subtle ways for aiding attainment of harmony between the mind and nature is the Japanese nomenclature for the human face. The names of physical parts of the face are the same as for parts of plants. The eyes are seeds, the ears are fruit, the nose is a flower, and the teeth are leaves.

The quality of nature that creates life in oriental thought is the life force—the *chi* in China and the *ki* in Japan. On both the human body and the earth's surface there are said to be special places where the life force is of unusual abundance and quality. It also connects pathways or meridians through which extra energy flows. These places on the body are referred to as acupuncture points. In the landscape, they are special holy places, *sei-chi* where strong spirits, *kami* in the Shinto tradition, are said to reside. The Japanese have a strong feeling for place, taking special care to acknowledge *sei-chi* as possessing a more spiritual quality *(reiteki),* in numerous ways.

In the Shinto tradition, the boundary and entry point to a holy place is indicated with a *torii* ("gate"), and the place is elaborately decorated with gardens, temples and shrines, marking special natural objects with a special straw rope with tassels *(shimenawa),* hung over special rocks or wrapped around special trees where special ceremonies and rituals are performed. All these activities call attention to the place and honor its power, seeking to gain favor from the spiritual forces *(kami)* present, and driving away evil forces. Architecture and landscaping at a *sei-chi* in Japan not only mark their location and provide religious symbolism, they help to serve as conduits for the *kami* to enter more directly human life and thus the design can be seen as invocation.

Hence, pine trees are often planted around shrines together with special trees and stones which are felt to be conducive to serving as temporary vessel for the *kami;* these *yorishiro* are given special recognition. Additional *yorishiro* include banners, wands, flags, light poles, dolls and puppets. Such decoration typically adds to the beauty of a place, but the Japanese name for places of spiritual significance is *sei-chi,* which means literally "sacred place" and is distinguished from the term *nadokoro* which is used to describe places of extraordinary beauty. The two may be the same, but not necessarily so.

One seeks out *sei-chi* with reverence, because *kami* can possess objects and people, resulting in special powers. According to Carmen Blacker, in her study of Japanese shamanism, *The Catalpa Bow,* an essential quality of the *kami* is their amorality. Their nature is

> neither good nor bad, but can manifest itself as benign or destructive to human interests according to the treatment it receives....Treatment which all *kami* find pleasing consists of assiduous worship, correct offerings, and above all purity on the part of the worshipper. Frequent visits to the shrine, copious offerings of dried fish, rice wine, fruit, lengths of cloth, swords, spears, horses are all calculated to win its favor (1986:41).

In Japan, there are two primary religions, Shintoism, the traditional religion, and Buddhism. They have, in some cases, become syncretized and, in other cases, remained distinct in their practice. There are also many other religions with smaller followings. While each religion has its own special customs and practices related to *sei-chi,* a belief in their existence as natural phenomena, apart from any human activities, is shared by most, except for Christians. One of the most important differences between Shintoism and Buddhism in regard to *sei-chi* is that Shintoism is more protective of sacred sites, placing greater restrictions on visiting them and making offerings to show proper respect. There are at least 80,000 shrines marking *sei-chi* in Japan and over 20,000 Shinto priests serving them.

During 1991 and 1992, I had the good fortune to make two lecture trips to Japan. During these visits, thanks to my gracious hosts, I had the chance to visit some of the *sei-chi* of Japan. In this paper, I will briefly describe some of the special holy places in the vicinity of two Japanese cities of Honshu, the main island—Sendai in the north and Nara in the south. I will conclude with briefly comparing Japanese practices and concepts with those in North America.

## Sendai

In November of 1991, the city of Sendai in Tohoku Province was the host for the Fourth Spirit of Place Symposium. This five-year symposium series is designed to explore the modern significance of the ancient belief about the unique power of place (Swan, 1990, 1991, 1992, 1996). In contrast to the Spirit of Place symposia held in the United States in 1988, 1989, 1990, and 1993, each of which drew some 40-60 speakers and crowds ranging from 125 to 375, the Spirit of Place Symposium held in Sendai drew 6,000, including representatives from the Japanese local, provincial and federal government. The size of this meeting was ample evidence of the interest and support for the spirit of place concept in Japan.

Sendai is a modern city of 700,000, located some two hours north of Tokyo by bullet train *(shinkansin)*. It had been heavily damaged by fire bombs during World War II and so most of the buildings are new. Sendai is called *mori no miyako* which means "the city of the trees," and most major streets are indeed lined with trees. It is an eastern coastal city tucked between the mountains and the ocean, with ten colleges and universities and many corporate research facilities as well as farming, fishing and forestry industries.

Compared with other parts of Japan, Sendai is a "new city," developed with the efforts of the Shogun Masamune Date (1567-1636). Arriving in Sendai, one of the first special places one sees, rising up along the banks of the Hirose River, is a prominent hill to the west. Aoba Hill is the site of the Aoba ("green leaf") Castle of Masamune Date, preserved as a popular park—Aobayama-Koen Park. On top of the 433-foot-high hill is a statue of the shogun riding a horse and wearing his helmet, decorated with a large crescent moon. The castle was destroyed in 1945 by bombing and so the Gokoku Shrine now covers most of the area once occupied by the castle.

According to tradition, spirits of deceased ancestors may become *kami*, and animals, such as birds, deer and foxes, serve as messengers of the gods, e.g., the powerful mountain god Yamanokami. Near Masamune Date's statue is a second one of a *taka* or hawk, commemorating the legend that the emperor Jimu (660-585 B.C.) was guided to victory in battle by a golden hawk. Aside from the enjoyable view from the top, visitors can also often see many hawks, kites, ravens and crows flying around the hill, evidencing the power of this place. In the Orient, as well as elsewhere, an abundance of animals, especially of one species is commonly recognized as a sign of being a special place.

To the north, some 35 minutes by train, lies Matsushima Bay, which is one of the most beautiful natural areas in Japan. It is in fact one of three places the Japanese call their Three Big Scenic Wonders. In the bay, there are some 250 small, pine-covered rocky islands, each with a distinctive shape and many unusual rock formations. At the entrance to Matsushima Bay is the Zuiganji Temple which has been declared a national treasure. Erected in 1606 by Masamune Date, this wooden building with many ornate carvings and paintings, and two ancient plum trees brought from Korea in 1592, is a training seminary for Zen Buddhist priests. In nearby rock outcroppings are ancient natural caves once used by monks to practice meditation.

Visitors to this park make offerings and receive small paper prayers which they tie on the branches of trees to ask the help of the *kami* to make the predictions come true and ward off evil spirits. Just inside the gate is a modest stone shrine to honor the Eel God whose presence is known by the abundance of eels commonly found in Matsushima Bay.

To the south of Sendai, high in the interior mountains, is another *sei-chi,* Akyotaki Park, which protects and honors a spectacular waterfall. Visitors to the park may walk down a simple gravel path to see the cascading water, as in any other park in the world, or they may take the path that leads to the Shinto shrine which honors the god Fudo, said to be the shaman god, the God of Fire who stands for truth and justice. Taking this second path, the visitor becomes a pilgrim.

The word "Shinto" means literally "the *kami* way," and there are four principal elements of Shinto worship—purification *(harai),* offering *(shinsen),* prayer *(norito),* and symbolic feast *(naori;* Ono, 1962:51). You know that you are entering a special place by passing under the overhead arch, the *torii.* You then proceed to a sacred spring where you wash you mouth and the tips of your fingers to purify your mind. Then you move to a small stand where candles, amulets and artifacts are displayed. This is the first place to make an offering. Traditionally offerings include money, food, drink, materials and symbolic objects. You make an offering and then burn some incense in a large urn to dispel evil. A second offering may then be made in a wooden collection box at the foot of the shrine. Then you pray, bowing slightly, then deeply twice, clapping your hands twice, before saying any prayer. At the end of the prayer you make a deep bow and a slight bow and you ring the massive gong at the feet of the statue honoring the god, before setting a foot on the gravel path to the waterfall. There is a debate about the purpose of ringing the giant bell. Some say it calls the attention of the *kami,* others insist it drives away evil. Moving down the gravel path to the waterfall, you pass many paper fortunes tied to branches and small piles of stones which mark similar hopes and wishes.

Aside from its natural beauty, the cascading waterfall is of special value. Spiritual seekers traditionally stayed in small caves beside and under the waterfall, fasting and meditating, hoping for enlightenment. Blacker (1986:91) states that shamanic training in Japan once called for neophytes to stand directly in the cascading waterfall for extended periods of time. While standing under a waterfall, aspirants would recite various chants and prayers. On the way back from the waterfall, outside the area of worship, some local vendors offer pickled snakes and other amulets for sale, as well as rattles, candles, incense, jewelry, and carved wooden objects which may be used for celebration.

# Nara

The city of Nara in southern Honshu was originally surrounded by an agricultural area, especially known for its rice and fine cloth. Founded in 710 by Emperor Kammu, it was the capital of Japan before Kyoto. A famous attraction of the Nara area is Nara-Koen Park, home of about one thousand tame deer who roam freely among numerous temples and shrines. The origin of honoring deer dates back to a time long ago, when, it is said, an old man, a powerful *kami,* arrived with an important message, riding on the back of a white deer.

In the vicinity of Nara-Koen Park, there are many places of special significance. Mount Wakakusa is a hill covered with lush natural vegetation. It is set afire each year on January 15 by fifteen priests, insuring ample new green growth for the deer of the park. The Kasuga Tashi Shrine, founded in 768 by the Fujiwara family, is famous for its numerous lanterns (more than 2,000) made out of stone and decorated with symbols of the sacred deer. In the Shinto tradition, lighting lanterns is a method of communicating with the *kami.* The lanterns are lit twice a year, February 2 or 3 and August 15, and each year the Kasugamatsuri Festival is held on March 13. There are four shrines, surrounding an art gallery. In the Shinto tradition, shrines may be torn down and rebuilt every twenty years to purify the site. The Kasuga Tashi Shrine has been rebuilt over fifty times. At the shrine, there are many *sakaki* (evergreen trees, *Cleyera ochnacca),* sacred in Shinto tradition.

Within the Nara area lies Tenri, a religious city and the home base of the Tenrikyo Religion. The Tenrikyo Religion was born at 8:00 a.m. on October 26, 1836 when 41-year-old Miki Nakayama, a housewife of the rich farming family, Nakayama, had a divine revelation. She said that God the Parent, Tenri-O-no-Mikoto, spoke to her. As with many prophets, people initially did not understand, and she and her family suffered many hardships, but slowly her teachings gained respect. Between 1869 and 1882, her teachings were written down and preserved in the Ofudesaki ("holy book"), consisting of 1711 verses, written in the Japanese *waka* style. It serves today as the principal scripture for the Tenrikyo Religion which now has more than 16,000 churches and three million followers world-wide.

At the core of the Tenrikyo Religion is the belief that you can fully benefit from this religion through entering a mental state akin to that of the foundress and that, once this happens, and you follow the religious practices with devotion and good spirit, you as a devotee will receive guidance, healing, and recognize omens. In some respect, the beliefs are quite similar to Jung's concepts of synchronicity (Inoue, 1988).

In honor of the foundress, a magnificent wooden temple, the Oysato (the "Parental Home"), has been erected in Nara, marking the exact place where

Miki Nakayama first had her revelations. The main sanctuary, which is said to be the largest wooden building in the world, contains an Inner Sanctuary and four surrounding worship halls which all face the Inner Sanctuary. In the center of the Inner Sanctuary is a hexagonal wooden platform, the Kanrodai, rising from the floor. This marks the exact place of the foundress' revelations. It is called the Jiba or "Place of Human Creation." There is a hole in the roof overhead above the Jiba. All worship halls have beautifully polished wooden floors and are covered with an elaborate wooden structure.

Twice daily, at sunrise and sunset, thousands of people, from near and far, gather in the Oysato for service, led by priests. People kneel in all four directions, facing the Jiba and perform a series of mudras and chants which begin with *Ashiki o harote tasuke tamae, Tenri-O-no-Mikoto,"* which is translated as "Sweeping away evils, please, save us, Tenri-O-no-Mikoto." Evidence of the power of this place and the religious services can be found nearby in a large collection of crutches, canes and wheelchairs which have been discarded by people who reportedly have been healed by their visit to the Oysato. Nearby schools and hospitals carry on the teaching and healing work for the Tenrikyo church. Several times a year as many as a quarter million of people assemble at the Oysato to express their devotion.

On the hills northwest of Tenri is Mount Miwa, another *sei-chi.* A number of shrines dot the landscape along a gravel path that gently ascends the mountain. The most magnificent is the Suwa Shrine. Shinto priests dispense fortunes, perform ceremonies and invite monetary offerings from pilgrims to show their respect for the *kami.* There are a number of revered shrines whose deity is the white snake. Legend has it that, in ancient times, one of the *kami* transformed himself into a white snake to gain access to a beautiful girl. In this disguise, he entered her compound and had sex with her. The child from this bonding became the leader of a new clan with great power. As evidence of the truth of this legend, it is said that all descendants have a small patch of skin that is scaly like that of a snake.

Along the path ascending the mountain, one of the most interesting shrines honors the God of Sake (alcoholic beverage). It is said that, in ancient times, monkeys taught the people to make sake and that sake has a spiritual origin. According to legend, sake was once used by a hero to defeat an eight-headed god of nature who came into villages to ravish young women. No man could defeat this god and so the hero devised a plan to use sake. When the god came into the village to pillage, the hero invited him to sit down and drink. The god accepted the offer and liked the sake so much that he became intoxicated. When the god was inebriated, the hero beheaded him. Today anyone can consume sake for entertainment, Shintoist and Ainu still brew and drink sake during religious rites. Aside from creating good feelings, one of the main powers of sake is to make all people equal and foster friendship.

Further down the path, past the sake shrine, you come to a sacred waterfall. You may drink from the water which, some believe, is good for health.
Most people turn back at this point, but serious pilgrims can rent a white
scarf to wear around the neck when climbing to the summit of the mountain
along a steep and narrow trail. The white scarf is for protection as powerful
spiritual forces are present. Along the way you see many *shimenawa*, marking special rocks and trees, and there are trailside shrines to honor the white
snake deity.

Descending from the mountain, we explored more of the shrines with
many works of art. On the summit of a nearby hill, there is a plaque which
tells how shrines and *torii* in the area have been erected on special lines of
subtle forces to channel energies between sacred mountains (very similar to
the concept of ley lines in England).

The strength of Shintoism, as expressed in shrine worship, is in its emphasis on direct invocation of spiritual forces through ritual. Theoretical
questions and philosophical discourses are set aside and people go directly
to the *kami* and seek blessings and powers. This makes Shintoism a living
religion, renewed every time and more mutable, resulting in dynamic ethic,
as pointed out by Sokyo Ono, "In Shinto ethics, nothing—sex, wealth, killing, etc.—is regarded as unconditionally evil" (1962:105).

## Onsen

Japan has much volcanic activity. One consequence is an abundance of
hot springs which are called *onsen*. There are *onsen* all over Japan, most
have been recognized in some fashion, because public bathing is a Japanese
pastime. Some of the springs on the mountains have been incorporated into
the development of resorts, some are in private homes and others in large
resorts and hotel complexes. The chemistry of the water varies. One of the
springs I visited had an especially strong healing quality. It was rich in iron
and had a dark reddish-brown color. Nearby pools had hot and cold water.
After bathing, one is invited to enjoy tea and elegant meals served in traditional Japanese fashion.

In contrast, in downtown Nara, another natural *onsen* has been developed as part of a weekend retreat, featuring massage, movie theaters, restau-
rants, and pachinko parlors. In this spa, there are a number of pools with
water of various temperatures as well as a special pool containing herbs. In
Japan today, a serious public health problem is *karoshi,* which means working oneself into illness, even death. As an antidote to stress at work, some
Japanese simple spend the weekend at such a resort.

## Discussion

The Japanese landscape is dotted with many *sei-chi* of all descriptions—caves, rivers, hot springs, mountains, hills, waterfalls, etc. In contrast to North America, where sacred space is defined solely by human-made buildings or scarcely, at best, marked by indigenous tribes, the Japanese take special measures to insure that their sacred places are well-known and honored. Elaborate shrines and temples are placed at special sites or at their threshold and local spirits, associated with each place, are known and respected in ceremonies, rituals and arts. Similar shrines may be found at many homes, both inside and outside, integrating distant spirits with those which preside over the home. The result of the extensive marking of *sei-chi* elevates the overall feeling of sanctity of the land and provides a constant reminder of how nature, spirit and mind are interconnected. Religious rituals, ranging from formal festivals and ceremonies to individuals going on pilgrimages to make offerings and invoke the gods at certain places, draw upon centuries of respect for natural powers and enrich Japanese life. The visitor comes away wondering if somehow Japan is more sacred than North America.

There is a sharp contrast between Japanese attitudes toward proper behavior toward sacred places and those of native people indigenous to North America. In Japan one makes a great amount of effort to honor and respect certain places and invites as many people as possible to come and pay homage to them. There are special customs relating to how you show respect for *sei-chi,* such as making offerings, wearing a white scarf to visit a special place, and taking no photos. People are encouraged to come and visit and learn from first-hand experience what the powers of these places are like, because the places are there to benefit everyone who shows proper respect. Indian tribes of South and Central America traditionally paid more public attention to their sacred places, sometimes erecting large temples to honor various gods and spirits. In North America, however, such human-made structures are virtually non-existent, except for the burial mounds of the Midwest. Among Native American Indians, sacred places are frequently secret and not visited, except perhaps by shamans and/or select leaders.

The difference in attitudes toward sacred places can be explained by differences in the nature of the religious practices in each area. Shintoism, an indigenous religion of Japan, is a nature-oriented, polytheistic religion with many shamanic qualities. The mountains, caves, waterfalls, and forest groves are the homes of *kami,* and each is worshipped through special rituals and shrines. Buddhism is more a commemorative religion, and yet there are still shamanic elements in some Buddhist sects. In Japan, Buddhism has frequently incorporated many aspects of Shintoism and even blended with it in some cases. Much the same has happened with Confucianism and even Christianity to a certain extent. One consequence is that various religious orders have staked claim to specific *sei-chi,* especially the spirit mountains *(reizan).* The most prominent Shinto mountains are Mount Fuji and Mount Nantai. Syncretic Shinto-Buddhist sects gather at Mount Yamabushi, where an ascetic mountain tradition flourishes. At Mount Ontake, a favorite place of *yo* ("pilgrim clubs), mediums assemble and perform the *yorigito* ritual to predict the future and manifest other psychic powers. Farther north, the Ainu of Hokkaido are people with a core shamanic religion closest to North America Indians, however, according to Hitoshi Watanabe, "there are no longer living Ainu who have (fully) personally experienced traditional Ainu life" (1971:v).

Nonetheless, when cultures move from shamanic to commemorative religions, replacing shamans with priests, then public rites become more common place and serve to anchor cultural values and customs, creating community as well as invoking spirituality. An important question that one is faced after having seen and visited the sacred places of Japan and studied sacred places of North America, concerns diminished powers of place through widespread, respectful recognition of the place. In a world with a growing population and galloping technological developments, this question seems very important for Japan as well as inhabitants of other nations. It has relevance for both heritage preservation as well as the mental and ecological health of the society, and the social customs regarding the spiritual values of nature.

One of the criticisms made against modern Japanese culture is that while the Japanese inherit their love for nature and have developed extraordinary landscape and horticulture arts to maximize natural beauty, they prefer to watch and tame natural environments and then regard them from a distance rather than coexist with them in a more dynamic state (Kim, in a speech, 1991). In my limited experience, it seems that, in modern Japan, there is reluctance to go out into nature and appreciate it without any human alteration, in contrast to the United States where many recreationists go hiking and backpacking in the American Wilderness Preservation System. This distancing from nature may be linked to the modern Japanese tendency to avoid individuation through personal exploration of the deeper mythic and symbolic meanings of dreams and visions of the unconscious, preferring instead to conform to group standards (Kauai, 1991). Nature has a tendency to loosen ego boundaries, facilitating exploration of the unconscious through dreams and visions, etc. (Swan, 1992). To access the unconscious, due to the pressures of modern life, barriers need to be removed.

In contrast to the Japanese preference to regard natural beauty aided by human actions, and modern Americans who create parks and reserves to preserve wilderness, the circumpolar Inuit have no word for "park," as they traditionally live in "wild" places. Modern Inuit refer to parks and wilderness areas, designated by modern society, as "places white people play." Inuit, like Sami, bushmen, and other traditional hunter-gatherers live in a constant state of dynamic interplay with nature, essential for their survival because in nature lies their source of food.

Regardless of our cultural heritage, there is a common urge among all people to make contact with sacred places (Swan, 1990). In modern society this can be a source of serious problems for land managers and heritage preservationists. At Stonehenge in England, visits to the original stone circle are heavily restricted due to the number of tourists who want to visit this place. An importance difference between use of Stonehenge and Japanese sacred places, however, is that Stonehenge is not considered by most people to be a center for ongoing active religious practice, but rather a historical artifact, representing a previous religion and culture. The difference in cultural perception of places between modern and traditional societies is one example of how mind and nature have become split in modern culture, resulting in alienation within, pollution and destruction of the natural world outside. In a modern world, where material values are given so much weight, it would seem that we could learn much from the Japanese legacy of sacred places and the cultural values they preserve. Translated to other soil, they could help shape values of love for nature and guide us to create a more ecologically harmonious world.

## Acknowledgements

I wish to thank Fumio Suda, Tadaaki Kanno, Akio Inoue, Tomohide Cho, Mr. and Mrs. Takashi Tsumura, and the many other gracious Japanese for supporting my visits to Japan and introducing me to Japanese culture and thought.

## References

Blacker, Carmen. *The Catalpa Bow: A Study of Shamanistic Practices in Japan.* London, England: Unwin Hyman Ltd., 1989.

Inoue, Akio. "'Signs Coincided' and the Way of the 'Divine Model,'" *Tenri Journal of Religion, 22* (December, 1988).

Kauai, "Internal and External Dimensions of Human Environment," paper presented at the Tenri Yamato Culture Congress, Tenri, Nara-ken, Japan, November 1992.

Kurita, Isamu. *Nihon no Kokoro* [Japanese Mind]. Tokyo: Maruzen Co., Ltd., 1992, p.123.

Ono, Sokyo. *Shinto: The Kami Way.* Tokyo: Charles E. Tuttle and Co., 1962.

Shimizu, Yoshitaka. Keynote speech at the Spirit of Place Symposium, Sendai, Japan, November 25, 1991.

Swan, James. *Nature as Teacher and Healer.* New York: Villard-Random House, 1992.

____. *The Power of Place.* Wheaton, IL: Quest Books, 1991.

____. *Sacred Places.* Santa Fe, NM: Bear and Co., 1990.

____, and Roberta Swan. *Working With the Spirit of Place.* Wheaton, IL: Quest Books, 1996.

Ueda, Makoto. *Basho and His Interpreters: Selected Hokku with Commentary.* Stanford, CA: Stanford University Press, 1991, p.102.

Watanake, Hitoshi. *The Ainu Ecosystem.* Seattle, WA: University of Washington Press, 1972.

# DISCUSSION

With Alwyn, Leikam, and Swan

*Hall:* I want to direct my comments to both James Swan and William Leikam, your presentations struck me deeply. I am from Western Montana and spent three years working for the Western Montana Department of State Lands. This experience is kind of the reason why I am here and not there. Do you know the state regulatory agencies because they hold the permits for those lands? Montana politics are as bad as California's. However, to have the land being taken care of, we do have the Environmental Policy Act.

*Leikam:* I know a little bit about what is happening there. The early release of the land to the Zortman Mines has been carried down through time. Part of the battle has to do with grandfathering of the Zortman Mines. Nobody is getting anywhere with this whole issue. The problem is that part of Spirit Mountain is on and part of it is off the reservation. Somebody asked me how they could help. I did not bring the address for Red Thunder Incorporated but the address can easily be obtained. They are legal and belong to the traditionalist movement devoted to saving Spirit Mountain.

*Heinze:* Bill's address is in the List of Abstracts so people can write to him.

*Hall:* It is a Gordian knot. In another case, a copper miner from Butt, Montana, which is five hundred miles to the West, had mystical and healing experiences. So a sacred place has arisen above one of the larger copper mines and a 150-foot statue of Our Lady of the Rockies, based on Our Lady of Guadalupe, has been erected. The permission was passed by the Department of State Lands. There is an Environmental Impact Statement, Gary Moon's office (he was a forester), said "yes." So this 150-foot statue now gazes at you, from the Rocky Mountains. It can be very startling in the fog.

*Skaife:* I like to make a comment about Mt. Shasta which recently received historic designation. The local business community is well organized and has endorsed it. In our time, it is extremely important that people living outside of the area also communicate the value of the mountain. Everybody can help and there are two ways to do it. I will put my address on the blackboard or you can contact "Save Mt. Shasta" and become politically connected so you can give your input. We have pretty much forgotten that the mountain has value not only for the few people who live around it. It is timely for you now to help.

*Morgenstern:* I have a question to Jim because I will be going to Japan. The question is, if you pick a place where you would go to look at shamanism, not the traditional Buddhism or the traditional Shintoism, where would you go and who would you see?

*Swan:* Get hold of the book, called *The Catalpa Bow, A Study of Shamanic Practices in Japan,* by Carmen Blacker (London: Unwin Hyman, Ltd., 1989). It is the best single source I know of. If you can't find it, go to the bookstore in Japantown.

Mt. Ontaka in the north, for example, is a place where a group of shamans go every year and prophesy all around the mountain. They are primarily women who act as mediums for the spirit of the mountain.

*Rivers:* I want to honor all of you for your beauty and your grace. May the Spirit of Place touch you and the work you do for Spirit Mountain! I heard horror stories about not just physical but also spiritual destruction. I think it moves all of us. I noticed all people in the room, when we were watching the video, felt connected. It is sad that tragedy connects us but it gives us an opportunity to come together and heal some wounds, not only to protect the land but also to help each other heal.

I also want to thank for the presentation on Celtic traditions, my mother is Celtic and she is beginning to remember. Furthermore, James Swan, thanks for your work so the people can see the beauty of the place.

I want to share something that happened to me this summer as part of our training technique. Since I am not Indian, I still follow traditional processes of my husband in honoring and protecting the sacred sites. I do this work to bring this realization to others. So I went to a particular place which is considered to be one of the higher places in our area in northern California. It had been part of the Go-Road controversy and was under environmental, not religious protection which is something we still have to work on. When I traveled up there, the mountain touched my heart and demonstrated that our work has to do with understanding and protecting a place. It is appreciated and we are heard. So I commend you for what you do and hope that you will continue and have the strength to do so and the blessings.

*Scott:* Siona, I want to thank you for recognizing the importance of White Buffalo-Calf Woman returning to the people. This is an auspicious time for all native people. I would like to remind you that in the late eighteen hundreds there was a massacre that took place at Wounded Knee. Men, women and children were literally slaughtered. But there has been a change, rather than a biological slaughter, there is now an ecological genocide going on. Spirit Mountain is just one example. The Havasupi Reservation is also in dire need of assistance. They are strip mining and trying to do uranium mining. We have nuclear testing sites on the reservations in Oklahoma and Nevada. All of this is an example of how the native consciousness is like a thorn in the political European consciousness. They don't want to recognize that. There was a newspaper article citing the ratio of Downs Syndrome children among minorities. Native Americans were not even mentioned as a minority. This is the type of untouchability that we don't want to address today. It goes back to our sense of not having a place, a motif, to move west, not having any possibility to put down any roots anymore. It is a symbol of our lack of connection, a place is not only a geographical but a spiritual place.

There is an anecdote I would like to share with you. I had an experience a few years ago when I went to the Black Hills to a Gathering of Eagles over which a medicine man by the name of Yellow Horse was presiding. Representatives of cultures from all over the world convened in the Black Hills and the Elders came to share ceremonies, to share their wisdom, and essentially to be there for the people. We had also aboriginal elders, virtually every race was present.

Yellow Horse had a vision in his tipi. The vision came from Black Elk, Crazy Horse, and Sitting Bull. On the fourth day, we consummated this vision and placed a Medicine Wheel for all nations in the Black Hills. My adopted grandmother, with the staff of seven eagle feathers, led this procession up into the Black Hills in a ceremony of great depth and beauty. Each person placed a stone in the circle and then we all came down and celebrated. The wheel still exists in Custer, South Dakota. It is a way of connecting. So I want to encourage you all to get involved. Know about your place not only spiritually but also geographically. We are so busy in our lives, we never step out and smell the sweetness of the trees or whatever is there. So I honor all the work you are doing. It is really important.

*Leikam:* I think if you set out to destroy a culture, especially a traditional culture, you would not even have to kill anyone. You wouldn't to have wage war in the ordinary sense, all you have to do is to destroy the sacred sites. What I showed you is not the only kind of destruction of sacred sites, New Agers are trying to get back to the land. I just recently learned that, in the Dakotas, New Agers are going to sacred sites where native people have held ceremony and tied prayer bundles to sacred trees. New Agers have taken these sacred bundles off the trees, leaving their beer cans at the sacred sites. On Mt. Shasta also, destruction is going on by the New Age people coming into the Sacred Hot Springs.

*Heinze:* They even left crystals on Mt. Shasta. If you don't know a place and don't know the ceremony, don't invent one. Don't change a sacred place which has been established by different people for different purposes. Respect the place and ask for permission before you do anything. I am very satisfied with these presentations because they brought up that we have to become more involved in these burning issues. If you have energy to spare, I strongly encourage you to get in touch with our speakers.

*Marks:* I just want to make the comment that the white race is a minority on this planet.

*Flower:* I was talking with Ife this morning, about abuse. One definition of abuse is failing to ask permission.

*Heinze:* The motto of our conference is: Respect the differences. When you don't know the differences, inquire. Second: Be ready for a relationship which is not a one-way street. This leads to the third expectation—reciprocity. To give you an example: I am glad that Pai Ely is here but I saw people swarming around him, trying to get a private reading. Did you think of reciprocity? It may not be money, maybe a flower? I think it is very bad taste to receive something and not show your appreciation. It should be a little bit more than just a thank you. Whatever it is: Bake a cake, embrace him, make a donation to his temple! Reciprocity is also connected with sacred sites. We should be grateful and protect them. Wrong help can move in like a Sherman tank and cause more damage than good. We should ask for permission first and inquire how we can help.

# HIGH TECH SHAMANISM: ENTERING ALTERED STATES OF CONSCIOUSNESS USING THE SCIENCE OF SOUND

Morningstar

High Tech shamanism is a term I coined to describe a portion of the shamanic world which utilizes modern technology to enhance the process of entering into and exploring states of extraordinary reality. When I began to look at shamanism as a practice that uses tools to assist its practitioners to enter realms of extraordinary reality to make contact with their higher self, i.e., directly with God or God Consciousness, I observed how an ordinary drum, beat in a particular manner, might possibly have a high tech equivalent. Furthermore, sounds of specific frequencies, played through stereo earphones, might have their high tech chemical equivalent (some exotic substances).

I am a physicist who just happened to have some experiences in the realm of extraordinary reality. I could not stop exploring. My path took me from the scientific teachings of the 50s and 60s into a study of parapsychology, healing, and from there into just about every nook and cranny that presented itself and seemed worthwhile, and I had time to explore. It has taken me about twenty-five years to return to something that begins to resemble physics.

My intention for the past year has been to explore extraordinary reality utilizing modern technology and excluding all forms of chemistry. However, there was an important period that lasted several years during which time chemicals in various forms were used to induce states of extraordinary reality.

The original journey began over twenty-five years ago, in 1968, when I had two spontaneous psychic experiences. During the first, I discovered, much to my surprise, that under the right conditions, I could be amazingly clairvoyant and accurate. I felt like Thomas Edison must have felt when he discovered lightning was made of electricity. Like most enthusiastic neophytes in any field I wanted to bring this knowledge to the world, but quickly found out that this, and many more experiences yet to come, were going to form a body of experiences that did not lend itself to mass dissemination or scientific investigation. Within five months of that first spontaneous psychic experience in 1968, I had a second equally profound experience.

I woke up, became very aware of the fullness of my bladder, got out of bed and headed for the bathroom. I tried to find a light switch somewhere along the path and became increasingly frustrated as I tried every available light switch in the hallway. Finally, I ended up back at the bed. When I tried to turn on the bed lamp, I noticed a body lying in the bed. I looked closely and it was me. If clairvoyance was difficult to explain, an out-of-body experience was even harder.

For most of my life thereafter, "ordinary reality" would involve technical and business pursuits during "normal" business hours and metaphysical pursuits during much of my free time.

In 1978, while in a First Aid Station of a nuclear power plant construction project I was involved with, I channeled healing energy to a co-worker who had a cancer growing on his ear. He was looking for the name of a good local surgeon and so we went to the First Aid Station together to talk to the manager in charge to see if he could recommend a surgeon. While my co-worker was talking to the manager, something inside told me to touch him ever so lightly on the arm and send him some healing energy. Immediately upon doing this I felt as though I had a door slammed on my face. It was the same excruciating pain I had previously experienced when inadvertently hitting myself on the finger with a hammer.

While I was trying to recover from the pain, my co-worker concluded his conversation and left the First Aid Station. When we met the next morning, I was still in pretty bad shape. He appeared to be in a neutral place. I decided not to tell him what I had done or what had happened to me but I had a book in mind I wanted him to read about spiritual healing. I asked him if he did much reading. He said he only read one book, the Bible, and made it clear that he wasn't interested in reading any other book. Why was that, I asked? He said that about five years ago Jesus had appeared to him on the sidewalk of a small town in Tennessee and had told him to study the bible every day. He walked into the first church he found and began to read and study the bible every day. I asked him if by reading another book he might be able to heal himself of his cancer, would he consider reading this other book. He said he didn't have to worry about cancer any more because he had been healed. "How do you know that?" I inquired. He said, that after he went out the back door of the First Aid Station he met Jesus for the second time. Jesus told him, he had been healed. I asked him if he had any idea what caused Jesus to appear to him in that particular place at that particular time. He said, he didn't. I didn't say anything and really couldn't say anything. I was very grateful for that entire experience and felt that I had direct communication with God.

There were quite a few notable experiences from 1980 to 1990 but none so great as what was to come in 1991 when the doors opened to the world of teacher plants and sacred substances. I was scared to use these plants even though two of the teachers I had been with the longest offered their assistance. I wanted a personal consultant and found a mentor with thirty years experience. After about a dozen experiences which spanned over the next two years, I finally came to the conclusion that I couldn't put as much faith and trust in what I was experiencing under the influence of a sacred substance than I could in the three experiences I previously related. They all took place without any use of chemical substances.

Logic told me that while my mind was under the influence of a sacred substance I needed to be in a state of total surrender in which I couldn't be evaluating anything because it would take me out of the state of surrender. I was therefore incapable of distinguishing between what was important to my personal and spiritual growth and what was fundamentally entertainment, what was spiritual and what was hallucination, what was an out-of-body experience and what was the separation of the mind from the body by the anesthetic effects of a substance.

I have always paid close attention to what is called "mind set" and "setting." I believe this concept is one of the most important regardless of the means or process by which exploration into extraordinary reality is achieved. I therefore decided to develop techniques that would verify or validate experiences in extraordinary reality so that my mind could evaluate the experiences at some other time without disturbing the state of surrender that I felt was necessary to have the experience in the first place. I wanted to know with almost absolute certainty that what I was receiving was not a figment of my imagination or my ability to hallucinate.

First, I would pick a place, time and setting that I believed would bring me as close to God as I could get in ordinary reality.

Second, after arriving at the place, prior to the actual time of the journey, I would ask for a one-in-a-million miracle to occur in ordinary reality either immediately upon the conclusion of the experience or within twenty-four hours thereafter.

Third, the miracle had to be artfully crafted so that absolutely nothing needed to be done by me in order for the miracle to occur.

The first time I used this technique I was at a conference with a spiritual leader from India named Mata Amritanandamayi. She is affectionately called Ma or the Holy Mother by her followers. I was operating on the belief that if I attained a state of extraordinary reality within her auric field, I should have an incredibly wonderful spiritual experience.

It was Friday night at precisely sunset when the drumming and chanting began. I parked my motor home within earshot of the chanting. As I thought about what to ask for, I noticed a very beautiful woman sitting by herself about 40 feet from me. Both of us were at the very back of the place which was actually outside on a lawn. She was looking at Ma and chanting as was everyone else and didn't seem to take any notice of me at all. I then said that if what I am about to experience in the motor home is really important and valid then I want this woman to spend the night with me, sleeping in my motor home. Having declared my miracle, I got up, walked toward the motor home, perhaps passing as close as 20 feet from her, but intentionally not looking at or disturbing her.

I took what was for me a very large amount of a substance and totally surrendered to the experience. I became aware that I had died and that my soul had transcended to another plane of existence. I found myself in a hallway, sitting on a plain wooden bench with no back. It definitely felt like I was in the uppermost part of a large football stadium, looking at someone inside the announcer's booth through a wall with glass windows from about waist height up to the ceiling.

There was a grey-haired man in the booth, operating a machine which controlled the view outside of the window. Sometimes he would be looking at two people doing something. At other times, it looked like the entire stadium was flying over mountain scenes. I could see people's lips moving but I couldn't hear any sound. I watched for a long time, looked up and down the long hallway and finally decided I wanted to find out who this man was, where I was, and what was supposed to happen next.

No sooner did I have these thoughts when he looked around at me, held up one finger in a gesture to indicate that he would be through in a minute or two. I immediately thought we must be using telepathy to communicate so I sat down and waited. Soon the scene on the screen became very peaceful and the grey-haired man opened the door and came out into the hall.

"Am I really dead?" I asked. "Yes, you are," he answered. I don't remember feeling any emotion when he said this. It just seemed like a very natural, very normal experience.

"Am I in heaven?" "No." "Am I in hell?" "No." "Then where am I? Who are you?" I asked. What was going on? He sort of half smiled and said, "I am God, this is where I work. What I do here is to look in on the lives of everyone on the planet and when things are getting too good in their lives, I create a little tension or stress. And when things are getting too bad in their lives, I create something that is wonderful. I just keep stirring the pot in people's lives so they don't get too set in their ways and stay conscious about things. I am sort of a prankster, if you know what I mean, and what I practice could be called 'crazy wisdom.'"

"Does heaven exist?" "Yes." "Where is it?" "Back on earth." "And hell?" "It's all there too." "So you are sort of a Cosmic Comedian and the fact that heaven and hell co-exist on earth at all times depends upon each individual person's awareness, a Cosmic Joke. Right?" "Right!" "And what you are telling me is that there is no reason for me to continue to remain here because there is nothing here to do, so I might as well return to earth and live life according to my awareness in either heaven or hell. I can choose which ever I want at all times." "That's right," he said. "Anything else we need to discuss?" "Nothing I can think of." "O.K." "Then send me back."

It took quite a few minutes for me to be able to get up, wash and make my way back to the chanting throng. It was about 3:00 a.m. I was conscious of being sweaty and smelly and did not think it appropriate that I should receive *darshan* from Ma. Ma is a living Hindu saint. No matter how many hundreds or thousands of people come to receive *darshan* from her each day, she will touch and hug each one until all have been given *darshan*. I read she is the only living Hindu saint who will make sure that everyone in the audience has been personally touched by her before she ends the session.

When I arrived there were no more women in the women's line, left of the audience, all of the women had received *darshan*. Ma was giving *darshan* to the next to last man in the men's line. The last man was in a wheel chair about six feet from Ma's pillow seat. His back was facing me like a solid wall. I was about ten feet behind him and conscious that I was probably the only one besides the man in the wheel chair that Ma had not yet given *darshan* to.

Instead of having the man in the wheel chair go to Ma, Ma got up and knelt in front of him, treating him as though he were the saint. I could see enough of her to know that she was on her knees and bowed over him. It was very touching to see her rubbing his feet in this position.

As she began to work with him, I spontaneously began to channel healing energy to him. As soon as I began doing this, Ma peeked out from behind the wheel chair and looked straight at me as if she had sensed the energy flow and was responding to it. She smiled, I smiled back. I asked her telepathically, "Ma, do you know about the Cosmic Joke?" She smiled and then nodded her head. Then I said telepathically, "Ma, you know that the Cosmic Joke is that this is both heaven and hell?" Again, she smiled and nodded her head. Then I asked, "Ma, do you know that God is really a Comedian, a Cosmic Comedian?" For the third time she smiled and nodded her head. "Ma, do all the Saints and Masters from all religions know about this and don't tell anyone because no one would believe them? Ma, is the reason, why all the living Saints and Masters always appear to be happy because they know life is really a sort of Cosmic Joke?" For the last time she smiled and nodded her head, ducked back behind the wheel chair where I couldn't see her face and returned to rubbing and kissing the feet of the crippled man.

Then she got up, looked at me and at the drummers and made a movie director-like signal indicating they should cut the drumming. She walked over to me, smiled at me, patted me on the head and left with a crowd of at least fifty to one hundred of the most faithful devotees.

Remembering the miracle, I decided to look straight down at my feet and do nothing that would attract the beautiful woman I wanted to spend the night with. All I could see out of my peripheral vision were pairs of bare feet going in every possible direction. It seemed like hundreds of pairs of feet passing by. Time also was passing by very slowly. Because I had my head down with my chin tucked in, I could smell myself even more and was really grateful Ma didn't want me to receive *darshan* which would have involved ending up hugging me like a child. The pat on the head was more than sufficient to constitute *darshan* for me under the circumstances.

A female voice asked me, "Are you alright?" I looked up. It was her. What happened next is a wonderful cosmic comedy. She had been totally aware of me from the time I left the motor home until I returned. She had been totally aware of my communications with Ma but not their exact content. She was not feeling good about sleeping in a very cold room she was sharing with five women and accepted my invitation to spend the night in my heated motor home. Then, just when I thought I was actually going to get to spend the night with her, she tells me that the very tall man approaching from the left was her fiancee who will understand the importance of her spending the night with me. Even though I questioned her about it, she insisted he would understand and I began to believe she was behaving as if she were under a magic spell. The Cosmic Comedian had struck again. I realized that the miracle had happened and what I really didn't need to was not pressing the issue of her actually spending the night me. She was engaged but even though I barely knew her, I wanted her to be with me and not with him. Her fiancee turned out not to be as understanding as she thought he would be. He never let her out of his sight and consequently I never got to speak to her again. I admit that I still think about her from time to time, probably always will, and yes, I sometimes wonder what would have happened if I hadn't broken the magic spell.

Once I developed the concept of finding the perfect spiritual setting, followed by asking for a miracle to occur in ordinary reality, variations on the theme began to appear.

In one case there was a one-minute gap in my memory about which I had no recollection, but I intuitively knew it was important. I hired the director of a School of Hypnotherapy to hypnotise me so that I could recall what happened in the lost time. The one lost minute turned out to be one and a half hours worth of memory.

The director of the school was a very straight conservative women in her fifties, authoritarian, systematic and very no-nonsense. At one point, I saw a separate spirit-like form identifying itself as being my soul or essence, entering my body. I experienced waves of energy unlike anything I had ever experienced before, all being under hypnosis. Then it came out of my body, the waves stopped and we agreed to set up a channel for communication. I told the director of hypnosis to stop prompting me so I could allow the energy to use my voice to communicate. The director said it is already communicating. I asked how and she proceeded to tell me that when she was looking at me, I had been transfigured into an olive-skinned, dark, curly-haired mediterranean- looking man in his 30s. The shock of her statement took me out of trance. Later on, she said she had read about things like this in professional hypnosis magazines but this was the only time in her 25 years in the field that she had actually experienced it. I repeated this experiment with another hypnotist about one month later and a similar phenomenon occurred.

There are now within me a number of such experiences that have been confirmed by miracles. All were important philosophical or spiritual teachings. Interestingly, none were precognitive warnings or instructions as to how I should live my life. Each has been duly noted and recorded in my mind and has been integrated into my model of extraordinary reality. They have influenced the way I think and behave and I am comfortable with them. I still don't know how true they are but now it feels safe for me to believe in them with far fewer reservations.

In the past eleven months I have focused on substance-free methods, primarily involving sound waves. I affectionately refer to what I have experienced as being beeped, booped and bopped. Based upon what I read in OMNI magazine, I ended up going to the Monroe Institute in Virginia. After that I went to the AHA spa in Malibu, California, and finally, and most importantly, to the home of a good friend and mentor Jack Houck.

My body and mind have been exposed to many hours of auditory, vibratory and optical input under a variety of conditions of "mind set" and "setting." So far to date I have not had a single experience within this branch of science that equals what I have experienced with either no tools or with substances being the primary tool. However, there is a very powerful intuitive feeling within me that believes that the process pioneered by Jack Houck and inventor Bob Beck may be the key to opening the door to non-substance extraordinary experiences that could become more widely available, thus avoiding the risk potentially inherent in the use of substance. A few terms need to be explained at this point, they are:

1. MAW - MAW stands for mental access window. When the predominate frequency of an individual electroencephalogram (EEG) is between two frequencies, such as 7.81 and 7.83 cps, the probability of extraordinary experiences and high mental performance appears to increase. A sort of uni-

versal MAW has been defined for all human beings in the frequency range known as the "Schuman Resonance."

2. Schuman Resonance - In 1952, a German mathematician, Schuman, postulated that the hundred or more lightning bolts striking throughout the earth's surface every second stimulate the cavity between the earth's surface and the ionosphere and resonate at extremely low frequencies (ELF) below 11 cps. In 1961, the U.S. National Bureau of Standards actually measured these magnetic field oscillations. Due to various factors such as changes in the ionosphere, the frequency range of the Schuman Resonance can change somewhat every day.

Bob Beck theorized that when a person's predominant brain wave frequencies synchronize with the Schumann resonance (appr. 8 cpm), the person's mind then can easily access information throughout the world. He built equipment which Jack Houck was kind enough to let me have for several sessions. Although I didn't have any extraordinary experiences, I was able to see the strong possibility. Currently, I am working with a group of electronic shamans to develop new equipment which I will be able to demonstrate and talk about at next year's conference.

# SOUL: IN AND OF THE WORLD

Julien Puzey

That the Self advances and confirms the myriad things is delusion.
That the myriad things advance and confirm the Self is enlightenment.
*Dogen (1986:69)*

Like so many of us, I was taught to believe that the road to the good, moral, spiritual life was achieved by being *in* but *not of* the world. Both, the body which housed the spirit and the world which that body inhabited, were profane—not sacred.

This paper will explore the sacredness of being *both in* and *of* the world—the experience of ensoulment. For the purpose of this paper, *ensoulment* is defined as *consciousness of being alive in a living world.* Specifically, we will look at five areas:

1. Ensoulment in early childhood,
2. ensoulment as being multi-sensory and primarily non-verbal,
3. the role of the natural world in ensoulment,
4. ensoulment and identification of the sacred, and

5. accessing the integrative-metaphoric modes of ensoulment.

Ensoulment, access to Other, bonding with Earth, may well be the primary developmental task of early childhood—a task which requires full-bodied multi-sensory participation in the natural world.

The experience of ensoulment in childhood is a natural response to a living Earth—a response of one living being to another. The dual processes of making sense and of making soul is the sacred ground of the child.

Thomas Moore tells us that "The ensouled body is in communion with the body of the world and finds its health in that intimacy" (1992:173).

The ensouled, Earth-bonded child lives naturally in a state which many adults attempt to achieve or recover.

> It is significant that adult memories of childhood, even when nostalgic and romantic, seldom suggest the need to be a child but refer to a deep desire to renew the ability to perceive as a child and to participate with the whole bodily self in the forms, colors, and motions, the sights and sounds of the external world of nature and artifact (Shepard, 1969:130).

Heinz Werner (1948), the German developmental psychologist, paid close attention to the qualities of the perceptual world in early childhood—from eighteen months to six years. (It is important to distinguish Werner's work on perception as being different from the work of others, e.g., Piaget who focused on cognition.) In Werner's work we are challenged to look at thinking as a non-verbal process. Additionally, he gifts us with insights into the metaphoric foundations of our humanness.

According to Werner, children experience the world *synaesthetically*. The senses of seeing, hearing, smelling, tasting, and touching often merge. One specific form of synaesthesia is *chromaesthesia* or color hearing. Individuals who experience chromaesthesia experience certain sounds as having specific colors—and not just "pure tones" but natural voices—Bird, Cricket, Wind, and Thunder. Further, any one of the voices may include a wide spectrum. Three-year-old Tara Sobel reported Thunder speaking in pink, blue, and deep avocado green (Sobel, 1991:4).

To my knowledge, Tara is not an "exceptional" child in any way other than in what she heard and how she was empowered by her perception—perhaps, that is what exceptional is.

Allowing ourselves access to our own synaesthesia—risking a reality beyond poetry, once again, Cloud sings, Flower offers wisdom, and the "imaginary" slice of Moon offered us by the child, tastes like lemon custard.

Beyond being merely interesting or even mind-expanding, the existence in children of the synaesthetic sense suggests a biological foundation for metaphor (Sobel, 1991:4). The unfolding of those skills and the maintenance of the metaphoric soul-making process requires access to the natural world.

World Soul and Human Soul are co-catalysts. Maintaining that relationship is the domain of the shamanic.

> The relationship of mind to nature is the crucial question for man's ecology. If we deny that mind requires anything in its environment save other minds, we imply that the quality of natural surroundings is not very important, indeed, place is expendable (Shepard, 1969:122).

I do spend a lot of time thinking about the kinds of environments in which we can unfold and be who we truly are in all of our humanness. I am not as certain that we need an evolutionary leap as much as we need a re-balancing of our *all too peopled* environments.

What I do know is that when we institutionalize, we also de-humanize. Characteristic of our institutions, whether they be day care, school, church, prison or rest home, is decreased access to the natural world.

As we become isolated from other beings and from Earth and as we decrease our interest in other than strictly human concerns, we may, indeed, not only lose our souls, but, cease to be authentically human.

I return, in my mind, again and again to the statement which David Bower made in reference to the California condor and wonder if it is not also true for the human:

> A condor is five per cent feathers, flesh, blood and bone. All the rest is place [environment]. Condors are soaring manifestations of the place that coded their genes. That place requires space to nest in, to teach fledglings, to roost in, unmolested, to bathe and drink (Sessions, 1985:156).

The soul's environment must be Other—must be other than strictly, merely *peopled!*

The soul does not merely identify with—soul knows itself to be Tree, Rock, Soil, Ocean. Ruth-Inge Heinze has given us this account of her conscious ensoulment in childhood:

> My family lived in Berlin which, at that time, was the capital of Germany and a big city. When I was still of pre-school age, we went to the Baltic Sea in summer. One day, I found myself alone, standing on the beach. The sea touched the sky and there I was, breathing with the waves. I entered the rhythm of the waves. There was a sudden channeling of energy—the sun, the wind, the sea—going through me. I became the sun, wind, and sea. There was no "I" anymore for "I" had merged with everything else. A door opened. All sensory perceptions became one. Sounds, smells, shapes, melted into brilliant light. The pulsating energy went right through me. I was part of this energy (in Jamal, 1987:69).

Ruth-Inge Heinze's account poignantly illustrates that the community necessary for the soul's unfoldment includes kith as well as *kin. Kith* is all the other, non-humans in the environment we call home. The child is held in nurturing embrace by the non-humans.

In a paper, entitled "A Mouthful of Flowers: Ecological and Spiritual Metaphors From Early Childhood," educator David Sobel reports:

> The empathy of young children extends to nonliving organisms like the moon and the clouds. As the metaphoric tendency of early childhood bridges the gap between images and concepts in language, it also bridges the gap between unlike organisms and creates a kind of interspecies empathy, cultivation of this empathy in early childhood is one of the foundations of living lightly on the planet (1991:6-7).

Similarly, we hear from Stephen Trimble in the recenty published *Geography of Childhood:*

> By forging connections with plants, animals, and land, by finding some relationship to Earth, individuals can gain a sense of worth. Herein lies security. Edith Cobb, in analyzing the roots of creativity in great thinkers found that many had experienced a pivotal childhood "discontinuity, an awareness of [one's] own unique separateness and identity, and also a continuity, a renewal of relationship with nature." Cobb marveled at what can grow from this paradox: "...a delighted awareness that knowing and being are in some way coincident and continuous...and that this kind of knowing is in itself an achievement of psychological balance" (Nabhan and Trimble, 1994:22-23).

What Edith Cobb refers to as "psychological balance" is known and referred to by others as direct, uncontestable knowledge of the sacred. The experience of ensoulment in childhood is the touchstone or litmus test for discernment of the sacred and of the authentically shamanic.

Continuing the narrative of her childhood experience, Ruth-Inge Heinze confirms its significance:

> This was the first time I got a glimpse of what shamans experience. They learn how to tap this energy and offer themselves to become channels through which the energy can flow.
>
> I could not talk about this experience. My parents thought I had a heat stroke and so kept me in bed, in the dark, for a couple of days. This gave me time to reintegrate and return to my family.
>
> As a child, I did not know what to do with this vision. There was no one with whom I could talk about it, since people would think I was crazy. However, every time I have similar experiences, I remember the first time. That experience became a measuring rod for me as to whether future visions were genuine or just fictions of my imagination (in Jamal, 1987:70).

Were Edith Cobb alive, researching and writing today, she may very well used the words "genius" and "shaman" interchangeably:

> The key point, bearing on later human genius in adulthood, is what Cobb calls "plasticity of response to environment and the child's primary aesthetic adaptation to environment." Cobb notes that this original childhood experience may be extended through memory into a lifelong renewal of the early power to learn and evolve." This accounts for the ever-fresh joy in new discovery which certain persons of genius continue to exhibit into advanced age, while ordinary

people glumly settle for "nothing new under the sun." She further notes that genius does not result from accumulation of information but from continued openness of the entire organism to new information from the outer world.

...In Cobb's collection of autobiographies, she notes that it is to this particular period in childhood that these creative thinkers "return in memory in order to renew the power and impulses to create at its very source."...Cobb wrote that the child seems to experience both "an awareness of his own unique separateness and identity, and also continuity, a renewal of relationship with nature as process" (La Chapelle, 1978:63-64).

And there is hope for adults—hope for the healing restoration of our souls. We can both regain and sustain a sense of conscious ensoulment, but, we can't get there by "trying"—at least in our typical power-over kinds of ways:

But I can't go out and try to see this way. I'll fail, I'll go mad. All I can do is try to gag the commentator, to hush the noise of the useless babble that keeps me from seeing just as surely as a newspaper dangled before my eyes....The world's spiritual geniuses seem to discover universally that the mind's muddy river, this ceaseless flow of trivia and trash, cannot be damned, and that trying to damn it is a waste of effort, that might lead to madness. Instead you must allow the muddy river to flow unheeded in the dim channels of consciousness; you raise your sights; you look along it mildly, acknowledging its presence without interest and gazing beyond it into the realms of the real where subjects and objects act and rest purely, without utterance (Dillard, 1974:83).

Although, more really accessible in childhood, the potential for conscious ensoulment is available throughout the human life span:

Bob Samples in his book The Metaphoric Mind, differentiates between the logical-rational mode of thought and the integrative metaphoric. Cognitive thought, as portrayed by Piaget, has discrete stages of development....But the metaphoric [soul making] modes do not appear to distribute themselves developmentally (Sobel, 1991:11).

## *In and of* the world:

It is a crime of deception—convincing people that their own visceral experience of the world hardly matters, and that predigested images hold more truth....We need to return to learning about the land by being on the land, or, better, in the thick of it. That is the best way we can stay in touch with the fates of its creatures, its earthbound wisdom. That is the best way we can be in touch with ourselves (Nabhan and Trimble, 1994:107).

Wilfred Pelletier provides us with an illustration of soul recovery in adulthood. A hint of what awaits us as we cease "trying" and once again risk to taste the moon:

The one day I came smack into reality. I suppose it sounds silly, but what happened was that I saw a dandelion. Here I was, a middle-aged person surrounded with dandelions all my life. Then I saw one. But there was nothing that stood between me and that dandelion, that's what I mean; no classifications, no categories, no words, not even the word "dandelion." Nothing. and that dandelion was not just a thing, one of a million yellow things that were bright and pretty and very common. That dandelion was a being, a living being that accepted and included me totally: I felt like I was standing in the center of the sun with the cool petals going out from my feet and into the distance forever.

I said I saw a dandelion for the first time. But it really wasn't the first time. I learned that because there was a flash of remembrance in that experience—no when or where, just a flash—but enough so I know that when I was a very young child I lived in that reality all the time....Perhaps that is a way of saying what happened. "I" was there, but there was no longer an observer and an observed...no separate and isolated individuals. There was only one inclusive totality with nothing left out....It was flowing...It was all flowing.

I'm not really dependable anymore by white standards. But, I'm getting freer and freer. Others are finding out, they're going back to the land, more and more of them. And that's the only real seat of learning there has ever been. They'll learn from the land, all they need to know, all there is to know. If they stay there long enough, they'll learn that they *are* the land....

Wherever you are is home. And the Earth is paradise and wherever you set your feet is holy land....You don't live off it like a parasite. You live in it, and it in you, or you don't survive (1973:122-123).

## References

Bower, David. "The Condor and a Sense of Place," *The Condor Question*. Mill Valley, CA: Friends of the Earth, 1981.

Cobb, Edith. *The Ecology of Imagination in Childhood*. Dallas, TX: Spring Publications, 1993.

_____ . "The Ecology of Imagination in Childhood," *Daedalus, 88:3* (1959):537-548.

Dillard, Annie. *Pilgrim at Tinker Creek*. New York: Harper Magazine Press, 1974.

Dogen, Eihei. "Genjo koan," *Moon in a Dewdrop,* ed. Kazuaki Tanahoshi. San Francisco, CA: North Point Press, 1986.

Heinze, Ruth-Inge, "Profile 6: Ruth-Inge Heinze," *Shape Shifters: Shaman Women in Contemporary Society,* ed. Michele Jamal. Harmondsworth, Middlesex, England: Arkana, Penguin Books, Ltd., 1987, pp. 69-70.

Jamal, Michele, *Shape Shifters: Shaman Women in Contemporary Society.* Harmondsworth, Middlesex, England: Arkana, Penguin Books, Ltd., 1987.

La Chapelle, Dolores. *Sacred Land Sacred Sex Rapture of the Deep*. Silverton, CO: Finn Hill Arts Publications, 1988.

_____ . *Earth Wisdom*. Silverton, Co: Finn Hill Arts Publications, 1978.

_____ . *Earth Festivals*. Silverton, CO: Finn Hill Arts Publications, 1974.

Moore, Thomas. *Care of the Soul*. New York: Harper Collins Publishers, 1992.

Nabhan, Gary Paul and Stephen Trimble. *The Geography of Childhood.* Boston, MA: Beacon Press, 1994.

Samples, Bob. *The Metaphoric Mind.* Reading, MA: Addison Wesley, 1976.

Sessions, George. *Deep Ecology.* Salt Lake City, UT: Peregrine Smith, 1985.

Shepard, Paul and Daniel McKinley. *The Subversive Science.* Boston, MA: Houghton Mifflin Company, 1969.

Sobel, David. "A Mouthful of Flowers: Ecological and Spiritual Metaphors From Early Childhood," *Holistic Education Review* (Fall 1991):3-11.

Werner, Heinz. *Comparative Psychology of Mental Development.* New York: International Universities Press, 1948

# CIRCLING THE BAY: CARRYING INCA GOLD TO NORTH AMERICA

Gini DuPraw Anderson

A number of ancient prophecies point to the present era as a time of transition in human existence. The Inca version comes from *Pachacuti*, whose reign over the empire preceded the coming of the conquistadores. The prophecy attributed to him describes five hundred years of cultural decimation and struggle that would be followed by five hundred years of healing during which the ancient wisdom, carefully guarded through generations of oppression, would become one of the pieces necessary for humankind—and all of Nature—to emerge to a new level of existence.[1] To a number of Inca shamans alive today, that era has now begun.

All of Nature exists through reciprocity, or *ayni* and they say it is the enactment of reciprocity which will bring about the transformation. Through *ayni*, knowledge and power is bestowed as gift by all Beings in Nature, and it must be reciprocated by sharing one's own highest and best knowledge and power with others. It is on this basis that the Incas have begun to share with people outside their lineage the knowledge upon which the "Circling the Bay" project is based. The project is a personal response to their bequest and the continuous cycling can help us reach subtler and light energies, and in this way help to maintain the balance between heaven and earth.

In 1991, I was invited with a small group of people from North America to participate in *Hatun Carpay* or the Great Passage. I was told that these teachings were shared with people outside the Inca lineage for the first time. It is time, they say, for the eagle of North America and the condor of South America to fly together. A creation is in process and the gifts from both are needed to give birth to a higher level of consciousness.

There is a progressive unfolding of a vision; especially powerful here is the role of our own consciousness and our intention, of our purposeful participation in the creation of the vision. It came to me through dreamtime and through direct teaching from the Incas (especially through the Qu'ro shaman Americo Yabar), it gave impetus and shaped my own image of this unfolding process.

The most encompassing form of vision came to me recently: In space, there is a weaver and, in his listening fingers, are golden strands, vibrating with vitality. The strands come from sacred places on Earth and, as they are gathered together, the weaver is creating a golden net to encircle the planet; within it, a new era has begun. The net is three-dimensional, woven from within and without. The elements of creation (Earth, Air, Fire, and Water) are one dimension of the net; others are the varied expressions of the Life Force (i.e., different forms of life that include the Stone, the Plant, and the Animal People); the third dimension is human intention. As human beings become conscious expressions of the Life Force, we participate in the weaving of the Web of Life, reaching toward the highest expression.

The Incas believe that certain places in Nature, sacred sites, are gateways to elemental knowledge and the wisdom of the Spirit of Nature. With Don Juan Nunez del Prado, anthropologist and shaman, the shaman Don Buenaventura Sanchez, we travelled to *huacas* or power spots in Peru and Bolivia. *Huacas* are places where some natural phenomenon (it could be a striking rock formation or a place where water emerges from the Earth) both marks the place and becomes the vehicle through which knowledge is transmitted.

According to Don Juan, we take in Spirit through four bands that encircle and permeate our bodies. Interaction with certain places of power opens the bands and deepens our relationship with Nature. The four bands are related to the four directions of the medicine wheel which the Incas consider the pathway to knowledge. For them, each of the elements is related to a particular location in the human body. The first band, which is black, is at the base of the spine and is related to water. The second, which is red, is at the belly and related to the earth. The third is of gold and is at the heart, related to the fire of the Sun. The fourth is of silver and at the throat, related to air. This painting of the four bands is the rendition of one of the women who was involved in the first group I worked with in California.

The Inca say there is no fundamental distinction between a person, a rock, a tree, or an animal: the Life Force runs through them all. They are all

Beings and each carries its own perception, its own body of knowledge. The power of these special places facilitates interaction with them. One form this interaction takes is through shamanic journeys among the three realms of the universe (the upper world or *hanan pacha;* the ordinary world or *kai pacha,* and the lower world or *uhu pacha).* The *ayni* which takes place during these journeys affects the ordering of the universe.

Feeding is the basis of reciprocity in the relationship between humans and the Nature People. One form is through a *despacho,* or offering, which the shaman prepares to address the spirit world, usually the sacred mountains. Certain elements are always the same, e.g., the use of coca leaves, symbols of the four directions, and of Male and Female. The shaman adds other items that might be relevant to the request and that might tempt the spirits, being of universal appeal—chocolate, good-smelling blossoms, a bit of sparkle or colored ribbons. When Don Juan and Don Buenaventura assembled the offerings, the *despachos* were passed around, each of us blowing on them three times to imbue the objects with our Life Force, bringing us into a more personal and active involvement with them. The *despachos* were then burned so that the smoke would carry our prayers to the Spirits.

Another form of feeding is related to the dense energy we accumulate in the course of our ordinary lives—*hucha,* they call it. It is the residue of our unfinished business, e.g., pain, anger, helplessness, demeaning attitudes about ourselves and others, etc. The release of what we cannot digest frees us to reach toward higher planes, and that which we release becomes food for *Pachamama.* It is energy compost. The Incas don't speak of bad or good, but rather dense energy or light and it is only dense because it is not where it belongs or in the form that it belongs.

The process of release is called "eating *hucha.*" It involves focusing on a beam of sunlight entering the body through the seventh chakra. Imagine a mouth in the belly, just in front of the intestines. Feed the mouth the residue of unfinished business (sorrow, painful memories, shame, etc.) and watch the mouth chew, swallow, consume, and release it. See it going into the Earth, compost for new growth. Offer it to Mother Earth for that purpose. And bring the Light from the Sun into the top of the head, into the emptied spaces, filling them with brilliance. Because life continues to challenge the process becomes an ongoing practice to be repeated often, whenever it is necessary.

Clearly, sacred places can be found all over the Earth. In 1991, when I returned from Peru to California which has been my home for nearly thirty years, I wanted to find these places, to honor them and to continue to learn from them. Incas believe that when you are born, there is a prominent aspect of Nature with whose essence you are involved for your lifetime (called *itu*).[2] I was born near Lake Michigan, a large body of fresh water; now the power of San Francisco Bay, near my home, is so palpable for me. For this reason, I wanted to constellate my search for sacred sites in such a way as to place the Bay in the center of the sites I worked with.

Working with some friends, we created a list of twelve places to visit. They included six sacred mountains around the Bay—Tamalpais, Ring, Diablo, Hamilton, Umunhum, and San Bruno. Six additional sites were chosen; other sites are explored on people's recommendations of places at which they had a significant experience of Nature.

We followed a general format at each site.

1. passing a talking stick, everyone spoke of the state of her heart, mind, spirit, and body, shared relevant dreams and mentioned personal needs or intentions for her spiritual work on that particular day;

2. purifying by water or by smudging and calling the powers of the four directions, Father Sky, and Mother Earth;

3. approaching the sites, we move in silence, with an awareness of walking on our Mother, the Earth, surrounded by all the forms of her children; intending a personal surrender or opening, wherever possible, we walked toward our destination through a forest (often bay laurel and oak). The dappled light, alternating shadow and light, assist our transition into non-ordinary reality. We allowed ourselves to attend to all forms of perception — fleeting images, sounds and sensations whose origins were not apparent, dreams before or after the visits, etc.;

4. making an offering at each site, including a crystal that had been part of a cluster, along with personal contributions, tucking it into the crevice of a tree or a hollowed-out spot in the Earth;

5. proceeding then with whatever work was specific to the site. The land informed our work.

Each spot offered a unique relationship to the Nature People.

Our first site, De La Vega Trail, is in a unique valley between Berkeley and Oakland. The high walls of the valley protect it remarkably well from the noise of both communities and descending into the valley, we had a sense of entering the body of the Mother, enfolded by the verdant hills. At a grotto, two small waterfalls tumble side by side next to the trail; we used the Inca water ceremony to purify the four bands. Each person took water into the hand, brought it to each of the four bands, and swirled it in a counterclockwise motion, with the intention of purifying or releasing anything that would obstruct the connection between us and the Elemental Powers.

A grove of tall, straight cypress trees on the floor of the valley became the focus of our work. A community of humans began communicating with a community of Tree People, exchanging personal histories with individual trees, singing or chanting to the trees, rattling or drumming, and paying attention to the resonance or response in whatever way it might be experienced. We worked with the trees as models for our own connection between heaven and earth. In a walking meditation, we incorporated breath. We sent our roots into the earth, brought nourishment up our trunks, and connected with all the universe-particularly the light of the Sun. We raised our arms toward the sky, as the trees raise their branches and brought our arms down with the exhalation, sending the energy brought from the universe into the ground, as the tree channels light from the sun. The trees provided a strong sense of that connection, modelling both receiving light and extending into the earth. Becoming centered, we felt the light of the universe flowing through us, which was an excellent preparation for the practice of eating *hucha*.

Eating *hucha* was repeated at each site we visited and people were encouraged to use it between our site visits to continue releasing dense energy, obstacles to the flow of spirit. One woman had a Rolling Stone mouth which she encouraged by saying, "Eat, Igor!" Another, not comfortable with the imagery, developed her own—the trash icon of her Mac computer which she emptied regularly.

At Ring Mountain, we created a group *mesa,* a collection of personal power objects we carried for some time before the event, with the expressed intention of imbuing them with the highest spiritual intention for our work. We placed the objects on a woven cloth, wrapped them up, and drew energy to the *mesa* through drumming, dancing, and chanting. An enormous phallic-shaped boulder served as a vehicle to empower each individual's intention. We took turns standing with our backs to the boulder, with the power objects placed at the third chakra. Drawing power from the Earth, a member of the group placed her forehead against the power objects, and with three deep breaths, created a loop of intention through the *mesa,* the stone, the receiver, and the Earth.

An enormous boulder elsewhere on Ring Mountain was shaped like a vulva. Petroglyphs suggest that this site was used in fertility ceremonies several thousand years ago. Vandalism has marked the stone, and when we had spent some time in the practice of eating *hucha* for ourselves, we processed some of the dense energy carried by the stone. Because of the striking masculine and feminine shapes of the boulders on Ring Mountain, we journeyed about balance of male and female. (On subsequent occasions, I have used this site for fertility rituals as well.)

At the Marin Headlands, we began our work with the elements. Water was the only element for which a mountain site was not used. Kirby Cove marks the site where the waters of the Pacific Ocean and San Francisco Bay mingle and make the site very special. As we walked in silence from the rolling hills of the headland toward the beach, our process of slowing down from ordinary life and entering another way of being present, was very much affected by the beauty around us. Striped layers of sedimentary rock on the cliff next to the path revealed the action of tectonic plates and looked like the waving staff lines of a piece of music, as if the Earth were singing the song of the cliffs. The fragrance of gray-green eucalyptus wafted through the air as the path descended. The air was permeated by the aroma of the white eucalyptus blossoms and the button seed pods strewn on the bed of fallen bark.

On the opposite side of the path, a cypress grove lingered on the bluffs above the water and we engaged in the practice of eating *hucha*. We worked with the release of our dense energy and then began to work with the dense energy of the water itself, i.e., the energy of pollution carried by the water. Americo Yabar, a shaman from the Qu'ro tribe, said once that all fields of energy can ultimately be cleared through this practice.3 We allowed ourselves to become conscious of the pain, because there was something to do with it.

Emerging from the cypress grove onto a bluff overlooking the water where the ocean and the bay meet to exchange the gifts of their day's journeys, we used drumming, chanting and shamanic journeying to the Spirit of the Waters. Some of us commented afterwards:

> I became the water. For a while I was a waterfall, then a stream, then a river, and felt myself flowing over everything I came to. I have never felt such a close connection between myself and what I was touching. I was in complete contact with everything.

> I felt the cell-by-cell exchange between the salt water and the fresh water, and the exchange was the essence of all that the Ocean and the Bay experience separately. It was a blending and a disseminating.

The first major peak we worked with was Mt.Tamalpais which overlooks the Pacific Ocean. Walking in silence in a bay and oak forest, where the light shifts with every step, is a mind-altering experience. Emerging from the forest, we climbed a high bluff to a grove of oak trees, surrounded by the ancient sentinels of their long-dead sisters, and left an offering to the mountain in the hollow trunk of a fallen tree.

As I drummed within the grove, I used the events of the mountains's history to take people back in time, gathering the threads of their personal lineage:

> In 1880, the last grizzly bear was trapped on Tamalpais: you had an ancestor who was alive on that day. In the early 1800s, the Europeans began to settle Marin and, within two decades, the Native Americans were decimated. You had an ancestor who was alive on that day. Seven thousand years ago, the Miwoks, migrants from Siberia, lived on the slopes of Mount Tamalpais. Your lineage goes back to that day. 18,000 years ago the last global ice age peaked and the sea level was thirty miles west of the mountain. Your lineage goes back to that

day. 65-150 million years ago, the uplift of plate movements formed Mount Tamalpais. You have a lineage that goes back to that day.

Gather the threads of your lineage and come forward, through the forming of the mountain, the ice age, the migration from Siberia, the sprouting of the oldest redwood tree, the Europeans settling Marin, to the trapping of the last grizzly bear, to being back here on the mountain, on this day in 1994. Welcome these ancestors into your body and open your eyes (see also, Fairley, 1987).

Nearby, a moonscape of serpentine scree gave off a gray-green glow. Seated on a large natural boulder of serpentine, the vista encompassed the Bay, the Ocean, and the coastline to the South. The outcropping was used by Native Americans as a holy place, and has magnetic anomalies due to magnetized minerals in the serpentine (Devereux, 1989). As we sat there, a great tranquility came over us. People reported a sense of contentment, of being home, of being profoundly in touch with the Earth. (On two separate occasions, I have taken people to this site and they both were surprised to find the place familiar to them and had very similar experiences. Each reported that on this site, many years, an intense feeling of "being home," a sense of belonging had come to them and they knew the Bay Area was to be the place where they would put down roots.) Honoring the site, we created a spiral of some serpentine stones in front of the seat and used it as a labyrinth in which to walk, replacing the stones before we left.

Mount Diablo in the East Bay looms above the surrounding valleys. From its summit, on a clear day, one can see 40,000 square miles out to the Farallones in the Pacific Ocean, north to Mount Shasta, across the Sacramento Valley to the Sierras (Martin and Martin, 1993). Sandstone caves and rocky outcroppings are scattered over the mountain. It became the site at which we focussed on our connection to the element Fire.

Prayer sticks were made during the day as we spread out on the mountain in silent contemplation. The sticks, prepared for a fire ceremony, were related to aspects of ourselves that were in need of transformation, attitudes or habits whose energy needed to be released, so that we would no longer be bound by them. Chanting and dancing, we called the presence of Fire and its balancing element, Water, and made our offerings to the Fire.

At the summit, before dawn, we began a practice which continued through-out the rest of the year. We began calling in the powers of the places we had visited, honoring and welcoming the Nature Spirits. We chanted the visual images, the animals and birds, the sounds and smells, the plants, the elements. With each call, we took time to experience them in every perceptual mode possible, strengthening our capacity to envision and to invoke. In this way, we began the creation of a web of energy that stretches from each site to each other site, encompassing the Bay.

Just below the summit, a rocky outcropping (Devil's Elbow) faces east;

we sat there in the pre-dawn light, with the rosy red glow of the rising sun illuminating the mist in the valleys below, blanketing the rocks of the mountain itself, and filling the air around us. We were literally bathed in the glow of the sunrise and felt our bodies absorbing the light.

On San Bruno Mountain, Indians tossed the shells of their oyster meals onto a mount next to a stream. Five thousand years later, we walked on the shell fragments becoming Earth, returning to the Mother. Our group climbed through a grove of oak and buckeye toward the summit, again enjoying the shift in consciousness that the patterns of light and shadow induce. Only the low, bowing grass had made a bargain with the fierce wind and found a home. The summit's rounded hilltops, surveying the ocean on one side and the bay on the other, are continually bathed by the wind.

Two women spread on the ground a cape of woven reeds gathered from the Bay shore. Kneeling in a circle around the fragrant tules, one by one we lay on the cape with our faces turned toward the drifting clouds. Sound encircled us, as we invoked the presence of the Wind which continually stroked our hair, face, and body. Each of us experienced a sense of transcendence, being taken by the wind, floating through space, out of the body.

At the foot of the mountain, the Bay is an enormous womb and around it we found ourselves deeply implanted, nourished. We returned our Life Force to the Earth and the Water which host our very existence.

Our pilgrimage continues. We return to one of the sites each month. People go singly or in twos or threes, deepening our relationships with one another and with the Nature People. A second group of people made the same pilgrimage the following year. At times, both groups meet at a site and on full moons there is an open fire ceremony. Several new groups are soon to begin.

I believe that a thought-form is unfolding and that the work done at sacred sites is pivotal to the healing of the planet. And as we come into that awareness and understand the opportunity of our own participation, we will experience ourselves present together in Paradise, without ever leaving home.

## Notes

1. Shamanic work with Don Juan Nunez del Prado, Hatun Carpay, Peru, 1991.

2. Shamanic work with Americo Yabar, *Cronos, Logos and Eros.* Big Sur, CA, 1993.

3. Shamanic work with Americo Yabar, *Cronos, Logos and Eros,* Sedona, Arizona, 1994.

## References

Devereux, P. *Earthmind.* New York: Harper, 1980.

Fairley, L. *Mount Tamalpais, a History.* San Francisco, CA: Scottwall Association, 1987.

Martin, D. and B. Martin. *Northern California Discovery Guide.* Columbia, CA: Pinecone Press, 1993.

# DISCUSSION

### With Dupraw Anderson, Morningstar, and Puzey

*Mied:* Julien, who wrote the book you quoted from?

*Puzey:* In *The Ecology of Imagination in Childhood,* published in 1993, Edith Cobbs collected autobiographies of 300 individuals who were considered to be geniuses in the Western world. What these people had in common was a conscious ensoulment experience in childhood and this ensoulment experience shaped their cosmology. Like it litmus test, it determined what was authentically sacred throughout their lifetime. Cobbs' work was done before serious research was conducted on shamanism. When she refers to the geniuses of the world, we are reminded of the shamanic journey. People remained healthy despite of the unhealthy roles they had to play.

*Denig:* As a comment to Virginia, 1991 was the year where the Indians in Peru began to open up, so it does not really matter who got there first.

I want to share one of my experiences about Less work. Last year I talked about what turned out to become an illness of two years. I met Les last year and spent some time with him. It was not so much that he offered to work on me but that I just knew I needed help. Those of you who saw me last year, will remember that my abdomen was extended. Now I know I was processing a lot of things that needed to be brought up and out to be looked at.

Les was behind me. I remember music, incense and candles, and that Janet was holding my feet. Suddenly I began to cry, to moan, and it seemed that there were many, many voices. It was revealed to me that my mother had thirteen babies and only three of us survived. It was only many years later when my youngest sister married that she learned she was RH negative. We then understood what had happened. All of the babies had been born at home and, at that time, they did not know about RH negative. Some of the children lived a few hours, a few days, a few weeks, the longest one survived seven months. It finally got to the point that Mama was not even giving names to these babies because, she thought, she would lose them any day. I found that in my abdomen I was carrying all ten of my brothers and sisters and I gave voice and name to them. What I was protecting them against was my father's violence. When the last baby died, I thought my father had hit it, because it disappeared one night and was never mentioned again. I don't know whether this really happened or not but I knew that my father was capable of doing something like that. I had gathered all ten of my brothers and sisters in my abdomen and Les' suggestion was that I give them a job to do. Now they are protecting me, they are working with me. They are present in many forms and a few of them have gone on. But there was something in the way Les worked, his touch was instantaneous. When he touched me at a point below the belly button, the wailing began and the voices of the children at last were heard.

*Morgenstern (Morningstar)*: What was interesting about that night was that I had eavesdropped on a healing Shelley Thomson had done. Shelley had been working with a friend of mine who was experiencing a negative force. She knew that one of the ways to deal with the force was giving it a job. And when it turned out that you had these ten entities to deal with I just remembered what I had heard Shelley do and I said, "eh, you got all these resources, use them." Shelly had been my teacher and then I was able to help you.

My experience of healing women is that they hold a lot of stuff, just below the belly button, just above the pubic area. We heard at least half a dozen references to the womb area in the last couple of days, haven't we? When I work with a woman, with her permission, of course, I press my hand into this area and I keep pressing. When it starts to hurt, it starts to heal. It is amazing but it works.

*Mied:* Virginia, I was really struck by your description of eating *hucha,* because Carol had asked Ron after the presentation how we combine spirit with emotional courage and that was a direct description. Ron's response to her was, "receive while working." Receiving is exactly like we do in meditation. The image we use for release is—releasing it to the River of Forgetfulness. When I get stuck with a client and it feels like a difficult moment, I plant my feet on the ground and I am really conscious of releasing through the bottom of my feet. I keep releasing until it breaks through.

I also want to mention the ensoulment of children. I really look forward to reading your whole paper, Julien. I don't have a lot of children in my space but when I am with children I am very aware whether there is something or not. I never named it but I am conscious of looking for what you called "ensoulment" and pulling it forward. I can acknowledge that I have an energy relationship to what you have said.

*Puzey:* I think a lot of the problems in our culture are emotional difficulties. They manifest in a way that we either feel dead or the world is too much. When we are talking about the loss of soul, we talk about our relationship of being alive and the aliveness of the world, this reciprocity Ruth-Inge is talking about.

*Mied:* Another way to talk about healing is that I look into a person's eyes and grab on to that light and then take away everything else, until that light is present all the time.

*Denig:* Eating *hucha* has also to do with freeing our body and freeing ourselves to see spirit more completely. How much joy can there be if there is that openness!

This wonderful cape is the creation of two women who worked at Kirby Cove, the place where the waters of San Francisco Bay and the Pacific Ocean mingle and exchange their *ayni.* The women received directions from the ancestors to make a ceremonial cape and they did not even know how to handle fibers or anything else. You can see the development they went through in the course of making it and how much more space is given to the incoming and the flow of spirit.

*Coffey:* I first want to honor Ruth-Inge's alchemy in putting us together. Julien talking first about the creation of soul in humans and soul in nature and then Gini's speech dealing with it so concretely. It was remarkable. And Les talked about bringing in electronics, a wonderful combination.

Gini, I live in the Bay Area and I could hardly contain myself. I want to thank you for what you are doing. I hope that this spirit is coming into everyone so that we all are able, like Jim Swan talked about Japan, to understand the sacred places inmidst of a very urban environment.

*Olsen:* Eating *hucha* really brought the last year into a prospective for me. In *Time Magazine,* they talked about nuclear terror. Plutonium is now coming out of Russia and is sold on the Third World Market. Also, the population conference is starting this week in Egypt. There is now a new unholy alliance between the Vatican and the Islamic fundamentalists over the issue of women's fertility rights and so forth. I was getting increasingly depressed and reminded why I left NASA twenty years ago. I have not accomplished anything in the last twenty years. Furthermore, the population curves are still the same. In 1950, the world population was 2-1/2 billion and by 2050, one hundred years later, it will be either 10 billion or 12.5 billion, depending how you look at the figures. That's a fivefold multiplication of the world's population in our lifetime, in one hundred years. It is not a question of why should

I be here, it is a question of why should I stay and really feel it in my body. Coming to this conference, I feel that there is a lot of more space on the planet than there will be in Egypt. So the transformation is not taken place on a physical level, it is taking place on a spiritual level—the ensoulment; and there is a lot more to talk about.

*Coffey:* I just want to comment on the power of the process, giving us a way to move out of denial. If we have something to do with the pain we see, with the desecration we experience, we can allow ourselves to be more conscious of it.

*Flower:* I am also honoring Ruth in the way she has put groups of people together. I was touched by you, Julien. You spoke of bonding with the earth as one of the primary tasks in early childhood. We think in terms of bonding with parents, bonding with the mother. When we create our sacred sites, we should also think of who is the mother and the quality of empowerment. The empowerment begins with the creating of an altar in our living room, with creating a space in our backyard, a circle around the Bay Area. We wouldn't need to run to Sedona, as beautiful as it is, or go to Stonehenge in England. There are places right here which we can preserve and with which we can grow. We can expand their energy. The personal empowerment each one of us can gain at sacred sites is very important.

*Heinze:* I really don't deserve the compliment, you deserve it because you gave me an early abstract by October and when I get all papers by July 1, it is fairly easy to weave the themes together.

# TUNING INTO SOURCE THROUGH TRANCE DANCE AND TONING

Sandia Rising Star

Shamans and healers from indigenous cultures all over the planet use dance, sound, music and breath as means of producing altered states, curing ailments and connecting to source.

Trance dance is a moving meditation, a vehicle for emptying the mind of "thought" so that we can truly be present to Spirit, to that quiet place in the center of our Being. It puts us more in touch with our "expanded" selves, that powerful place where magic happens and healing is both generated and experienced.

In trance dance, as I use it, there is an emphasis on letting go of control, of allowing the body to go into "natural" movement. I encourage shaking, bouncing and swinging actions primarily since these types of movement seem to most readily facilitate emptying out and shifting into an altered state. It is also best to keep the eyes closed or almost closed to help block out exterior stimuli and to maintain an inner focus.

The deep breathing that accompanies this type of movement is another tool used to clear the mind and go inside. It gives the body "permission" to let go and may even bring up some deep-seated emotional issues that need healing. I refer to the use of deep breathing in re-birthing and other types of breath work and the profound experience that often occurs in that process.

The use of the voice through "toning" is yet another tool we shall use for clearing out and tuning in to our inner essence. The vibration of sound (just as the vibrations of movement and breath) can be used to clear out each of the chakras and help restore the body to harmony and resonance. The system of toning that I use deals with the three main body cavities, the head, the heart and the hara.

Let us begin by swirling high tones around the inside of the head as if it were a brass bowl, allowing them to break up, clear and calm all the mental chatter. Now send some tones up through the crown chakra opening it up to the light, to Spirit.

Start to allow the tones to trickle down through the throat chakra to the heart (you can feel the vibration with your hand on your heart) and let it swirl around your heart. Allow yourself to feel LOVE generating from your heart and bath your whole being in it. Now fill the circle with LOVE—imagine a huge bowl full of rainbows, LOVE of all colors. Place one or more persons in the center of this bowl of LOVE, persons who you know need healing and visualize the rainbows swathing them in LOVE. Now fill this bowl so full of LOVE that a huge rainbow begins to grow out of it and surrounds the entire earth in all directions and returns, cleansing and healing as it goes. Breathe in some of this wonderful rainbow of LOVE for yourself.

And now begin to let the tones drop deeper down through the solar plexus and into the pelvis or hara. Let the tones go as deep as they can and swirl them around, cleansing and healing the second and first chakras. Now allow them to open the base of the pelvis! Send a beam of light straight down into the earth, to the center, the heart of the Mother and anchor it on a strong root as you surrender to the earth's pull.

Begin to stretch and twist and breathe as you rise, letting any sounds come forth that want to. Now let your body feel an inner pulsing, begin bouncing and shaking and swinging in response to the beat of the drums and your inner rhythm, keeping your eyes closed half way. [Tempo gradually increases until it reaches a very fast pace, then it slowly diminishes to stillness.]

Let us now weave our voices together in harmonious, free-toning as we come together toward the center of the circle and experience this state of blissful peace and well-being!

# THE TYRANT'S GAME: THE WARRIOR'S DANCE WITH TYRANTS AND CONFLICT

Caroll O'Connell

The Tyrant's Game is a ceremony which I created and ran with a group of shamanic practitioners. The ceremony comes out of a practice taught by Grandfather Harley Swiftdeer, a Metis medicine man, trained by the grandmothers of the Cherokee tradition. The ceremony is based on a wheel taught by Swiftdeer, called the Tyrant's Wheel. Everything Swiftdeer teaches, he can put on a wheel or circle. The main wheel of the teachings he shares is called the Star Maiden Circle Key Driver Wheel. This is a psycho-spiritual map, describing how we manifest the different aspects of our human consciousness. The Tyrant's Wheel portrays the way how the eight aspects, described by the Star Maiden Circle Key Driver Wheel, are expressed when a "tyrant," a person (or institution), acting from the place of each aspect, tries to interfere with the free expression of another person's energy. Appended to this paper is the Tyrant's Wheel which places around a circle the eight different styles or manifestations of hostile, provocative or energy stealing kinds of behavior attributed to specific tyrants.

The recreation of Swiftdeer's practice in ceremonial form called the Tyrant's Game came as a result of working with a group of 15-20 practitioners with whom I had been doing other ceremonies and practices given by Swiftdeer. We had attempted to work with the Tyrant Wheel teachings in a format that had one person, placed in the center of a circle, being "attacked" by a group of people sitting around her or him, each acting out a style of attack mapped on the tyrant wheel. The person in the center had the task to deflect, redirect, or counterattack the attacks, possibly with humor. The basic challenge was to "count coup," to avoid giving one's power away in the attack and, if possible, turn the situation around so that the attacker see themselves and become aware of what they are doing. The intention behind this format was to exercise and strengthen the "Warrior" response to situations in life.

Given that this exercise was done in a group that was fairly intimate, there existed a high degree of safety with the kind of attacks we made on each other. There were some terrific laughs coming from the contest of the battling "Warriors" and "Tyrants," but I also saw the "warriors" getting emotionally wounded. In the spirit of the Sacred Law of the Cherokee we held as an overriding principle of our work: "Let nothing be done to harm the children (or the child within)." I proposed to the group to redesign the exercise with a ceremonial container to deal with raw woundedness that was emerging out of the process.

What I came up with was approaching the Warrior in a different way. The focus is on discovering one's vulnerabilities and learning to respond in a new way so that one does not give one's power away out of these vulnerabilities. The premise is that the ways in which we are vulnerable to attack arises out of wounds we have experienced in the past, usually in our childhood. Often the experience of these wounds is held in our unconscious as beliefs about these experiences. When we consciously allow ourselves to experience our vulnerability, we can gain access to old patterns, assumptions and beliefs that are underlying our automatic response to a stimuli when we feel attacked or threatened. When we see and change our beliefs about past incidents where we experienced a wounding, we are freed up to have a genuine response in the moment. We are no longer merely reacting out of what is triggered by the charge from the old wounding experience which resembles the present situation, activated by the present "tyrant" or current conflict.

The concept of the Warrior that we were working with is of a person who never gives his/her power away for any reason at any time. My understanding of this principle of the Warrior is that the Warrior stays in his/her own power, which means to stay with his/her genuine response to any stimuli. Reacting from beliefs and protective mechanisms, arising from old wounds, is giving one's power away to an old program. The design of the Tyrant Game Ceremony was then to provide a process in which participants could sort out their true responses from reactions arising from old patterns and beliefs that are probably not appropriate to the current context. Additionally, the ceremony was to provide the opportunity for participants to practice skills to keep them centered in their response to a Tyrant's attack.

The ceremony began with all participants making a prayer, stating the intention of the ceremony. Included were at least six "Tyrants" (the direction of the West and East were not acted out because the physically brutal tyrant is in the West and, in the East, the institutional Tyrant; i.e., church, state, school's ability to impede choice). Also participating were one or two

"Grandparents" who were acting as the symbolic Higher Self *(hokkshedeh)*, guides and protectors of the "Child" who is the Warrior going into the Tyrant Circle to discover his/her vulnerabilities and practice ways to stay centered in his/her power.

Next, the participants, acting as Tyrants, formed two lines, facing each other, each line representing the *yin* or *yang* polarity. The Tyrants danced in place while the Grandparents drummed and moved back and forth behind the lines. The Child lay between the two lines, being balanced by the movement of the polarities. When the Grandparents determined that the energy had been raised and balanced appropriately, the Tyrants were directed into one line, alternating the polarities from each of the dance lines to form the Tyrant Circle. The Grandparents then took the Child to the South opening of the circle (which, in the Star Maiden Circle, is the place of the Child and of Trust and Innocence). The position of the South is not occupied by a Tyrant although this is the place of the distracting energy stealing, "whining Child" Tyrant. This position on the circle is left open for the Child, so that s/he may sit in this gate of the circle and face all his/her Tyrants at once.

The Grandparents then spoke to the Child to find out what amount of protection or intervention the Child wanted from the Grandparents while under attack from his/her Tyrants. The Grandparents had stated initially that if they see the Child getting hurt, they would declare that a Tyrant had made a "hit" and would interrupt the attacks so that the Child had an opportunity to reflect on the experience of the attack. The talk with the Child was to determine what other safeguards the Child felt were needed and to generally strengthen the symbolic presence of the higher guiding and protective intelligence within the Child. The talk also served to sensitize the Child to his/her vulnerabilities in meeting his/her Tyrants rather than fortifying him/herself against the attacks or his/her own feeling arising from the attacks. When the talk was complete, the Child sat down in the South and the Grandparents moved to the outer perimeter of the Tyrant Circle. The Tyrants began their attacks, speaking one at a time and staying aware of a specific tyrant style, as represented on the Tyrant Wheel. When the Child felt hurt by an attack, the Child reported that s/he had been "hit." At this point the Child was asked to make a simple statement of the experience of hurt, such as, "I feel ashamed, stupid, or betrayed." The Tyrant, making the hit, then announced from which tyrant style s/he has made the hit. The Grandparents kept track of the information from the Child and the respective Tyrant to discuss their observations in more depth with the Child later. The Grandparents then signalled the Tyrants to continue their attacks, stopping each time when the Child indicated that it had been hit or when the Grandparents saw the Child had been hurt and was not reporting a hit. This procedure continued for 15 to 30 minutes while the Child and the Grandparents gathered experiences and information on the dynamics and patterns of the attacks which had "hit" the Child.

While the Ceremony proceeded, each participant had a different focus to hold. The Child's primary focus was on itself; how is it physically and emotionally experiencing the Tyrant's energy and words. The Child was using the Tyrant's barrage to find where its own "buttons" were. The degree of sensitivity or the charge on a button triggered by a Tyrant's attack may be comfortable enough for the Child to try to respond to the attack. If the Child so elects, it can attempt to respond in a way that redirects the energy *(yang)* or receives *(yin)* the energy of the Tyrant without taking on or retaining the invalidation or information of the attack which would stimulate the Child's inner Tyrant of the Southeast which pertains to self-concepts.

The Grandparents need to be sensitive to the momentum of the Tyrant's energies in assisting the Child to connect with its sensitivity to the attacks. At the same time, the Grandparents must calibrate the momentum of the attack so that the Child's focus does not go primarily into the "protect" mode, i.e., shielding, watching for the attack rather then observing its own experience.

The Tyrants need to be as ruthless and direct as they can. They need to be clear on the direction or position on the Tyrant's Wheel they are express-ing and be simultaneously aware of what energies the Child is most likely to be vulnerable to and what was the impact of the preceding Tyrant. It is the Child's and the Grandparents' job to stop the Tyrants. It is the Tyrants' job to keep the collective energy of the Tyrant Circle moving.

When the Child wants to stop or when the Grandparents determine stop-ping is appropriate, they take the Child away from the circle. the Tyrants remain in their places. The Child and the Grandparents go more deeply into the experiences of the hits. They identify and explore core areas of sensitiv-ity, as revealed by the information reported by the Child and the nature of the attacks, represented by the particular tyrant style on the Tyrant Wheel. Here, with the combined skill and insight of the Grandparents and the Child who is now returned to the stance of the Warrior, in conjunction with the ceremonial focus and intent, beliefs formed from old experiences can be accessed.

For example: The Child who was a woman in this particular case, repeat-edly experienced a hit when her Tyrants told her, in various ways, that her way of dressing and presenting herself was unappealing and in poor taste. Even though she knew her Tyrant friends were deliberately trying to get to her, she was anxious that this was really how they saw her and started to feel unattractive and wondered if the colors she was wearing went together. Her self-concept had been effected. The surface level of this information was that her sense of herself could easily be influenced by others. The Tyrant, doing the damage here, was her own inner Tyrant of the Southeast which turned the external information against her. The remedy for her was to make a different choice about how she will feel and regard herself. A deeper level of information may come from looking at what style of Tyrant had impacted her in this way. The Tyrant of the Northeast attacks all manners of one's expression so as to leave the individual with a belief that s/he is not able to do anything well or even right. The Tyrant of the North attempts to undermine another person's knowledge or ideas, often setting him/herself up as the final arbitrator, judge, and definer of reality. Both of these Tyrants had been active in creating the hits that put this woman into the place of negative self-concept, corresponding to the Southeast on the Tyrant Wheel. This indicated that some parental wounding had also been triggered. The woman was then assisted in making a conscious link to where she was still controlled by her critical parent's message about her physical appearance and creativity in dressing herself. Exploring the parental messages further, the woman found old beliefs about the limits of her creativity. Thus, the real or antecedent tyrants were identified from the stimulation of the Tyrants during the ceremony. For example, the Inner Tyrant of the Southeast who imposed a negative self-concept, although, as an adult, she has a choice about how she regards herself. Also identified was the internalized critical and judgmental parent whose messages she is still acting on instead of responding from her choice to the current Tyrant's re-evoking of parental wounding.

Getting to this level of information often brings up emotions to be released in which the Grandparents support the Child. The Grandparents and the Child then move into creating ways to empower the Child to respond, free of pain and fear of the wounding which had been uncovered.[1] The Child is then sent hack into the Circle for a "replay" of the hits that have been explored and worked with by the Child and the Grandparents outside the Circle. The Tyrants are instructed on what is needed and asked to intensify the energy of the hit, even by moving towards the Child from their position on the Circle. At no time, however, does any one other than the Grandparents physically touch the Child. The Grandparents may coach the Child as the Child finds its new centeredness in responding to the attack.

The ceremony closes with the Child facing its Tyrants, one at a time, starting in the Southwest, thanking each Tyrant for the teaching. The Child proceeds around the circle in this manner, moving sunwise. All may embrace and sing when the Child has expressed its gratitude.

This closing is particularly symbolic of the focus and intent of the entire ceremony. Looking at our Tyrants as stimulating both our responses and reactions allows us to see the Tyrants as teachers and means to self-knowledge and skills. The primary experience of the Tyrants shifts from being the enemies who would hurt us or impede our exercise of choice. We, in turn, are no longer the "victim," powerless or intimidated in relation to the Tyrants. The Child's act of embracing the Tyrants within the Ceremonial Circle is a further symbolic act of embracing aspects of oneself, represented by the map of the self contained within the Tyrant Wheel as a form of the Star Maiden Circle Key Driver Wheel. Gratitude is felt and expressed for the part others plaid in bringing to our focus and attention what we need to have brought up out of our unconscious for healing and release. The physical warmth and closeness reminds us that we are safe and that we are embracing aspects of ourselves, always within our own Circle.

In the Tyrant Game ceremonial dance of the Warrior/Child and the Tyrants, the nature of conflicts can also be seen in a new way. The challenges or attacks that are experienced as conflict provide opportunities of what really matters to us. The Tyrant Game Ceremony illustrates what is the source of our response. Conflict in our lives can, if we use it consciously (within the approach of the Tyrant Game Ceremony), reveal to us where we are not living fully in alignment with our own genuine responses and values because we are acting from limitations on our choices. These limiting beliefs most often originated in experiences we had as young children or precognitively, before we had the awareness about our choices and our limitations. So it is by the presence of conflict in our lives that we can learn where we have passively or actively agreed to limit our choice in our lives and, correspondingly, surrendered our power and unique sacred expression. This requires the willingness to regard Tyrants or conflicts as bringing us to our next step toward empowerment and self-knowledge. Each attack itself carries within it a piece of ourselves that is wanting to be empowered or healed. Then, in the manner of the Warrior who is awakening to his/her own sacredness through conscious experience of the conflict, the sacredness of the Tyrants is also recognized. The attack is no longer a question of oneself or the other prevailing. The self is realized in the interface of the other.

The teachings I received from the Tyrant Game Ceremony about resolving conflict are (1) that conflict is to be received as a friend. And, as with a friend, we can often pick our timing. (2) the awareness of the fundamental value and desirability of conflict, when handled consciously and creatively, can reflect our own material that wants to be revealed so that choices and self-expression aare expanded. And (3) this way of regarding conflict and Ttyrants" gives the ability to resolve conflict because we can choose a role other than "victim" and we are able to heal our part of the dynamic of conflict which also ends the attraction of a particular conflict pattern in our life.

## Note

1.   I have found, subsequent to the ceremony being run in the manner I have described, that the awareness of old wounds does not necessarily reduce the

vulnerability. From my own practice, I know that the most effective way to release the influence of the old beliefs or messages, coming from earlier wounds or incidents, is by placing in the unconscious a form of forgiveness that releases the energy of the incident out of our energy field. The spoken words of the forgiveness are:

"It is safe, right and good that forgiveness is the releasing of all the energy around an incident or wounding, allowing the person who caused the wounding to carry it."

This is mentally placed into the back of the head in the area of the pituitary gland. Clients create an image of a flower or blossom in which the words are being received. The statement of forgiveness is repeated and received into another blossom-like center which clients creates in the front of their heads, in the area of the pineal gland. Once this basic definition of forgiveness has been placed in the unconscious and conscious, clients can make the simple statement into the back and front of their head:

"I forgive my mother, father, etc, for...[describe the incident]."

Limited or otherwise inappropriate beliefs can also be replaced in a similar fashion. This healing process was developed by Gail Montgomery who has worked for ten years with the Star Maiden Circle Key Driver Wheel in her shamanic/psychotherapeutic practice. She developed techniques of releasing from the unconscious in a process she calls "consciousness up-dating." I use these processes in working with clients in my meditation practice, utilizing the same focus on vulnerabilities as in the Tyrant's Game Ceremony.

# The Tyrant's Masks

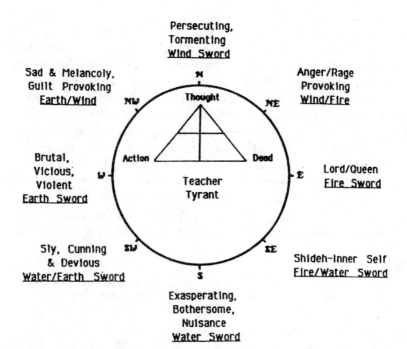

## The Star Maiden's Circle Infinity Movement
(Use this wheel to create your infinity movement)

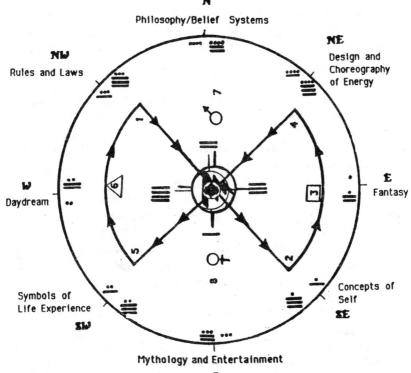

**N**
Philosophy/Belief Systems

**NE**
Design and
Choreography
of Energy

**NW**
Rules and Laws

**W**
Daydream

**E**
Fantasy

Symbols of
Life Experience

**SW**

Concepts of
Self

**SE**

Mythology and Entertainment

**S**

# AWAKENING
# THE MUTANT CATERPILLAR
# USING DREAM REENTRY HEALING

Fred C. Olsen

## The Problem: The Mutant Caterpillar

Once upon a time there was a civilization of caterpillars who forgot their true nature. They forgot that they were destined to become butterflies. They were a very intellectual and hard-working species of caterpillar. The greater their knowledge and success at building caterpillar cities and nations and creating ideas and tools, the more distant and alienated they became from their real nature.

As time went on, their memories faded. Even thoughts or dreams of a world of higher and subtler dimensions terrified them. When a butterfly did appear, they captured it. They pinned it to an altar so they could admire and worship it. They created a religion and rituals to worship it. When they died, if they believed right or worked hard enough they might go to a caterpillar heaven, where they could be nearer to the butterfly god.

Any caterpillar who could see and feel and know the truth of his or her nature and talk about it or even begin to live it, frightened the caterpillars who were addicted to the world that they had inherited and created. It was dangerous to awaken from the illusion. Denial was so pervasive and insidious that it became the implicit ethic and law of the land.

The caterpillar culture became increasingly unstable and violent. The available resources became scarce and were horded by a few. Even those who wanted change couldn't figure out how to turn the tide. They tried to make changes from the viewpoint of the illusion itself. It was too frightening to trust the natural calling to become a butterfly. This most simple solution for these mutant caterpillars became the most difficult to embrace because of the addiction to the limitations of the world they had created.

We are the mutant caterpillars. We are the addicts of a limited dimensionality. But where can we look? What can we do? How can we lift the veil of our illusion to see and embrace our real selves?

## The Solution: Lifting the Veil at the Edge of the World

We can begin to look in a variety of directions to find tears in the veil. Two radically different sources are available. The Aborigines in Australia may have never lost it. Great thinkers like David Bohm may have rediscovered it at the edges of our "civilized" world.

*Dreamtime and the "Real People"* - A clue lies with people who did not succumb to the illusion. One example is the Aborigines of Australia. They maintain a real connection to their butterfly nature—the non-dimensionality of Dreamtime. In an interview for the *Dream Network Journal,* Marlo Morgan, Ph.D., author of the book *Mutant Message from Downunder,* shared what she learned from the "Real People."

The Australian Aborigines enter Dreamtime to receive information to assist them with their basic questions.

To them "there are different levels of Dreamtime," just as there are different levels of consciousness....Dreams are the Shadow of Reality. Everything that happens here is also available in the dream world. All answers are there.

Gifted members of the tribe called Dream Catchers are available to give guidance in any situation. They do this by drawing out the feelings that arise in Dreamtime. "Mutants only enter the dream state through sleep, but Real People are aware of dream consciousness while awake....To them, Dreamtime is always going on; it never finishes." They even know how to enter sleep with their eyes open and being fully conscious.

They see us as mutant—not real—partly because of our addictions. One of our main addictions is dimensionality. To the Aborigines, real people have no addictions, they are not caught up in dimensionality. To them consciousness is a continuum that spans from the physical to higher domains.

*The Implicate Order and the Physics of Reality*—David Bohm, one of the great physicist/philosophers of our time, spoke about the "implicate order." He used simple metaphors to convey a sense of reality that flows infinitely beyond any fixations that we attempt to impose. In *Science, Order and Creativity,* Bohm and Peat discussed the imperative for our very survival to re-access the natural creative intelligence that we have lost because we live in a false consciousness of illusion, delusion and collusion.

String theory suggests a universe of at least ten dimensions. If we are able to have eyes to see increasing dimensions of reality then we once again may remember and trust our true nature.

What may distinguish so-called "civilized man" from "real people" are our discontinuities of thought, feeling, value, action and image in contrast to the flow and the subtle continuum of what is real and seems illusive in our state of addiction.

The very attempt to pin down, to dissect and to control the flow of nature and consciousness may be the root and cause of our demise. This very impulse separates, isolates, divides and destroys the connective tissue of life itself.

From inside our addictive prison of limited dimensionality, the corona of the numinous seems terrifying and unreal. Even when we do receive, acknowledge, and study, we often do so with the intent of a mutant caterpillar who captures and pins the butterfly to the wall in order to control, admire and worship it rather than to embody its nature, essence and freedom.

The path to the butterfly cannot be explained to the mutant caterpillar. It makes no sense whatsoever. Rather the caterpillar has to enter into a state of awareness in which it can see, sense, feel and trust its butterfly nature. This is actually pretty easy to do because it is natural to the caterpillar. Yet it is the most difficult challenge because of the massive investment in denial of the goodness and value of our real nature.

*Awakening the Mutant Caterpillar*—The key to awakening is to bypass or dissolve the illusion altogether. The caterpillar is first led to look into a mirror, reflecting its real nature. Then it is guided on an exploration into the world that is revealed therein. When the caterpillar discovers that this world is not an escape from reality but is what is real, safe and even fun, then the veil of illusion dissolves and the world transforms.

Real caterpillars don't forget their calling to be butterflies. Humans, on the other hand, have trouble remembering. We need a constant reminder.

*Dream Reentry Healing: A Vehicle to Explore Reality*—The Dream Reentry Healing process is fun and a safe and direct way to access and explore this inner reality. It provides us with training wings to fly on. It is a process that helps as safely reenter and explore the dimensions of our true nature and release the veil of illusion. It is a way to reenter Dreamtime and to explore the dimensions of the Implicate Order—what I call the "Implicate Domain."

*The Play Ethic: The Hidden Secret of Creative Intelligence*—For both the Aborigines and David Bohm this exploration of reality has more to do with play than work. The essence of creative intelligence is rooted in the playful curiosity of discovery and exploration of a child. It is about discovery and expression rather than control. This may be why the scriptures say "You cannot enter into the kingdom of heaven unless you become as little children."

*Dream Reentry Healing: A Test Flight*—Rather than go through elaborate explanations of the Dream Reentry Healing process, we will take a simple test flight on our butterfly wings. That is where the fun comes in. How many of you would like to have some fun? Let's go on a little journey together.

The rules of the game are very simple. I'll ask a question. If you see or feel a response you raise your hand. When most of you have raised your hands, I'll ask another question. When you see or feel a response to my question, you raise your hand again, until I invite you to return to the room and share your journey.

There are three basic launching points in the Dream Reentry Healing process. The first is a remembered dream. The second is a physical sensation in the body or a physical symptom. The third is an emotional issue or scene from waking life that has a charge to it. Usually, I have you chose. When exploring a group consciousness, we can chose a common launching point.

*Dream Reentry Healing: A Tool for Group Healing and Transformation*—For the purpose of this particular journey, I recommend we all leave from a common departure point. This departure allows us to explore the inner world of a group, organization or community and discover its collective butterfly nature.

We are all part of the energy of this conference. We have a shared life together because we have come to this place for a common purpose. Each of us relates to this body in our own way and from our own state of being.

So, right now, tune into the place in your body where you feel connected to the community. Raise your hand when you are there.

Now, go there, to the place in your body where you feel your connection to this community. Raise your hand when you see a picture.

Now, notice yourself there—in the picture or in relation to the picture. Notice where you are in the picture. Raise your hand when you are aware of yourself there.

Notice how old you are there—right now in the picture. Raise your hand when you have that age.

What are you wearing? Raise your hand when you are aware of your outfit or dress. Notice what you are feeling as the self in the picture. Raise your hand when you have that feeling.

Notice where that feeling lives in your body in the picture. Raise your hand when you have the location.

Go there. Raise your hand when you have a picture.

Notice your self there. How old are you? What are you wearing? Raise your hand when you have a sense of your age and dress in that picture.

Now notice what you want to do in this picture. Raise your hand when you are aware of what you want to do.

Notice what you need in order to do that. Where do you need to go to meet that need? Notice what happens when you take that action in this picture. Raise your hand when you have acted.

Notice what you are feeling now in the picture. How is it different? Raise your hand when you have a sense of that.

Now take the present feeling back to the original picture. What is happening there now? Raise your hand when you are there, with this new feeling.

How old are you now? What are you wearing? Notice what you want to do now in this picture, from the new feeling. And what happens when you do it? Notice what happens when you act from this new feeling. Raise your hand when you have acted.

Take this all in. Notice any changes. Notice anything that is incomplete. When you are ready, return to the group.

## Sharing Stories from the Inside

How many of you were able to follow the journey to the end?
How many got a result?
How many got stuck or diverted along the way?

That is okay. What we took was a two-level test flight into the imaginal world using some of the basic keys of the Dream Reentry Healing Process. A full-blown process with a guide can go much further and we are able to track your own flight path more closely.

For the purpose of demonstration I have asked a set of questions to illustrate some of the keys to the Dream Reentry Healing process. I operated blind and yet you each could follow your own journey.

As a group we can share the story of our journey with each other. Common themes will surface along with our relationship to the deeper and more subtle dimensions of the group consciousness. In the playful domain of this reality, understanding, healing and group transformation are often safer, more complete and more real than in many other approaches to organizational development and transformation.

## *References*

Bohm, David and David Peat. *Science, Order, and Creativity.* New York: Bantam New Age Books, 1987.

Morgan, Marlo. "Dreams are the Shadow of Reality: The Real People live Their Myths," an interview with Roberta Ossana," *Dream Network, 13:2* (1994).

# A VISION QUEST STORY

Barton Stone

For ten years we have been guiding people of all ages and walks of life into the California desert for a solitary encounter with wilderness within a ceremonial framework.

Vision questing is an ancient human process of personal initiation and renewal that has been recently revived and revised to suit the needs of contemporary people. It is a time for looking into the soul, finding a new direction or source, a test of survival, and a trial by loneliness.

The heart of the quest is a three- or four-day solo period when questers fast from food and sit up the last night in their Medicine Wheel, a circle of stones representing the formative elements of their lives.

We see ourselves as guides, not shamans. Our premise is that we each have the answers within ourselves and that wilderness provides a powerful setting for realizing them, no authorities or intermediaries are necessary. In wilderness, we understand that the earth can heal us, that we are all in this together and must each find our thread to the answer and the healing of us all.

In preparation for the trip, we help questers to bring to full consciousness the most meaningful issues they wish to confront during this sacred time and space. Afterward, they are helped to process what for some may have been an ordeal, but the journey throughout is theirs.

As in any meaningful and important ceremony, the quest involves a progression from the separation phase of withdrawal, to the liminal phase of transformation, and to the reincorporation phase of return to the world. It is a hero/heroine's journey intended to bring vision and meaning into our lives by opening us to a mythic dimension, and then giving to others the gifts of spirit, life purpose, vision and healing that have been abundantly received during the quest.

The vision quest almost always begins with a loss. One's usual way is not working. A decision is made to go for help, not to experts or teachers or outside higher powers, but to the Earth herself, her deserts and mountains. It begins in fear and loneliness, for our trust in earth processes has taken a beating over generations of alienation from the wilderness within and without.

The first step has been taken toward the threshold of surrender, giving up the supports of comfort, familiarity, addictions, all old friends, toward the threshold of the wild. It is a time of grief and bravery.

It continues through the liminal phase of the journey, the time alone, where the vision and insights are discovered. For many, this is their first time alone in the wilderness. Without books, radio, or even food, there is little to distract the quester.

A fundamental law at this time is to pay attention. Not only for reasons of safety, but because spirit often comes in subtle and surprising ways. One must be alert to receive it.

In this quiet time, the earth, the sky, the sun, and the winds, occasional animals, take on a new and personal meaning. Days of silence allow communion with rocks, stars, the elements.

During the last night, questers sit inside a medicine circle made of rocks, each representing some part of their life. The entire universe is represented in the stones of the medicine circle. Special care is given to the rocks that are placed in the four cardinal directions, each carrying the symbols and powers belonging to that direction—the south representing the child, loving, open, innocent and playful, the west representing the place of introspection, the depths of the soul, change, transformation, the north the long cold nights, the winds, the wisdom of the elders, life made into medicine, the east the dawn of a new day, the ability to see far and to move from intuition. All of these are of equal importance and must be incorporated and brought into balance, both within the individual and into the world itself.

Reincorporation is the process of re-entering what we call "the little round of life."—coming back, saying the first words to people, eating a meal, telling our story. The questers usually receive a name that refers to some part of the natural and spirit world which brought them special gifts and strengths during their time alone—Moon Dancer, Humble Heart, Keeper of Dreams, Loving Wind, Coyote Healer.

All the spirits in the desert seem to welcome us and lend their support. To be open to nature, to self, to each other, to spirit, and to take on the medicine that each has come into this life-walk to express, and perhaps most importantly, to relinquish seeing oneself as a victim—this becomes the goal. In the re-incorporation phase the lessons learned are shared with others and the commitment is made to carry them back to our people and into the everyday world.

We especially feel the benefits during the part of the trip when everyone is back safely from their time alone, in a very precious transparent space. They tell their stories in the safety of the circle of other questers in a similar space, held in the surrounding beauty of the desert. These individual stories, woven together make a collective story which we feel is important to the new paradigm we are struggling toward in order to live in harmony on the Earth.

Occasionally people return feeling that nothing has happened to them. Questers receive feedback from us as we take them back through their experience, helping them understand the significance of what passed before their eyes, their minds and souls. Usually, after they have told their story and heard it told back to them, they realize that the mountains have danced and the spirits have brought them wondrous gifts.

On the last night a drum beat welcomes the questers to a larger circle lit with candles a good distance from base camp. Questers and guides alike are in ceremonial garments with faces painted. The drumming provides an entrance into an altered state and along with rattling and dancing, celebrates the ending of this part of the quest. Entering the circle, questers are smudged with sage, sprinkled with blue cornmeal, and invited to sip the sacred waters of life. After more ritual, questers are asked to sing or dance their experience of the last three days and nights. They are reminded to let the song and dance move through them with the impulse of spirit.

Questers then return home to work and lifestyle, and the guide remains available to process later aspects of each person's vision, everything is done with an attitude of mindfulness and attention to detail. The reintegration into society can take as long as a year or more. We often think of this part as the most difficult and challenging part of the quest.

Far from instant enlightenment, the vision quest, like anything worthwhile, takes hard work. It is often painful, even dangerous. Much of the psychological processing has to do with giving up our old, worn out stories, finding new and better ones. The quest concerns healing, growth, navigating through all the storms and shoals of life to that place of peace and prosperity for all humankind. It is one more path on the journey to wholeness.

The following vision quest story was chosen because it is rather typical and because this quester was so articulate.

## Margaret: Questing After Breast Cancer Surgery

Right after I had found out I had breast cancer, I went on a quest in the desert—ten days far away from phones, family, and friends, alone in nature, looking at and listening to myself as I grappled with my newest challenge.

Getting ready was easy. The less I took, the less I had to worry about. I had no responsibility for food or equipment other than to borrow a big tarp and buy some nylon cord to improvise a shelter. I decided to take only the basic bed roll and clothing, minimal toiletries (who needs to wash?), no frills like tapes or books, except my journal. Even my camera was a distraction from the inner explorations I wanted to make.

My quest was about dying and about which therapies to choose to heal myself. I also wanted to take stock of my life, my relationships, and my attitudes to my suddenly fragile body.

We were four questers—a woman about my age, experiencing a recurrence of breast cancer, a psychic healer, a 21-year-old ready to experience a rite of passage, and me. Our leaders would counsel, support, and feed us during the ten days and keep the home fires burning at base camp during our three days alone.

Up at dawn, we drove all day, through magnificent Yosemite Park into the high deserts of Inyo Recreational Area. We filled every one of our seventy- gallon water jugs before branching off onto the dusty tracks through scrubby pines and junipers. We were amazed at the profusion of flowers in bloom. This is a desert?

My biggest fear was about sleeping alone on the ground in the desert in the dark, but I gratefully snuggled into my sleeping bag in the cool night air and fell instantly asleep. I discovered that the Milky Way and the starry heavens gave enough light to reveal the shapes of trees and rocks. In the profound stillness, I could hear that no creature was stirring near me. When the ivory moon rose of the hill, I was enchanted by the serene beauty that surrounded me. There was no need for fear.

We spent two days preparing for our adventure alone, ranging widely over the land looking for the perfect spot. My buddies hiked miles to sites with views of snow-capped peaks. Feeling fragile and vulnerable, I wanted an embracing sort of place, where my inner little girl would feel mothered and safe. In a dry wash, I found the perfect spot by a mother tree where I could spread my bedroll within its sheltering arms. Near my tree was a flat place for the circle of rocks which would represent my life. I knew this was my place, because in the center of the space was a six-inch-high juniper tree with cancerous growths all over it.

Next morning as the sun rose, I drank a quick cup of tea, hefted my tarp and water jugs, and silently left camp. It was moving to watch my buddies, similarly burdened, walk quietly away, alone into the desert.

When I reached my place, about a mile from base camp, I didn't know what to do first. Set up camp? Build my wheel? Go for a walk? Normally, I would have grounded myself by eating, but now I was fasting for three days. Purification seemed appropriate. I stripped, washed the strategic bits in a cupful of water, put on a fresh shirt, more for ceremony than because I needed clothes and smudged myself, using the sage and juniper which grew all around.

Refreshed on all levels, I set up my altars, one by the sick juniper, and the other by my bed. I made camp, such as it was. Four gallons of water in the shade was my kitchen, my toothbrush and comb on a rock my bathroom, my tarp over a branch my living room and bedroom. Now what? Eat, of course.

Not eating was a revelation. Like most women, I spend hours every day, buying food, cooking and eating, washing up. My life revolves around meal times. Without that structure, the whole day opens up, giving me huge chunks of uninterrupted time. Although I had never fasted for longer than a day, I found it pretty easy. Every time I felt hungry, I drank some water. I didn't long for pizza, but for a toasted English muffin spread with mashed bananas and for some big juicy oranges. By the third day, my belly was a bit hollow and I tended to get dizzy going uphill, but I felt energetic and surprisingly good.

By eight a.m., I was all settled in. Now I had to face myself. I had a few tasks—to build my stone circle, make a list of intentions for my life, and an inventory of the addictions I wanted to root out. I would stay in this place for three days and nights, remaining awake the last night in my stone circle, fasting and praying for guidance.

It took me three days to construct my circle. After I had placed stones for the four directions, I began to identify the people and concerns of my innermost heart. I placed rocks for my children, my parents and siblings, my cancer, my future, fear of a poverty-stricken old age, for the abusers in my life, for a lover, and others. Born in Scotland, I am a Celt and dearly love stone circles, of which there are many in Scotland. Creating this one was instinctual. There was no right or wrong way to do it, no tradition I was following. I was creating the great mandala of my life at that moment. On the third day, I began recording my conversations with each of the rocks in my journal, an enlightening process that went on for many hours.

My creativity flowed during these shapeless long days. I bound my intentions list onto cross sticks with brightly colored yarns to make a brilliant god's eye which attracted many gorgeous humming birds. When my inner little girl was sad and lonely, I made her a comforting little doll out of a handkerchief and some yarn. My gourd rattle was shaped like a breast with a splotch just where my cancer was. With my pocket knife, I carved the ugly marks into a lovely strong butterfly, symbolically transforming myself.

Butterflies were everywhere among the flowers. As I sat quietly, they would come to sip the moisture and salts from my skin. Sometimes there were five fluttering delicately through the hairs on my arms, unrolling their fantastic long tongues to taste me. I wrote this "Desert Song."

Wind sings in ancient pines
Rocks and sage sit silent in the sun
Butterflies kiss me—all are One.

Amidst all the life around me, Death, the Faceless One, was sitting behind my left shoulder, especially during the long nights. I came to see that my life is in my own hands. I choose my death—and I'm not ready, so back off, you old menace. You can't fool me with your tricks.

On the third day, it was overcast and rainy. I would stay in my circle from sunset until the sun rose. I folded and refolded my tarp until I was sure I could keep myself and my sleeping bag warm and dry. I did a healing ceremony for the sick little juniper in my circle, talking to it, watering it, cutting of all the cancerous growths.

Towards sunset, I began dancing around the outside of my circle, chanting and singing. Faster and faster I danced, my songs becoming loud yells, until I stepped in the eastern gate of the circle and closed it behind me, setting the rock in place. As I collapsed breathlessly, I could hear faint drumming and yelling in the distance. Someone, probably at base camp, was answering me.

It was a long, long night. I sang all the songs I could think of, serious and silly ones and prayed for guidance, chanted, talked to each rock and listened for its answers. When I got dangerously sleepy, I'd dance around the inner perimeter, shuffling cautiously in the starlight. Distant thunder rolled and menaced, occasional lightning streaked spectacularly into the dark hills. I know I slept because I woke up when my face hit the sand. No spirit or animal came to visit me, though I heard an owl hooting as I prayed for wisdom. I took great delight in peeing on my abusers' rock that long night. Take that, you jerks. You have no power over me.

I welcomed the sliver of moon climbing over the horizon and watched the eastern sky pale as I sang, "No one can hold back the dawn." When, at last, I could leave, I found little desire to return to camp and people and talking. Not even food was enticing. These three days had been some of the deepest, most introspective and valuable days of my life, face to face with my fears, my strengths, my loves and hates, my failings, my disease.

Meandering slowly back to base camp, after obliterating all traces of my bivouac, I was sad that I had received no vision. Then, as I rested after breaking my fast, I received my answers at last. I would choose only alternative therapies—no chemotherapy, no radiation, no radical mastectomy. I would start with a macrobiotic diet, add herbal remedies and oxygen, visualize healing myself, do Hatha Yoga and meditate, draw and paint my tumor and listen to what it has to tell me, have my lump removed but keep all my lymph nodes intact. I saw that this is my body that I must take responsibility for healing it.

Integrating the discoveries of the time alone and reintegrating with other people was a slow and delicate process. I felt fragile, speechless, empowered, but vulnerable. In the evening, we sang harmonies and chanted together rather than talking. I was grateful we had a couple of days left before returning to regular life.

I have returned changed, deepened, more open to myself, my inner voice, and to the natural world around me.

There are many stories, each one very special and very different. Some people see visions, others hear voices, many simply have a calm and reassuring experience of knowing. Ah ha. However, unfailingly we watch as the desert responds to each person and it gives them exactly what they need, exactly what they have been searching for, whether they knew it or not.

# DISCUSSION

## With O'Connell, Olsen, and Stone

*Fellows*: Have you read *Hope for the Flowers* (New York: Paulist Press, 1972)? It is a children's book about two caterpillars, a boy and a girl caterpillar. They end up climbing this caterpillar pillar because they want to find out what's on the top. The female caterpillar comes back because she did not like stepping over everybody in the process of going up but the male caterpillar goes to the top. When he is on the top, he sees all the other caterpillar pillars around him and is kind of disappointed. But when he looks up, he sees the female caterpillar who has become a butterfly. I shortened this story. It reminds me of what you said.

Talking about nature: Once I went out into nature for my own healing. When I was lying in the grass and the sun was coming through in the oak grove, a butterfly came fluttering by. It landed on my cheek and then flew off. I made a Haiku, "Butterfly who kissed my cheek. I, a flower?"

*Burns:* Carol, I liked your presentation. I don't have exactly a question but just some comments to see whether you have a response. When I listened to you, I was reminded of my years with my spiritual teacher. His form was different. His style of teaching was very loving. We never doubted his love but he would be very confrontational when he would see us acting out of a frozen emotional response. He would call us about it. It was a kind of experience similar to what you were describing. What it did for those of us who wanted to be in close association, was, it would empower us in our every-day life. We would treat everything in the same way. We would try to identify these situations and see them as teaching experiences. One of the most powerful insights I got out of this attitude was the ability to see the importance of being transparent to the energy. I was able to see tyrants as giving forces and energies that themselves have limitations. When I had the compassion to see their limitations, they lost their power. I found also that it needed a lot of integration. The confrontation was not really something we needed, we should go ahead and do the process ourselves, engage in it and integrate it. Since I have been teaching myself, I am, for years, integrating and processing.

*O'Connell:* My experience was applying it to my own every-day life in dealing with conflict. You do learn specific tyrant styles, so it is easy to become more conscious and able to identify how you have been hit. That gives you more of a representational symbol of what it may relate to in your own childhood, your own history. It's in layers. If you take a current situation, who is this really? It is a clearing process and, for me, it is a process of forgiveness. Going as far back as possible, clearing it and then bringing it forward, that's the way I work with my clients's conflicts, too. The first step is realizing that the person who is hitting you is always giving what you need.

*Scott: K'ola lece leco.* I guess, I am a fierce traditionalist when it comes to native lifeways but I want to qualify. I think what you do, Barton, is good. But when you desecrate a sacred site, you can injure the spirituality and heart of the people. You mentioned New Agers going in and desecrating sacred sites, this applies equally to ceremonies. The Lakota say, "do it this way, and the ancestors will honor you." Some of us, however, like to dabble We take a little bit here and a little bit there and get an amalgam which is a desecration of a spiritual way of being. Recently, I called a man who was advertising sweat lodges and I asked him who his teacher was or if he had ever done a sweat lodge before. He said he never had done one before and he didn't have a teacher but he wanted to do sweat lodges anyway. For me, this is ravishing people and false advertising. If you are not careful, you can do tremendous harm to people and to nations.

Also, I guess I have to do this on the record, in all of my experiences with native people, which is not extensive, never have I experienced grandparents being tyrants for the children. It is important to recognize that one advocate of a particular nation is not necessarily the nation and I know that the Cherokee people are not necessarily aligned with the visions of Mr. Swiftdeer. He uses essentially a synthesis of many different traditions which form the body of his work. It does not necessarily reflect the feelings, the spirituality, and the cosmology of the Cherokee. This does, however, not negate the beauty of his work as a metaphor for how we as adults can treat each other. I want, however, to clarify that it is important to honor tradition as it has been passed on and see how it fits within our own matrix of understanding. We must try to be as sensitive as possible to those ways if we wish to adhere to them. When we are not honoring the people as a whole, we also are not honoring the ancestors who came before us.

*Olsen:* I like to respond. I also do appreciate and value traditions. The tradition I had to struggle with was leaving the traditional Christian orientation. There is a quotation from the Proverbs that I do hold to and that is, "A wise man takes from that is old and that is new." A new synthesis is coming up. Part of the native traditions is to really have the roots there but also have the branches to move forward, rather than being stuck in the tradition. This may be a trite statement, but there is a story. A woman who made pot roast, always cut the ends off before she put the roast into the pot. After three generations, people said, "why do you do that?" And they went back to the grandmother and the grandmother said, "because the pot was too small."

*Stone:* I really would not think of telling anyone not to go by some traditional way if they wanted to do so, neither would I accept anyone telling me not to amalgamate and synthesize, innovate and invent. I feel the attitude you are expressing, Phillip, is one which has the danger of doing great harm because it can have a chilling effect on people finding their own way to Spirit. They may be working toward this great project that I mentioned at the beginning of my presentation—the reunion of earth and spirit. If someone wants to do a traditional Indian vision quest, I would certainly send him/her to traditional Indians to do that. We make no claim to do that, we try to offer an experience which suits the people who come to us. If anyone has any suggestions of a better way, let me know.

*O'Connell:* I want to clarify too, I don't hold this game as a Cherokee ceremony. Swiftdeer also did not teach this particular Tyrant Wheel as a Cherokee ceremony. In fact, a lot of his ideas came from Carlos Castaneda's book about the tyrants. This is all in the public domain. My recreation of the ceremony came out of Swiftdeer's teaching of being a warrior. However, it has not been out of the alignment with the sacred principle of the Cherokee, "Let nothing be done to harm the children." Out of the clear alignment with that principle, I just sat down and the grandmothers gave me the ceremony.

*Heinze:* Carroll also did not let the grandparents be the tyrants, on the contrary, the grandparents were the protectors of the child.

*Rothenberger:* I would like to say that I think we live in a very complex time. Each of us has a particular job to do and I think our company is symbolic of that. I think some of us, now at this time, work to keep sacred and protect the traditional ways. Others, what I certainly am involved in, are saying, we live at a unique time in history, we are experiencing a unique change over time. For some of us it is to see what is appropriate now. We want to see what speaks to this time and then we do our part. Even honoring the ancestors, we would say, "Who knows who we really are? Which lifetime? Which ancestors?" So it seems to me for each of us, we are true to whatever our explorations tell us. We are here, at this time, in the most deep way, to honor our particular ancestors and the ancestors of all life that brought us to this time. I think there is room for all of us to do our work and to support each other.

*Heinze*: Phoenix is rising. Bart's clear answer proves it. We rose from the ashes. We really did.

*Stone:* Before I give up the microphone, I want to publicly express gratitude to this remarkable jay, doing bridgework here, letting us into its reality, in such a charming way.

*Heinze*: Allowing both voices to be heard, calmly and accepting, and reciprocity balancing the situation.

# META ART III

Wolfgang Gersch

*[music: Manfred Man, "Medicine Song"]*
Kara Young: "I really like using paper. I like to use soft material and I like using low-tech. I don't like to use very much equipment. I even shifted from using a drill and a paint stir and pulp my paper by using a water hose which takes no electricity and the sound is a lot better. So I use water as the machine or force to pulp the paper."

"My "Open Doors" are something I just started doing in January. The image has been with me for quite a while, at least nine months. And I started by pouring, creating the base. It means I pour the paper and leave the opening, about six month before."

*[music: Enja]*
"I push through on some level, to get to it, almost each time I do the work. It's like I need to go through some transition period before I really get into it. And it feels intimidating, it feels difficult—the challenge of creating."

"The first "Open Door" I did in January. Doors are much more challenging, they are much more exciting for me to do and they are much more revealing. I am used to have people when I exhibit my work and they would say to me, 'What's behind the closed door?' And I always say, 'Your imagination.'"

"Now, I am showing what my imagination is! And I am giving a picture of myself. I am still questioning what it all means. I am looking for the answers or let the answers come, not pushing them. I am curious from where these images come? Why am I drawn to them."

"It's not new! But, when I first started my work about six years ago, similar imagery came up and I didn't know how internal the imagery was or whether I was just repeating things I saw."

*[music: Tony Scott "Music for Zen Meditation"]*

"Nature is a place I like to be more. As a culture, I do the work because I have to. It is just the drive, I need to do it."

*Wolfgang:* "What do you mean you have to do it? Is it such a strong desire?"

*Kara:* "I have to do it, there is nothing else to do. This is what I am supposed to do. And I do it because I want to see what is coming out. I want to see what the end product will be. The more I put it out, the more I know myself. I see where my inner world resides."

*[music: "Blue Buddha"]*

"And it is drawing me back to things I have put aside in the past, due to conflict or other types of people."

"I am hopeful for the planet. It may not include us humans. I see us human beings on a transition course, on a collision course. Maybe this is the only way how we can get there. When I see plants and trees growing up through the middle of rocks or on side walks, the forces of nature are so strong. I am sure the planet will be okay. I am not the sure about us humans, but the planet will be okay."

*[music: Manfred Man, "Medicine Song"]*

*Wolfgang:* "Hello, I am Wolfgang Gersch. I am the visionary and creator of Meta Art Studios and what it puts out into the world. Meta Art Studios create beautiful visions about our inner and outer journeys, connecting with ourselves and the world in which we live. We want to learn to protect our world, to cherish and to pass it on to our children's children in a good shape."

*[music: "Blue Buddha"]*

"Over the last few years, the influence of computers has also entered my life and my consciousness more and more. I am wondering how the visual imagery of the future will be impacted and transformed by the technology and the advancement in the computer field. I have done quite a few studies and research about this over the last few years."

*[music: William Aura, "Peace"]*

"I have created more images on the computer where there is no original like a painting or a piece of art, we had so far in history—pictures to hang onto the wall or to look up in a book."

*[music: Ragas and Sagas]*

"I had even paintings of mine which actually burned in the Oakland Hill Fire. All what I have left now are some electronic files and data of these originals. Now, with the advancement of the computer technology, these images could be brought back to life, not in the sense that I could recreate the original paintings but they could be reproduced in very high quality on a canvas, with electronic controlled airbrush equipment."

*[music: Peter Gabriel, "Shaking the Tree"]*

"I like especially to show that there is more than one reality, that there is more than one way to see the world around us."

"I like to show in my paintings which are in transition with many viewpoints, that the viewer can pick today this viewpoint and tomorrow a different one, explore and see the world from different angles and viewpoints and in a more holistic way."

*[music: Peter Gabriel, "Digging in the Dirt"]*

"Painting is as primal as, for language, are sounds. Music and dancing are ancient forms of self-expression."

"For me as an artist, it is not so important that the viewer really knows what I am trying to say. It is rather an interactive contact. The viewer sees my art to contemplate and it could show him much about himself, what he sees and in what he believes. Maybe, he can see what I, as the artist, might have seen or wanted to see or dreamed to see."

*[music: Brian Eno, "Nerve Net"]*

# SKY DANCERS: JOURNEY TO DAKINI PLACES OF TIBET

Leila Castle

I was fortunate to go, in the summer of 1991, on a pilgrimage to Dakini places in Tibet with Tsultrim Allione, author of Women of Wisdom. She was leading a small group of twenty-five women, mainly her students, to practice at sacred sites and she had asked me to assist her. I have been traveling to sacred sites since 1975 and am involved with geomancy and goddess traditions for many years, so to go with Tsultrim to the sacred feminine sites of Tibet was a great treasure.

The goddesses in Tibetan Buddhism are called *dakinis,* a Sanskrit word meaning "sky dancers," or "those who move in the sky" and "are enlightened female beings." The sites we went to were power places of the *dakinis.* The Red Citadel of Machig Lapdron who first transmitted the Chod practice in the 11th century, Drigung charnel grounds and Vajra Yogini mandala and Shoto Terdrom and the cave of Yeshe Tsogyel, the 8th century consort of Padmasambhava, the founder of Tibetan Buddhism.

I have started burning juniper I gathered at eighteen thousand feet near the cave of Yeshe Tsogyel so you can experience some of the fragrances of Tibet. Juniper is burned as an offering in Tibet. It mixes with the scent of yak butter and yak dung used as fuel.

## Sangri Kharmar—The Red Citadel of Machig Lapdron

The entire pilgrimage lasted one month. We were going through altitude sickness when we crossed the river which is called the Great Purifier on the way to Sangri Kharmar which was the hermitage of Machig Lapdron, one of the most revered women teachers in Tibet. She lived in the eleventh century and was considered an emanation of Yeshe Tsogyel. Machig Lapdron came from a Bon family and she integrated this with the early Buddhist teachings and became the founder of the Chod practice and lineage, the only practice originating from a Tibetan woman and taught by all schools of Tibetan Buddhism today. The Chod practice is a method of cutting off demons, the root of egoic attachment. It is traditional done in desolate places such as charnel grounds with practitioners singing a melodious song while playing a drum and a bell, calling the demons to come feed from their body which they offer as a feast. It is the destruction of the ego. The slides show the rebuilt monastery that was destroyed by the Chinese army and then rebuilt. In the shrine room is a *tanka* of Machig Lapdron dancing.

We were able to practice in the shrine room. For the Tibetan's it was very reaffirming to see us practice after the Chinese had tried to wipe out their tradition. There was a stone which, it is said, was thrown into the river by the bodhisattvas as a sign where Machig should live. The stone lies directly across from her cave. This is the entrance to the cave where we were able to practice too. The crack inside is the entrance to the 108 charnel grounds, things may actually have been transported through this crack. Things came out of it and things disappeared. Many of us had visions of the charnel grounds and of actually being there. There was a statue of Machig Lapdron and her bowl. You hold the bowl in your right hand and the drum in your left hand. There was a stupa opposite the cave and we were going into a meditation cave right next the stupa. It is beautifully decorated with mani stones carved with mantras. We collected the earth from inside the cave. It is medicinal and used for blessing. The stones are red, the essence of the feminine, the red of the menstrual blood.

## Mandala of Vajra Yogini—Drigung Dundro or Sky Burial Site

Drigung Til is the seat of the Drigung Kagyupas in the lineage of Milarepa. The monastery (*(gompa)* was destroyed and rebuilt three times. The entire area is considered to be the mandala of Vajra Yogini, a dakini form of the Great Mother, also called the Diamond Sow. The sky burial site is her body, the stone altar where bodies are offered to the vultures is her heart. The stones there are the actual heart of Vajra Yogini. If your body is offered here, it is conceived that you achieve instant enlightenment. One stone is Vajra Yogini's breast, it is surrounded by four other stones. As we descended down the cliff, a rainbow appeared. It is said to be connected by a rainbow to one of the main charnel grounds in India.

## Shoto Terdrom and the Cave of Yeshe Tsogyel

The destination of our pilgrimage was Shoto Terdrom which means "Box of Treasures." It refers to its *terma* tradition. Terma are treasures of teachings, hidden primarily by Padmasambhava and Yeshe Tsogyel when they both lived here in the 8th century.

We came to visit a present incarnation of Yeshe Tsogyel, the dakini Tenzin Chron. When Yeshe Tsogyel died, her body dissolved into rainbow light and she promised she would always emanate her form at this site. We were really amazed when we descended to the village of Terdrom to see this triangle shape in the sky. In Buddhism, this is the symbol of the Great Mother who is considered to be space. There was a nunnery and many lay practitioners who were incredibly friendly. There was a stupa next to the river and hot springs. Where the two rivers converge, they create a vulva shape. The story goes that Padmasambhava threw his *dorje* from his cave to create a tunnel which drained a poisonous lake and the hot springs emerged. Mantras are carved in the rocks. The supernatural is daily life reality for these people. It is a magical culture which is barely hanging on, as you well know. The spot is shown where Padmasambhava leaned against the rock and melted it with his shoulders. Offerings were placed there. There is a place where he put his bowl. And we saw the cave where he and Yeshe Tsogyel practiced. There is a footprint of Yeshe Tsogyel with her boot on and a print of her bare foot. The nuns took me one day to a boulder with her hand print and I put my hand into it. It was quite extraordinary. When you touch clay and draw away, it has a sort of tackiness. Her hand print had this too. It was not carved it was really melted into the rock.

After the others had left, three of us were hiking up to the hermitage at 18,000 feet where Tenzin Chodron lived. We had heard before that she is very elusive. People had gone there to see her and were told that she was not there to find out that the woman who had told them Tenzin was not there was Tenzin Chodron herself. We wondered which one of the women she really was. But she was really not there what we discovered later on.

We were allowed to stay inside the shrine room. One nun took us to Yeshe Tsogyel's cave, straight up. You go inch by inch, a triangle shape of the Great Mother was the entrance to her cave. It was like going into her *yoni*. There were wild flowers everywhere. We practiced in the inner cave. I don't have time to tell all the stories but everyone on this trip was really transformed. Wild yaks were all over the landscape which is dangerous because they loosen rocks and rocks which then come down roaring down the cliffs. There were even higher caves, one is called the Assembly Hall of the Dakinis. All of this is in a book by Keity Dawson, *Sky Dancers* (London: Arkana, 1984) which recalls the life of Yeshe Tsogyel. We could not go there because we did not have time and our bodies could not adjust fast enough to the altitude. It was also very dangerous to hike.

Nomads passed us by. The Tibetans are extraordinary people. They embody their teachings, aside from the hardships they are enduring, they are radiant and genuinely kind. Tsultrim is recognized as an emanation of Mad and M is recognized as emanation of Yeshe Tsogyel, like the Russian dolls, one inside the other.

This is Tenzin Chodron whom we finally met. Tsultrim's daughter had hiked and found her working on a prayer wheel. We had been separated from her by the floods. We did not realize that we were flooded the whole time we were there. She spoke to us briefly and was extremely concerned about our safety. She was very protective and blessed us. She was extremely gentle and very powerful at the same time, very kind and very knowing. It was really a teaching of the sacred feminine. I thank her and all the Tibetan people for keeping this alive. I want to leave you with this image of a dakini in our times.

# PERSISTENCE OF SPIRIT:
# REVERED SITES IN BRITAIN

Cindy A. Pavlinac

Today's holy buildings frequently hold ancient secrets in their dark corners. Cathedrals and country churches were often built on ancient sacred ground and determined explorers can locate remnants of simple shrines and trickles from holy wells. Medieval pilgrimage stops and routes frequently traveled near prehistoric sites and the modern pilgrim witnesses the persistence of spirit at special places. Ancient holy sites contain a mosaic of beliefs, interweaving Earth mysteries with Sky God lore in a complex land/spirit/sky scape. The reawakening interest in ancient sacred sites reflects the modern search of the human psyche for wholeness and meaning.

As an artist interested in expressions of the sacred, I travel as a pilgrim, seeking unexpected alignments, remnants of balance, and clues to ancient wisdom. As a photographer, I create images out of phantoms in the corner of my eye, working ceremonially, intuitively, and determinately to communicate the beauty and power and presence of place.

A prehistoric sacred site is a precious entity. Often developed over thousands of years, sites are becoming increasingly vulnerable to modern technological intrusions, objectifying craziness, possessive ownership, and tourists. Yet a sacred site transcends our sense of time and space. It is alive in a terrain integrating local topography, plants, smells, seasons, weather, animals, sky, sun, moon, planets, stars, people. Folklore tempts with seductive descriptions of buried treasure, veiled realms, and underground passageways. Legends of dancers being turned to stone may recall ancient celebrations and tales of tunnels between sites may be reminders of ceremonies which activated and connected sacred sites to their neighbors and perhaps, to sites all around the world.

Ancient sanctuaries are a repository for human memory. The megalithic sites in Britain include massive earthworks, dolmens, single standing stones, chambered burial tombs, and stone circles, four to eight thousand years old. Many, if not most, were constructed on sites already in use, giving a specific place perhaps at least several thousand more years of continued human attention, song, dance, and prayer.

Northern European megalithic sites were built when wandering people began to settle into agricultural lifeways. Usually near rivers or the ocean and often on geomagnetic, mineral, and underground water veins, the sites were conceived at a major evolutionary shift in human consciousness and, as such, can offer us an opportunity for mental and spiritual archaeology. What we unearth is our own subconscious, concern with the interaction of the psyche with environment, a look at the last balanced point in Western consciousness between a deep alliance with Nature and the rise of technology and science. An ancient sacred site is a whole.

A place like Stonehenge is a precinct extending into the local topography to the visible horizon. Preserving the full experience of a place like Stonehenge for future researchers and pilgrims would require protecting not only the famous circle of megaliths and trilithons but the earthwork henge, avenues and dozens of burial mounds in its vicinity, as well as astronomically important horizon features, some of which have yet to be discovered. It is a testimony to the power of a sacred site that despite busy roads, military helicopters and tank maneuvers, and millions of visitors a year, most of whom spend less than a half hour outside their car or tour bus, Stonehenge still functions as an astronomical observatory. For a sacred site is not just a place but an event. The Heel Stone, for instance, has obligingly shifted sideways to compensate for a 4,000 year difference so the solstice sun still rises and sets on its alignment.

A sacred site's field of influence ripples through time and entering its precinct we can time travel. To be at an ancient sanctuary during an astronomical event is a profound experience. Watching the sun sink through the trilithon portals of Stonehenge on the Winter Solstice is to experience a burning away of time. One's self disappears into the theater of turning earth and sky. Light beams and shadow enter through the eyes to burn directly into the soul, conveying information on physical, intellectual, intuitive, emotional and spiritual levels simultaneously. By participating in a site as event, I knew the site. And the site entered my mind, fixing an orientation and sensitizing me to sacred geography, appearing in my thoughts and dreams, waking me for solstice ever after, no matter in what time zone I sleep.

The megalithic builders were sky watchers and amazingly complicated alignments have been rediscovered in the last few decades by modern observers, mathematicians, astronomers and computer scientists. Not only are there convincing solar solstice markers, as related in local folk wisdom, but there now seem to be many more alignments for moon rising and setting, and, most incredibly, the Major Lunar Standstill, the extreme northern and southern rising points in a 18.6-year cycle. A solar calendar could be accurately constructed, given a stick and enough sun to make a shadow, within a few years. But an accurate lunar calendar of the complexity found in Britain, which includes sightings from a single arrangement of standing stones to coordinate alignments in various directions across neighboring stones to distant hills, mountains, even islands dozens of miles away, many marked with cairns, barrows, or standing stones, could take generations to observe, build and verify. One wonders at their techniques for divining correct placement and right relation to create simple temples of stone which participate in complex celestial events. The stone circles themselves, of which over 900 have been identified so far, are self-contained expressions of sophisticated sacred geometry, comparable to medieval cathedrals. There is growing evidence that Stonehenge was primarily a lunar calendar and that the current mania for summer solstice sunrise says a lot about our culture's priorities, and could also illustrate the cognitive shift some 4,000 years ago in neolithic consciousness from matrifocal land based people to solar and sky god worshipping patriarchal nomads on horseback.

Ancient sky watchers created a ceremonial calendar to celebrate astronomy in the landscape with fairs, festivals and games. It has long been speculated, beginning with the fifteenth century English gentlemen antiquarians who looted prehistoric graves for mantelpiece trophies, and country peasants who buried, dragged away and split in bonfires the pagan stones, that the strange stone circles may have been gathering places for feasting, trading, judgment and amnesty. Although the megalithic builders have vanished or have been assimilated by conquering tribes like the Celts, shadows of their festival days have survived into our modern calendar. Cross-quarter days, halfway between solstice and equinox, mark important seasonal and religious festivals, suggesting they were inherited from a very old solar calendar with well established feast days and celebrations on the eight major subdivisions of the year. The Celtic calendar also preserved these eighth divisions beginning the year November 1 with the Feast of Samhain, when veils between the worlds were thinnest. Our Halloween and All Saints' Day are celebrated November 1 and All Souls Day is November 2. Christmas is near Winter Solstice, Imbolc and St.Brigit's Day on February 1, Candlemas and Groundhog Day February 2, Lady Day is March 25 near Spring Equinox. The summer half of the Celtic year began May 1 with the lighting of fires on Beltane. Summer Solstice is near June 24, Midsummer Day and Feast Day of St.John the Baptist. August 1 is Lammas and the Feast of St.Peter. Michaelmas, the Festival of St.Michael and all the Angels is September 25, just after the autumn Equinox Thus important dates of the ancient solar calendar have become modern holidays, a displacement technique, wrought at ancient holy sites as well as festivals.

A personal relationship to land and nature is fundamental to our psyche and well being. There is a place within me obsessed with travel to holy locations, a place with such intense need to linger within fields of sacredness that I become homesick if I am too long away. The inner soul landscape is fed, refined, caressed by visiting external sacred landscapes. I will end with nine minutes of slides accompanied by music, an artist's response to meeting, dancing, singing, breathing with the land. We go first to England's stone circles, barrows, and earthworks held visually in the context and drama of sacred landscape, with a few crosses and medieval cathedrals to show the continuity of honoring place and use of sacred geometry. The second half goes to Brittany, France, with chambered tombs, standing stones, 40 feet tall, stone rows miles long and carved stones deep in tombs. All the photographs are my original images and the music was composed and performed by my favorite traveling companion, Martin Gregory.

Enjoy these images of ancient sacred places as holistic systems of knowing, intellect still close to nature, places built for purposes of the spirit before the Age of Reason declared nature a machine. Allow boundaries to soften, sift through landscape layers of time, accessing ancient memory banks to fuse with contemporary consciousness. We are a whole community dreaming together.

# DISCUSSION

With Castle, Gersch, and Pavlinac

*Seidel:* I feel the presence of ritual very strongly in the two presentations of ancient sites, in Tibet with prayer wheels and stupas and then, of course, the stones in England. IT is part of their power.

I was wondering, Wolfgang, you had some pictures of your friend Kara outside, does she work outdoors? How does this enter her art process? Also, do you have any ritual process in your studio? And finally, how do you exhibit your computer images?

*Gersch:* Kara Young is my partner, lover and wife. We met in America in 1981 and have been together ever since. She has become this magnificent artist. The photos I showed were taken at a recent wilderness trip with Coquelicot around Lake Tahoe. I was showing her other side, collecting and searching for her imagery in nature. We both are not visiting that intensely ritual sites around the planet. We have not done extensive traveling yet. We look at our world and other artists and draw on our own resources. Kara Young has been living in the United States all her life and has a deep affinity toward the American Indian culture.

You were also asking me about my own inspiration and how I exhibit computer work?

*Seidel:* I was asking if there was any ritual practice in your work and how you exhibit your work. Are your computer images exhibited in galleries?

*Gersch:* Briefly, I have been born and raised in Germany and then broadened my horizon from an early Catholic induction which I was not taking on too well. I searched for mysticism and metaphysics around the planet and developed a more personal and private style of relating to planetary consciousness and metaphysics from different cultures, respecting and honoring them. I am trying my own way without taking too much from another culture when I don't understand it.

Some of my work is shown in galleries and exhibitions and there is my mural art. My computer art is definitely shown on computers. New means of electronic messenging is coming now into its own being.

*Pavlinac:* I also want to add that I have an art background and it was not only working with Indians. It was about medicine wheels and about honoring the land, asking for respect. I was taught how to behave on the land, how to pray and how to sing in ways that I had not known were possible. I also apply it to my own culture and my genetic lineage.

*Marks:* Ten years ago, when I came here, I was the first artist. I had this idea that art and shamanism work well together. At that time, it was sort of new. It is remarkable that artists and creativity make a tremendous comeback. It all shut down during the industrial revolution. People became consumers and artists retreated to the avantgarde. With computers, with media, inadvertently everything that threw us out is bringing us back. I feel a tremendous hope for peace. Through the process of bringing shamanism together with these new media, with technology, all of us on the planet have a million more choices than we had before. Choices is what's all about. I see the artists supported here today. They bring us all together. Thank you.

*Heinze:* Thank you, Carolina. There is a book by Andreas Lommel, *Shamanism, The Beginning of Art* (transl. Michael Bullock. New York/Toronto: McGraw Hill Book, Co., 1967). Shamans were also the first artists. You can look at the cave art in Altamira in Spain and Les Eyzies in France, for example. Themes have come full circle and I really appreciate they have entered this conference, too.

*Chase:* Shamans were also the first scientists.

*Heinze:* Yes, and the first healers, and weather makers. I want to thank the last three presenters for a worthy finale. We can now take the memory of the three days and nights devoted to the exploration of shamanism and healing back into our lives and our dreams.

# WISE OLD STORIES

Luisah Teish

First of all, I want to say to you, "Alafia," and your response is, "Shalafia ni." We greet each other by wishing that you have good health and be at peace with your mate and you have returned the same thing to me in responding to this wish.

From my point of view, this story telling is happening right after the presentation where the child spirit was invoked. I always say that I am telling stories to children from 3 to 93. It has to be the innocent, open, ancient, young self who comes to the circle.

In order to receive the gift of story telling, you have to bring three things. You have to bring attention. I had a beautiful experience the other day. My daughter and I were in the car, sitting in front of our house and there was a little boy on his bicycle. He was pumping and making a sound. He was going, "shackalacka shackalacka," and then he stopped and you saw him just looking and it was such a stop. When my daughter and I were looking out of the car window, it was as if we were watching something out of another dimension. He was so concentrated. We wanted to see what he was looking at. And he had been stopped by a butterfly. Here was his intense concentration, he did not exhale. He did not bat an eyelid, he just looked at this butterfly. And he took it in what it felt like. I did not time it, forty-five second of the rest of the world being gone and just him and this butterfly. You saw him take it in and then he went, "shackalacka, shackalacka," returning immediately back to what he had been doing before.

The next day the little boy had two other little girls in front of my fence. I consciously had planted both a butterfly and a hummingbird garden in my front yard. So all these butterflies were fluttering in front of my house and he had gathered two little girls and brought them over there and they were all looking at the butterflies. So I started, "This is a monarch and this is a cabbage," and I said, "what are you doing? Don't catch them, because you will hurt them. If you pick them up, you damage their wings." And he said, "We never do that!" That child reminded me of what happens when a child pays attention, everything stops and the whole miracle of creation is seen. It is that kind of attention that is necessary to reap the benefit of story telling.

The other thing is "cooperation." Because, sometimes, especially in African story telling, it is call and response, you have to be listening. You are not a spectator out there, your act of watching is part of story telling. Sometimes, there are stories when the story teller cannot continue, until you respond. So story telling is very different from television. There is no fourth wall between the story teller and the audience, in fact, there should be an alchemical process going on. I am making love to all of you right now. Do you feel it? (laugher) That's Oshun, she had to come out. (laughter)

What I really need is your imagination because we are going to go into "no time," into ancient time, into magical places where almost anything can happen. So I want to pull on the ancient selves and have everybody look at the fire for a few minutes. Recognize, we are doing now what our ancestors have done for centuries, all over the world, in hot climates and in cold climates, all times of the year. There is the incredible truth that human beings love to draw around the fire and tell stories.

In most cultures, the story of the quest for fire is always one where a trickster steals the flames from a deity. There is almost no culture where the sun just drops a piece of fire and says, "Here, humans, have it." It is true, it is always a struggle to get it. Somebody gets chased by a volcano, by lava, or somebody sneaked up and pinched a piece of the sun's butt or something like that. And there is always a consequence for having acquired fire. So this is a very ancient and sacred thing, sitting here and looking at the fire. Looking for example at Madame Pele on Hawaii or Agayu of Africa who lives in the belly of the volcano and makes fresh earth for us, creates new land masses and burns away decay.

So in coming here tonight, I came to tell tales. And when I was sitting in the room in there, I was saying to myself, "Maybe, I should do...but you didn't originally plan" and then I come out here and there are moving lizards which is a clear sign for me to "I should do...."

This story has to do with a contest between Obatala who is the Lord of the Clouds and Olocu who is the Old Man at the Bottom of the Ocean. Before I even start, there are some here who are children of Obatala and they will agree with the way this story ends. And there are other children here who are children of Olocu and they will say, "there is a twist in this tale, something is missing." And it is true, we can find in our folklore proverbs that say one thing and there are others which say, "Ah, but yes...." It is a very brief little tale but it is fitting for the beginning.

\*       \*       \*

At one time when the land and the sky had been existing in peace here on earth, Elegba, the trickster, started a rumor. And Elegba said he heard that Olocu at the very bottom of the ocean was threatening to rise up in a tidal wave and overtake the land. When this rumor was circulated around the earth, the issue came up who would defend the land and it was Obatala, the Lord of the Clouds, who thought it was his job to set proper limits on that. And so Elegba ran down to the bottom of the ocean and informed Olocu that the challenge would be met. Olocu went to the very bottom and came up to the surface, dressed in magnificent robes of seaweed. Obatala looked down and thought to himself, "hm, what now must I do?" because the clouds are particular about getting soiled. So Obatala decided that the smartest thing to do was to send one of his messengers. So he scooped up Chameleon and send Chameleon to earth. Chameleon landed on Olocu's robe and immediately turned the color of seaweed. So Olocu went back down to the bottom of the ocean and he surfaced again, dressed in corral and pearls, threatening to overtake the land. Olocu moved in on the shore but then, pop, Chameleon fell on his sleeve and immediately turned into corral and pearl and Olocu said, "eh, eh" and went back to the bottom of the ocean and came up again, pop, changed, down, up again, pop, changed. Seven times Olocu went down and seven times Olocu surfaced, seven times Chameleon matched Olocu perfectly. After that Olocu realized that if the owner of the clouds could match him every time, he should change his intention.

At least, this is the story we are told, but I am not so sure. I wonder because the powers of the ocean are as mighty as those of the clouds. And when you look at the art of the town of Benine, you often see Olocu, the mudfish, standing on the surface of the earth, holding a Chameleon in each hand. (laughter)

\*     \*     \*

The next story is called the "Wishing Star." It is one of those light fire stories, it is not the story I usually tell about the quest of fire. All these stories are so wonderful, it is hard to decide which one to tell. In order for this story to work, you have to consider that we are approaching dark morning in creation. It is the time before the sun has come up, in the beginning of time. Now, as I start this story, begin to think seriously about what is going on in your life and I want you to think about seriously, if you could have one real wish granted to night, what would that be? Because, at the end of the story, I will ask you to wish on the Wishing Star.

\*     \*     \*

What's that thing? What are we going to do with it. My friend Elegba was the first one to see it. He was just walking along, early one morning, minding his own business, when suddenly, whoa, that thing came flying out of the sky. But when he tried to touch it, it was hot. He decided to call his mama. "Yemaya, will you come look at this thing?" Yemaya was in the kitchen cooking her breakfast. She really did not want to be called, but since she had been called, so she came and said, "Honey, what's that thing? What are we going to do with it?" Elegba said, "I don't know, Mama. I was just walking along, minding my own business when suddenly, whoa, that thing came flying out of the sky." And Yemaya looked at it and said, "well, it's hot." And so she fanned her skirt around it and cooled it off with some ocean water. But she still did not know what it was and what she was going to do with it. So she decided to call her husband and. she called, "Ogun, Honey, would you come and look at this thing, please?" Now, Ogun was in the backyard working on his car and he really did not want to be called. But since she called, he came and said, "What's that thing? What are you going to do with it?" And Yemaya said, "I don't know, Honey, but it was awfully hot and I cooled it off." And Elegba said, "I was just walking along, minding my own business, Daddy, when, whoa, this thing came flying out of the sky." And Ogun said, "Oh yeah, I am telling what I am going to do with it." And he got a heavy, heavy chain and wrapped it around that thing and locked it up. But he still did not know what it was or what he was going to do with it. So he decided to call his brother, "he, Shango, man, come, check out this thing." Now Shango was standing at the corner, talking to his girl friend and he really did not want to be called. But since they called him, he came and he said, "What's this thing? What are you going to do with it?" Ogun said, "I don't know, man, but I chained it up." And Yemaya said, "it was awfully hot and I cooled it down." And Elegba said, "I was just walking along, minding my own business, Uncle, when, whoa, this thing came flying out of the sky." Shango said, "oh yeah, I tell you what I am going to do with it." He reached out and grabbed that thing by the chain and whirled it around and he hurled it across a lightning bolt. And it went flying through the sky, with them running behind and it landed in front of Nanabubuku's house. Now, when Old Woman woke up and she saw them standing and she saw that thing, what did she say? [audience] "What's that thing? What are you going to do with it?" "Whose thing is this?" Shango said, "It is not mine, Grandmother, I just brought it here" and Ogun said, "I chained it up," and Yemaya said, "It was awfully hot and I cooled it down." And Elegba said, "I was just walking along, minding my own business, Grandmother, when, whoa, that thing came flying out of the sky." And they began to argue over whose thing it was. And Old Woman said, "You all discuss it and let me know." And she slept for a hundred years. Do you know, when she woke up they were still arguing whose thing it was. Old Woman said, "Well, you don't know what it is and you don't know whose thing it is and you don't know where it came from, I will do that." And she put it in the sky and it has been up there ever since.

I want to ask you a question. How many of you have seen the sky at night? Could you raise your hands? Have you seen this great big ball of light that is in the sky at night? What is that thing? [audience] The Moon. Sometimes the moon has had too much to eat that's what we call a full moon. And sometimes the moon goes on a crazy diet and gets real skinny and looks like a crooked banana. That's called the crescent moon. And sometimes, when the moon has been on that diet, we see an itty bitty star hanging around the moon's belly button. That's called the Star in Crescent. The next time you look up and see that star hanging around the moon's belly button, I want you to point one finger at it and make a wish very, very carefully. And say, "that's what it is. That's what they did with it. And it's mine, the Wishing Star."

You see what I do. I take old stories and put them in modern language and adapt them to modern situations so that the original meaning of the story is not lost to us. The truth is that every problem that we are facing has been faced by our ancestors before. So it is very important to allow people to understand that the stories are still relevant. So I do what I call "return tales," I take them and turn them over one more time.

This one is a remake of an old story. I can't remember who I heard it from. Some of our tales have been put into anthologies and some are learned from elders. When I am in the presence of elders, I eavesdrop, a lot. That way I get a lot of good stories.

For this one, I want you to imagine the ocean. And I want you to see a rock in the water and the mist rises from the waves around the rock. Hear the sound of the waves! Smell the salt water in the air! Feel the rhythm of the ocean! And allow yourselves to be caressed by these powers.

      \*         \*        \*

There he sits, the mermaid's lover, alone on his rock. There he sits, awaiting her return, imagine his reality to have been with her. Once upon a time, there was a boy child who spent his time, sitting on a rock by the side of the shore. When the other children were playing games, he sat there. When the others were studying their lesson, he languished. When others were fast asleep, he stared out and gazed. One day, while he was sitting on his rock, he looked out and he saw something shimmering in the ocean. He thought he saw a wisp of hair, he thought he saw the glitter of scales. And, lo and behold, there was a splash in a wave and he saw the mermaid's tail. He was enchanted and watched her move, up and down, up and down, up and down. And love struck him as only a mermaid's love can. She moved toward him and he beheld a sight more beautiful than anything he had seen in his life. There she was, her skin blue-black, hair the color of seaweed, luminescent eyes like pearls, angular breasts, and a fish-scale body of blue and purple, with a hint of corral in her tail. And he fell in love as only a young man can. He reached his hands out to touch her and she warned, "No, no! You are not allowed to love me" and disappeared in the waves, undulating. He ran, ran, ran to his brother and he said, "Oh, brother, I was down at the ocean today and I saw her." And his brother said, "No, ah, ah, don't go back! I am warning you. I know about her. Don't go back!" But the young man was not listening and the next evening, you would find him sitting on that rock, looking for that tail, listening to that wisp on the waves. And he stretched out his hands for her and she said, "No, no, no, it is better for you not to love." Unable to contain himself, he ran to his father and said, "Father, I have seen her, I have seen the mermaid." And his father said, "Boy, stay away from her. Men have been lost at sea." But his words fell on deaf ears and again the young man was found sitting on that rock, longing with desire and being pulled to the water. He stretched out his hand, almost touching her hair and she said, "Better for you not to love." She flipped away from him this time and he hungered for the touch of the seaweed. He wanted to run his fingers against her scales. He wanted to follow her into the sea. And he ran to his mother and he said, "Mother, I met the woman of the ocean and I love her." And in that moment, the mother gave up the life of her son, because she knew, what every woman knows, the power of the mermaid. And she knew that her son was lost to her for ever. But fulfilling her obligations, she said, "Son, don't! Son, don't!" but he disappeared back to the rock.

There he sat and the mermaid surfaced and, this time, took his hands and pulled him into the water. And as they went down into the sea, his skin turned to scales. And as they went further into the water, his legs turned to a tail, his arms to fins, his lungs to gills, and his eyes moved to the side of his head. There, at the bottom of the ocean, he saw a great castle. She took him into that place and there they made love as no human has made love before. He was quite pleased with the wife of his. Everyday she washed for him and he did not notice the apron she used. Everyday she cooked for him and he did not notice the weight in her pocket. Everyday she took care of him and he was unaware of the danger lurking between her thighs. Every night she went into a secret chamber and closed the door behind her. And there came the time when there was no other way to test her love except to ask for entry into her secret chamber.

He asked and she refused. He asked again and she refused. He asked again and she refused. And he said, "Aren't you my wife?" At which point the weight in her apron became most heavy and she said, "I will let you into my inner chamber. Here you will see my secret under one condition that you never tell anybody what you see." And he approved and so she pushed against the door and a light so bright came through it that it almost blinded him. And as he stepped into the room, he saw a floor made of pearls, walls of corral, a ceiling of crystal and every treasure that ever had been lost at sea was casually lying about. He looked upon these riches and thought to himself, "My father could stop working." He looked at these riches and thought to himself, "My brother need not go to school." He looked at these riches and saw his mother drenched in wealth. At that moment, he opened his mouth and said, "Wait, until I tell Mother." And when he said, "Mo-ther," she grabbed his tongue, went into her apron pocket and, whack, cut off his tongue with a machete. She said, "Now, go and tell that."

Shocked, he ran from the secret room. He ran out of the castle, feeling himself changing but he was too frightened and too much in a hurry to notice what was happening with his body. He ran with a trail of blood behind him. He ran, carrying heartbreak, and when he broke the surface of the water, he returned to his rock. But when he looked at himself, he still had a tail. When he looked at himself, he still had fins. When he looked at himself, his eyes were still on the side of his head. And, most importantly, his ability to speak was gone. And so it is, that sometimes when you go down to the ocean and watch very carefully, you can see the mermaid's lover, sitting on the rock, hoping that you understand his story. If you listen carefully, you can hear him, going, "Oop, oop. Oop, oop. Oop, oop."

*          *          *

The last story is an important story for me because I made myself a promise some years ago, to take very seriously this business of story telling and to recognize story telling's power not only to teach and guide but to heal. I consider this to be one of my healing tales. Often, in folklore, catalytic and eruptive occurrences in nature will be described as rape. And those of us who study folklore and its symbolism, understand this. But the people who don't, the people who take the story at face value, often misunderstand and think that rape in the story is some sort of ancient endorsement of that violent act. The story I am about to tell you is a remake of an old tale that is supposed to explain how different bodies of water got on the surface of the earth. You will feel the relationship between the moon and the water. In the original tale, Yemaya, who is the Goddess of the Ocean, is chased down by her son who is the space between the ocean and the sky. He rapes her and her breast break open and water is everywhere. And her belly bursts open and all the other deities come out. We really don't need that story. You know what I am saying, we really needn't tell our children all that. We need to tell our boys and girls a very different version. So what I have done is I created, what I consider, my healing version of the story and it is called, "The Day Her Belly Burst" and it is dedicated to all the women in the audience, all the mothers and daughters.

*          *          *

Once upon a time, there was a beautiful woman by the name of Yemaya who looked into the waters of the ocean. There she saw her own reflection and she said, "Who is that beautiful woman? I thought that I was the prettiest thing that the world had ever seen." And then she looked upon that woman and there was a rumbling in her belly and it grew and it grew, and it grew, until it exploded and covered the earth with rivers, lakes, streams.

And Yemaya looked into the water of a lake and again she saw that woman and she said, "Who is that beautiful woman? I thought that I was the prettiest thing that the world had ever seen." And a rumbling came into her belly and it grew and it grew and it grew, until exploded and sprinkled the night sky with stars and a full moon.

Yemaya looked into the light of the moon and there she saw that woman and she said, "Who is that beautiful woman? I thought that I was the finest thing the world had ever seen." This caused a rumbling in her belly and it grew and it grew and it grew, until it exploded and before her stood thousands of beautiful women. "Who are you beautiful women? I thought that I was the loveliest thing that the world had ever seen." And the women looked deep into the eyes of Yemaya and there they saw their own reflection and they said, "You are, Mama, we are just you."

*        *        *

You want to sing a song to Yemaya? The "asesu," yes, this is everybody's favorite song. It is a very simple song. We have some very elaborate ones, but this is a simple song which seems to have caught on quite well. It has call and response. I will sing one verse and then you sing it. And when you are secure in it, I will call the different names of Yemaya. When I stop calling, you may want to call the names of other goddesses of the ocean from other traditions. I would like for us to do that. Yemaya is that big body of water that touches everything. She is fluid and connected, in every way. There is a little twist in the song. You think it is going one way but it is going the other. How many people here are recovering Catholics? Now, this is not a Gregorian chant; they are beautiful, but this is not one. You sort of want to imagine drums behind it and the feeling of undulation in the ocean.

Yemaya asesu, asesu Yemaya. Yemaya asesu, asesu Yemaya.
Yemaya olodo, olodo Yemaya. Yemaya olodo, olodo Yemaya.

# COYOTE AND THE FIREFLIES

Barton Stone

Everything was darkness one time when Coyote woke up. He rubbed his eyes and then opened them really wide. He must be blind! The sun has died! He thought all the things a coyote might think waking up to total darkness in a panic. Finally, he saw tiny sparks of light in the distance and, with much stumbling and bumping through the woods, made his way there.

Fireflies! Their green-golden lights winked on for seconds at a time, like moving stars above an open meadow. Coyote was so relieved! He went over to one of them and said, "Firefly, I'm so glad to see you! It's really, really dark and I'm very, very busy. Give me your light so I can see my way."

"Oh, Coyote, I'm sure you have very important things to do, but I won't give up my light."

He tried another one.

"If you really loved me, you'd give me your light."

"I *do* love you, Coyote, but I would never give up my light."

Coyote trotted over to another firefly.

"Hey, you! Give me that light or I'll eat you up."

"Coyote, you can eat me if you must, but I will not give up my light!"

Coyote could see that the direct approach was getting him nowhere with these fireflies and he was beginning to get angry now. He put on his most authoritative face, drew himself very tall and went over to the next firefly.

"Excuse me. I don't think you're qualified to shine that light. I want to see your license, also your diploma, your firefly certificate, and your current monthly dues receipt. Otherwise I'll have to confiscate your light."

"Oh, Coyote, I'm afraid, I don't have any of those things. Qualified or not, this is my light, and I will shine it till I die."

He tried again.

"If you will, please, just give me that light I'll love you always, yes, I will and I'll tell everyone how wonderful you are."

"Well, I *do* want everyone to love me, Coyote, but still I will not give away my light for anything."

Coyote went to another one.

"Hey you, Firefly! You're too old to shine that light. Shining a light like that at your age could burn out your brain cells. I'm willing to take it off your hands for free and protect your sanity."

"Oh, no, Coyote! I was already old when I got this light and now I'm not willing to give it up, crazy or not."

In a frenzy, Coyote dashed over to another one.

"Watch out! Shining that light could hurt someone and you'd be responsible. You're taking a very dangerous risk here. Think of your loved ones. Better turn it over to me for safekeeping."

"No, Coyote. Whatever the risk is, I will take it, for this light is my passion and I will not give it up."

In despair, Coyote curled himself up into a ball of fur, covering his eyes with his paws and allowing himself to sink into now welcome darkness. He didn't see the fireflies as they gathered together and made a glow of light all around him.

When he opened his eyes again, the glow was bright like the dawn. The sun's first rays struck jewels in the dew on the meadow and on his bushy tail. Coyote saw delight.

# LIST OF PRESENTERS

Virginia DuPraw Anderson, Ph.D.
19 Irving, Atherton, CA 94027

Janet Bray
2028A Piner Road, Santa Rosa, CA 95403

Jean Burns, Ph.D.
1525 153rd Ave, San Leandro, CA 94578
(510) 481-7507

Leila Castle
POB 302, Pt.Reyes, CA 94956
(415) 663-11954

Josephine A. Coffey
248 Dublin, San Francisco CA 94112
(415) 585-6506

Elizabeth and Robert Cogburn
Box 11, Arroyo Seco at Taos, NM 87514
(505) 776-8723

Madrina Denig
Casilla 624, Cusco, Peru
011-51-84-236-639 or
4364 Bonita Rd, Ste 181, Bonita, CA 91902
(619) 267-5271

Pai Ely (Manoel Rabelo Pereira)
Lar de Ita, Rua Frederico Ozanan, 175,
52280-500, Recife PE, Brazil

Paula Engelhorn, MA, ATR
5115 Gold Lake Dr., Santa Rosa CA 95405
(707) 539-7745

Elaine Fellows
400 Santa Clara, Oakland, CA 94610
(510) 836-1117

Panna Flower
P.O. Box 207, Morton, PA 19070-0207
(215) 544-9254

Wolfgang Gersch, Meta-Art Studios
255 Stuyvesant Dr., San Anselmo CA 94960
(415) 258-8210

Coquelicot Rudiak-Gillard
2813 Esaw St., Minden NV 89423
(702) 267-4982

Felicitas D. Goodman, Ph.D.
114 E Duncan St, Columbus OH 43202
(614) 267-9310 or
Route #5, Box 358-A, Santa Fe, NM 87501
(505) 455-2749

William Gough, Ph.D.
442 Knoll Drive, Los Altos CA 94024
(415) 941-7462

C. Jess Groesbeck, M.D.
1888 Spring Oaks Dr., Springville, UT 84663
(801) 489-8448, 224-6001 or
2025 P St. Sacramento CA 95814
(916) 441-4419

Ruth-Inge Heinze, Ph.D.
2321 Russell #3A, Berkeley CA 94705
(510) 849-3791

Jürgen W. Kremer, Ph.D.
CISS, 765 Ashbury St., San Francisco CA 94117
(415) 753-6100 x253

Stanley Krippner, Ph.D., Saybrook Institute
450 Pacific, Suite 300, San Francisco CA 94133
(415) 433-9200; 826-9295

Rowena Pattee Kryder, Ph.D.
POB 940, Mt. Shasta CA 96067
(916) 938-2142

William C. Leikam
530 Kendall Ave #l, Palo Alto CA 94306
(415) 856-3041

Carolina Marks
1427 Milvia, Berkeley, CA 94709
(510) 527-2356

Joanne and Ron Mied
711 Diablo Blvd #19, Novato, CA 94947
(415) 898-0067

Raymond Miller and Mary Wimmer
2619 5th Avenue, #403, Seattle, WA 98121
(206) 448-6314

Les Morgenstern
9193 Molt River Circle, Fountain Valley, CA 92708
(714) 965-8177; 1-800-677-3973

Jack Norton and Jana Rivers
Native American Studies,
Humboldt State University, Arcata CA 95520
(707) 826-4329; 839-4010 or
1920 Acacia Ct., McKinleyville, CA 95521
(707) 839-4010

Carol L. O'Connell
POB 58, New Hope, PA 18938
(215) 862-0226

Fred Olsen
241 Joost St., San Francisco, CA 94131
(415) 333-7326

Cindy A. Pavlinac, M.A.
128 Morning Sun Avenue, Mill Valley, CA 94941-4113
(415) 381-9685

Tomas Pinkson, Ph.D.
240 Miller Ave, Mill Valley, CA 94945
(415) 381-3909

Mena E. and Dominic Potts, Ph.D. and Attorney
Fernwood Forest, Fernwood Road, Wintersville, OH 43952
(614) 264-4444; off. 282-7000

Julien Puzey
864 Roosevelt Ave, Salt Lake City, UT 84105
(801) 484-7344

Cheri Quincy, M.D.
Santa Rosa Medical Group
4275 Montgomery Dr, Santa Rosa, CA 95405
(707) 539-3511 or
3644 Alta Vista Ave, Santa Rosa, CA 95404
(707) 579-0750

Lillian Rhinehard, M.A., MFCC.
1475 Los Alamos Rd, Santa Rosa CA 95409
(707) 539-0153

Beverly A. Rubik, Ph.D.
Center for Frontier Science, Temple University
Ritter Hall 00300, Philadelphia PA 19122
(215) 204-8487

Phillip Scott
310 Channing Way #216, San Rafael, CA 94903
(415) 479-5002

Sandia Rising Star
POB 1226, Middletown, CA 95461
(707) 987-2228

James A. Swan, Ph.D.
Box 637, Mill Valley CA 94941
(415) 383-5064

Howard Teich, Ph.D.
3368 Sacramento St., San Francisco, CA 94118 or
1200 Gough 17-D, San Francisco, CA 94109
(415) 931-9893

Luisah Teish
1026 53rd St., Oakland, CA 94608
(510) 654-8644

Larissa Vilenskaya, Ph.D.
Psi Research, 405 El Camino Real #250, Menlo Park, CA 94025
(415) 960-2448

ellen Helga Weiland
765 West Pebble Beach, Ashland, OR 97520
(503) 482-3300